Foundations for the LPC

Foundations for the LPC

Part 1 Professional conduct

Kathryn Wright, LLB, Solicitor (non-practising)
Clare Firth, LLB, Solicitor (non-practising), Senior Lecturer in Legal Practice,
Director of Legal Practice, University of Sheffield

Part 2 Revenue law

Lucy Crompton, LLB, LLM, Solicitor (non-practising), Senior Lecturer,
Manchester Metropolitan University
Clare Firth, LLB, Solicitor (non-practising), Senior Lecturer in Legal Practice,
Director of Legal Practice, University of Sheffield
Helen Fox, LLB, Solicitor (non-practising), Senior Lecturer (part time), Staffordshire University
Frances Seabridge, LLB, Solicitor (non-practising), Teaching Fellow in Law at Aston University
Susan Wigglesworth, LLB, Solicitor, Freelance Lecturer in Law

Part 3 Wills and administration of estates

Clare Firth, LLB, Solicitor (non-practising), Senior Lecturer in Legal Practice,
Director of Legal Practice, University of Sheffield

Part 4 Human rights

Elizabeth Smart, LLB, LLM, Executive MBA, Solicitor (non-practising), Professor, Head of
Law, Sheffield Hallam University

OXFORD
UNIVERSITY PRESS

OXFORD
UNIVERSITY PRESS

Great Clarendon Street, Oxford, OX2 6DP,
United Kingdom

Oxford University Press is a department of the University of Oxford.
It furthers the University's objective of excellence in research, scholarship,
and education by publishing worldwide. Oxford is a registered trade mark of
Oxford University Press in the UK and in certain other countries

Eighteenth edition 2014
Nineteenth edition 2015
Twentieth edition 2016

Impression: 1

Published in the United States of America by Oxford University Press
198 Madison Avenue, New York, NY 10016, United States of America

British Library Cataloguing in Publication Data

Data available

ISBN 978–0–19–878766–2

Printed in Great Britain by
Bell & Bain Ltd., Glasgow

OUTLINE CONTENTS

Preface   xiii
Guide to the Online Resource Centre   xiv
Acknowledgements   xvi
Table of Cases   xvii
Table of Statutes   xix
Table of Statutory Instruments   xxiii
Table of International Treaties and Conventions   xxiv
Table of Code of Conduct and Other Rules   xxv

PART 1   **Professional conduct**   **1**
          1   Introduction   3
          2   Financial services   37
          3   Money laundering   53

PART 2   **Revenue law**   **59**
          4   Introduction to revenue law   61
          5   Income tax   66
          6   Capital gains tax   82
          7   Inheritance tax   90
          8   Corporation tax   125
          9   Value added tax   140
          10   Taxation of sole proprietors and partnerships   149
          11   Taxation of trusts and settlements   159

PART 3   **Wills and administration of estates**   **171**
          12   Introduction to wills and administration of estates   173
          13   Entitlement to the estate   174
          14   Application for a grant of representation   209
          15   Post-grant practice   249

PART 4   **Human rights**   **283**
          16   Human rights   285

APPENDIX 1   Answers to self-test questions   305
APPENDIX 2   Investments   307

Index   311

DETAILED CONTENTS

Preface   xiii

Guide to the Online Resource Centre   xiv

Acknowledgements   xvi

Table of Cases   xvii

Table of Statutes   xix

Table of Statutory Instruments   xxiii

Table of International Treaties and Conventions   xxiv

Table of Code of Conduct and Other Rules   xxv

PART 1   **Professional conduct**   1

1   **Introduction**   3

1.1   Regulation   3

1.2   A brief history of legal ethics   4

1.3   What is going to be covered?   5

1.4   What being a member of the profession and a good solicitor means 6

1.5   The Handbook   9

1.6   Practical application of the OFR Code   14

1.7   Professional conduct and the LPC core subject areas   23

1.8   Professional conduct: checkpoints   27

1.9   Suggested solutions to Chapter 1 activities   27

2   **Financial services**   37

2.1   Introduction   37

2.2   Relevance to solicitors   42

2.3   The regulatory regime   44

2.4   Financial promotions   44

2.5   Solicitors regulated by the Solicitors Regulation Authority   45

2.6   Conclusion: solicitors and the financial services legislation   50

2.7   Commentary to scenarios   51

3   **Money laundering**   53

3.1   Introduction   53

3.2   Money laundering   53

3.3   The legislation   54

3.4   The offences   54

3.5   Relevance to solicitors   55

3.6   Money laundering: checkpoints   57

PART 2	**Revenue law**	**59**

4	**Introduction to revenue law**	**61**
4.1	Introduction	61
4.2	Why do we tax?	61
4.3	The changing nature of taxation	61
4.4	European context	62
4.5	Sources of revenue law	62
4.6	Introduction to the main taxes	62
4.7	Tax planning	64
4.8	Administration of taxes	64
4.9	Appeals	65

5	**Income tax**	**66**
5.1	Chapter outline	66
5.2	Introduction to income tax	66
5.3	Sources of income tax law	67
5.4	Collection and payment of income tax	67
5.5	Allowances and rates of income tax	69
5.6	Calculation of income tax	69
5.7	Sources of taxable income	73
5.8	Charitable giving	79
5.9	Summary	80

6	**Capital gains tax**	**82**
6.1	Introduction	82
6.2	The principles of CGT	82
6.3	Who is liable for capital gains tax?	82
6.4	Disposal of assets	82
6.5	What are chargeable assets?	83
6.6	How is the capital gain calculated?	83
6.7	The rate of CGT	83
6.8	Capital losses	84
6.9	More than one disposal in a tax year	85
6.10	Exemptions and reliefs	85
6.11	Death of a taxpayer	87
6.12	Case study: Arthur Pickering Deceased	88
6.13	Conclusion: checkpoints	89

7	**Inheritance tax**	**90**
7.1	Introduction: basic structure of inheritance tax	90
7.2	The charge to inheritance tax	91
7.3	Potentially exempt transfers	92
7.4	The transfer of value on death	93
7.5	The occasions to tax	93
7.6	The charge to tax and a lifetime chargeable transfer	99
7.7	The charge to tax and an LCT where the transferor dies within seven years of the LCT	105
7.8	The charge to tax and a PET	109
7.9	The charge to tax and death	110
7.10	Gifts subject to a reservation	118
7.11	Liability, burden, and payment of tax	118
7.12	Tax planning	121
7.13	Conclusion: checkpoints	121
7.14	Commentary to exercises	122

8	**Corporation tax**	**125**
8.1	Introduction to corporation tax	125
8.2	Calculating the income profits of a limited company	125
8.3	Calculating the capital gains of a limited company	126
8.4	Roll-over relief	127

8.5	Capital losses	127
8.6	Trading losses	128
8.7	Capital Allowances ('CA')	129
8.8	Calculating corporation tax	132
8.9	Payment of CT	132
8.10	The payment of dividends	133
8.11	Close companies	133
8.12	Taxation of close companies	134
8.13	Steps to a complete CT calculation	136
8.14	Conclusion: checkpoints	139

9	**Value added tax**	**140**
9.1	Introduction	140
9.2	Sources of VAT law	140
9.3	When is VAT charged?	140
9.4	What are the rates of VAT?	141
9.5	Input and output VAT	143
9.6	Registration	144
9.7	The tax point	144
9.8	Accounting for VAT	144
9.9	Doing VAT calculations	146
9.10	Conclusion: checkpoints	148

10	**Taxation of sole proprietors and partnerships**	**149**
10.1	Introduction	149
10.2	Sole trader liability to income tax and VAT	149
10.3	Partners' liability to income tax	150
10.4	Calculating the trading profit of sole traders and partners	151
10.5	Charge on income	152
10.6	Capital gains and capital losses	153
10.7	Trading losses	153
10.8	The basis of assessment of trading profits	154
10.9	Overlap relief	155
10.10	A change in the membership of a partnership	156
10.11	Division of profits and losses between partners	157
10.12	Terminal loss relief	157
10.13	Start-up loss relief	158
10.14	Carry forward relief on incorporation of a business	158
10.15	Conclusion: checkpoints	158

11	**Taxation of trusts and settlements**	**159**
11.1	Introduction and background	159
11.2	Inheritance tax	160
11.3	Capital gains tax	164
11.4	Income tax	167
11.5	Conclusion: checkpoints	168

PART 3	**Wills and administration of estates**	**171**

12	**Introduction to wills and administration of estates**	**173**
12.1	Introduction	173
12.2	Breakdown of the task	173

13	**Entitlement to the estate**	**174**
13.1	Basic structure of entitlement to the estate	174
13.2	Wills	174
13.3	Validity of wills	175
13.4	Revocation of a will	179
13.5	Alterations in wills	182
13.6	Incorporation by reference	183

13.7   Failure of gifts by will   184
13.8   Gifts to children in wills   188
13.9   Wills: checkpoints   189
13.10   Intestacy   190
13.11   Intestacy: the basic position   191
13.12   Entitlement where there is a surviving spouse (or a surviving civil partner) of the intestate   192
13.13   Issue of the intestate   194
13.14   Other relatives of the intestate   195
13.15   The Crown   195
13.16   Inheritance tax and intestacy   196
13.17   Intestacy: checkpoints   196
13.18   Property not passing under the will or the intestacy rules   198
13.19   Property passing outside the will or intestacy rules   198
13.20   Property not forming part of the succession estate but forming part of the deceased's estate for inheritance tax purposes   200
13.21   Property not forming part of the deceased's estate for succession or inheritance tax purposes   200
13.22   Property not passing under the will or the intestacy rules: checkpoints   200
13.23   Provision for family and dependants   201
13.24   The basis of the claim for provision   201
13.25   The application   201
13.26   The applicant   202
13.27   Reasonable financial provision   203
13.28   The guidelines   204
13.29   Family provision orders   206
13.30   Property available for financial provision orders   207
13.31   Family provision: checkpoints   207

14   Application for a grant of representation   209
14.1   Introduction   209
14.2   Grants of representation   209
14.3   Responsibilities of solicitors instructed by personal representatives   210
14.4   The effect of the issue of a grant   211
14.5   Grant not necessary   211
14.6   Types of grant   212
14.7   Personal representatives: capacity   214
14.8   Personal representatives: several claimants   215
14.9   Personal representatives: number   216
14.10   Personal representatives: renunciation/power reserved   216
14.11   Grants of representation: checkpoints   217
14.12   Obtaining the grant: practice overview   218
14.13   Registering the death   220
14.14   Preparing the papers to lead the grant   220
14.15   Funds for payment of inheritance tax   220
14.16   Swearing or affirming the Oath   222
14.17   Lodging the papers   222
14.18   Obtaining the grant: practice overview: checkpoints   222
14.19   The court's requirements: Oaths   223
14.20   The requirements generally   224
14.21   Oath for executors   224
14.22   Oath for administrators with will annexed   231
14.23   Oath for administrators   234
14.24   Further affidavit evidence   238
14.25   The court's requirements: checkpoints   239
14.26   HMRC's requirements   240
14.27   Excepted estates   241
14.28   Form IHT 400   244
14.29   Form IHT 400 Calculation   247
14.30   Summary   247
14.31   HMRC's requirements: checkpoints   248

15   **Post-grant practice**   **249**

15.1   Introduction   249
15.2   Duties and powers of personal representatives   249
15.3   Duties of personal representatives   249
15.4   Administrative powers of personal representatives   251
15.5   Duties and powers of personal representatives: checkpoints   257
15.6   Administering the estate   257
15.7   Protection of personal representatives   257
15.8   Financial services   260
15.9   Collecting/realising the assets   261
15.10   Payment of debts (solvent estate)   263
15.11   Payment of debts (insolvent estate)   265
15.12   Post-death changes   266
15.13   Administering the estate: checkpoints   268
15.14   Distributing the estate   270
15.15   Payment of legacies   270
15.16   Ascertainment of residue   272
15.17   Estate accounts   275
15.18   Assents   277
15.19   Financial services   278
15.20   Beneficiaries' rights and remedies   279
15.21   Distributing the assets: checkpoints   281

PART 4   **Human rights**   **283**

16   **Human rights**   **285**

16.1   Introduction   285
16.2   General principles   286
16.3   European and international doctrines   286
16.4   The Convention rights   290
16.5   Judicial remedies   303
16.6   Conclusion: checkpoints   304
16.7   Bibliography   304

APPENDIX 1 Answers to self-test questions   305

APPENDIX 2 Investments   307

Index   311

PREFACE

This book provides foundations for study on the Legal Practice Course, containing materials relating to the Core and Pervasive areas (other than Accounts and Skills) identified in the 'Outcomes for the course' defined by the Solicitors Regulation Authority. Accounts and Skills are each the subject of a dedicated volume in the *Legal Practice Course Guide* series. The principles introduced here will be further developed in the Core Practice and Elective areas of the Course.

The chapters on Revenue law take into account the effects and planned changes of the Budget introduced by the Chancellor of the Exchequer in March 2017. However, they do not reflect changes that may have been made subsequently.

Susan Wigglesworth would like to express her gratitude to Angela Fountain, Director, RBA Wealth Management.

The authors are, as ever, grateful for the support and assistance afforded to them on this occasion by members of the Higher Education Division at Oxford University Press.

Clare Firth
Sheffield
April 2017

GUIDE TO THE ONLINE RESOURCE CENTRE

Online Resource Centres are websites that have been developed to provide students and lecturers with ready-to-use teaching and learning resources. They are free of charge, designed to complement the textbook and offer additional materials that are suited to electronic delivery.

The Online Resource Centre to accompany this book can be found at
www.oxfordtextbooks.co.uk/orc/foundations17_18/

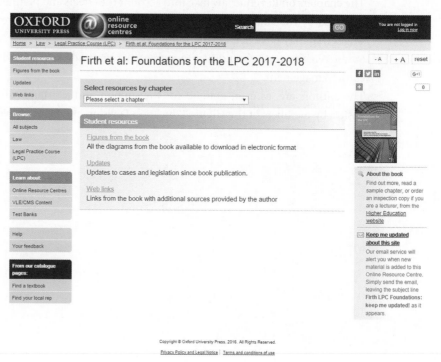

Student resources

Student resources are open access and free to use.

Updates

Updates on changes to key legislation and procedures.

Useful websites and resources

Useful links and resources selected by the authors and organised by chapter to provide you with additional information on the areas covered in the book.

Figures from the book

Lecturers can access figures featured in the book online in a format suitable for use in Power Point slides or inserting into handouts. Use these diagrams to complement your teaching and encourage your students to get the most from this book.

ACKNOWLEDGEMENTS

In Chapter 14, the forms of Oath for Executors, for Administrators with the will annexed, and for Administrators are reproduced by kind permission of Oyez Professional Services Limited for educational purposes only.

TABLE OF CASES

Adams (Dec'd), Re [1990] Ch 601 . . . 182

Amin v Secretary of State for the Home Department [2003] UKHL 51 . . . 287

Appleton, Re (1885) 29 ChD 893 . . . 274

Atlan v United Kingdom (Application 36533/97) [2001] Crim LR 819 (ECtHR) . . . 296

Attorney-General's Reference (No 3 of 2000) [2002] 1 Cr App R 29 . . . 297–8, 299

Austin and Saxby v Commissioner of Police of the Metropolis [2005] HRLR 20; [2007] EWCA Civ 989; [2005] HRLR 20 . . . 292

Banks v Goodfellow (1870) LR 5; (1870) QB 549 . . . 175, 176

Barrett v Bem [2012] EWCA Civ 52 . . . 178

Beckles v United Kingdom (Application 44652/98) (2003) 36 EHRR 13 . . . 295

Benjamin, Re [1902] 1 Ch 723 . . . 259

Brodie's Will Trustees v IRC (1933) 17 TC 432 . . . 168

Callaghan, Re [1984] Fam 1 . . . 204, 205

Chalcraft, In the Goods of [1948] P 222; [1948] 1 All ER 700 . . . 178

Chaplin, Re [1950] Ch 507; [1950] 2 All ER 155 . . . 194

Charles v Fraser [2010] EWHC 2154 . . . 180

Charman v Charman (No 4) [2007] 1 FLR 1246 (CA) . . . 205

Collins, Re [1975] 1 WLR 309; [1975] 1 All ER 321 . . . 194, 251

Collins, Re [1990] Fam 56 . . . 204

Commissioner of Stamp Duties (Queensland) v Livingston [1965] AC 694 . . . 279

Condron v United Kingdom (Application 35718/97), 2 May 2000 . . . 295

Cook, In the Estate of [1960] 1 WLR 353; [1960] 1 All ER 689 . . . 178

Coventry, Re [1980] Ch 461 . . . 205

Cradock v Piper (1850) 1 Mac & G 664 . . . 275

Crispin's Will Trusts, Re [1975] Ch 245; [1974] 3 WLR 657; [1974] 3 All ER 772 . . . 194

Cunard's Trustees v IRC [1946] 1 All ER 159 . . . 168

Douglas and Others v Hello! Ltd [2001] QB 467 . . . 289

Duce and Boots Cash Chemists (Southern) Ltd's Contract, Re [1937] Ch 642 . . . 278

DWS, Re (Dec'd) [2001] Ch 568 . . . 267

Evans v Westcombe, Law Society's Gazette, 10 March 1999 . . . 259

Eve, Re [1956] Ch 479; [1956] 3 WLR 69; 3 [1956] All ER 321 . . . 264

Fitt v United Kingdom (2000) 30 EHRR 480 . . . 296

G Mayor Cooke, Re 5 TLR 407 . . . 4

GHR Co Ltd v IRC [1943] KB 303 . . . 277

Goodwin v United Kingdom (1996) 22 EHRR 123 . . . 302

Gully v Dix [2004] 1 FCR 453 . . . 202, 203

Handyside v United Kingdom (1976) 1 EHRR 737 . . . 288, 301

Harman v Harman (1686) 2 Show 492; 3 Mod Rep 115; Comb 35 . . . 266

Hobbs v Knight (1838) 1 Curt 769 . . . 182

Hokkanen v Finland (1994) 19 EHRR 139 . . . 289

Ireland v United Kingdom (1978) 2 EHRR 25 . . . 291

Jasper v United Kingdom (2000) 30 EHRR 441 . . . 296

Jemma Trust Company Ltd v Liptrott [2004] 1 WLR 646 . . . 274

Kane v Radley-Kane [1998] 3 WLR 617 . . . 251

Khan v United Kingdom [2000] Crim LR 684 . . . 302

King's Will Trusts, Re [1964] Ch 542 . . . 278

Knatchbull v Fearnhead (1837) 3 M & C 122; 1 Jur 687 . . . 257

Lamy v Belgium (1989) 11 EHRR 529 . . . 292

Ludi v Switzerland (1992) 15 EHRR 173 . . . 299

McCann v United Kingdom (1995) 21 EHRR 97 . . . 287, 290

McVeigh, O'Neill and Evans v United Kingdom, (Applications 8022/77, 8025/77, and 8027/77) (1981) 25 DR 15 . . . 300

Malone v United Kingdom (1984) 7 EHRR 14 . . . 288

Miller v Miller; McFarlane v McFarlane [2006] UKHL 24 . . . 205

Ministry of Health v Simpson [1951] AC 251 . . . 280

Neuminster v Austria (1968) 1 EHRR 91 . . . 289

Northcote's Will Trust, Re [1949] 1 All ER 442 . . . 275

Nottingham City Council v Amin [2000] 1 WLR 1071 . . . 298, 299

Observer and Guardian v United Kingdom (1991) 14 EHRR 153 . . . 302

Osman v United Kingdom (1998) 29 EHRR 245 . . . 287

Parker v Felgate (1883) 8 PD 171 . . . 175, 176

Pearce, Re [1909] 1 Ch 819 . . . 270

PG and JH v United Kingdom (Application 44787/98) *The Times*, 19 October 2001 (ECtHR) . . . 297

Pilkington v IRC [1964] AC 612 . . . 256

R v Birtles [1969] 1 WLR 1047 . . . 301

R v Cole, R v Keet [2007] EWCA Crim 1924 . . . 295

R v Director of Public Prosecutions, *ex parte* Kebilene [1999] 3 WLR 972 . . . 294

R v Doldur [2000] Crim LR 178 . . . 295

R v Doubtfire (2000) *The Times*, 28 December . . . 296

R v G; R v Looseley *See* Attorney-General's Reference (No 3 of 2000) [2002] 1 Cr App R . . . 29

R v Moon [2004] EWCA Crim 2872 . . . 298

R v Smurthwaite and Gill [1994] 1 All ER 898 . . . 298, 301

R (D) v Secretary of State for the Home Department [2006] 3 All ER 946, CA; [2005] UKHRR 917 . . . 287

R (Laporte) v Gloucestershire Chief Constable [2006] UKHL 55; [2007] 2 WLR 46 . . . 292

R (O) v Harrow Crown Court [2006] UKHL 42; [2006] 3 WLR 195 . . . 292

Reynold's Will Trusts, Re [1966] 1 WLR 19; [1966] 3 All ER 686 . . . 194

Rooke, Re [1933] Ch 970 . . . 270

Rowe and Davis v United Kingdom (2000) 30 EHRR 1 . . . 296

Salabiaku v France (1991) 13 EHRR 379 . . . 293

Soering v United Kingdom (1989) 11 EHRR 439 . . . 288

Spracklan's Estate, Re [1938] 2 All ER 345 . . . 181

SW and CR v United Kingdom (1995) 21 EHRR 363 . . . 300

T and V v United Kingdom (Applications 24724/94 and 24888/94) 16 December 1999 . . . 293

Teixera de Castro v Portugal (1998) 28 EHRR 101 . . . 297, 298, 299

Townson v Tickell [1819] B & Ald 31 . . . 267

Van Colle v Chief Constable of Hertfordshire [2008] UKHL 50 . . . 287

Wemhoff v Germany (1968) 1 EHRR 55 . . . 292

White v White [2003] 3 WLR 1571 (HL) . . . 205

Wood v Smith [1993] Ch 90 . . . 178

X and Y v Netherlands (1985) 8 EHRR 235 . . . 300

TABLE OF STATUTES

Administration of Estates Act 1925 . . . 251
    s 10(2) . . . 266
    s 25 . . . 249, 250
    s 33 . . . 271
    s 33(1) . . . 191
    s 34(3) . . . 263
    s 35 . . . 263, 264, 265
    s 36 . . . 277
    s 36(2) . . . 278
    s 36(4) . . . 277, 278
    s 36(5) . . . 278
    s 36(6) . . . 278
    s 36(7) . . . 278
    s 36(10) . . . 278
    s 39 . . . 251
    s 41 . . . 251, 271
    s 42 . . . 252, 271
    Pt IV (ss 45–52) . . . 191
    s 46 . . . 195
    s 47 . . . 191
    s 55(1)(ix) . . . 270
    s 55(1)(x) . . . 193
    Sch 1
        Pt II . . . 263
Administration of Estates (Small Payments) Act
    1965 . . . 212, 221
Administration of Justice Act 1932
    s 2 . . . 210
Administration of Justice Act 1982 . . . 180
    s 17 . . . 177
    s 20 . . . 260
Administration of Justice Act 1985
    s 50 . . . 215, 275
Adoption Act 1976 . . . 188
    s 39 . . . 195
    s 45 . . . 260
Anti-Terrorism, Crime and Security Act 2001 . . . 54
Apportionment Act 1870 . . . 275

Bail Act 1976 . . . 292
Building Societies Act 1986 . . . 212

Capital Allowances Act 2001 . . . 129, 151
Capital Transfer Tax Act 1984 *See* Inheritance Tax
    Act 1984
Children Act 1989
    s 3 . . . 252
    s 3(3) . . . 252
    s 6 . . . 181

Civil Evidence Act 1995
    s 1 . . . 204
Civil Partnership Act 2004 . . . 181, 191, 198
Corporation Tax Act 2009 . . . 64, 125
Corporation Tax Act 2010 . . . 64, 125, 128
    s 37 . . . 128, 153
    s 38 . . . 128, 153
Criminal Evidence (Amendment) Act 1997 . . . 300
Criminal Justice Act 2003 . . . 294
    s 114 . . . 294
    s 114(2) . . . 295
    s 115 . . . 294
Criminal Justice and Public Order Act 1994 . . . 295
    s 25(1) . . . 292
    s 34 . . . 295
Criminal Procedure and Investigations Act 1996 . . . 294

Equality Act 2010 . . . 18
Estates of Deceased Persons (Forfeiture Rule and Law of
    Succession) Act 2011 . . . 267
    s 1 . . . 267
    s 2 . . . 267
    s 3 . . . 192

Family Law Reform Act 1987 . . . 188, 195
    s 18 . . . 195
    s 18(2) . . . 195
Fatal Accidents Act 1976 . . . 262
Finance Acts . . . 62
Finance Act 1986
    s 100 . . . 91
    s 102 . . . 118
Finance Act 2005
    s 55 . . . 132
Finance Act 2006 . . . 92, 159, 160, 162
Finance Act 2012
    s 209 . . . 97
Finance (No 2) Act 2015 . . . 90
Financial Services Act 1986 . . . 39, 257
    s 3 . . . 39
Financial Services Act 2012 . . . 37, 39
Financial Services and Markets Act 2000 . . . 37, 39–44, 47,
    49, 50, 52, 260, 261, 305
    s 1B . . . 39
    s 1B(2) . . . 305
    s 1C(2)(d) . . . 39
    s 1F . . . 305
    s 19 . . . 39, 48, 260
    s 19(2) . . . 39

s 21(1) . . . 44
s 22 . . . 40, 305
s 22(1)(b) . . . 40
s 22(5) . . . 40
s 23 . . . 39, 305
s 26 . . . 39
s 28 . . . 39
s 31 . . . 40
s 38 . . . 40
s 40 . . . 40
Pt XX (ss 325–333) . . . 40, 43, 44, 45, 48, 49, 51, 52, 260,
    261
s 327 . . . 43, 47
s 327(6) . . . 43
Forfeiture Act 1982 . . . 267

Human Rights Act 1998 . . . 285, 286, 289, 297, 303, 304
s 2 . . . 304
s 2(1) . . . 286
s 3 . . . 285, 286
s 4 . . . 285
s 6 . . . 289
s 6(1) . . . 286
s 6(3) . . . 286
s 8(1) . . . 303
Sch 1 . . . 290
Sch 2 . . . 304

Income and Corporation Taxes Act 1988 . . . 64
Income Tax Act 2007 . . . 63, 67, 69, 151
s 3 . . . 70
Pt 2, Chp 2 (ss 6–21) . . . 69
s 11 . . . 67
s 14 . . . 67
s 15 . . . 67
s 72 . . . 158
s 86 . . . 158
s 89 . . . 157
Pt 10 (ss 518–564) . . . 70
Pt 12 (ss 615–681) . . . 70
Pt 13 (ss 682–809) . . . 70
Income Tax (Earnings and Pensions) Act 2003 . . . 63, 67
Pt 2 (ss 3–61) . . . 70
Pt 9 (ss 565–654) . . . 70
Pt 10 (ss 655–681) . . . 70
Income Tax (Trading and Other Income) Act 2005 . . . 63, 67,
    125, 149
Pt 2 (ss 3–259) . . . 70, 125
Pt 3 (ss 260–364) . . . 70
Pt 4 (ss 365–573) . . . 70
Pt 5 (ss 574–689) . . . 70
Inheritance (Provision for Family and
    Dependants) Act 1975 . . . 174, 201, 218, 223,
    259, 267, 268, 269
s 1(1) . . . 201, 202, 207
s 1(1)(a) . . . 202
s 1(1)(b) . . . 202
s 1(1)(ba) . . . 202
s 1(1)(c) . . . 202
s 1(1)(d) . . . 203
s 1(1)(e) . . . 203
s 1(2) . . . 203

s 1(2)(a) . . . 203
s 1(2)(b) . . . 204
s 2 . . . 204, 206
s 2(1) . . . 206
s 3(1) . . . 204
s 3(2) . . . 203, 205
s 3(2A) . . . 206
s 3(3) . . . 206
s 3(3)(aa) . . . 206
s 3(4) . . . 206
s 3(5) . . . 204
s 9 . . . 207
s 10 . . . 201, 207
s 11 . . . 201, 207
s 14 . . . 203
s 15 . . . 202
s 15A . . . 202
s 19(1) . . . 206
s 25(1) . . . 207
Inheritance Tax Act 1984 . . . 63, 91, 96, 160
s 1 . . . 91
s 1(3) . . . 91
s 2 . . . 91
s 3 . . . 91
s 3A . . . 92
s 4 . . . 110, 111
s 6 . . . 92
s 8A . . . 114
s 11 . . . 92
s 18 . . . 94
s 19(3A) . . . 122
s 20 . . . 102
s 21 . . . 103
s 22 . . . 102, 103
s 23 . . . 95
s 24 . . . 95
s 25 . . . 95
s 43(2) . . . 160
s 47 . . . 92
s 48 . . . 92
s 49 . . . 162–3
s 49A . . . 162
s 58 . . . 161
s 65 . . . 161
ss 71A–71F . . . 162
s 73 . . . 164
s 86 . . . 164
s 88 . . . 164
s 92 . . . 164
s 125 . . . 112
s 131 . . . 105, 108
s 141 . . . 112
s 142 . . . 268
s 144 . . . 161
s 151 . . . 164
s 161 . . . 94
s 176 . . . 111
ss 178–189 . . . 112
ss 190–198 . . . 111
Inheritance and Trustees' Powers Act 2014 . . . 191, 237
s 3(1) . . . 193
s 3(2) . . . 193

s 5 . . . 195
s 8 . . . 255
s 9 . . . 256
s 9(2) . . . 256
s 9(3)(b) . . . 256
s 10(1) . . . 256
s 10(2) . . . 256
s 10(4) . . . 256
s 10(5) . . . 256
Sch 2 . . . 201
    para 2(3) . . . 203
    para 4 . . . 206
    para 5(2) . . . 205
    para 5(3) . . . 206
    para 6 . . . 201
    para 7 . . . 207
Intestates' Estates Act 1952
Sch 2 . . . 194
Investigatory Powers Act 2017 . . . 301

Judgments Act 1838
s 17 . . . 266

Land Registration Act 2002 . . . 273, 277
Law of Property Act 1925
s 27 . . . 256
s 184 . . . 186
Law Reform (Miscellaneous Provisions) Act 1934
s 1(1) . . . 262
Legal Services Act 2007 . . . 3, 4
Legitimacy Act 1976 . . . 188
s 5 . . . 195
s 10 . . . 195

Marriage (Same Sex Couples) Act 2014 . . . 191
s 1 . . . 180
Sch 3 . . . 180
Married Women's Property Act 1882
s 11 . . . 198, 219, 221
Mental Capacity Act 2005 . . . 175–6
s 1 . . . 175, 176
s 2 . . . 175
s 3 . . . 175, 176
s 16 . . . 176
Code of Practice . . . 175, 176
Mental Health Act 1983 . . . 177

Obscene Publications Act 1959 . . . 288

Police Act 1997
Pt III (ss 91–108) . . . 300
Police and Criminal Evidence Act 1984
s 78 . . . 297, 298, 299
s 78(1) . . . 297
Code C . . . 298
Prevention of Terrorism Act 1989
s 16A . . . 294
s 16B . . . 294
Proceeds of Crime Act 2002 . . . 54, 55
ss 327–329 . . . 54

ss 330–332 . . . 54
s 333A . . . 54
s 340(11) . . . 54

Regulation of Investigatory Powers Act 2000 . . . 301
Pt II (ss 26–48) . . . 300

Senior Courts Act 1981
s 109 . . . 240
s 114 . . . 215, 216
s 116 . . . 215
Settled Land Act 1925 . . . 228
Statute of Westminster 1 (1275)
Ch 29 . . . 4

Taxation of Chargeable Gains Act 1992 . . . 63,
    82, 164
s 3 . . . 165
s 18(3) . . . 165
s 60 . . . 164
s 62 . . . 268
s 68 . . . 164
s 71 . . . 166
s 72 . . . 166
s 73 . . . 166
s 76 . . . 166
s 152 . . . 166
s 165 . . . 165
s 225 . . . 166
s 260 . . . 165
Sch 1 . . . 165
Terrorism Act 2000 . . . 54
Trustee Act 1925 . . . 251
s 15 . . . 252
s 19 . . . 252
s 20 . . . 252
s 25 . . . 253
s 27 . . . 223, 257, 258, 259, 266, 269
s 27(2) . . . 258
s 31 . . . 167, 168, 255, 256
s 31(1) . . . 255
s 31(2) . . . 255
s 32 . . . 256
s 42 . . . 275, 276
s 61 . . . 280
s 63 . . . 271, 276
Trustee Act 2000 . . . 249, 250, 251, 254
s 1 . . . 250, 252
s 3 . . . 254
s 4 . . . 254
s 5 . . . 255
s 8 . . . 255
s 11 . . . 253
s 12 . . . 253
s 14 . . . 253
s 15 . . . 253
s 21 . . . 253
s 22 . . . 253
s 23 . . . 253
s 28 . . . 274
s 28(4) . . . 18 7

s 28(4)(a) . . . 187
s 29 . . . 274
s 31 . . . 253
s 34 . . . 252
s 35 . . . 249
Trustee Delegation Act 1999
s 5 . . . 253
Trusts (Capital and Income) Act 2013 . . . 250
Trusts of Land and Appointment of Trustees Act
    1996 . . . 228, 251, 252
s 6(3) . . . 255

Value Added Tax Act 1994 . . . 64, 140
Sch 7 . . . 142
Sch 8 . . . 142
Sch 9 . . . 142

Wills Act 1837
s 9 . . . 177, 178, 183, 189, 238
s 15 . . . 179, 187, 213, 274
s 18 . . . 180
s 18(3) . . . 180
s 18(4) . . . 180
s 18A(1) . . . 181
s 18B . . . 181
s 18C . . . 181
s 20 . . . 181, 182
s 21 . . . 182–3
s 24 . . . 184
s 33 . . . 186, 187, 190
Wills Act 1963 . . . 175

TABLE OF STATUTORY INSTRUMENTS

UK Statutory Instruments

Administration of Insolvent Estates of Deceased Persons
Order 1986 (SI 1986 No 1999) . . . 266

County Court Jurisdiction Order 2014 (SI 2014 No
503) . . . 210

Financial Promotions Order 2005 (SI 2005 No 1529
as amended) *See* Financial Services and Markets
Act 2000 (Financial Promotion) Order 2005 (SI 2005
No 1529)

Financial Services and Markets Act 2000 (Designated
Professional Bodies) Order 2001 (SI 2001 No
1226) . . . 43

Financial Services and Markets Act 2000 (Exemption) Order
2001 (SI 2001 No 1201) . . . 40

Financial Services and Markets Act 2000 (Financial
Promotion) Order 2005 (SI 2005 No 1529) . . . 44, 47

  Art 55 . . . 47

  Art 55A . . . 47

Financial Services and Markets Act 2000 (Professions)
(Non-Exempt Activities) Order 2001 (SI 2001 No
1227) . . . 43

Financial Services and Markets Act 2000 (Regulated
Activities) Order 2001 (SI 2001 No 544) . . . 41, 45, 48,
49, 50, 51, 260, 305

  Art 22 . . . 41, 305

  Art 29 . . . 41, 305

  Art 60 . . . 41, 305

  Art 66 . . . 41, 42, 45, 52, 260, 261, 305

  Art 67 . . . 42, 45, 47, 51, 52

  Art 72C . . . 42, 45, 46

  Pt III (Arts 73–89) . . . 42, 305

Housing Benefit (Amendment) Regulations 2012
(SI 2012 No 3040) . . . 79

Inheritance Tax (Delivery of Accounts) (Excepted
Estates) (Amendment) Regulations 2011 (SI 2011 No
214) . . . 241, 243

Inheritance Tax (Delivery of Accounts) (Excepted
Estates) (Amendment) Regulations 2014 (SI 2014 No
488) . . . 241

Inheritance Tax (Delivery of Accounts) (Excepted Estates)
Regulations 2004 (SI 2004 No 2543) . . . 241

Money Laundering Regulations 2007 (SI 2007 No
2157) . . . 53–6

  reg 5 . . . 55

  reg 5(a) . . . 56

  reg 6 . . . 55

  reg 7 . . . 55

  reg 11 . . . 56

  reg 16(4) . . . 55

  reg 19 . . . 55

  reg 20(1)(b) . . . 55

  reg 20(2)(d)(i) . . . 55

  reg 21 . . . 55

Non-Contentious Probate (Amendment) Rules 1991 (SI 1991
No 1876) . . . 210

Non-Contentious Probate Rules 1987 (SI 1987/2024) . . .
210

  r 9 . . . 224

  r 12 . . . 238

  r 13 . . . 238

  r 14 . . . 238

  r 15 . . . 239

  r 20 . . . 212–13, 214, 217, 218, 223, 231, 240

  r 21 . . . 213

  r 22 . . . 213, 214, 217, 218, 223, 231, 234, 237, 240

  r 22(4) . . . 214

  r 25 . . . 216

  r 27 . . . 214, 215, 216, 229, 230

  r 27(1A) . . . 229

  r 35 . . . 215

  r 37 . . . 217

  r 37(2) . . . 217

Proceeds of Crime Act 2002 (Business in the Regulated Sector
and Supervisory Authorities) Order 2007 (SI 2007 No
3287)

  Art 1(1)(n) . . . 54

Solicitors' (Non-Contentious Business) Remuneration Order
2009 (SI 2009 No 1931) . . . 273

European Secondary Legislation

Money Laundering Directives . . . 53

VAT Directive (2006/112) . . . 140

TABLE OF INTERNATIONAL TREATIES AND CONVENTIONS

European Convention on Human Rights and Fundamental
    Freedoms 1950 . . . 195, 285, 286, 304
  Art 2 . . . 286, 287, 290
  Art 2(2) . . . 286
  Art 3 . . . 291
  Art 4 . . . 291
  Art 5 . . . 291–3
  Art 5(1)(c) . . . 291, 292
  Art 5(3) . . . 292
  Art 5(4) . . . 292
  Art 6 . . . 289, 292, 293–7, 299, 302, 304
  Art 6(1) . . . 293, 296, 297
  Art 6(2) . . . 293, 294
  Art 6(3)(b) . . . 294
  Art 6(3)(c) . . . 294
  Art 7 . . . 299, 300
  Art 8 . . . 287, 297, 299, 300–1, 302

  Art 8(1) . . . 302
  Art 8(2) . . . 287, 300, 302
  Art 9 . . . 301
  Art 10 . . . 288, 289, 292, 301–2, 303
  Art 10(2) . . . 289, 301
  Art 11 . . . 292, 302, 303
  Art 12 . . . 302
  Art 14 . . . 302–3
  Art 16 . . . 303
  Art 17 . . . 303
  Art 18 . . . 303
First Protocol . . . 290
  Art 1 . . . 303
  Art 2 . . . 303
  Art 3 . . . 303
Sixth Protocol . . . 303

TABLE OF CODE OF CONDUCT AND OTHER RULES

Solicitors' Accounts Rules 1998 . . . 9
Solicitors' Investment Business Rules . . . 257
SRA Code of Conduct 2007 . . . 4, 7, 9, 12, 13, 16,
    18–22, 24, 28
   r 1 . . . 11, 12
   r 1.01–1.06 . . . 11
   r 2 . . . 15, 16, 18, 250
SRA Code of Conduct 2011 . . . 3–36
   Section 1 (Chs 1–6) . . . 5, 14, 18
     Ch 2 . . . 18
     Ch 3 . . . 19–20
     Ch 4 . . . 20–2
     Ch 5 . . . 22, 25
   Section 2 (Chs 7–9) . . . 5
   Section 3 (Ch 10) . . . 5
   Section 4 (Chs 11–12) . . . 5
     Ch 11 . . . 22–3
   Section 5 (Chs 13–15) . . . 5
     Ch 14 . . . 19, 20, 23, 30, 34
   Indicative Behaviours . . . 5, 9, 11, 13, 15, 20, 24
     IB(1.7) . . . 30
     IB(1.9) . . . 30
     IB(1.11) . . . 29
     IB(1.12) . . . 29
     IB(1.16) . . . 15
     IB(1.17) . . . 15
     IB(1.19) . . . 15
     IB(1.22) . . . 16, 29
     IB(1.25) . . . 32
     IB(1.26) . . . 17
     IB(3.3) . . . 24
     IB(3.4) . . . 24
     IB(3.5) . . . 31
     IB(3.7) . . . 24, 31
     IB(3.7)(a) . . . 34
     IB(3.12) . . . 31
     IB(3.14) . . . 24
     IB(4.2) . . . 31
     IB(4.3) . . . 31
     IB(4.6) . . . 31
     IB(5.4) . . . 35
     IB(5.5) . . . 35
     IB(5.9) . . . 35
     IB(11.5) . . . 23
   Outcomes . . . 5, 7, 9, 11, 13–36

O(1.3) . . . 17
O(1.4) . . . 30
O(1.9) . . . 16, 17, 29
O(1.10) . . . 16
O(1.11) . . . 16
O(1.13) . . . 15, 28, 35
O(1.14) . . . 16
O(3.1) . . . 19, 30, 32
O(3.2) . . . 19, 32
O(3.3) . . . 19, 30, 32
O(3.4) . . . 19
O(3.5) . . . 19, 20, 30
O(3.6) . . . 19, 20, 26, 30, 36
O(3.6)(a)–(d) . . . 19
O(3.7) . . . 19, 20, 26, 30, 31, 36
O(3.7)(a)–(e) . . . 20
O(4.1) . . . 21, 33, 34
O(4.2) . . . 21, 33, 34
O(4.3) . . . 21, 33
O(4.4) . . . 31
O(5.1)–O(5.8) . . . 26
O(5.1) . . . 35
O(5.2) . . . 35
O(5.4) . . . 35
O(11.2) . . . 23
Principles . . . 5, 7, 8, 9, 10, 11–13, 20, 24, 30–4, 36
   Principles 1–9 . . . 12
   Principle 1 . . . 26
   Principle 2 . . . 20, 24, 26, 30
   Principle 3 . . . 24, 30
   Principle 4 . . . 13, 20, 24, 27
   Principle 5 . . . 8, 9, 17, 20, 24, 30
   Principle 6 . . . 6, 8, 20, 26
   Principle 8 . . . 9, 14
   Principle 10 . . . 12, 13
SRA Financial Services (Conduct of Business) Rules
   2001 . . . 46, 47, 50, 260, 305, 306
SRA Financial Services (Scope) Rules 2001 . . . 43, 46–7, 48,
   49, 50, 51, 260, 305, 306
   r 4(a) . . . 46
   r 4(b) . . . 46
   r 4(c) . . . 46, 47
   r 5 . . . 261
SRA Recognised Bodies Regulations 2009 . . . 9

Part 1

Professional conduct

1   Introduction   3
2   Financial services   37
3   Money laundering   53

Introduction

1.1 Regulation

The Solicitors Regulation Authority ('SRA') is the independent regulatory body of the Law Society in England and Wales. They set the principles and code of conduct which solicitors and law firms in England and Wales must abide by in order to provide legal services. The code of conduct currently in force was introduced on 6 October 2011. For the purposes of this chapter and to differentiate between the old and new codes, this new code will be referred to as the outcomes-focused regulation code ('the OFR Code'). The OFR code was a major change from the strict rules-based approach which had been in force prior to this date and many in the legal sector were concerned by the changes to compliance the OFR Code would introduce. The purpose of the OFR Code was to provide a more flexible approach to the governance of legal service providers.

1.1.1 The OFR Code and consumers

The SRA's intention was that the OFR Code would encourage a higher standard of service for consumers by making it clear what *outcomes* clients should expect from legal service providers. The SRA hoped that by reducing strict rules and bureaucracy legal service providers would be able to focus on improving services and providing excellent customer care.

This also meant that the SRA could focus its time, not on ensuring all firms were complying strictly with all rules, but on high-risk firms, and high-risk activities, to ensure consumers were protected.

1.1.2 Other changes to the legal profession?

Not only has the OFR Code of Conduct been introduced but we have also seen the emergence of alternative business structures ('ABSs') which were made possible due to the Legal Service Act 2007 ('LSA'). The SRA began accepting applications from prospective ABSs in January 2012 and licensed the first ABS in March 2012. By 2017 there have been more than 600 ABSs enter the market. These ABSs allow for the ownership of legal service providers, which had been restricted to lawyers, to be open to anyone deemed 'fit or proper'. So for example an insurance company or a supermarket—hence the much discussed term 'Tesco law' which has been widely commented on by the media and professionals alike.

Although there was some concern from existing legal firms that ABSs would have a detrimental effect on their business, this has not happened in practice. Research has shown that the introduction of ABS businesses has benefited the market more widely as ABS firms are more likely to be innovative than other regulated legal services firms. These new, innovative providers have increased competition in the market, which encourages a wider variety of legal services in the market that are more accessible and affordable to consumers.

The timeline for the introduction of the outcomes-focused approach and introduction of ABSs is set out in **Figure 1.1**.

Figure 1.1   Timeline of SRA Handbook implementation

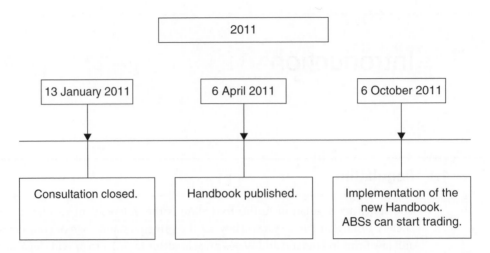

1.2 A brief history of legal ethics

One of the earliest examples of regulation of the legal profession can be found in Chapter 29 of the Statute of Westminster 1 (1275) in which 'deceit or collusion' by lawyers was forbidden. *Re G Mayor Cooke* 5 TLR 407 is an example of common law identifying these ethical principles. In this case it was stated that an act of professional misconduct is committed by a lawyer who does something which is 'dishonourable to him as a man and dishonourable to his profession'.

These ethical principles which have been honoured by lawyers since medieval times were not committed to any real written form until the second half of the twentieth century. In 1960 the Law Society's *A Guide to the Professional Conduct and Etiquette of Solicitors* was first published; this contained the original set of rules. This was only superseded on 1 July 2007 by the implementation of the Law Society's Code of Conduct.

You will see from this chapter that you could argue that the regulation of the legal profession has gone full circle—originally a profession which required no absolute written code (as a lawyer acted within one rule—that being to act honourably) to a profession governed by the Code of Conduct 2007 (a set of mandatory rules of compliance often criticised as too detailed, complicated, and rigid) to the OFR Code which reverts back to lawyers upholding a number of basic principles. How they uphold those principles is not strictly regulated.

1.2.1 Why the need for change?

The LSA was passed in 2007. It represented a key stage in the process of a number of government reviews and recommendations which included the removal of restrictions on competition within the legal profession in relation to the structure, ownership, and management of law firms and the development of ABSs for legal service firms. It was felt that the implementation of a new form of regulation, based on the firm rather than an individual solicitor, was required in order to deliver the objectives of the LSA.

There were concerns that the regulations in the Code of Conduct 2007 (the '2007 Code') were too strict and inflexible for the changing legal market. The legal market was and still is seeing a significant increase in the export of legal services, new technology, different and innovative ways of attracting new clients and developing the business, and, as mentioned, the introduction of ABSs. It was felt by both practitioners and regulators that a new approach to regulation was needed to keep abreast of these changes.

There were also concerns, particularly from the City firms, that the existing regulation for the larger firms serving the corporate sector was not fit for purpose and the SRA's rules focus did not protect adequately the needs of corporate clients. Many City firms at the time of consultation mooted that they should be governed by an alternative set of rules. This did not come to fruition though. The SRA introduced one set of regulations—the OFR Code. The SRA hoped this would be a 'one size fits all' regulation as it allows for more flexibility—a regulation fit for all legal service providers from the large City firms to the sole practitioners and also the new ABSs.

The OFR Code is flexible and wide-ranging. The SRA felt that the rules-based approach focused on strict compliance rather than on the primary aim, which was to achieve the best outcome for the client. The OFR Code provides a clear focus on the achievement of positive outcomes for consumers and gives firms flexibility to decide how those outcomes are best achieved.

The OFR Code therefore focuses on the quality of what a solicitor is delivering to a client, rather than prescribing how legal service providers reach that stage. The benefits are the ability to adapt to a particular type of firm and to the needs of a particular client base and the ability to eliminate rules-driven bureaucracy which can create unproductive costs.

The OFR Code has been reviewed and updated a number of times since it was first introduced with minor updates and amendments. It is now version 18 of the OFR Code. It is worth noting at this point that at the time of going to print a consultation is underway to once again change the code of conduct which governs legal providers. The SRA plan to radically simplify the OFR Code, but more importantly are proposing two separate codes—a Code of Conduct for Solicitors and a Code of Conduct for Firms. As and when this comes into practice is unclear at this point.

It is also worth mentioning that the route for becoming a solicitor has also been under review. All students training to be solicitors will be required to take the new SQE (solicitors qualifying examination), currently timetabled to be introduced in September 2019. For some of you this may come into force whilst you are studying for a law degree, the GDL, or LPC. The SRA have advised during any transitionary period domestic candidates who have started a qualifying law degree, CPE, LPC, or period of recognised training before September 2019 would be able to choose whether or not to qualify under the old route (subject to availability) or to take the SQE. Meanwhile, people who start a law degree or postgraduate conversion course in September 2019 or after may no longer qualify through the existing route and must take the SQE.

1.3　What is going to be covered?

In the first section of this chapter we will look at what being a member of the profession and a good solicitor means, the Handbook, and the OFR Code in general.

In the second section of the chapter we will look at the practical application of the OFR Code and will look in detail at the principles (the 'Principles'), the outcomes (the 'Outcomes'), and indicative behaviours ('Indicative Behaviours') in the OFR Code (reproduced with the kind permission of the Law Society) which are most relevant to you at this stage of your legal career as a student and trainee.

The OFR Code covers the following:

- 1st section—You and your client;
- 2nd section —You and your business;
- 3rd section—You and your regulator;
- 4th section—You and others; and
- 5th section—Applications, waivers, and interpretations.

We will be mainly concentrating on the first section of the OFR Code dealing with 'You and your client', as this is the area which you need to be very familiar with during the LPC and when you start your time in practice. We will also look in brief at areas in the fourth section—particularly in relation to undertakings. The other parts of the OFR Code are of course important and you must be aware of what they cover, but for your purposes at this level of your study we will not be concentrating on them.

The third section of this chapter highlights the areas in the core subjects which you will study on the LPC where professional conduct issues typically occur:

- property law and practice;
- litigation; and
- business law and practice.

Throughout the chapter, to assist you with your learning and knowledge of the OFR Code, there will be activities to do. There will also be example scenarios from everyday practice where you will be asked to consider how you might achieve the Outcomes for your clients. **Suggested solutions** to these activities and scenarios are provided at the end of this chapter at **1.9**. You should check your answers against these suggested solutions in **1.9** as you attempt each activity.

1.4   What being a member of the profession and a good solicitor means

> **Activity 1**
>
> What do you think clients want from their legal advisers? Try to think of as many diverse ideas as you can.

1.4.1   Act professionally

The public demands a high standard of professionalism from the legal profession, but the nature of what 'acting professionally' actually encompasses can be difficult to define. The standard is extremely high not only in order to fulfil your professional duties and obligations, but also in order to satisfy ever-increasing client demands and expectations.

The following is a non-exhaustive list of what you should be aiming to achieve in order to maintain a high standard of professionalism:

- Have high ethical standards including honesty and integrity;
- Have respect for all people you deal with or work with;
- Have a positive attitude;
- Be competent;
- Be flexible;
- Be commercially aware;
- Understand confidentiality;
- Have good communication skills;
- Have good time management;
- Be punctual;
- Understand financial management.

1.4.2   Enrolling as a student member

All LPC students must enrol as students with the SRA. In order to enrol and be accepted by the SRA as a member of the profession you must confirm you are of good character and suitable for the profession. You will (if you are presently studying the LPC) already have done this and seen the type of behaviour or past convictions which might preclude you from working as a lawyer. Even though you are not yet in contact with clients, the principles of professional conduct apply to student members. Student members are subject to the same constraints and responsibilities as those which apply to qualified solicitors.

As a law student, already governed by principles of professional conduct, a higher than normal standard of behaviour is expected. Look at Principle 6 set out in the OFR Code. You must 'behave in a way that maintains the trust the public place in you'. Professional rules are strictly enforced.

The SRA will take an interest in the behaviour of prospective solicitors. It is likely to take disciplinary action if issues such as criminal convictions, dishonesty, bankruptcy, or LPC assessment offences arise. Examples of dishonesty and potential offences would include copying someone else's answer, plagiarism, or making a false declaration that the assessment submission is your own work.

The spirit of the OFR Code and its rules of professional conduct are summarised by the SRA in its introduction to the Handbook:

This Handbook sets out the standards and requirements which we expect our regulated community to achieve and observe, for the benefit of the clients they serve and in the general public interest. Our approach to regulation (ie authorisation, supervision and enforcement) is outcomes-focused and risk-based so that clients receive services in a manner which best suits their own particular needs, and depending on how services are provided (eg whether in-house or through private practice).

1.4.3 Commercial and client awareness

In the increasingly competitive environment in which all solicitors now operate, it is more important than ever to provide outstanding service to clients. One of the key elements of continuing success for any lawyer, or his or her firm, is to recognise that they must put the needs of the client first. Reread the last sentence of the introduction to the Handbook. Note the emphasis on an individual client and his or her needs. Being a lawyer is not just about being technically good, it is also about being client-focused and ensuring your clients receive a service appropriate to their needs. What is suitable for one client may not be suitable for another.

The success or failure of a solicitor's practice depends largely on how it deals with its clients, in addition, of course, to the quality of the legal services delivered. Technical excellence is critical for a solicitor and clients will expect their solicitor to have this technical excellence, but that is only the beginning. Clients in today's market expect their legal adviser to provide so much more than technical ability.

Clients want their solicitors to:

- be attuned to their ever-changing needs;
- understand their individual situation and concerns;
- deliver on time at an appropriate cost;
- 'add value' to the relationship;
- (if they are corporate clients) be as commercially focused as they are; and
- (if they are corporate clients) understand their business.

By acting within the OFR Code you should be achieving these 'wants' but should remember that the Outcomes in the OFR Code are a fluid concept: what may satisfy one type of client may not satisfy another. Each firm will need to review their client base and ascertain whether their existing systems and requirements will suit their specific clients under the OFR Code. A firm may have to have very different systems in place to meet different client type needs particularly if they are a firm practising a wide range of legal services. It will not be enough for firms to assume that, if they were meeting the rules of the 2007 Code, they are achieving the Outcomes in the OFR Code.

Clients' expectations of solicitors continue to increase as does the firm's drive to deliver continued excellence in client service. Even when you have satisfied a client it is vital to consider what else you can do to improve the relationship and add further value. Solicitors are working in an increasingly competitive market which looks certain to become even more challenging with the introduction of the ABSs.

1.4.4 Time and costs recording

A crucial part of your job will be recording your time. This is important both for the client and the firm in order to achieve the Outcomes of the OFR Code and act within the Principles of the Handbook. All firms have some form of time-recording system. As a trainee this can be one of the hardest skills you need to learn. Time is recorded on a six-minute basis. Each six-minute period of time is one unit. If you write a short letter which only takes you two minutes to dictate you would charge one unit. So you round up to the nearest six minutes. If you spend half an hour writing or dictating a more complicated letter then you would record five units of time. Each activity you undertake as a solicitor will have a different code for time-recording purposes; so there will be different codes for letter-writing, making or receiving a telephone call, attending court, attending on a client, preparation or perusing a file. All of these are examples of chargeable activities; that is, activities which you can charge to your client for work undertaken on their transaction or file.

There will also be codes which relate to non-chargeable activities. Examples of these might be training, internal meetings, or marketing and networking. These are activities which you will have to attend to as part of your job but you cannot record these to a client's matter as they do not form part of the client retainer or rules of engagement.

Each client will have a number; it is to that client and number that time is recorded. This is necessary in order to provide the most accurate picture of how the firm spends time and to allow proper informed management and strategic decisions to be made. Most firms will have targets which they expect their fee-earners to achieve in relation to the amount of chargeable time which must be recorded in a day.

There are several different time-recording and case management programmes used by firms. The importance of accurate time recording is paramount. The purpose and value of time recording is not only so that a client's costs can be recorded and billed accurately and correctly but also to provide financial information on the basis of which the partners can make sensible and informed decisions about their firm. If fee-earners do not record time accurately, the partners of the firm may, as a result, make decisions based on incorrect information. This could have a seriously detrimental effect on the profit and/or the overall financial stability of the firm.

The firm is a business and it is for the partners to make decisions based on financial sense. The time-recording system allows them to have at their fingertips information on the chargeable and non-chargeable time for all individual lawyers and departments. This will allow partners in a firm or managing directors of an ABS to identify departmental difficulties and allow better decisions to be taken on matters such as work allocation.

In the current competitive and difficult financial market, it will also give crucial information in relation to variations in fee-earner workloads, which will assist with recruitment and staffing decisions.

'Imaginative' and 'creative' time recording is fraudulent. From a business perspective, it also reduces the value of the relevant information and can lead to misconceived decisions being made. It will therefore be impossible to assess true productivity and profitability of fee-earners and/or departments, types of work, and clients. This will have a direct impact on the firm's ability to comply with the Principles of the OFR Code, particularly the last four Principles of the OFR Code relating to good business management (see **1.5.3**).

1.4.5   Be organised

Under Principle 5 of the Handbook, you must provide a proper standard of service to your client. In order to achieve this you need to be organised and have excellent time management skills. Learning how to prioritise is crucial.

You may not comply with Principle 5 or Principle 6 of the OFR Code if you are disorganised. A lack of organisation could damage rapport with your client or could damage your professional reputation and that of the firm. You could also be opening yourself up to potential negligence claims arising from missed deadlines.

Activity 2

Spend a few minutes thinking of processes you could implement to ensure you have good time management skills.

Activity 3

Test your 'natural clock'. Use a clock or watch with a second hand. Shut your eyes for what you think is one minute. When you think a minute has passed open your eyes and check your watch or clock. Do you have a good natural clock? If not, you know this is a skill you will need to improve.

Most people naturally think 60 seconds lasts longer than it actually does.

1.4.6   Dictation and note taking

Another vital skill that you will have to learn is dictation. Although some firms will expect you to do some of your own typing and administration jobs, most firms appreciate that it is more cost-effective to employ support staff to help you with this aspect of your job. It is usually quicker for you to dictate a letter and/or document and have a secretary with excellent touch-typing skills then transfer this to paper. This is a much better use of your time and better for the client who is paying for your skills on a timed basis. This will ensure you are achieving the Principles not only in relation to providing your client with a proper standard of service (Principle 5) but also in relation to managers of the legal service provider ensuring the business is run effectively (Principle 8).

It is also important that you record by way of a note on your file each and every conversation with clients, other professionals, or solicitors on each transaction. If it is not a communication in a written form (a copy of which can go on the file) there is no way to record what has been discussed other than a written record of the conversation. Again this would normally be dictated by the fee-earner and typed up and added to the file. But think commercially: if it is a very quick conversation then write the note by hand so you are not needlessly taking up secretarial time. You must always bear in mind that your firm is a business. This business sense is at the heart of the OFR Code.

1.4.7   Professional conduct and the LPC

Professional conduct cannot be considered in isolation. It pervades all aspects of a solicitor's life and work; for that reason it is also studied on the LPC as a pervasive topic. It will be covered in all of your core subjects and where applicable in your elective subject choices.

When considering whether you are complying with the OFR Code you need to ensure you are aware of the matters noted in **Figure 1.2**.

Figure 1.2   Professional conduct diagram

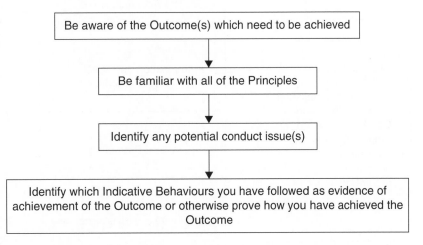

1.5   The Handbook

1.5.1   Structure of the Handbook

Until the implementation of the Handbook, the regulatory regime consisted of the Solicitors' Code of Conduct 2007, the Solicitors' Accounts Rules 1998, the SRA Recognised Bodies Regulations 2009, and the client financial protection (ie indemnity insurance and compensation fund requirements). The Handbook replaced all of these regulations in a single structure and brought together the key regulatory elements in seven sections. The Handbook does not just regulate solicitors in traditional firms but also regulates new entrants to the legal profession, for example ABSs. Clients of all types of legal practice will receive the same level of protection from the SRA.

There is no printed version of a 'rule book'. The Handbook is an online-only resource. The benefit of this is that it allows for flexibility without the need to reprint the Code with any updating changes. However, there has also been concern expressed that this flexibility may lead to problems. It is easy for the SRA to update and change the OFR Code and Handbook but more difficult for legal service providers to keep on top of the OFR Code and its current requirements.

You can access the OFR Code and other elements of the Handbook on the SRA website http://www.sra.org.uk. You can also use the SRA website to check for any amendments. Please note that due to the flexible nature of the OFR Code there may have been minor amendments since this textbook was published. In order to keep you up to date with amendments another resource available to you is www.oxfordtextbooks.co.uk/orc/foundations17_18/.

Figure 1.3 shows a snapshot of how the Handbook is structured. This was provided to practitioners by the SRA on 6 April 2011 when the final version of the Handbook was launched.

Figure 1.3   Code of conduct structure diagram

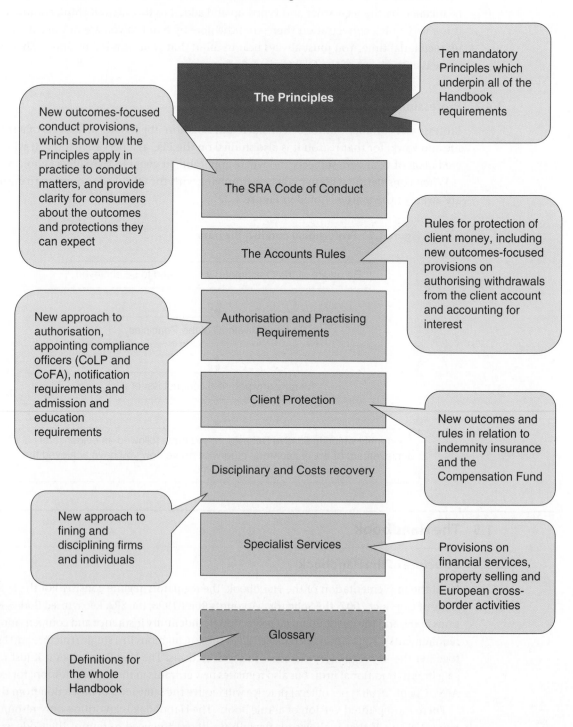

For the purposes of the rest of this chapter we will be focusing on the Principles and the SRA Code of Conduct (defined in this chapter as the OFR Code) as it is these, as a student and trainee, you need to be most familiar with as you carry out your studies and enter practice.

1.5.2 Background to the Handbook

In October 2008 Lord Hunt of Wirral was commissioned by the Law Society to write a report into the regulation of legal services and to consider what was needed to establish best modern practice. His findings confirmed the view that there needed to be a radical overhaul. He further concluded that the SRA needed greater expertise and understanding and a more sophisticated approach that recognised the varied needs of different sectors of the profession.

Lord Hunt advised a return to reinvigorated professional values—a return to principle-based regulation. He went on further to state that Rule 1 of the 2007 Code should become the overarching philosophy, a statement of core ethics that embrace the importance of justice and the rule of law, integrity, independence, the paramountcy of clients' interests, and standards of service. The writer was fortunate enough to attend one of Lord Hunt's presentations during the gathering of information and input from the profession for his report. The clear message from the presentation was the need to return to the early implied regulation governing the profession, that being to act within the instinctive guiding principles of professionalism, decency, trusted adviser, and duty to the client.

See Rule 1 of the 2007 Code as set out in **Figure 1.4**. In addition to this Rule 1 there were then 24 rules to supplement this with extensive guidance for each rule. All rules and guidance were mandatory.

Figure 1.4   Rule 1 of the 2007 Code

	Rule
1.01 Justice and the rule of law	You must uphold the rule of law and the proper administration of justice.
1.02 Integrity	You must act with integrity.
1.03 Independence	You must not allow your independence to be compromised.
1.04 Best interests of clients	You must act in the best interests of each client.
1.05 Standard of service	You must provide a good standard of service to your clients.
1.06 Public confidence	You must not behave in a way that is likely to diminish the trust the public places in you or the legal profession.

It is interesting to set out Rule 1 of the 2007 Code as you will see that the view of Lord Hunt of Wirral, and many other commentators and practitioners, was in fact widely adopted by the SRA when drafting the Principles for the Handbook.

1.5.3 The Principles

The Handbook is underpinned by ten overarching Principles, some of which are new and others which have been based on existing core duties. The Principles are amplified by Outcomes which firms are expected to achieve. The only *mandatory* parts of the Handbook are the Principles and Outcomes. These are intended to cover those areas which are genuinely needed to protect clients and the public and to deliver high standards of service. The rest of the Handbook, including the Indicative Behaviours and guidance, are *advisory* only (with the exception of specific areas such as accounts).

The ten Principles underpin the regime and everything in the Handbook, not just the OFR Code. The OFR Code then sets the Principles in context. The Principles define the fundamental ethical and professional standards expected of all firms and individuals when providing legal services. The introduction to the Principles in the Handbook advises that the Principles should be your starting point when faced with an ethical dilemma.

The ten Principles of the OFR Code are set out in **Figure 1.5**.

Figure 1.5   Ten Principles of the OFR Code

You must:

1. uphold the rule of law and the proper administration of justice;

2. act with integrity;

3. not allow your independence to be compromised;

4. act in the best interests of each client;

5. provide a proper standard of service to your clients;

6. behave in a way that maintains the trust the public places in you and in the provision of legal services;

> These first 6 Principles are carried over in their entirety from the 2007 Code.

7. comply with your legal and regulatory obligations and deal with your regulators and ombudsmen in an open, timely and co-operative manner;

8. run your business or carry out your role in the business effectively and in accordance with proper governance and sound financial and risk management principles;

9. run your business or carry out your role in the business in a way that encourages equality of opportunity and respect for diversity;

10. protect client money and assets.

Consider these Principles next to the old Rule 1. You can see that the old Rule 1 was in its entirety adopted, with the addition of four new Principles.

The first six Principles (being the same as from the old Rule 1) have long been established as the professional standards required from the legal profession. Indeed, the guidance to Rule 1 as set out in the 2007 Code confirms this approach:

A modern just society needs a legal profession which adopts high standards of integrity and professionalism. The core duties contained in rule 1 set the standards which will meet the needs of both clients and society …

The aim of the Principles is to ensure a solicitor's responsibility to his or her clients and to society is upheld. As a rough guide, Principles 1 and 6 address the responsibility a solicitor has to society and Principles 2, 3, 4, and 5 address the responsibilities a solicitor has to his or her client.

The four new Principles have been included to assist with the new OFR approach.

Principle 7 adds as a mandatory obligation the need to comply with the regulator. There was under the old regime a high level of non-compliance in certain areas, including failure to disclose referral fees and non-payment of compensation awarded by the Legal Complaints Service. This Principle also assists the SRA with its gathering of information, which is a large part of the OFR approach, allowing the SRA to monitor risk as an ongoing relationship with firms rather than having to deal with an incident after it has happened or with a complaint once it has been made, or even in very serious cases having to shut down a firm once an incident has occurred.

Principle 8 was included to try and tackle the large number of firm insolvencies in the last few years and the large number of firms in the Assigned Risks Pool. The Assigned Risks Pool provides indemnity insurance cover for firms which cannot get cover from qualifying insurers or cannot reasonably afford the terms available to them. This might be because the firm has a poor claims record, a major claim outstanding but not yet decided, or other risk factors. This Principle therefore makes it mandatory that the firm is run based on sound commercial awareness.

Principle 9 is an important addition as it tries to differentiate between the different client types, whether they are sophisticated bodies corporate or vulnerable individuals. This Principle also covers the treatment of employees.

Principle 10 is also a valuable addition, particularly in the current climate with the increase in mortgage fraud. This goes to the heart of the duty in Principle 4, which is to act in the best interests of your client by protecting their assets which have been entrusted to your firm.

The last four new Principles are drafted very widely and look like catch-all provisions but they effectively duplicate duties already imposed on the legal profession through various legislative and regulatory frameworks.

You should review the Principles in the Handbook. In addition to the Principles there are notes which should be read in conjunction with the Principles providing additional guidance on what these mean.

If the Principles are breached then the enforcement approach by the SRA will depend on all of the circumstances of each individual case. The primary aim of the SRA is to achieve the right outcome for the consumer.

1.5.4   The Code of Conduct ('OFR Code')

In addition to the ten Principles, the OFR Code contains the Outcomes. The Outcomes are mandatory and when achieved will help to ensure compliance with the Principles. These Outcomes should be an explanation of what the successful application of the Principles should look like to a client instructing a legal professional. The mandatory Outcomes can be achieved in a variety of ways depending on the particular transaction and circumstances. Whereas previously the legal profession and firms had the detailed rules to guide them in their actions, the legal service providers are being allowed to decide for themselves and make considered decisions how best to translate the Principles into a successful client outcome. This means greater judgement on the part of the legal service provider. Some say this is a positive step allowing solicitors to go it alone and make informed decisions as to how best to translate the Principles and Outcomes into a successful client outcome. This differs from the 'hand-held approach' of the 2007 Code. However, the flexibility of the OFR Code might also widen the opportunity for some practitioners to avoid their professional duties without the strict rule-based requirements of old, thus keeping them in line.

The Outcomes are then supplemented with the non-mandatory Indicative Behaviours to aid compliance and understanding by practioners. The Indicative Behaviours are not exhaustive. These are provided to give some assurance that if you follow the Indicative Behaviours your firm '*may*' be achieving the Outcomes. The word *may* is important. There is no certainty that even if you or your firm are/is following the Indicative Behaviours you will then be compliant with the OFR Code. Firms are encouraged to consider how they can best achieve the Outcomes, taking into account the nature and size of the firm, their particular circumstances, and, crucially, the needs of their particular clients. It is up to the legal service provider to prove how it has achieved the Outcomes.

This flexible, individualistic approach was intended to achieve a move away from the old detailed rule book which received so much 'bad press' amongst practitioners, especially City firms, and the new approach links to the slogan of the OFR Code—'freedom in practice'. However, hand in hand with this approach it must be understood that you have no certainty that your firm is compliant. The SRA has also stated that it does not act as a 'safe harbour' to firms seeking approval for an activity.

1.5.5   Compliance officers

One of the more substantial regulatory changes in the OFR Code is the requirement for firms to appoint a Compliance Officer for Legal Practice ('CoLP') and a Compliance Officer for Finance and Administration ('CoFA'). In order to hold these posts you need to be of sufficient seniority and hold a position of sufficient responsibility to fulfil the role. The person appointed must therefore, within the firm, have sufficient authority and credence to put in place systems, controls, and governance to ensure good compliance with the Handbook. It is for the firm to ensure that these nominated officers have sufficient authority to ensure the systems will work effectively. The officers will provide a point of contact for the SRA on matters concerning compliance. Even though the OFR Code seems to impose ultimate responsibility on the CoLP and CoFA, the guidance notes state that the existence of these compliance officers in a firm is not a substitute for the firm's and manager's responsibilities.

Concern has been expressed in relation to the roles of the CoLP and CoFA and how their responsibilities have been drafted in the Handbook. The Law Society is so concerned by the prospect of these officers becoming personally exposed under the Handbook that it is considering a scheme to shore up their position as it felt it was wrong that the officers should be held personally liable for the behaviour of others.

1.6 Practical application of the OFR Code

1.6.1 You and your client

Before you read this section of this chapter you should review the first section of the OFR Code which covers 'You and your client'. The Outcomes in this section show how the Principles apply in the context of client care.

Section 1 of the OFR Code covers:

- client care;
- equality and diversity;
- conflicts of interest;
- confidentiality and disclosure;
- your clients and the court; and
- your client and introductions to third parties.

1.6.1.1 Client care (Chapter 1 of section 1 of the OFR Code)

There are 16 Outcomes relating to client care. These cover providing a proper standard of service, giving clients the appropriate level of information about the services they will receive, and supplying information as to how much this will cost. For the purpose of this chapter we are going to concentrate on those areas of professional conduct which you will encounter during your LPC and training.

1.6.1.2 Client care and costs

You must remember that your firm is running a business and in order to comply with Principle 8, and the Handbook in general, the amount you can bill a client and the fees you are able to generate are crucial. As mentioned previously, it is no longer good enough to be an excellent technical lawyer: you need to be able to go out there and win clients and fees and then retain those clients. It is also worth noting that it is not negligence or errors which garner the most complaints from clients in relation to their lawyers, it is the costs associated with these services.

You may, when you enter practice, be shocked or embarrassed by your charge out rate. You may feel that you do not yet have the expertise to be charged out by your firm at such an expensive rate. An average trainee charge out rate is likely to be in the region of £100–£165 per hour. For City firms this figure could be much higher. However, a trainee's limited experience has been taken into account by the firm when it sets a trainee's charge out rate. Partners and more senior lawyers will be charged out at substantially more. Do not get into the habit of undercharging. Record your time correctly. This reiterates the requirement always to act professionally as discussed in **1.4.1**. If you are surprised by your charge out rate, imagine how surprised a client might be, particularly if they have never had the need of a solicitor before. It is imperative that your client has its eyes wide open in relation to the likely cost of a matter. Better this is all laid out in the open and the client is kept up to date with this as the transaction continues rather than surprising the client with a large bill at the end. This is when the complaints start. You must get over any discomfort you may feel in discussing the potential cost of something.

1.6.1.3 Costs in general

Rule 2 in the 2007 Code governed all aspects of costs information and was very detailed, setting out clear guidance on the information which clients had to be given at the outset and during a transaction. Information in relation to costs also had to be in writing. You will see from Outcome **O(1.13)** that this has been replaced by an obligation to provide the best possible information.

O(1.13) *clients* receive the best possible information, both at the outset and when appropriate as their matter progresses, about the likely overall cost of their matter;

There is no obligation to provide this information in writing any more, but Indicative Behaviour **IB(1.19)** suggests this information should be in a clear and accessible form appropriate to the needs and circumstances of the client. The Indicative Behaviours also cover explaining to your client not only how your costs might be charged but warning the client that they may have to pay another person's costs, perhaps in a litigation matter, and whether the client may be entitled to public funding or a conditional fee agreement. Remember that the Indicative Behaviours are not mandatory but if you do not follow them you may be asked to prove how you have otherwise met the Outcomes.

Activity 4

What different ways can you think of to ensure the following different client types have the best possible information in relation to costs and their transaction and thereby achieve **O(1.13)**?

(a) An illiterate client.

(b) A client who does not speak English.

(c) A medium-sized corporate client.

(d) A large corporate, experienced, legal service user.

1.6.1.4 Publicly funded clients

It is important to think about clients individually. Cost information for different types of clients will vary depending on the type of work you are doing for them, the nature of your firm, and the type of client. Clearly you will be achieving **O(1.13)** if you do not discuss the possibility of public funding when acting on behalf of a corporate client (to do so would in fact be wrong). However, if you are acting for an individual whose financial situation would indicate that they may be entitled to public funding and you do not discuss this option with them (which is covered in **IB(1.16)**) then it would be for you to prove to the SRA how you achieved **O(1.13)** without giving this information.

Activity 5

You are acting for a client whose father has just died. Your firm was instructed to deal with the probate. On the basis of your initial instructions you gave your client a quote confirming that your costs would be £1,000 plus VAT. However, you have now received correspondence from another firm of solicitors advising they have been instructed to contest the will of your client's father. The matter is now clearly more complicated than originally anticipated. What should you do to ensure you are achieving the Outcomes?

1.6.1.5 Conditional fee agreements

Conditional fee agreements only arise in litigation. **IB(1.17)** provides guidance suggesting that if you enter into a fee agreement with your client then the client should be given all relevant information in relation to that agreement. Again, remember that the Indicative Behaviours are not mandatory. They merely offer assistance to a solicitor to advise how they can achieve the Outcomes. However, if you have a conditional fee agreement with your client and your client does not have all the relevant information given to them in relation to the agreement then, because you did not follow the Indicative Behaviours (but may have achieved the Outcome in a different way), it will be for you to prove to the SRA how you have achieved the Outcome.

1.6.1.6   Client care and complaints

Outcomes **O(1.9)**, **O(1.10)**, **O(1.11)**, and **O(1.14)** all cover how a client's complaints should be handled and the information which a client should be given at the outset of their matter. You will note in **O(1.9)** that the obligation to provide information to clients in relation to their right to complain confirms that this must be in writing and must be given at the outset of the matter.

O(1.9) *clients* are informed in writing at the outset of their matter of their right to complain and how *complaints* can be made;

Again, Rule 2 of the 2007 Code sets out the rules in relation to providing complaints information to clients. This had the same requirement as **O(1.9)**. At the start of the matter the client had to be given in writing information that they could complain if they were unhappy with the service they received and who they could complain to. It was, however, also mandatory to have a written complaints procedure which had to be highlighted to the client and provided to them on their request. You will note that this obligation to have a written complaints procedure is not in the Outcomes. However, look at **IB(1.22)**, which supports the new **O(1.9)**. This suggests that, by having a written complaints procedure, which should be brought to the client's attention, this may achieve the Outcome.

It would appear therefore on the surface that little has changed. Although it is no longer compulsory to have a written complaints procedure, most, if not all, firms will already have this in place, so continue to do so under the OFR regime in the knowledge that if this satisfied the old 2007 Code then it should for the most part continue to satisfy the Outcomes. By having the written procedure firms are following the Indicative Behaviours which albeit not mandatory are guidance as to how you can achieve the Outcomes. The difference will be in making sure the written complaints procedure is satisfying the needs of all client types.

Activity 6

On the information provided, which of the following scenarios would not achieve the required Outcomes?

(a) A client who has been referred to you, emails you and gives you some background details on a transaction he wants to instruct you on. You send him a brief email back just introducing yourself and commenting on his email. The client responds and confirms that he wants to instruct you. You email him a letter and include within this letter information on the client's right to complain if there is an issue and the estimated cost of the matter.

(b) An angry client contacts the firm's receptionist and says, 'I want to make a complaint and don't tell me I can't because I know I am entitled to because the solicitor told me I could in the first letter he ever wrote to me!' The receptionist gives very clear oral instructions about the procedure available to the client.

(c) A client who has been referred to you comes into the office to see you. He decides on the spot that he is so keen to instruct you that you discuss with him at this first interview the likely costs and the fact that if he so wishes in the future he can make a complaint, and how to go about that. You go back to your desk and open a file. Part of the firm's opening file procedure is a checklist. You tick the boxes in relation to the OFR Code's costs and complaints requirements as having been met.

> **Activity 7**
>
> You work for a firm that has in place a written complaints procedure. This runs to 20 pages and is very detailed. You act for a client who has had a very limited education and whom you know struggles with reading and writing. He rings up the receptionist to complain. She refers him to the letter sent out at the start of the transaction, which in fact contained a copy of the complaints procedure and she advises him he needs to read this and follow the suggested procedure.
>
> Has your firm achieved **O(1.9)**? If not, how could you suggest amending this procedure for this client?

1.6.1.7 Client care and instructions and resources

Look at **O(1.3)**.

O(1.3) when deciding whether to act, or terminate your instructions, you comply with the law and the Code;

As a solicitor, you can decide whether you wish to act for a client or not, but when making that decision you need to comply with the law and the OFR Code. However, look at **IB(1.26)**. You may not have complied with the OFR Code if you terminate instructions with a client without good reason and without providing reasonable notice. You should not therefore refuse to act or terminate instructions based on any difference in political or social views with a client. You need to base your decision on good reason. It would be for you to prove to the SRA that your decision for refusing or terminating instructions was based on good reason.

Compliance with the Outcomes should ensure that both solicitors and clients are clear as to their responsibilities and expectations. Clients whose expectations have been properly managed are less likely to complain about the service they receive, but more likely to be impressed with the service and to re-instruct the solicitor or law firm in question.

> **Activity 8**
>
> Which of the following do you think would be reasonable reasons for refusing or terminating instructions and would therefore be achieving **O(1.3)**?
>
> (a) You have been acting on behalf of a client who has not paid her bills despite your accounts department having written to her twice and spoken to her four times in the last three months asking for payment.
>
> (b) You are contacted by a potential client who has been accused of criminal damage. He set fire to an abortion clinic as he is vehemently opposed to abortion. You in fact believe in a woman's right to choose and decide not to accept his instructions.
>
> (c) A potential client tells you that they have heard you are the best divorce lawyer in the country and that if you manage to agree a divorce settlement of over £15 million for them they will give you a £5,000 bonus at the end of the matter.
>
> (d) You acted previously for a client, Tom Smith. A new client wants to instruct you in bringing an action against Tom.
>
> (e) You have been acting on behalf of a client whom you don't like. This month when you sent her an interim bill she paid it late. You decide to terminate her retainer.

When deciding whether to accept instructions you should never allow your pride to take over when considering whether or not your firm has the resources to act on behalf of a client. Look at Principle 5. You must provide your client with a proper standard of service.

> **Activity 9**
>
> Read the following scenario, then look at the Outcomes in the OFR Code. Is your firm able to act for the client? Explain your answer.
>
>   You are a trainee at a firm which only offers property advice services. A client for whom you have acted for many years in relation to his successful property investment business contacts you for advice on an employment matter. An employee is claiming constructive dismissal. The client wants you to act because he trusts you.

1.6.1.8   Client care in general

Most firms will already have in place a client care letter. City firms tend to use the phrase 'terms and conditions of business' or 'engagement letters', which will contain the information required in relation to costs and complaints. These are sent out to clients at the start of each transaction or, if a firm acts for a client on a retainer basis, may simply be reviewed with the client each year rather than sent out for each and every transaction the firm is instructed on.

These satisfied the requirements in Rule 2 of the 2007 Code. Most firms have continued to use these client care letters in order to satisfy the Outcomes in section 1 of the Code 'You and your client'. However, there is a subtle shift in emphasis which you need to watch out for. Previously, a firm may have had a perfect client care letter which ticked all the rule boxes of the detailed Rule 2 in the 2007 Code. However, this may not be satisfactory for your particular client if they do not understand the information provided to them because it is too detailed or complex. In this scenario, under the OFR Code you will not have satisfied the Outcomes. Firms which already have effective and extensive systems in place to ensure that client care is the focus of their engagement will still under the OFR Code have to carry out a thorough check of these systems and procedures to check that they are compliant with achieving the Outcomes.

Many larger firms will have in place rules of practice with which they require their fee-earners to comply to ensure complete client satisfaction. These will be going a long way towards satisfying the subtle shift to ensuring each individual client is cared for rather than just a tick-box system which was required under the 2007 Code.

Typical rules include:

- All incoming correspondence must receive a reply within 24 hours of receipt.
- Each incoming call must be dealt with as promptly and efficiently as possible.
- If a fee-earner is unavailable or for some justifiable reason unable to take that call immediately, then the call must be returned on the same day.
- A fee-earner must sit down with a client and understand its business and needs and react and carry out its transaction accordingly.
- When a client file is removed from the office it must not be read whilst travelling on public transport.
- A client file or any matter relating to a client or the business of the firm must not be discussed in public where there is any likelihood of being overheard.
- Particular care should be taken in any communication to ensure that what is written or communicated is intended and in a suitable form for your particular client.

1.6.2   Equality and diversity (Chapter 2 of section 1 of the OFR Code)

As mentioned previously in this chapter you have a duty as a solicitor at all times to be seen as professional and to have integrity. Review the Outcomes in Chapter 2 of section 1 of the OFR Code in relation to this. None of the requirements to act within the Equality Act 2010 or to act in any way which would discriminate against any particular person or group of people should be a surprise to you. However, it is worth noting that these Outcomes are intended to cover both your relationship with clients and with your colleagues within your firm.

1.6.3   Conflicts of interest (Chapter 3 of section 1 of the OFR Code)

Conflicts of interest can be one of the most difficult areas to assess and do catch practitioners out. The problem is that there are circumstances, albeit limited, when you can act if there is a 'conflict of interest' and the decision as to whether a conflict exists can be fluid as the transaction progresses, so it must be an ongoing monitoring process. You should have Chapter 3 of section 1 on 'Conflicts of interest' to hand as you read this so you can review the different Outcomes and Indicative Behaviours as they are mentioned.

Due to the practical difficulties of assessing and dealing with conflicts this was, in the drafting of the OFR Code, one of the most contentious areas particularly in relation to property transactions. This will be covered in more detail later in **1.7.1** when we look at conduct issues relating to property law and practice.

At the start of a transaction most firms will run what is called a conflict check. This checks a firm's database to assess whether the firm has had any dealing with either the instructing client or the other party to the transaction. This information is the starting point to ascertain if there is, or is likely to be, a conflict of interest. Under the 2007 Code this conflict check was a requirement—a mandatory rule. During the drafting stage of the OFR Code it had been intended that the requirement to have these systems in place was only to be an Indicative Behaviour and therefore not mandatory. However, during the consultation process carried out with practitioners it was clear that this was felt by many to be almost one step too far and cause for concern. In the final version of the OFR Code released on 6 April 2011 the original draft Indicative Behaviours were upgraded to Outcomes. Look at **O(3.1)–O(3.3)**. Clearly, whether the firm is a sole practitioner with a small client base or an international City firm, the systems and procedures in place are likely to vary. The way in which such a conflict check will be undertaken will depend on the size and nature of the firm. It might be enough in a very small sole-practitioner firm to check a filing cabinet manually but clearly this is not going to be sufficient in a larger firm.

There is the basic rule that you cannot act if there is a conflict of interest between you and your client. See **O(3.4)**. This is called an 'own interest conflict' in the OFR Code. So if you were buying property from a client this would be an 'own interest conflict' and you could not act.

Prohibition on acting in conflict situations

O(3.4) you do not act if there is an *own interest conflict* or a significant risk of an *own interest conflict*;

O(3.5) you do not act if there is a *client conflict*, or a significant risk of a *client conflict*, unless the circumstances set out in Outcomes 3.6 and 3.7 apply;

However, look at **O(3.5)**. You can act in limited circumstances if there is a conflict between two or more clients. This Outcome essentially reflects the rules and guidance of the 2007 Code. You can act in **O(3.6)** if there is a client conflict and the clients have a 'substantially common interest' or in **O(3.7)** if there is a client conflict and the clients are competing for the same objective.

It is necessary first to look at 'substantially common interest' and see what this means. It is defined in Chapter 14 of the OFR Code. There needs to be a strong consensus between the conflicting clients on how any common purpose is to be achieved and any area of conflict has to be peripheral to the common purpose. In addition you need to achieve **O(3.6)(a)–(d)**.

Exceptions where you may act with appropriate safeguards, where there is a client conflict

O(3.6) where there is a *client conflict* and the *clients* have a *substantially common interest* in relation to a matter or a particular aspect of it, you only act if:

(a) you have explained the relevant issues and risks to the *clients* and you have a reasonable belief that they understand those issues and risks;

(b) all the *clients* have given informed consent in writing to you acting;

(c) you are satisfied that it is reasonable for you to act for all the *clients* and that it is in their best interests; and

(d) you are satisfied that the benefits to the *clients* of you doing so outweigh the risks.

In other words, you can only act if the parties have had the relevant issues and risks explained to them, if all the clients have given their consent to your acting on behalf of both of them in writing, if you are satisfied that it is reasonable for you to act for all of the clients, and if you believe that the benefits to the clients of your doing so outweigh the risks. You can see then that it is only going to be in limited circumstances that you will be able to satisfy all of these requirements.

You can also act for both parties competing for the same objective which is defined in Chapter 14 as *asset, contract or business opportunity* if you satisfy **O(3.7)(a)–(e)**. The Indicative Behaviours will help you to ascertain if there is a conflict or a potential conflict and whether you can act or whether you should refuse instructions.

Outcomes **O(3.6)** and **O(3.7)** are intended to apply to specialised areas of legal services where the clients are sophisticated users of those services and they conclude that they would rather use their retained solicitors than seek out new advisers. Often the large City firms or small specialist firms will act for several of the large PLC companies and will find their existing clients both want to instruct them in relation to the same transaction because of their expertise in their business or the market place. The SRA suggests that it should be rare for a firm to rely on O(3.7). Indeed, this Outcome should be relied upon with extreme caution. It is likely to be only the City firms which will try and use this.

If you cannot satisfy either of the exceptions in **O(3.6)** or **O(3.7)**, **O(3.5)** will apply and you will have to refuse to act for a client (if you have not already started acting). If you have already started acting for a client as no conflict existed at the start of the matter and a conflict arises during the transaction, you will have to stop acting for one of the clients. In deciding who you have to stop acting for, you would also at this stage need to think about your duty of confidentiality.

One area that City firms pushed for was to change the definition of 'conflict of interest' and 'client conflict' to relate only to current clients. This has not been incorporated and remains the same as the 2007 Code to include any client whether former or current. The definition of client in Chapter 14 of the OFR Code makes this clear.

It is also worth noting that there may be times where you should still refuse to act for two clients even if there is no conflict of interest because you would be breaching the Principles. This was discussed briefly in **Activity 8**. So, for example, if you were instructed to act on behalf of one client on the acquisition of a business where your firm had previously acted for that business and held confidential information in relation to it, there is no conflict per se. Remember, conflict is defined as between clients in the *same or related matter*. Here you acted for the business on a previous matter. It is not therefore a conflict but you would hold information which was material to the new client. As a result you would not be able to act because to do so would be breaching the overriding Principles 2, 4, 5, and 6.

Activity 10

Jot down whether or not you could act in this scenario.

You are a trainee at a firm which is well known for expertise in the telecoms industry. You have two long-standing clients, Phone PLC and Broadband Unlimited PLC, both large telecoms companies. Both companies contact your firm asking you to act on their behalf in relation to a tender to purchase a recently liquidated telecoms business.

1.6.4 Confidentiality and disclosure (Chapter 4 of section 1 of the OFR Code)

Keeping the affairs of your client confidential is central to the relationship you have with a client and is fundamental to your ability to comply with the Principles. You should read Chapter 4 of section 1 of the OFR Code before you read this section of this chapter.

Your duty to keep your client's affairs confidential continues even though the retainer between you and your client is terminated and even on the death of your client. It is also not just the individual solicitor who has a duty to keep the affairs of his client confidential but *all* members of the firm.

Your duty of confidentiality exists at all times and is set out in **O(4.1)**.

O(4.1) you keep the affairs of *clients* confidential unless disclosure is required or permitted by law or the *client* consents;

O(4.2) any individual who is advising a *client* makes that *client* aware of all information material to that retainer of which the individual has personal knowledge;

O(4.3) you ensure that where your duty of confidentiality to one *client* comes into conflict with your duty of disclosure to another *client*, your duty of confidentiality takes precedence;

As it stands, this is not difficult to comply with or complicated. However, this must be read in conjunction with **O(4.2)**. You have a duty of confidentiality but you also have a duty to advise a client of any information which is material to them. The problem arises if you are acting for more than one client. A conflict may arise between the clients if your duty of confidentiality with one client conflicts with your duty to disclose information which is relevant and material to another client's matter. The Outcomes confirm how you need to deal with this situation. Look at **O(4.3)**. The duty of confidentiality takes precedence. This is the same as was set out in the 2007 Code. The duty of confidentiality always overrides the duty of disclosure.

To achieve the Outcomes you must disclose material information to a client but you must also keep information confidential. If you are unable to do this because to achieve your duty of confidentiality in **O(4.1)** you are unable to tell the other affected client of the information which is material to them because of **O(4.3)**, then you will need to cease acting for the client to whom you owe the duty of disclosure, and not tell that client why because of your duty of confidentiality to the other client.

Activity 11

Match up the following potential confidentiality situations with the suggested solutions or methods of achieving the Outcomes.

You work in a criminal practice. You hear your client on his mobile negotiating to buy firearms for a planned burglary.	You may be able to act but you would need to put in place safeguards, would need consent to act, and should deem it reasonable to act with those safeguards in place.
You outsource photocopying to an external printers. The next day an article in the press appears revealing information obtained from the material you outsourced.	You should not reveal this information.
You work for a large City firm. Your firm has acted for Client X who you know has financial issues. You are instructed by a private investor who intends to lend money to Client X.	You may still be able to show you have achieved the Outcomes if you can prove to the SRA you made sufficient checks to ensure client confidentiality.
An old client rings to say his mother has died and your firm prepared her will. He says his mother told him that she left her house to his son. He asks you to check this before he tells his son.	You should contact the police.

Conflicts, confidentiality, and disclosure is a lot about instinct and the more experienced you become in practice the more your instinct will become honed and you will begin to sense when situations do not feel right. You need to assess every individual situation and scenario to make sure you are acting within the Handbook.

Activity 12

Read the scenario about Tony and Dougie and circle or underline areas when you think there may be a conduct issue or the potential for a conduct issue to arise. Have a look at the solution to see how your instinct is doing so far.

Tony and Dougie McGovern come to see you and instruct you to act on their behalf. They run a building firm together. Tony set the firm up when he left school at 16 and Dougie joined him three years later when he also left school at 16. Tony had built up a considerable amount of goodwill when he was on his own.

Tony and Dougie tell you that up until now they have done building work to other people's houses but now want to take advantage of their skills and buy up properties, do them up, and sell them on. They are hoping this will be more profitable. They tell you that they want all of the properties put into their joint names even though Tony will be the one funding the purchases initially. They also tell you that they want to hold the properties as tenants in common but to be held in equal parts.

Tony says he is really busy and any correspondence whether by phone, letter, or email should be via Dougie. Dougie will discuss anything he needs to with Tony and will then get back to you.

Several weeks later you receive the official copies from the seller's solicitor in relation to a property they want to buy and begin to do the work. Dougie rings you unexpectedly and says he wants to instruct you to act for him also in relation to a personal matter. He tells you his wife is threatening to divorce him as she has found out he has been having an affair. He says he is really worried as she has said she is going to take him for everything he has! He doesn't want Tony to know as he thinks Tony will be really angry with him and worried about the financial effect on their business. He tells you to press on buying the property and not to do anything at the moment as he is going to try and talk his wife round but he wanted to give you a 'heads up' as he may need to instruct you if his wife refuses to listen.

What should you do now? What conduct issues does this scenario raise?

1.6.5 Your client and the court (Chapter 5 of section 1 of the OFR Code)

It is essential when you are acting as a litigator or trainee in a litigation department that you understand the additional Outcomes you must achieve. These will be looked at later in this chapter when discussed in context with what you will cover on the LPC in your civil and criminal litigation core subject.

1.6.6 You and others: relations with third parties (Chapter 11 of section 4 of the OFR Code)

It is worth noting that in the preface to the Outcomes it is specifically set out that the conduct requirement dealing with your relations to third parties extends beyond professional and business matters. It also ensures you do not use your professional title as a lawyer to advance your personal interest. This is inherent in any event under the Principles but the importance of how you act in your personal capacity, not just professional capacity, is again reiterated here.

In the 2007 Code there were specific rules dealing with how you needed to deal with other solicitors or members of the profession but these detailed rules have not been reproduced in the OFR Code. You need to go back to your overarching Principles, note the requirement to act with integrity, and behave in a manner which maintains the trust the public have placed in you.

This goes back to the overarching Principle: always act with integrity. Deal with other professionals in the same manner you would like to be treated.

The element of Chapter 11 on which we are going to concentrate for the purpose of this chapter is the undertaking point.

Look at the definition of undertaking as set out in Chapter 14 of the OFR Code. You will note how widely this extends. Anyone in a firm who gives a statement which someone else reasonably relies upon, whether given orally or in writing, will have given an undertaking. Relate this then to the Outcomes in Chapter 11.

O(11.2) you perform all *undertakings* given by you within an agreed timescale or within a reasonable amount of time;

Note the requirement to perform an undertaking within the agreed timescale or within a reasonable period of time. It is important therefore to ensure you never say you will do something when you have no control over whether or not that act can be achieved. Most firms will have very detailed guidelines as to when and how undertakings can be given. Note **IB(11.5)** which confirms that your firm may be meeting the Outcomes if you have a record of each undertaking given. This can be administratively quite time-consuming but it is very important so that a firm can keep track of what has been promised and ensure these are met.

Activity 13

Review this scenario.

It is 8pm and you are still in the office working—it has been a long day! You have just finished speaking with the solicitor on the other side of your transaction. You have finally managed to agree a contentious clause in a contract on behalf of a client. You tell the other solicitor while on the telephone that you will engross (prepare final versions of) the agreement and put the documents in the post, before you go home tonight, for signature by all parties. You also say that you will send with the documents some money for a survey which the other solicitor's clients had paid for and which your client had said they would meet the cost of. Your client had promised earlier in the day that they would drop a cheque off for you in the morning for this amount. You follow your conversation up with an email confirming the points discussed and confirming you would send the agreement and money.

At which point has an undertaking been given? What are the issues with this undertaking?

1.7   Professional conduct and the LPC core subject areas

1.7.1   Property law and practice

1.7.1.1   Introduction

In practice the specific areas of professional conduct which arise in relation to property arise in relation to acting for both the seller and buyer in property transactions, acting for both the lender and borrower in property transactions, and dealing with more than one prospective buyer in a conveyancing transaction. The other more sinister aspect of professional conduct and property can be seen in the huge rise in the use of property transactions for mortgage fraud and money laundering. This will be considered in more detail in **Chapter 3** of this textbook.

The conveyancing market has changed considerably over the last few years. Conveyancing was for many firms the 'bread and butter' of their income. However, this is no longer the case. The number of sole practitioners and smaller high street firms has dropped significantly over the last ten years and with this so has the traditional conveyancing model. This has been replaced to a large extent by bulk conveyancing. New case management software has replaced much of the personal contact between a client and lawyer. Clients can now access their file directly within the case management system to see how things are progressing and what stage of the transaction their file is at. The rise and then fall of the property market has also had a drastic effect not only on the residential property market but also the commercial property market and those law firms which rely on this type of work.

1.7.1.2   Conflicts of interest in property transactions

Professional conduct issues that arise in property transactions, whether residential or commercial conveyancing, centre on the issues of conflicts of interests or the potential for conflict. If you are a litigator then it is clear you cannot act for both the defendant and claimant as their requirements clearly conflict. However, this is not always so easy to spot in a non-contentious matter and you may feel able to act for both parties in such a scenario.

In the 2007 Code there were distinct rules dealing with acting for a buyer and seller and acting for a borrower and lender. Originally the SRA's intention had been to remove specific reference to property transactions from the conflict provisions, thereby ensuring that that situation was considered the same as any other potential conflict situation—that is, you cannot act if a conflict exists or arises except in limited circumstances. However, this was met with considerable concern from practitioners and the Law Society as to the confusion this would cause.

The OFR Code does follow the SRA's initial intention to some extent, as it does not contain any specific Outcomes which deal with acting for buyer and seller but it does in fact contain some Indicative Behaviours. Look at **IB(3.3)** and **IB(3.4)** which would suggest that you may have met the Outcomes if you decline to act for a buyer and seller when you would need to negotiate on the price of a property or where a builder is selling to a non-commercial client. Note also **IB(3.14)** which confirms that acting for a buyer and a seller may tend to show you have *not* met the Outcomes.

The position contained with the OFR Code actually reverses the 2007 Code where solicitors could act for a buyer and seller in specific limited circumstances. Under the OFR Code the Indicative Behaviours would suggest that you should not act—but always remember the Indicative Behaviours are not mandatory. Therefore, as with all Outcomes, it will be for the firm to show how it has achieved the Outcomes when acting for a buyer and seller in any given circumstance. The lack of specific Outcomes therefore does mean that you need to go back to basics and assess whether there is a conflict or a significant risk of a conflict occurring if you do act. If you are satisfied that no conflict exists then remember you would also then need to satisfy yourself that you can also achieve all of the Principles too. The SRA has noted that it is important to ensure the benefit of your acting for both a buyer and seller should be a benefit to the clients and not in your firm's own commercial interests.

The SRA has confirmed that acting for a buyer and seller is an area which carries a high risk and it does not expect firms routinely to act in these circumstances. The reasons why it is so high risk is because there would normally be some form of negotiating to be done over the price or some inequality in bargaining power which would make it very difficult to achieve Principle 4 on behalf of both clients. Remember also Principles 2, 3, and 5.

1.7.1.3   Acting for a borrower and lender

The position in relation to acting for a borrower and lender would seem to be not that far removed from the regulation in the 2007 Code, although far less detailed. If you look at **IB(3.7)** you may be showing evidence of complying with the Outcomes if when acting for a borrower and lender it is a standard mortgage and the certificate of title the lender asks you to use is in a form approved by the Council of Mortgage Lenders. The basics would therefore appear to be the same—that you can act in a residential situation for the buyer of a house who is taking out a mortgage, and act for the mortgage provider as well provided a conflict of interest does not arise during the transaction. You should not always assume that you can act in these circumstances. You need to consider conflict in every scenario. Remember this is just an Indicative Behaviour and it only *may* show that you have achieved the Outcomes.

If however you were acting in a commercial transaction it would be very unlikely because of **IB(3.7)** that you would be able to act for borrower and lender.

> **Activity 14**
>
> Why should the following situations make you look more closely at acting for the borrower and lender?
>
> > (a) You are acting for Simon who is buying a house. You are also acting for his mortgage provider. He tells you he is really relieved because the surveyor sent by the mortgage company to value the house missed the evidence of subsidence movement in his report to the mortgage provider so they have approved his loan. He doesn't think he would have got it otherwise!
> >
> > (b) You are still acting for Simon but this time there are no subsidence issues. However, he is not borrowing the money from a mortgage provider but from his father and his father has asked you to act for him too as it will make it easier.
> >
> > (c) You are doing your niece's conveyancing and you are lending her the money to buy her house. You are charging a commercial rate of interest.

1.7.1.4   Property law and practice and undertakings

We have already considered undertakings in **1.6.6** but it is worth noting that in conveyancing situations there are some undertakings automatically implied. Undertakings form part and parcel of the conveyancing transaction. For example, there are undertakings which assist with the procedure at exchange. You should be aware that these exist even though they may not be explicitly referred to. You will deal with these in more detail in the property law and practice core module on the LPC.

1.7.2 Litigation

1.7.2.1   Introduction

When considering litigation, the areas of professional conduct which most commonly arise are advice about funding and costs, refusing instructions to act as an advocate, your duty of disclosure and duty to the court, and appearing as an advocate. The most common question you will probably be asked by a layperson is: how can you defend a client if you know he or she is guilty? Your reading of the OFR Code will help you to answer this question.

The Outcomes you need to achieve in relation to your duties to the court and acting as an advocate are set out in Chapter 5 of section 1 of OFR Code. You should have this to hand as you read the scenario in **Activity 15**.

> **Activity 15**
>
> You work for a firm which specialises in criminal litigation. You are called to the police station late at night to represent a young man, Jack, in detention, who allegedly beat someone up last night. You take instructions from Jack and write down his story. He tells you that he didn't do it and the police have the wrong man and are trying to set him up because they don't like him and are always picking on him. He tells you that he doesn't work and is on benefits.
>
> You agree to act on behalf of Jack. You tell him you will prepare his proof of evidence and have it ready for him to check at the first court hearing.
>
> Jack enters a not guilty plea at the court hearing and afterwards you give him the proof of evidence which is several pages long, for him to read. He gives it back to you after one minute and says it is fine. You give him a pen and he signs it. The proof of evidence contains information from Jack which indicated he was at his girlfriend's when the incident took place and she will vouch for this. You draft Jack's defence statement on this basis and serve it on the prosecution.
>
> Some weeks later when the matter is listed for a pre-trial hearing, you meet Jack outside court as arranged. Jack tells you his girlfriend is running late maybe, he says, because she is reluctant to back up his

---

Activity 15—Continued

story. He says, 'Between you and me I bopped that lad but he deserved it. She is worried about lying in court—silly mare!'

You know that the 'other lad' who was allegedly beaten up by your client is a well-known drug dealer and actually you quite like Jack. He is just a scallywag rather than a criminal in your opinion! Anyway he told you all this as a friend and you want to keep on good terms with him. You decide not to do or say anything further based on the information he has just given you.

What conduct issues does this scenario highlight?

The issues contained in **Activity 15** relate to criminal litigation but the issues will be similar for commercial litigation. Instead of public funding you may need to advise clients in relation to conditional fee agreements and would need to advise them in full in relation to the possibility of having to meet the other parties' costs as well as your own. The other issues are the same as would face any litigator in court. Look at **O(5.1)–(5.8)** and remember too your overriding Principles 1, 2, and 6.

1.7.3 Business law and practice

1.7.3.1 Identifying your client

The main areas where you are going to come across conduct issues in a more corporate setting are in deciding who your client is and avoiding conflicts of interest. Deciding who your client is may sound quite straightforward but in a corporate or commercial sense this can actually be quite difficult.

Activity 16

You are instructed by Mr Red, Mr Green, and Mr Orange to incorporate a new business called Colour Me Happy Limited. They all intend to be directors and shareholders in the business. Mr Orange currently owns a property which he is going sell to Colour Me Happy Limited to be used as its new head office.

Who is your client?

1.7.3.2 Conflicts of interest

In **1.6.3** we already looked at the issues which you may encounter in relation to conflicts of interest in commercial transactions and the exceptions contained in **O(3.6)** and **O(3.7)** which are only likely to be utilised by sophisticated legal services users and therefore, more likely, the large corporate firms. This is a particularly tricky area and you should always remember that conflict-warning instinct which you should pay attention to.

Activity 17

You have been acting for Montgomery Limited for the past five years and have dealt with a number of legal issues for it, including incorporating the company initially and drafting the shareholders' agreement. You now receive instructions from one of the directors regarding a property he owns which is leased to the company. It appears the company is in financial difficulty and is in six months' arrears with its rent.

What professional conduct issues do you need to consider here?

1.8 Professional conduct: checkpoints

You should now be able to:

- identify how you should behave as a member of the profession;
- understand the overarching Principles which govern the legal profession;
- find your way around the OFR Code and understand how it works; and
- identify the areas of professional conduct which are most relevant to you at this stage of your studies.

1.9   Suggested solutions to Chapter 1 activities

Activity 1

- To do a good job!
- To provide clear advice and explanations.
- To be able to keep things confidential.
- To be proactive. A client does not want to feel it always has to ring you to find out what is happening or if anything is happening.
- To provide clear information as to how much the matter will cost.
- To communicate effectively.
- To understand how to treat a client—a client thinks he is like a consumer and therefore 'the customer is always right'.
- Note there are certain circumstances where this might not be true and by following your client's instructions you may in fact be breaching Principle 4 to act in a client's best interest. Imagine if your client were getting divorced and told you to delay matters as much as possible because he wanted to make things difficult for his wife. This would be following a client's instructions but would not be in his best interests and you would have to explain your duty to him.
- To help and inform the client in its decision-making process.
- To have good problem-solving skills.
- To be able to think outside the box and come up with innovative solutions or commercial recommendations.
- To always put the client's needs first.
- To be realistic and honest. It is better to tell a client at the outset it cannot win a case rather than let them litigate only to lose! This again goes directly to your ability to comply with the Principles. Don't waste your client's money or public funding!
- To follow instructions from the client (*subject to the comments above*).
- To manage the client's expectations. Don't tell a client you will be completing next week, or will send a letter out tonight if you won't be able to meet that deadline.
- To appreciate the importance of timing. Remember to a client its transaction is the only transaction! It doesn't know you have a mountain of paperwork on your desk to deal with nor should it need to know. You need to have excellent time management skills.
- To ascertain and understand the client's objectives. This goes directly to the goal of the OFR Code which is to achieve Outcomes for individual clients. It is not just a tick-box system the rules of which are applicable to *all* clients.
- To become familiar with the client's business in order to be able to always act in a client's best interests.

Activity 2

- Use a diary to keep track of all due dates, meetings, and scheduled activities.
- Make and use 'to do lists' every day.
- Anticipate deadlines and high stress periods and work these into your day/week.
- Set priorities and deadlines. Categorise 'to do list' tasks into high, medium, and low priorities and focus on high priorities first.
- Divide large tasks into several smaller parts. Focus on a small task to complete one part at a time. This will make a big project feel more manageable.
- Regularly ask yourself, 'What is the best use of my time right now?' Do that task.
- Schedule time for 10/15-minute breaks and 'interruptions'. That will leave you some time for the inevitable 'unplanned' jobs you will have to undertake.
- Don't forget to sleep, exercise, and eat! This will allow you to stay physically fit and mentally alert.
- Within limits learn to say no. Commit yourself only to those activities you have time for.
- Do one task at a time and finish it; avoid procrastination—get on and do the job.
- Many firms have clear desk policies so you will need to clear your desk at the end of the day. This is an excellent way of ensuring you are working in an organised and systematic fashion.

Activity 4

Remember under the OFR Code what will satisfy the Outcomes for one client will not necessarily satisfy the Outcomes for another.

(a) If your client is illiterate you will have to give them extra support and think of ways around this problem. You may initially advise them of the likely cost in a meeting with them and agree to phone weekly with an update. You may be able to set up an automated text service if your client can read numbers, updating them in relation to the costs during a transaction. A detailed letter discussing potential legal costs and disbursements is not going to meet this client's requirements and you would therefore not be achieving **O(1.13)**.

(b) You will need an interpreter either to translate a letter setting out the costs into the client's language or to interpret in a face-to-face meeting and discuss the costs. Again remember the ongoing requirement to keep your client informed of the potential costs. This will all need to be done in their language.

(c) It will probably be appropriate for a firm to send out what has been called a client care letter in the 2007 Code to this type of client at the start of a transaction and send updates in a written format as necessary. This will be a fairly detailed letter explaining charge out rates, disbursements, and estimates. Agree with your client how they would like this information—letter, email, fax.

(d) A large corporate, experienced, legal service user may not want or need detailed information in relation to costs at the start of the transaction. You could provide access to its case management file on your computer systems so it can have an ongoing view of the costs. The company may ask to pay you a set fee per month for continuous legal advice and just ask you to provide a breakdown of costs as and when needed.

Activity 5

New information has been received which means the likelihood is that the costs will be greater than originally envisaged. To achieve the Outcomes clients must receive, when appropriate and as the matter progresses, the best possible information in relation to costs. **O(1.13)** sets out this requirement.

Activity 5—Continued

Since you have received this new information you need to give the client an update on the likely increase in costs and potential costs of the other side if this matter becomes litigious. Look at **IB(1.11)**. This suggests that you need to explain your fees clearly and if and when they are likely to change. **IB(1.12)** says you should give warnings about any other payments which the client may be responsible for.

Although the IBs are not mandatory, remember their preamble confirms that if you follow them, you may tend to show you have achieved the Outcomes. If you do not achieve the Outcome and have not followed the IBs, it will be for you to prove to the SRA how, by any alternative means, you have met the Outcome.

Activity 6

This too may **achieve** the Outcomes. Note there is no requirement to have a **written** complaints procedure. You only have to tell a client that they can complain in writing. **IB(1.22)** suggests having one would achieve the Outcomes but remember the IBs are **not** mandatory.

(a) A client who has been referred to you emails you and gives you some background details on a transaction he wants to instruct you on. You send him a brief email back just introducing yourself and commenting on his email. The client responds and confirms that he wants to instruct you. You email him a letter and include within this letter information on the client's right to complain if there is an issue and the estimated cost of the matter.

This **achieves** the Outcomes as the fact a client can complain must under **O(1.9)** be given in writing at the start of the matter.

(b) An angry client contacts the firm's receptionist and says, 'I want to make a complaint and don't tell me I can't because I know I am entitled to because the solicitor told me I could in the first letter he ever wrote to me!' The receptionist gives very clear oral instructions about the procedure available to the client.

(c) A client who has been referred to you comes into the office to see you. He decides on the spot that he is so keen to instruct you that you discuss with him at this first interview the likely costs and the fact that if he so wishes in the future he can make a complaint, and how to go about that. You go back to your desk and open a file. Part of the firm's opening file procedure is a checklist. You tick the boxes in relation to the OFR Code's costs and complaints requirements as having been met.

This **does not achieve** the Outcomes. Under **O(1.9)** the client must be informed in writing that he has the right to complain.

Activity 7

The Outcomes in Chapter 1 in relation to client care do not provide specific information as to how you should give the client the information he needs to understand his engagement of you as his solicitor. This is because you need to focus on the Principles and ensure you are achieving the right Outcomes for your particular client. What is right for one client is not necessarily right for another. You need to take into account in every case a client's particular needs and circumstances.

In this case it is likely you will not have met the Outcomes because the receptionist has suggested the client read a detailed letter and work out what he needs to do next. You know his reading and writing skills are limited so this needs to be taken into account when considering the Outcomes for this particular client. There is probably too much complex information contained in this lengthy letter and this would affect the client's ability to read and understand the information contained within it. In these circumstances it would have been better for the receptionist to have talked the client through what he needed to do in very clear steps. Another option would have been to invite the client in to talk through his complaint with a dedicated complaints handler at the firm who could discuss his options with him.

Activity 8

(a) It would be reasonable to stop acting for this client. She has consistently not been paying her bills despite your chasing her for them. A solicitor is entitled to be paid for his/her services!

(b) Your reasons for refusal must be reasonable. You cannot refuse instructions based on a personal dislike of something or someone or their beliefs. You would however have to think carefully whether you could act in a client's best interests if you felt very strongly about this issue.

(c) You are not allowed to accept gifts from clients unless they take independent legal advice. Look at IB(1.9); you may be showing achievement of the Outcomes if you refuse to act in these circumstances. But in this instance this is more than a gift; this is almost a bribe which may affect your judgement when acting and would most certainly be in breach of Principle 3 and very likely Principles 2 and 5.

(d) You may think this is a conflict but it is not because this is not the 'same matter' which is required for a conflict to exist. Look at the definition of 'client conflict' in Chapter 14. However, there is some professional embarrassment here and you would not be able to comply with the Principles. You might feel unable to act for the new instructing client because you may feel inhibited to act in your client's best interests because of your previous relationship with Tom. You may be able to show reasonable reasons for refusing instructions in such a scenario.

Activity 9

You are a trainee at a firm which only offers property advice services. You are being asked by a client to advise on an employment matter. Remember you must provide your client with a good standard of service under Principle 5. Your firm does not appear to have the appropriate resources. O(1.4) states that you must have the resources, skill, and procedure to carry out your client's instructions. You cannot achieve O(1.4). IB(1.7) confirms that you must decline to act if you can't act in the client's best interests. In this scenario you would not have the expertise to achieve the Outcomes or the Principles. You must tell your client that they will need to appoint another solicitor. You could suggest solicitors who have the appropriate expertise.

Activity 10

This should have made your conflict-warning bell chime. Here you have two clients who want to instruct you in relation to the purchase of a telecoms business.

You need to look at the conflict Outcomes to see if you can achieve them and the Principles.

To satisfy O(3.1) and O(3.3) you should ensure your systems and controls are sufficient and suitable for your client base. Here you are a trainee at a large City firm. The large numbers of clients and transactions which your firm is likely to be involved with, along with the number of fee-earners involved, would suggest you would need a very rigorous and tested technical software program to cross-check your large client base and assess if there is a conflict. This should reveal the fact that you are being asked to act for two clients who wish to purchase the same business. On this basis there would appear to be a potential conflict.

This would potentially be a 'client conflict'. Remember under O(3.5) that you cannot act if there is a conflict of interest or risk of conflict of two or more clients in relation to the same or related matter unless the situation falls within one of the limited exceptions set out in O(3.6) and O(3.7).

O(3.6) allows you to act subject to appropriate safeguards if the clients have a *substantially common interest*. If you look at the definition of substantially common interest in Chapter 14, you will see this means where there is a clear common purpose. This is not the case here. They are each wanting to buy the business, not buy the business together.

Activity 10—Continued

O(3.7) allows you to act where the clients are *competing for the same objective.* You will note that this is defined as 'asset, contract or business opportunity', which is the case here. You can only act if:

(a) the clients are both aware that you are acting for two clients and both clients have confirmed in writing their consent for you to act in this situation;

(b) there is no other client conflict;

(c) different solicitors act for each client unless the clients specifically agree otherwise; and

(d) you are satisfied that it is reasonable for you to act and that your acting benefits the client more than any risk that might arise to them of your firm acting for both parties.

You also need to be aware of **IB(3.5)** and **IB(3.7)** which would suggest that you may be achieving the Outcomes only if you act in the above circumstances, if there is no unequal bargaining power, and if the clients are sophisticated users of legal services. Also look at **IB(3.12)** which goes further and would suggest that you may not be achieving the Outcomes if you act under the exception in **O(3.7)** if there is an unequal bargaining power.

Before deciding whether to act, you would need to check all of this in addition to ensuring you would also be meeting the Principles.

Activity 11

Match up the following potential confidentiality situations with possible solutions or methods of achieving the Outcomes.

You work in a criminal practice. You hear your client on his mobile negotiating to buy firearms for a planned burglary.	You should contact the police. *Such disclosure is permitted by law. Note IB(4.2).*
You outsource photocopying to an external printers. The next day an article in the press appears revealing information obtained from the material you outsourced.	You may still be able to show you have achieved the Outcomes if you can prove to the SRA you made sufficient checks to ensure client confidentiality. *See IB(4.3).*
An old client rings to say his mother has died and your firm prepared her will. He says his mother told him that she left her house to his son. He asks you to check this before he tells his son.	You should not reveal this information. *See IB(4.6). If you disclose the content of a will, this may suggest that you have not achieved the Outcomes.*
You act for Client X who you know has financial issues. You are instructed by a private investor who intends to lend money to Client X.	You may be able to act but you would need to put in place safeguards, would need consent to act, and should deem it reasonable to act with those safeguards in place. *See O(4.4).*

Activity 12

Read the scenario about Tony and Dougie and circle or underline areas when your conduct-warning chime starts to ring. Have a look at the solution to see how your instinct is doing so far.

Tony and Dougie McGovern come to see you and instruct you to act on behalf of them. Together they run a building firm.

There is nothing wrong with acting for two clients so long as you keep in mind that you can't act if a conflict exists or arises.

*Don't forget to achieve all of the basic client care Outcomes in relation to costs and complaints procedures and go through this with them. You also need to make sure you do a conflict check (your firm should ensure it has the appropriate systems in place to achieve this). Remember **O(3.1–3.3)**.*

Tony had built up a considerable amount of goodwill when he was on his own.

Your instinct (which should be quite honed by now!) should start to kick in. It would appear there is an imbalance in their interests in the business. Not an issue yet but you need to keep it in mind.

They tell you that they want all of the properties put into their joint names even though Tony will be the one funding the purchases initially. They also tell you that they want to hold the property as tenants in common but to be held in equal parts.

Your instinct should be in full mode now! Your instructions are to put the properties into joint names, albeit to be held as tenants in common but you are told this is to be on the basis of equal shares. So any equity in the property will be split equally even though it is Tony funding the purchases. Are you acting in each client's best interest? Will you be able to uphold the Principles?

Tony says he is really busy and any correspondence whether by phone, letter, or email should be via Dougie and Dougie will discuss anything he needs to with Tony and will then get back to you.

*You should be concerned by this. How can you ensure that Dougie is checking anything with Tony. Look at **IB(1.25)**. You need to make sure that you are satisfied that the person providing the instructions has the authority to do so. Get Tony to confirm this in writing.*

Several weeks later you receive the official copies from the seller's solicitor in relation to a property they want to buy and begin to do the work.

So long as you have satisfied yourself that there is no conflict and you have achieved the client care Outcomes it should be okay to go ahead and start work.

Activity 12—Continued

Dougie rings you unexpectedly and says he wants to instruct you to act for him also in relation to a personal matter. He tells you his wife is threatening to divorce him as she has found out he has been having an affair. He says he is really worried as she has said she is going to take him for everything he has! He doesn't want Tony to know as he thinks Tony will be really angry with him and worried about the financial effect on their business. He tells you to press on buying the property, not to tell Tony, and not to do anything at the moment as he is going to try and talk his wife round but he wanted to give you a 'heads up' as he may need to instruct you if his wife refuses to listen.

What should you do now?

On the face of it this is okay. You can act for one client on another matter so long as you always keep in mind the Outcomes you need to achieve and Principles you need to abide by. Outcomes in relation to conflict and confidentiality should be issues you should be thinking about at this stage.

At this point you should be very concerned. You know that Tony is funding the purchase of the property but that the equity will be held 50/50. The ownership of these assets would likely be taken into account in any financial settlement in a divorce.

Oh oh! You now hold information which is material to one client but which you are not able to tell him because of your need to keep affairs of a client confidential. **See O(4.1).** *Dougie has also specifically instructed you not to tell Tony.*

You should explain to Dougie what duties you need to comply with.

You need to explain your duty in **O(4.2)** *to tell Tony. However, remember you also have a duty to Dougie in* **O(4.1)** *to keep his information confidential. Note* **O(4.3).** *Your duty of confidentiality takes precedence over your duty of disclosure.*

You should tell Dougie that, unless he consents to your telling Tony of the threats from his wife, you will have to stop acting for Tony but you will not be able to tell Tony why you have to stop acting. Tony would obviously then be very suspicious! Dougie would probably have to end up telling Tony anyway! If Dougie gives you consent then you would be able to continue acting PROVIDED no conflict arose.

If Tony, on hearing of the problem, instructed you that he wanted the properties in his name only and Dougie did not agree with this, you should not continue to act for both of them. You could not act in both of their best interests.

Activity 13

At which point has an undertaking been given. What are the issues with this undertaking?

- As soon as you tell the solicitor on the telephone that you will put the documents in the post and send the money you have given an undertaking. Look at the definition in Chapter 14. An undertaking can be given orally and does not have to contain the word 'undertake'. You have at this point promised to do something which the other solicitor is relying on.

- It is 8 o'clock at night and therefore you cannot put the documents in the post. Last post in the UK is usually at 6pm. Therefore you will have breached this element of the undertaking. A breach but probably not too bad an error as you could make sure the documents were hand delivered the next day if the other solicitor's firm was close. Or you could ring the solicitor in the morning and confirm that you of course could not put them in the post last night but will do so today.

- More of an issue is the undertaking to send the money. You have given an undertaking to send some money based on a promise from your client to drop a cheque off in the morning. There are two issues with this. First the client may not drop the cheque off at all whereby your firm will have to meet the costs of this undertaking! Your firm will not be very happy with you! Secondly even if the client does drop off the cheque in the morning, cheques take at least five working days to clear so you still won't have funds in the morning—and the cheque might bounce!

- You should never give an undertaking to send money unless you have cleared funds from your client in your client account.

Activity 14

Why should the following situations make you look more closely at acting for the borrower and lender?

(a) This goes back to your conflict issues. You are acting for two clients here: the lender and the borrower. Until Simon told you about the subsidence movement you could act for both of them as long as there was not a conflict. Now a conflict has arisen. You hold material information which you have a duty to disclose under **O(4.2)** and a duty to Simon under **O(4.1)**. Remember your duty of confidentiality overrides your duty of disclosure. You would therefore have to stop acting for the bank and not tell it why unless Simon let you disclose the information to the lender.

(b) You cannot act for two or more clients where there is a conflict of interest. From the facts there does not appear to be any conflict between the parties. But note **IB(3.7)(a)**. The IBs would suggest that you would only be satisfying the Outcomes if the lender is a normal institutional lender. Here Simon's father is not a normal institutional lender. This would therefore fall under the general conflict Outcomes and Principles—that you can act if you can act in the best interests of *each* client and their interests do not conflict. If Simon's father instructed you to add an unusually high interest rate to the mortgage document then this would not be in Simon's best interest and a conflict would arise at this point. You should then not act for both.

(c) This is an 'own interest conflict'. You would be lending the money. Remember you can never act where there is a conflict or significant risk of conflict between you and your client. It would be difficult for you to prove in this scenario that you have met your niece's needs as you had such an inherent interest in the matter. You should not act.

Activity 15

What if any conduct issues does this scenario highlight?

He tells you he didn't do it.

You agree to act on behalf of Jack	*Don't forget to do your conflict check first!*
You take instructions from Jack and write down his story.	*You should take care when taking instructions to ensure the information is true. You do not have an additional duty to investigate whether it is true. You can take the information given to you at face value but if there are obvious holes in your client's story you need to be careful. Look at O(5.1) You must not knowingly or recklessly mislead the court.*
You tell him you will prepare his proof of evidence.	*Make sure you draft this in language appropriate for your particular client. Use clear, plain English so your client can understand it.*
He tells you that he doesn't work and is on benefits.	*You should be thinking about funding. Your client will probably be eligible for public funding. You need to satisfy O(1.13).*
He gives it back to you after one minute and says it is fine. You give him a pen and he signs it.	*Can your client really have read this in full in that time? Can he read? Is he too embarrassed to tell you? Remember you will be drafting his defence statement based on this and the defence statement is going to be relied upon in court!*
Jack tells you his girlfriend is running late maybe, he says, because she is reluctant to back up his story. He says, 'Between you and me I bopped that lad but he deserved it, she is worried about lying in court—silly mare!'	*At this point you should be very concerned! You have knowledge that the client is misleading the court. You will be in breach of O(5.1). He had told you he was at his girlfriend's and you put this information in his defence statement. You now know this is not true.*
You decide not to do or say anything further based on the information he has just given you.	*You **must** tell Jack of your duties to the court. Look at O(5.2) and O(5.4). You can advise Jack that he can maintain a not guilty plea and make the prosecution prove the case against him, but you cannot advance the defence statement which suggests he can't have done it as he was at his girlfriend's, as you now know this is not true. The defence statement will need to be withdrawn or amended. Look at IB(5.4), IB (5.5), and IB(5.9). You should advise Jack to allow you to withdraw or amend the defence statement. If he refuses to give you consent you should stop acting.*

Activity 16

Who is your client?

It is important to work out who you are instructed by and acting for. If you do not, there is a risk that you will be acting when there is a conflict of interests, or a significant risk of one which, as you know, will mean that you are not achieving the Outcomes.

You could be acting for the directors of the company, you could be acting for the shareholders of the company, or you could be acting for Mr Orange in his personal capacity as seller, or you could be acting for Colour Me Happy Limited, the company as the buyer.

You can see how in a business scenario it is not as easy as it may seem to answer the question of who is your client!

Activity 17

What professional conduct issues do you need to consider here?

Again it is important to consider who your client is. Is it the company Montgomery Limited as the tenant or is it the director who has contacted you as landlord? You would not be able to act for both here. Your conflict antenna should have suggested that there is going to be a conflict of interest here.

This is a contentious issue between a landlord and a tenant. Remember you cannot act for two clients where there is a conflict of interest or risk of a conflict. The tenant may argue there are good reasons for it withholding rent or dispute the fact entirely that it is in arrears!

The exceptions in **O(3.6)** and **O(3.7)** do not apply here as there is no common purpose nor are the clients competing for the same asset or business.

You should not act. It is very unlikely that you would be achieving the Outcomes in the OFR Code or the Principles.

 online resource centre

Visit the Online Resource Centre for more information and useful weblinks.
www.oxfordtextbooks.co.uk/orc/foundations17_18/

Financial services

2.1 Introduction

The first part of this chapter is a general introduction to the regulation of financial services. The Financial Services and Markets Act 2000 ('FSMA 2000') is put into context and the need for authorisation under the Act is explained. What is covered by the general prohibition is considered, as are the meanings of 'regulated activity' and 'specified investment'.

The second part (**2.5** onwards) discusses the position of solicitors, specifically those who are regulated by the Law Society, a 'designated professional body'.

To help you to assess your learning, a series of short-answer questions is included. Five scenarios are also set out to help you in the application of the financial services regulation to solicitors in their everyday work.

The FSMA 2000 has been amended by the Financial Services Act 2012. This introduced changes to the regulation of financial services, including the renaming of the Financial Services Authority as the Financial Conduct Authority ('FCA'). The changes took effect from 1 April 2013.

2.1.1 Investments

To appreciate the legislation and its effect fully it is helpful to understand what the legislation affects. The FSMA 2000 uses the term 'investment'. It helps, initially, to consider the word in its wider meaning, rather than in the narrower meaning which is given to it under the legislation.

A dictionary definition of 'investment' is 'monies *invested* for income or profit'. The definition of the verb 'to invest' is 'to commit monies to a particular use in order to earn a financial return'.

The meaning which is given to the word 'investment' in the FSMA 2000 does not include all investments in the wider meaning (the meaning of the word for the purposes of the FSMA 2000 is considered at **2.1.3.2**).

2.1.1.1 Financial return

The financial return—the income or profit—can be a return of income or capital, income being a recurring return and capital being a one-off benefit.

So an investment is something which will, it is hoped, bring in a return. Monies can be invested in a number of different ways. There are investments which will bring in solely income; investments which will bring in solely capital; and investments which will bring in a combination of both. The return received on an investment generally reflects the risk involved in making the investment.

2.1.1.2 The risk

The risk attached to an investment is the chance of the original money invested being lost to the investor. Some investments carry little (if any) risk and the return on these is usually predictable and on the low side, for example a building society deposit account. A deposit account pays a lower rate of interest than that paid on the more usual building society account people invest in—a building society share account—but the deposit account has the advantage that should the society find itself in difficulties the account holder is guaranteed first repayment from the funds available and so the chances of the investor losing his capital are negligible.

Other investments carry a much higher risk, for example shares on the stock market. The chance of a high return, by way of income (dividends) or capital growth, is there, but there is always a chance of the original investment being lost if, for example, the company goes into liquidation. An investor should always be aware of the risk attached to a particular investment, and investors should invest in those investments which carry a degree of risk only if they can afford to lose their original investment.

The diagram in **Figure 2.1** shows various investments building up the layers in a pyramid. The higher in the pyramid, the more risky the investment. A lottery, with no real chance of the stake being returned, floats above the pyramid.

2.1.1.3   Other considerations

There are a great number of investments on the market—bank or building society accounts, gilts, equities, unit trusts—and which investment a person makes depends very much on the investor's individual circumstances and requirements. Risk is not the only factor to be taken into account on making an investment; other considerations are:

(a) Will the capital be needed with only a short period of notice?

(b) Are there tax advantages which should be considered?

(c) One consideration which should not be overlooked: what will give the investor peace of mind?

Appendix 2 to this book gives details of a number of investments. It also contains an explanation of some of the 'jargon' used in the financial services sector, with which it is useful to be familiar.

Figure 2.1   Pyramid of risk

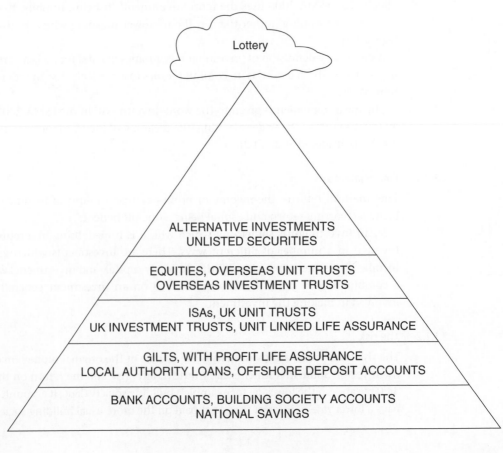

2.1.2   The background to the Financial Services and Markets Act 2000

With so many products on the market, investors often look for advice on which investment to make. Who can investors turn to?

Historically, and until 29 April 1988, investors could look to anyone for advice. The financial services industry was left to self-regulation with no one agency in overall control of the field. There was no requirement on financial advisers to have any qualifications, or for them to be registered or authorised. Anyone could advise a person about investments. This was found to be inadequate and gave rise, in the late 1970s and early 1980s, to a number of scandals in the investment sector, in which investors lost considerable sums of money through poor advice. In addition the investment markets were rapidly changing. In 1981, the then Secretary of State appointed Professor LCB Gower to carry out a review of the law on investor protection.

This review resulted in the Financial Services Act 1986, an Act which introduced measures to regulate 'investment business' and those who gave investment advice (or, in the words of the Act, those who carried on investment business). It achieved this by prohibiting a person from carrying on investment business in the UK unless that person was authorised under the Act, or was an exempt person (Financial Services Act 1986, s 3). The Financial Services Act 1986 came into force on 29 April 1988 and, until 1 December 2001, any investment business carried on after that date was caught by that Act.

At midnight on 30 November 2001, the FSMA 2000 came into force, repealing the Financial Services Act 1986. The FSMA 2000 was, itself, amended by the Financial Services Act 2012 and on 1 April 2013 a new regulatory framework was created to oversee the financial services industry.

2.1.2.1   The effect of the Act as amended

There are two financial regulators for the financial services industry: The Prudential Regulation Authority ('PRA') and the Financial Conduct Authority ('FCA'). The PRA supervises financial institutions. The FCA is an independent conduct of business regulator and regulates firms and financial advisers. It is with the FCA that we are concerned.

2.1.2.2   FCA's general duties

Set out in the FSMA 2000 are the statutory objectives that guide the FCA. The FCA's strategic objective is to ensure that the relevant markets function well. There are also three operational objectives: the consumer protection objective; the integrity objective; and the competition objective (FSMA 2000, s 1B). One of the aims of the FCA in meeting the consumer protection objective is to secure the appropriate degree of protection for consumers having regard to the differing degrees of risk involved with different kinds of investment. In addition, the differing degrees of experience and expertise that consumers may have in relation to different kinds of regulated activity are to be taken into account. One concept to which the FCA will also have regard is the general principle that consumers should take responsibility for their own decisions (FSMA 2000, s 1C(2)(d)).

2.1.2.3   The general prohibition

The FSMA 2000, s 19 prohibits a person from carrying on a regulated activity unless that person is authorised under the Act, or is an exempt person. Section 19(2) refers to this prohibition as 'the general prohibition'.

2.1.2.4   Sanctions

The FSMA 2000 sets out the sanctions for breaching the general prohibition. It is a criminal offence (FSMA 2000, s 23). In addition, any agreement made by a person in contravention of the general prohibition is unenforceable, and action can be taken to recover money or property paid or transferred and for compensation for any loss (FSMA 2000, s 26). The amount of compensation to be paid is set out in s 28 of the Act. Further, it is a criminal offence to make a false claim to be, or falsely to hold oneself out as, an authorised or exempt person.

2.1.2.5   Authorisation and exemption

To be able to carry on a regulated activity without contravening the general prohibition a person must be either an authorised person or an exempt person.

Section 31 sets out the categories of authorised persons for the purposes of the FSMA 2000. There are four categories, but this chapter is concerned only with the first—that of being a 'person' who has a Part 4A permission to carry on one or more regulated activities. The 'person' may be an individual, a body corporate, a partnership, or an unincorporated association (FSMA 2000, s 40). To have a Part 4A permission and so be authorised an application is made to the FCA. If granted Part 4A permission the authorised person is regulated by the FCA and is subject to the rules and regulations made by the FCA. These rules and regulations are set out in the FCA Rule Book.

The FSMA 2000, s 38 provides for the Treasury to permit specified persons or those falling within a specified class to be exempt from the general prohibition. An order has been made by the Treasury (the Financial Services and Markets Act 2000 (Exemption) Order 2001 (SI 2001 No 1201)) which provides for various persons to be exempt from the general prohibition. The exemptions are not comprehensive. However, the detail of the order is beyond the scope of this chapter.

The provision of relevance to most solicitors is that contained in FSMA 2000, Part XX. This grants an exemption from the general prohibition to members of the professions. This is explained in detail at **2.2**.

2.1.3   The need for authorisation

When is a person carrying on a regulated activity with the consequence that authorisation under the Act is required?

The FSMA 2000, s 22 provides:

22.—(1) An activity is a regulated activity for the purpose of this Act if it is an activity of a specified kind which is carried on by way of business and—

   (a) relates to an investment of a specified kind or

   (b) in the case of an activity of a kind which is also specified for the purposes of this paragraph, is carried on in relation to property of any kind.

[...]

   (4) 'Investment' includes any asset, right or interest.

   (5) 'Specified' means specified in an order made by the Treasury.

For the activity to be a regulated activity and caught by the general prohibition it must generally:

   (a) be an activity of a specified kind;

   (b) be carried on by way of business; and

   (c) relate to an investment of a specified kind.

There are some activities which do not have to relate to a specified investment (FSMA 2000, s 22(1)(b)).

Regulated activities and investments of a specified kind warrant further explanation (see **2.1.3.1** and **2.1.3.2**).

2.1.3.1   Regulated activities

The FSMA 2000 does not itself define what activities are regulated activities. This is left to secondary legislation, in that the Act provides for the Treasury to make an order specifying activities that are to be included in the definition of 'regulated activities' (FSMA 2000, s 22(5)). To date, the Treasury has made one order specifying the kind of activities which are regulated activities—the Financial Services and Markets Act 2000 (Regulated Activities) Order 2001 (SI 2001 No 544) ('RAO').

The specified activities listed at present include:

(a) dealing in investments as agent;

(b) arranging deals in investments;

(c) managing investments;

(d) advising on investments;

(e) entering as provider into a funeral plan contract; and

(f) entering into or administering regulated mortgage contracts.

2.1.3.1.1 *Dealing in investments as agent*

This involves the buying, selling, subscribing for, or underwriting of securities or contractually based investments as agent.

2.1.3.1.2 *Arranging deals in investments*

This could also be described as making arrangements for another person to *deal*. Simply recommending an investor to a broker would not be arranging. There must be some active participation.

2.1.3.1.3 *Managing investments*

This requires involvement in addition to just holding the investments, for example receiving dividends on shares which form part of a trust fund which a solicitor is administering; or on a trust fund which a solicitor is administering, deciding whether or not a rights issue for shares, offered by a company in whom the trust has shares, should be taken up.

2.1.3.1.4 *Advising on investments*

This involves giving advice to an investor on the merits of making a particular investment. It may be distinguished from the giving of generic advice on investments. For example, giving advice on the benefits of a repayment mortgage compared with an endowment mortgage is generic advice and is not caught by the Act.

2.1.3.1.5 *Entering as provider into a funeral plan contract*

A funeral plan contract is a contract under which, in return for the customer making a payment, the provider undertakes to provide a funeral in the UK for the customer (or another person). Where it is expected, or intended, that the funeral will take place within one month of the contract then the funeral plan contract is not caught by the legislation.

2.1.3.1.6 *Excluded activities*

In addition to listing the specified activities, the RAO also sets out exclusions that are applicable. Where an exclusion applies (and this can be defined by the investment subject to the activity, or by the activity itself), the activity does not fall under the FSMA 2000 and so no authorisation is required. The person can engage in the activity without fear of prosecution. Examples include: dealing with or through authorised persons (RAO, Art 22), unless a commission is received for which he does not account to the client; arranging deals with or through authorised persons (RAO, Art 29), unless a commission is received for which he does not account to the client; funeral contract plans where the plan is covered by insurance or trust arrangements (RAO, Art 60).

In addition to the exclusions set out as applicable to individual activities the RAO also sets out a number of exclusions that apply to several specified kinds of activity. Three exclusions which will be of relevance to solicitors are 'trustees, nominees and personal representatives' (RAO, Art 66), 'Activities carried on in the course of a profession or non-investment business' (RAO, Art 67), and 'Provision of information on an incidental basis' (RAO, Art 72C) (see **2.5.1**).

2.1.3.2   Specified investments

As with regulated activities, the Act does not itself define what investments are specified investments. This is also dealt with in the RAO (RAO, Part III). The investments listed in the RAO as specified investments include:

(a) deposits;

(b) contracts of insurance (this includes, for example, life policies, defective title indemnity, household and buildings insurance, after the event legal expenses insurance). So far as exclusions are concerned contracts of insurance are dealt with differently to other types of investments and are excluded from some exclusions, notably RAO, Articles 66 and 67 (see **2.5.1**);

(c) shares;

(d) instruments creating or acknowledging indebtedness;

(e) government and public securities, but excluding National Savings products;

(f) instruments giving entitlement to investments;

(g) certificates representing certain securities;

(h) units in a collective investment scheme;

(i) options;

(j) futures;

(k) funeral plan contracts; and

(l) regulated mortgage contracts.

Some investments which are not included, and consequently are not regulated by the Act, are:

(i) land;

(ii) currency; and

(iii) tangible assets, eg art, classic cars, etc.

2.2   Relevance to solicitors

So far as solicitors are concerned, the FSMA 2000 impacts on them. They are carrying on a business; their work involves investments specified under the FSMA 2000 (shares in an estate which the solicitor is administering; an endowment policy being cancelled on the sale of a property and the redemption of the mortgage); and solicitors frequently engage in a specified activity—dealing, arranging, managing, or advising. Furthermore, it is unlikely that the activity will be excluded under the Act. They are carrying on regulated activities. Consequently solicitors, on the face of it, need to be authorised to engage in their work which may fall to be regulated under the FSMA 2000.

2.2.1   The Law Society as a designated professional body

The regulated activities that most solicitors engage in are those which arise out of their main work as solicitors; they are incidental to their main work. For example, this would include selling shares in an estate that the solicitor is administering. Under the regime these activities are referred to as 'non-mainstream regulated activities'. Some solicitors do engage in regulated activities that are not incidental to their main work: for example, advising a client on what investments to make with an inheritance received. Such activities are termed 'mainstream regulated activities'.

The majority of solicitors do not engage in mainstream regulated activities but in non-mainstream regulated activities. While it was accepted by the Law Society that consumers needed protection, the Society's view was that all solicitors are regulated by the Law Society, their professional body. For solicitors carrying on only non-mainstream regulated activities the requirement also to be regulated by the FCA would not be in a consumer's best interests. The dual regulation would be onerous and expensive. The Treasury accepted this argument and FSMA 2000, Part XX was added to the FSMA 2000 while it was still a Bill.

This Part of the FSMA 2000 contains provision for members of a professional body who are engaging only in non-mainstream regulated activities to be exempt from the requirement to be authorised persons in order to carry out certain regulated activities. It grants an exemption from the general prohibition.

There are a number of conditions before the exemption is available:

(a) the professional body must be a designated professional body (DPB); and

(b) the professional body must also supervise and regulate the way in which its members carry on non-mainstream investment business.

2.2.2 Designated professional bodies

The Treasury has the power to designate such bodies, and by SI 2001 No 1226, eight professional bodies, including the Law Society, were designated for the purposes of FSMA 2000, Part XX. Other professional bodies designated include the Law Society of Scotland, the Law Society of Northern Ireland, the Institute of Chartered Accountants in England and Wales, and the Institute of Actuaries.

2.2.3 The Scope Rules

Although the Law Society is the designated professional body for solicitors in England and Wales, the Solicitors Regulation Authority, the independent regulatory body of the Law Society, supervises and regulates the way in which the non-mainstream regulated activities are carried on by practice rules, known as the Scope Rules. These fill in the detail of the DPB regime and are subject to approval by the FCA. The Scope Rules are considered in **2.5.2**.

2.2.4 Additional conditions to be satisfied

In order for the carrying on of the non-mainstream regulated activities to be exempt certain conditions need to be met (FSMA 2000, s 327). These conditions include the following:

(a) The person carrying on the regulated activities must be a member of a profession.

(b) That person must not receive a commission from a third party in respect of the regulated activities, unless he accounts to his client for the commission.

(c) The regulated activity must be provided in a way that is incidental to the provision of professional services.

(d) The investment to which the regulated activity relates must not be an investment specified in an order by the Treasury for the purposes of FSMA 2000, s 327(6).

This last condition means that there will be some regulated activities that do not come under the exemption to the general prohibition. Members of DPBs will not be able to undertake these activities, even though they appear to fit within the DPB regime. The Treasury has made an order under FSMA 2000, s 327(6), the Financial Services and Markets Act 2000 (Professions) (Non-Exempt Activities) Order 2001 (SI 2001 No 1227) ('NEAO'). The detail of the NEAO is beyond the scope of this chapter.

2.2.5 Solicitors carrying on mainstream regulated activities

Such solicitors will be subject to dual regulation. The regulated activities they undertake will not be covered by the DPB exemption and so they will need to apply to the FCA for permission to carry on regulated activities. Once granted authorisation they will then be subject to the FCA Rule Book.

The authorisation can be for different types of regulated activities. Which activity will determine what 'permission' is required from the FCA. If the application is made in the name of a firm, approved person(s) will be named. The authorisation will also dictate what controlled functions the approved persons can undertake.

The detail of the application for authorisation by the FCA and the appropriate regulations to which authorised persons are subject are beyond the scope of this chapter.

2.3 The regulatory regime

A diagrammatic representation of the regulatory regime and the role of the regulatory bodies is set out in **Figure** 2.2.

Figure 2.2   Regulatory regime

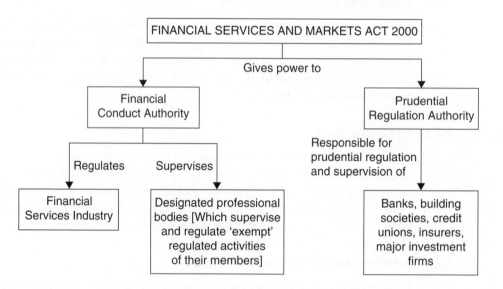

2.4 Financial promotions

In addition to the regulated activities regime and the general prohibition, the FSMA 2000 also sets out a second regime governing financial promotions. Section 21(1) states: 'A person ("A") must not in the course of business, communicate an invitation or inducement to engage in investment activity.' As with the regulated activities regime, the detail of the financial promotions regime is set out in secondary legislation—the Financial Services and Markets Act 2000 (Financial Promotion) Order 2005 (SI 2005 No 1529) ('FPO').

The terminology used in the financial promotions regime differs from that used in the regulated activities regime. For example, it uses the term 'controlled' rather than 'specified'. The activities and investments which fall within the legislation relating to financial promotions are similar to those falling within the regulated activities regime, but they are not identical.

The FPO defines 'communication' and distinguishes between 'real-time communications'—those made in a face-to-face situation or in a telephone conversation—and 'non-real-time communication'—which would include communications in writing (a letter, a publication, or a website) or by email.

The Part XX DPB regime does not cover financial promotions, and so solicitors undertaking non-mainstream regulated activities could still be caught by the financial promotions regime as they are not authorised by the FCA. There are several exemptions. Those relevant to solicitors engaging in exempt regulated activities under the DPB regime are discussed in more detail at 2.5.2.3.

2.5 Solicitors regulated by the Solicitors Regulation Authority

The purpose of this part of the chapter is to explain in more detail the ways in which solicitors can comply with the financial services legislation.

There are three methods of complying with the legislation:

(a) seeking authorisation from the FCA directly (see **2.2.5**);

(b) ensuring that the only activities undertaken are those which are classified as excluded under the legislation; and

(c) taking advantage of the Part XX exemption, and ensuring that the only regulated activities undertaken are those deemed exempt regulated activities under the regulation of the Solicitors Regulation Authority as the independent regulatory body of the Law Society in its role as a DPB.

The majority of solicitors will undertake only non-mainstream regulated activities and so the first method will be inappropriate. The second and third of these methods are discussed in **2.5.1** and **2.5.2**.

2.5.1 Excluded activities

The effect of carrying on only excluded regulated activities is that the activities do not come within the legislation and so no authorisation is needed. There are two types of excluded activities: those which apply depending on the investment which is subject to the activity; and those of a general application, which apply notwithstanding the investment. Examples of the first type are set out at **2.1.3.1.6**. Examples of the second type include trustees and personal representatives (RAO, Art 66), provision of non-investment services (RAO, Art 67), and provision of information on an incidental basis (RAO, Art 72C). These three exclusions are important to solicitors as many of the activities solicitors are engaging in on a day-to-day basis will come within their scope.

2.5.1.1 Trustees and personal representatives

Article 66 of the RAO provides for certain activities carried out by trustees and personal representatives to be excluded from the general prohibition. This means that solicitors acting in these capacities do not have to worry about authorisation. The activities excluded include arranging, managing, safeguarding and administering, and advising. There are two provisos to the exclusion. First, the investment to which the activity relates must not be a contract of insurance; and, secondly, the solicitor must receive only his costs for acting as trustee or personal representative; no additional remuneration must be received by him. In addition, the arranging or advising must be for, or to, a fellow trustee or personal representative, or for, or to, a beneficiary under the trust or will, or on intestacy.

2.5.1.2 Provision of non-investment services

The activities of dealing as agent, arranging, safeguarding, and administering and advising, when carried on in the course of a profession and when such that they might reasonably be regarded as a necessary part of other services provided in the course of that profession, are excluded from the general prohibition (RAO, Art 67). As with the exclusion for trustees and personal representatives, the investment to which the activity relates must not be a contract of insurance; and the solicitor must not receive additional remuneration for the activity. This exclusion will apply, for example, when arranging the sale of all the assets in an estate when administering it. However, where a decision has to be made as to which assets should be sold and which retained, it would be advisable to seek the advice of an authorised person.

2.5.1.3 Contracts of insurance

When the investment in question is a contract of insurance, the activities of arranging, managing, and safeguarding and administering are excluded from the general prohibition provided they are: (a) carried on in the course of a profession which does not otherwise consist of the carrying on of regulated activities; (b) consist of providing information to a (potential) policyholder; and (c) when the activity may reasonably be regarded as being incidental to that profession (RAO, Art 72C). The exclusion will apply, for example, when giving information to a conveyancing client with a view to arranging a defective title indemnity policy. The solicitor will be able to give the client the name and contact details of an authorised person who can advise the client. If more is involved, for example the filling in of forms, then the exclusion is not available.

2.5.2 Solicitors regulated by the Solicitors Regulation Authority as the independent regulatory body of the Law Society, a designated professional body

The Law Society is a designated professional body ('DPB'). The independent regulatory body of the Law Society, the Solicitors Regulation Authority ('SRA'), takes on the responsibility for regulating and supervising the way in which its members carry on non-mainstream regulated activities.

The SRA Financial Services (Scope) Rules 2001 ('the Scope Rules') and the SRA Financial Services (Conduct of Business) Rules 2001 ('the Conduct of Business Rules') set out the framework for the regulation. The Scope Rules set out the scope of the regulated activities which may be undertaken by solicitors. The Conduct of Business Rules regulate the way in which the exempt regulated activities are carried on.

The Scope Rules and Conduct of Business Rules are contained in the SRA Handbook in the Specialist Services section. The rules must be read in conjunction with the SRA Principles as the Principles apply to all aspects of practice, including the provision of financial services. The desired outcomes that apply to these specialist services are that financial services are provided to the same standard as required by the Financial Conduct Authority and in a manner that maintains confidence in the legal profession.

2.5.2.1 Scope Rules

The Scope Rules have been clearly drafted and are, with the Conduct of Business Rules, perhaps the most easily understood part of the financial services legislation affecting solicitors undertaking non-mainstream regulated activities.

The Scope Rules set out the conditions and restrictions with which solicitors' firms seeking to rely on the DPB regime must comply when carrying on regulated activities. They also prohibit solicitors from carrying on certain regulated activities and set out the effect of a breach of the Rules.

The Scope Rules can be found on the SRA website by using the following link: http://www.sra.org.uk/solicitors/handbook/finserscope/content.page

The Scope Rules should be read in full. However, three of the conditions warrant specific mention. A firm which carries on any regulated activities must ensure that:

(a) the activities arise out of, or are complementary to, the provision of a particular professional service to a particular client;

(b) the manner of the provision by the firm of any service in the course of carrying on the activities is incidental to the provision by the firm of professional services; and

(c) the firm accounts to the client for any pecuniary reward or other advantage which the firm receives from a third party (Scope Rules 4(a), (b), (c)).

The effect of the condition contained in Rule 4(a) is that the solicitor must first be acting for the client with regard to another matter, and the activity in question must arise out of, or as a result of, that first instruction, or be complementary to it. It is not possible for the solicitor to undertake a regulated activity in isolation.

For the condition in Rule 4(b) one factor that is taken into account is the proportion of the firm's work relating to regulated activities compared with the proportion of other professional services provided. If the proportion of regulated activity exceeds the other work, it is not incidental to it.

Under Rule 4(c) accounting to the client means that the commission or reward must be held to the order of the client.

At **2.2.4** it was pointed out that FSMA 2000, s 327 sets out additional conditions which need to be met in order for the carrying on of the non-mainstream regulated activities to be exempt. Compliance with the Scope Rules will ensure that these additional conditions are also met.

2.5.2.2   Conduct of Business Rules

As with the Scope Rules, the Conduct of Business Rules should be read in full. They set out what information clients must receive, how transactions should be effected, what records must be kept (including records of the transactions and any commissions received), and details of the safekeeping of clients' investments.

The SRA Financial Services (Conduct of Business) Rules 2001 can be found on the Solicitors Regulation Authority website by using the following link: http://www.sra.org.uk/solicitors/handbook/finserconduct/content.page. The Conduct of Business Rules apply only to solicitors relying on the DBP regime. However, it is recommended that firms relying on an exclusion to ensure that they are not breaching the FSMA 2000 also comply with the Rules as the distinction between the two methods of compliance is very fine.

2.5.2.3   Financial promotions

Solicitors carrying on exempt regulated activities under the DBP regime must be aware of the implications of the financial promotions regime as regulated by the Financial Promotions Order 2005 (SI 2005 No 1529 as amended) (FPO: see **2.4**). As they are not authorised by the FCA they will be subject to the restriction on financial promotions. They will have to ensure either that the content of the communication is approved by an authorised person (if it is not a real-time communication, as authorised persons are prohibited from approving real-time communications for unauthorised persons), or that the communication comes within an exemption. There are two relevant exemptions, one dealing with real-time communications and the second dealing with non-real-time communications. Together these two exemptions should cover most communications to clients.

2.5.2.3.1   *Real-time communications*

The exemption covering these communications is contained in Article 55 of the FPO. Briefly, the communication will be exempt provided the solicitor is relying on the DPB exemption; the person to whom the communication is made is an existing client; and the activity to which the communication relates is incidental to the provision of professional services and either is excluded under Article 67 of the RAO (provision of non-investment services: see **2.5.1.2**) or is an exempt regulated activity by virtue of the DPB exemption.

2.5.2.3.2   *Non-real-time communications*

The exemption covering these communications is contained in Article 55A of the FPO as amended. Where non-real-time communications are concerned, the communication will be exempt provided the solicitor is relying on the DPB exemption and the communication includes a specified statement. The statement is as follows:

The firm is not authorised under the Financial Services and Markets Act 2000 but we are able in certain circumstances to offer a limited range of investment services to clients because we are members of the Law Society. We can provide these investment services if they are an incidental part of the professional services we have been engaged to provide.

2.5.3   Self-test questions

2.5.3.1   The purpose and scope of financial regulation

You should now have an understanding of the purpose and scope of financial services regulation. To test your knowledge and understanding answer the following short-answer questions. The answers are set out in **Appendix 1**.

Q.1 What Act provides the framework for the current financial services statutory regime?

Q.2 What are the names of the regulators for the financial services industry?

Q.3 What is the FCA's strategic objective?

Q.4 What are the three operational objectives that guide the FCA?

Q.5 What is the effect of the general prohibition set out in FSMA 2000, s 19?

Q.6 What are the sanctions if the general prohibition is breached?

Q.7 What must a person be to carry on a regulated activity without contravening the general prohibition?

Q.8 What exemption to the general prohibition is contained in FSMA 2000, Part XX?

Q.9 Which section of the FSMA 2000 sets out the definition of 'regulated activity'?

Q.10 What characteristics must an activity have to be a regulated activity and caught by the general prohibition?

Q.11 Name a statutory instrument which defines what activities are regulated activities. Give the full reference and the usual abbreviation.

Q.12 Name a statutory instrument which defines what investments are specified investments. Give the full reference, the part, and the usual abbreviation.

Q.13 The majority of solicitors engage in non-mainstream regulated activities. What are non-mainstream regulated activities?

Q.14 The Law Society of England and Wales is a DPB. What is a DPB?

Q.15 FSMA 2000, Part XX states that a DPB must supervise and regulate the way in which its members carry on non-mainstream investments business. By what rules does the SRA, as the independent regulatory body of the Law Society, the DPB, supervise and regulate its members? Give the full titles of the rules and the short titles.

Q.16 There are two types of excluded activities. Those which apply depending on the type of investment involved and those which apply irrespective of the investment involved. For the exclusions to be applicable what must the solicitor do with any related commission received by him?

Q.17 Give three examples of activities which are excluded under the RAO.

Q.18 Which article in the RAO sets out the exclusion for trustees and personal representatives?

Q.19 What do the rules referred to in question 15 set out?

Q.20 (a) What is a real-time communication?

(b) What is non-real-time communication?

2.5.3.2 Solicitors and the financial services legislation

The following scenarios help you to put the legislation into context. They should assist you in understanding how the legislation impacts upon solicitors in their work.

For each of the scenarios you should ask five questions (these questions form a simplified version of the flow chart at **Figure 2.3**):

(a) Does the activity involve a specified investment?

(b) Is the activity capable of being a regulated activity under the RAO?

(c) If so, does it fall within any of the exclusions in the RAO?

(d) If not, is the activity capable of being an exempt regulated activity under Part XX?

(e) Does the activity fall within the Scope Rules?

Consider the scenarios. Assume that you are a trainee with Crookesmoors, and that the firm has not sought authorisation by the Financial Conduct Authority. Identify any financial services issues that arise. Decide whether you can act as requested. If you can act, state whether you are relying on an exclusion to the FSMA 2000 or whether the activity is an exempt regulated activity.

1. You are acting for a client in her divorce. As part of the financial provision agreement an endowment policy in your client's name is to be transferred to her husband. Are we able to deal with this?

    (a) Does the activity involve a specified investment?

    (b) Is the activity capable of being a regulated activity under the RAO?

    (c) If so, does it fall within any of the exclusions in the RAO?

    (d) If not, is the activity capable of being an exempt regulated activity under Part XX?

    (e) Does the activity fall within the Scope Rules?

2. A client has received £20,000 in damages from a personal injury claim in which one of the assistant solicitors in the litigation department acted. The client has asked for some advice on where he should invest the money. Can we advise him?

    (a) Does the activity involve a specified investment?

    (b) Is the activity capable of being a regulated activity under the RAO?

    (c) If so, does it fall within any of the exclusions in the RAO?

    (d) If not, is the activity capable of being an exempt regulated activity under Part XX?

    (e) Does the activity fall within the Scope Rules?

3. Two of the partners in the firm are the trustees of the TG Wilford Deceased Will Trust. They are the only trustees. The trust assets comprise some land and a holding of unit trusts. They have always undertaken a review of the assets each half year, selling and buying assets as they think best for the trust. Under the FSMA regime, can they continue with this practice?

    (a) Does the activity involve a specified investment?

    (b) Is the activity capable of being a regulated activity under the RAO?

    (c) If so, does it fall within any of the exclusions in the RAO?

    (d) If not, is the activity capable of being an exempt regulated activity under Part XX?

    (e) Does the activity fall within the Scope Rules?

4. An existing client asks for advice on whether he should buy a particular plot of land, which he will then develop. Can/should we advise him?

    (a) Does the activity involve a specified investment?

    (b) Is the activity capable of being a regulated activity under the RAO?

    (c) If so, does it fall within any of the exclusions in the RAO?

    (d) If not, is the activity capable of being an exempt regulated activity under Part XX?

    (e) Does the activity fall within the Scope Rules?

5. You are acting on behalf of James and Philip, the executors of their grandmother's estate. The estate is relatively small. It includes a house, some accounts with the Nationwide Building Society, and some shares in BG PLC, Centrica, and Abbey PLC. Under the will the residue will be divided among four grandchildren, who are all adults. All the assets are to be sold or closed to enable the funeral account, etc to be paid. Are you able to deal with these sales/closures?

    (a) Does the activity involve a specified investment?

    (b) Is the activity capable of being a regulated activity under the RAO?

    (c) If so, does it fall within any of the exclusions in the RAO?

    (d) If not, is the activity capable of being an exempt regulated activity under Part XX?

    (e) Does the activity fall within the Scope Rules?

2.6   Conclusion: solicitors and the financial services legislation

Where a solicitor is carrying on regulated activities the flow chart at **Figure** 2.3 sets out the questions to be asked to determine whether the activities come within the financial services regime, whether they are excluded and so no authorisation is required, or whether they will be exempt regulated activities under the DPB regime.

2.6.1   Checkpoints

You should now be able to demonstrate an:

- awareness of the purpose and scope of financial services regulation (**2.1**; **2.2**; **2.3**);
- understanding of the financial services regulatory framework in general (**2.3**);
- understanding of how the financial services regulatory framework applies and in particular in relation to solicitors' firms (**2.5**); and

Figure 2.3   Activities within the financial services regime

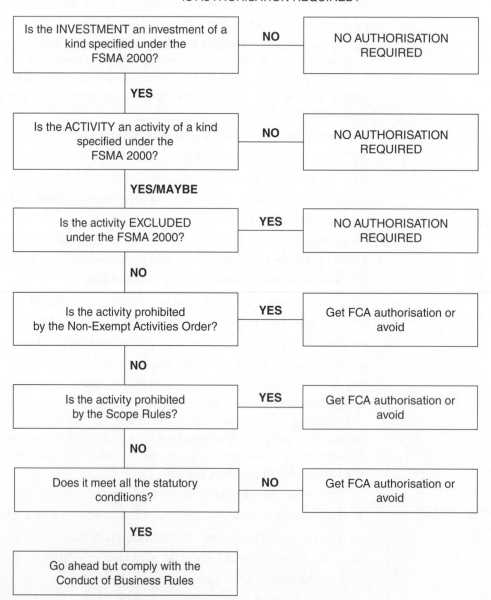

- ability to identify when financial services issues are raised in the type of transactions that you are likely to encounter as a trainee in a solicitors' firm that has exempt professional firm status (**2.5**; **2.6**; **2.7**).

2.7 Commentary to scenarios

(Scenarios set out at **2.5.3.2**)

1.

(a) Does the activity involve a specified investment? — *Yes, a contract of insurance.*

(b) Is the activity capable of being a regulated activity under the RAO? — *Yes, dealing.*

(c) If so, does it fall within any of the exclusions in the RAO? — *No, there are no exclusions relating to dealing.*

(d) If not, is the activity capable of being an exempt regulated activity under Part XX? — *In any event it does come within Part XX.*

(e) Does the activity fall within the Scope Rules? — *Yes. You can actually advise on and/or arrange the acquisition or disposal by way of assignment.*

Conclusion: You can deal with the transfer.

2.

(a) Does the activity involve a specified investment? — *Yes and to advise properly you need to be able to cover all types of investment as some will be specified investments.*

(b) Is the activity capable of being a regulated activity under the RAO? — *Yes, advising (see conclusion regarding generic advice).*

(c) If so, does it fall within any of the exclusions in the RAO? — *No, it does not fall within any of the exclusions. Article 67 (Provision of non-investment services) is not available as the activity could not be reasonably regarded as a necessary part of the other services provided to the client, ie acting in the personal injury claim.*

(d) If not, is the activity capable of being an exempt regulated activity under Part XX? — *No, it cannot be said to be incidental to the personal injury claim.*

There is room for considering that the activity does 'arise out of, or is complementary to, the provision of a particular professional service to a client'. However, to give this advice would not be meeting the spirit of the legislation. If in doubt you should ask yourself whether you, or the firm, has the expertise to give best advice.

(e) Does the activity fall within the Scope Rules? — *Not applicable.*

Conclusion: You cannot advise him on specific investments. To do so will be a breach of the financial services legislation.

However, you can give generic advice on the different types of investment open to him and their different characteristics.

You will need to put him in touch with an independent financial adviser—someone who will be authorised by the FCA and so able to carry on a regulated activity.

In doing so you will be ensuring that your client receives the best advice.

3.

(a)	Does the activity involve a specified investment?	*Yes, the unit trusts are. Land is not a specified investment however.*
(b)	Is the activity capable of being a regulated activity under the RAO?	*Yes, arranging, managing, administering, and advising.*
(c)	If so, does it fall within any of the exclusions in the RAO?	*Yes, Article 66—trustees and PRs. Unlikely that additional remuneration, ie commission, would be received. There is no need to answer any further questions.*

Conclusion: Yes, they can continue with their twice-yearly reviews.

4.

(a)	Does the activity involve a specified investment?	*No. Land is not caught by the FSMA. There is no need to answer any further questions.*

Conclusion: You can give him the advice he is seeking. No authorisation is needed. However, you need to consider whether you have the specialist knowledge to do so. It depends on exactly what he is seeking advice on. As we are looking at this at trainee level, it may be that the partner does have the necessary knowledge—it is more a question of identifying the thought process.

5.

(a)	Does the activity involve a specified investment?	*Yes, shares.*
(b)	Is the activity capable of being a regulated activity under the RAO?	*Yes, dealing or arranging.*
(c)	If so, does it fall within any of the exclusions in the RAO?	*Yes, Article 67—necessary.*
(d)	If not, is the activity capable of being an exempt regulated activity under Part XX?	*In any event it does come within Part XX. There is no need to answer any further questions.*

Conclusion: You can arrange the sale of the shares.

You do need to bear in mind the possible capital gains tax implications of the personal representatives selling rather than transferring relevant assets to beneficiaries and letting them sell.

Also bear in mind that in an estate where not all the assets need to be sold to pay debts, legacies, etc, you should be advising the personal representatives to take independent financial advice, to ensure that the clients receive the best advice. It may be that being in a position where some assets need realising, but not all, you come outside the 'necessary' exclusion. Independent advice should be sought.

 online resource centre Visit the Online Resource Centre for more information and useful weblinks.
www.oxfordtextbooks.co.uk/orc/foundations17_18/

Money laundering

3.1 Introduction

This chapter considers money laundering. We look at:

- the process of money laundering;
- the primary legislation and offences; and
- the relevance of the legislation to solicitors.

A concerted effort is being made within the EU to tighten up on money laundering. This is reflected by both the European Money Laundering Directives, which have led to changes in the UK legislation, in particular the Money Laundering Regulations ('MLR') (see **3.4.3**). Without a concerted worldwide effort to eradicate money laundering, any European legislation will have limited effect. There are still jurisdictions where no questions are asked about the provenance of funds.

The breadth of the regulation encompasses large-scale laundering of drugs money, to relatively small-scale fraud, such as benefit fraud by an individual. Solicitors are usually unwittingly involved in a money laundering scheme. They will avoid this by being conversant with the requirements of the money laundering legislation and fully complying with it. Solicitors in all areas of practice must be aware of the impact of the legislation. It is equally as important to a family practitioner as to a corporate lawyer.

In the UK, the National Crime Agency, which came into being in October 2013, replacing the Serious Organised Crime Agency ('SOCA'), is the body responsible within the UK for receiving and analysing all suspicious activity reports ('SARs') about money laundering. More information about the National Crime Agency can be found at http://www.nationalcrimeagency.gov.uk.

3.2 Money laundering

Before looking at details of the MLR it is helpful to understand what is meant by money laundering. Essentially it is the process by which 'dirty' monies—that is, the proceeds of crime—are 'washed' to give them the appearance of 'clean' money.

There are three stages in a money laundering transaction: placement, layering, and integration.

3.2.1 Stage one: placement

This is the stage at which the cash proceeds of the crime are put into a non-cash asset, for example buying investments with cash or buying a property with cash. Alternatively the money may be initially paid into a series of bank accounts. This stage will be the most difficult for the criminal because he will be disposing of cash. The initial cash may also be taken and invested 'offshore'; that is, taken out of the country and reintroduced to the country at the layering stage. This asset is then sold, or the money withdrawn from the bank, to enable layering to take place.

3.2.2 Stage two: layering

To avoid the money being readily traceable, the money will be passed through many transactions to create a trail which is not easily followed by the authorities. Money launderers may seek to pass money through a solicitor's client account as part of 'layering'. Law Society guidance makes it clear that money should be passed through the client account only where there is 'a genuine underlying legal transaction or some other valid reason to hold clients' money'.

3.2.3   Stage three: integration

The final stage is for the money to pass into a legitimate business or investment. By this stage, from the criminal's point of view, the proceeds will, it is hoped, not be readily traceable back to the proceeds of the original crime.

The impact of the legislation is that the scope of money laundering has been widened. Not only does it encompass the above, but also covers matters such as tax evasion (even of a minor nature) and benefit fraud.

3.3   The legislation

The primary legislation is contained within the Proceeds of Crime Act 2002 ('POCA 2002') as amended, the Terrorism Act 2000, and the Anti-Terrorism, Crime and Security Act 2001. The relevant legislation needs to be read in conjunction with the Money Laundering Regulations 2007 (SI 2007 No 2157).

3.4   The offences

Each Act sets out various offences.

3.4.1   Proceeds of Crime Act 2002

The POCA 2002 defines money laundering (s 340(11)) and creates a number of money laundering offences.

Those offences fall broadly into three areas:

- The first involves the *laundering* of proceeds of crime (POCA 2002, ss 327–9);
- The second centres around the *failure to report* a knowledge or suspicion of money laundering (POCA 2002, ss 330–2); and
- The final area relates to *tipping off* the person whom you know or suspect is laundering money about a money laundering disclosure or a money laundering investigation (POCA 2002, s 333A).

Everyone is subject to the POCA 2002, but the offences of 'failing to report' and 'tipping off' apply only to those who are engaged in business in the 'regulated sector'. Certain activities carried on by solicitors fall within the definition of activities in the regulated sector (Proceeds of Crime Act 2002 (Business in the Regulated Sector and Supervisory Authorities) Order 2007 (SI 2007 No 3287), Article 1(1)(n)).

3.4.2   Terrorism Act 2000 and the Anti-Terrorism, Crime and Security Act 2001

The offences established under these Acts are beyond the scope of this book.

3.4.3   Money Laundering Regulations 2007

These Regulations require the regulated sector to operate various systems with a view to minimising money laundering. A failure to comply with the requirements is a criminal offence.

The MLR apply to various persons, including independent legal professionals acting in the course of business in the UK.

3.5   Relevance to solicitors

As practising solicitors fall within the regulated sector and are independent legal profession-als for the purposes of the MLR it is important that the requirements are understood and complied with.

To ensure that he does not commit an offence of money laundering under the POCA 2002, if a solicitor knows or suspects that the proceeds of crime are involved in a particular matter then he must disclose his concerns. This disclosure will initially be to the Money Launder-ing Reporting Officer (see **3.5.1**) who must then make a decision whether or not to report the concerns to the National Crime Agency. The disclosure to the National Crime Agency by the Money Laundering Reporting Officer is termed an 'authorised disclosure' both for the purposes of the legislation, and when considering matters of professional conduct (see **3.5.2**).

To avoid an offence of tipping off, a solicitor must not mention his concerns or the fact that the matter has been referred to the National Crime Agency to his client.

3.5.1   MLR key requirements

The key requirements imposed on solicitors by the MLR are:

- to appoint a nominated officer, usually known as a Money Laundering Reporting Officer (reg 20(2)(d)(i));
- to apply customer due diligence measures (reg 7);
- to establish reporting procedures (reg 20(1)(b));
- to train staff (reg 21); and
- to keep records (reg 19).

3.5.1.1   Customer due diligence measures

Perhaps of most relevance to trainee solicitors are the customer due diligence (CDD) meas-ures. Under MLR, reg 5, 'Customer due diligence measures' means:

(a) identifying the customer and verifying the customer's identity on the basis of docu-ments, data or information obtained from a reliable and independent source;

(b) identifying, where there is a beneficial owner who is not the customer, the beneficial owner and taking adequate measures, on a risk-sensitive basis, to verify his identity so that the relevant person is satisfied that he knows who the beneficial owner is, includ-ing, in the case of a legal person, trust or similar legal arrangement, measures to under-stand the ownership and control structure of the person, trust or arrangement; and

(c) obtaining information on the purpose and intended nature of the business relationship.

Regulation 6 expands on the interpretation of 'beneficial owner'. MLR, reg 7 provides:

(1) . . . a relevant person must apply customer due diligence measures when he—

(a) establishes a business relationship;

(b) carries out an occasional transaction;

(c) suspects money laundering or terrorist financing;

(d) doubts the veracity or adequacy of documents, data or information previously obtained for the purposes of identification or verification.

(2) Subject to regulation 16(4), a relevant person must also apply customer due diligence measures at other appropriate times to existing customers on a risk-sensitive basis . . .

The purpose of the CDD measures is to ensure that firms know their clients and the purpose of the clients' business relationship with the firm. The better a firm knows its clients, the smaller the chance of the firm unwittingly being involved in money laundering. A client's identity is his name and address. Verifying that identify means seeing evidence of the name and address. It is important that this evidence is from a 'reliable and independent source' (MLR, reg 5(a)). Where you are using original documents to verify the identity, it is usual to ask for evidence containing a photograph of the client, such as a photo-driving licence or passport. An original utilities bill or bank statement can be used to verify the client's address. Verification can also be completed electronically or by obtaining the information from others who are also regulated.

If the firm does not deal on a face-to-face basis with the client (and the client has not been physically present for identification purposes) then enhanced measures are called for. These will usually be met by seeking additional evidence for verification of name and address.

Under the MLR it is important that the firm retains records of the documents used for the CDD measures for five years.

MLR, reg 11 provides that CDD measures must be undertaken before conducting the work for the client. It also specifies what can or cannot be done if the firm is unable to apply the CDD measures.

3.5.2 Professional conduct issues

The money laundering legislation gives rise to a number of professional conduct issues.

3.5.2.1 Confidentiality

A solicitor is under a duty to keep confidential to his or her firm the affairs of clients and to ensure that the staff do the same.

When making an authorised disclosure (**3.4.1**) the duty of confidentiality is overridden and a solicitor will not be breaching the duty of confidentiality.

3.5.2.2 Privilege

When acting for a client, some documents and information are protected by way of a privilege against disclosure and this is called legal professional privilege. Again, when making an authorised disclosure (**3.4.1**) this is overridden and a solicitor will not be breaching the legal or professional restrictions upon him of legal professional privilege.

The Law Society issues detailed anti-money laundering guidance for solicitors. The guidance takes account of all new developments, including relevant cases, and can be found on the Law Society's website:www.lawsociety.org.uk under anti-money laundering. The latest practice note on anti-money laundering can be found in the practice notes section of the practice support area of the Law Society's website:www.lawsociety.org.uk/support-services/advice/practice-notes/aml/.

The Law Society has previously issued a warning to all solicitors alerting them to circumstances in which they might be assisting money laundering. The causes for concern include:

(a) unusual settlement requests, for example settlements by cash, surprise payments by way of a third party cheque, or settlements which are reached too easily;

(b) unusual instructions, for example long-distance clients who have no apparent reason for instructing your firm, or if instructions change without a reasonable explanation;

(c) use of solicitors' client accounts—be cautious if you are instructed to do legal work, receive funds into your client account, but then the instructions are cancelled, and you are asked to return the money whether to your client or a third party;

(d) suspect territory, for example where a client is introduced by an overseas bank or third party based in a country where drug trafficking or terrorism may be prevalent;

(e) loss-making transactions—be alert to instructions which could lead to some financial loss to your client or a third party without a logical explanation, particularly where your client seems unconcerned.

3.6 Money laundering: checkpoints

You should now be able to:

- describe the process of money laundering (**3.2**);
- identify the primary offences (**3.4.1**);
- identify the relevance of the money laundering regime to solicitors (**3.5.1**; **3.5.2**).

Further guidance and details of the relevant legislation can be found on the Law Society's website: http://www.lawsociety.org.uk.

 online resource centre   Visit the Online Resource Centre for more information and useful weblinks.
www.oxfordtextbooks.co.uk/orc/foundations17_18/

Part 2

Revenue law

4   Introduction to revenue law   61
5   Income tax   66
6   Capital gains tax   82
7   Inheritance tax   90
8   Corporation tax   125
9   Value added tax   140
10 Taxation of sole proprietors and partnerships   149
11 Taxation of trusts and settlements   159

Part 2

Revenue law

Introduction to revenue law

4.1 Introduction

This chapter will introduce you to some of the essential principles of revenue law and to the main taxes that you will be studying on the LPC. The chapter will briefly deal with:

- the main taxes;
- the sources of tax law;
- who pays tax;
- the administration of the tax system; and
- appeals against tax decisions.

Revenue law (as the law on tax is generally known) is a 'core' topic on the Legal Practice Course and so is not studied in isolation. The study of taxation will pervade many of your compulsory and elective subjects on the LPC.

4.2 Why do we tax?

The main purpose of tax is to raise money for government expenditure. The government provides services that either cannot be provided by private enterprise, such as defence, or that policy dictates are better dealt with universally, such as social security benefits.

Taxation has other purposes beyond raising revenue. One of the main examples of this is using tax to redistribute wealth. For example, broadly speaking, the UK taxes the income of those in employment and uses some of the money to provide welfare benefits to the unemployed. How much revenue from taxation is spent for progressive purposes will vary from government to government.

4.3 The changing nature of taxation

Each year, the government will tinker with the taxation system. The Chancellor of the Exchequer will usually make a Budget Speech to the House of Commons in March or April of each year, containing proposed taxation measures for the following tax year. The House of Commons will debate the Budget and scrutinise the subsequent Finance Bill that is used to enact the Budget proposals. The political persuasion of the government of the time will inevitably influence its taxation policy.

The types and rates of tax have changed a lot over the years. For example, the top possible rate of income tax in the UK peaked at 99.25 per cent during the Second World War and it remained possible to pay 98 per cent income tax until as recently as 1974.

4.4   European context

The UK's membership of the EU means that, like other Member States, it has to accept some limitations on the extent to which it can impose taxes and customs duties. EU membership also brings a requirement to work towards harmonising indirect taxation (the taxation of goods and services). Value Added Tax is the main form of indirect taxation; this was introduced in 1973 as a direct result of the UK joining the EU. Once the UK has left the EU, it will no longer be required to harmonise its indirect taxation. It remains to be seen what changes the government might make to the VAT system. However, as VAT is a major source of taxation income, it is very unlikely to be abolished as a result of Brexit.

4.5   Sources of revenue law

Each of the main taxes you will study is statute based. The brief introduction to each tax at **4.6** will set out the statutory sources for that tax. These statutes apply as amended by subsequent Finance Acts. In addition, there is a significant body of case law interpreting the various taxes.

HM Revenue & Customs ('HMRC') administers these taxes and issues guidance on the interpretation of taxes. This guidance includes:

- Statements of practice: these set out what view HMRC will take about the application of specific tax provisions.
- Extra-statutory concessions: these set out circumstances in which HMRC will waive tax that would otherwise have to be paid. The taxpayer will have to meet the conditions of the concession to get the benefit of the waiver.

4.6   Introduction to the main taxes

This section will briefly introduce the five main taxes that you will study on the LPC. Each tax will be considered in more detail in its own chapter. These taxes are commonly known by their abbreviations:

- Income tax ('IT')
- Capital gains tax ('CGT')
- Inheritance tax ('IHT')
- Corporation tax ('CT')
- Value added tax ('VAT')

4.6.1   Income tax (IT)

Unsurprisingly, this is a tax on income, as opposed to capital. It is levied on most types of income, including wages, self-employed income, pension income, and interest on savings. Some income is not subject to IT, for example some welfare benefits.

4.6.1.1   Who pays IT?

IT may have to be paid by:

- individuals;
- partnerships—each partner pays IT on his share of the profits;
- personal representatives; and
- trustees

A company pays corporation tax (CT) on its income, not IT.

4.6.1.2   Sources of IT law

The main source of IT law is the Income Tax Act 2007. Other important statutes are the Income Tax (Trading and Other Income) Act 2005 and the Income Tax (Earnings and Pensions) Act 2003.

4.6.2   Capital gains tax (CGT)

CGT is a tax on the 'gain' (profit) made when an asset (for example shares or property) is sold, given away, or otherwise disposed of. It is important to appreciate that it is only the amount by which the asset has increased in value that is taxed, not the whole amount (if any) actually received for the asset.

4.6.2.1   Who pays CGT?

CGT may have to be paid by:

- individuals;
- partnerships—each partner pays IT on his share of gains made by the partnership;
- personal representatives—on disposals of the deceased's assets; and
- trustees—on disposals of trust assets.

A company pays CT on its capital gains, not CGT.

4.6.2.2   Sources of CGT law

The main statute is the Taxation of Chargeable Gains Act 1992.

4.6.3   Inheritance tax (IHT)

IHT is a tax levied on the value of a deceased person's estate. It may also be payable on certain gifts made and trusts created during his/her lifetime. Most estates do not have to pay IHT. Essentially, IHT is only due if the total value of the estate and certain gifts made by the deceased in the seven years before death exceeds a set threshold.

4.6.3.1   Who pays IHT?

IHT may have to be paid by:

- personal representatives on the deceased's estate;
- individuals on 'chargeable' transfers made during their lifetime;
- trustees on transfers into the trust in some circumstances; and
- companies, but only in very limited circumstances.

4.6.3.2   Sources of IHT law

The main statute is the Inheritance Tax Act 1984.

4.6.4   Corporation tax (CT)

CT is a tax on the taxable profits of limited companies and certain other organisations. CT is payable both on taxable income and on chargeable gains made by disposing of assets. Essentially, it is the company equivalent of IT and CGT.

4.6.4.1   Who pays CT?

CT may have to be paid by:

- limited companies; and
- other organisations, including charities and unincorporated associations such as members' clubs.

4.6.4.2   Sources of CT law

There are three main statutes governing CT. These are:

- Corporation Tax Act 2009;
- Corporation Tax Act 2010; and
- Income and Corporation Taxes Act 1988.

4.6.5   Value added tax (VAT)

VAT is a tax on most goods and services provided by VAT registered businesses.

4.6.5.1   Who pays VAT?

VAT is only paid to HMRC by businesses that are (or should be) registered for VAT and who have collected it from the consumers of their goods and services. VAT registered businesses may be run by individuals, partnerships, limited companies, or by other organisations.

4.6.5.2   Sources of VAT law

The main statute governing VAT is the Value Added Tax Act 1994.

4.7   Tax planning

A major area for tax advice in practice is the question of tax planning. Clients may seek advice about how to minimise their tax liability. Solicitors should be alert to tax issues even if the client does not ask and should advise the client about the tax implications of actions that they propose. You must only advise clients about *legitimate* ways of reducing their tax liabilities. It is important to understand the distinction between tax *avoidance*, which is legal, and tax *evasion*, which is not.

Tax avoidance is arranging one's affairs within the rules with a view to paying the smallest possible amount of tax, for example, by using tax-free savings accounts such as Individual Savings Accounts (ISA). This is a common and legitimate exercise.

Tax evasion is escaping tax by unlawful means. It usually has an element of dishonesty. This could be, for example, by providing false information in a tax return. Tax evasion is likely to be a criminal offence.

It is not always easy to see where the line is drawn between avoidance and evasion and clients may well seek advice about this.

4.8   Administration of taxes

Taxation is the responsibility of the Chancellor of the Exchequer, who heads the Treasury. The Chancellor delegates this responsibility to civil servants in HMRC and in the Treasury.

HMRC was created in 2005, replacing the Inland Revenue and HM Customs & Excise. HMRC is a non-ministerial government department. It is regulated by Commissioners who are permanent civil servants drawn from the top level of HMRC's management. The Commissioners make up the Board of HMRC, which is the body that issues statements of practice and extra-statutory concessions (see **4.5**).

HMRC and the Treasury work in partnership on taxation policy. Essentially, the Treasury develops the policies and HMRC maintains and implements them. HMRC's spending is overseen by a Treasury minister who reports to Parliament.

Inspectors of taxes are responsible for assessing the tax due and notifying the taxpayer of this. Often the taxpayer will be required to make a tax return. These are frequently submitted online with automatic calculations often possible.

Collectors of taxes are responsible for collecting tax, taking court proceedings if necessary. If the tax return is made online, the payment will often be made electronically as a matter of routine.

4.9 Appeals

If a taxpayer disagrees with the assessment of tax due, he can appeal. This should be done in writing within 30 days of the disputed decision. The taxpayer can also apply to postpone paying the tax that he says is being overcharged.

Most appeals are settled by the taxpayer and HMRC reaching agreement. If this is not possible, the taxpayer may ask for HMRC to review its decision. This would be done by an officer who was not involved in the original decision and the taxpayer would have the opportunity to put his case.

If the taxpayer does not agree with the outcome of a review, he can ask for his appeal to be heard by an independent tribunal. The review by HMRC is not mandatory—the taxpayer can proceed directly to the tribunal appeal if he wishes.

The relevant tribunal is called the First Tier Tribunal (Tax). The First Tier Tribunal's decisions can be appealed to the Upper Tier Tribunal (Tax and Chancery), with permission from the First Tier Tribunal.

online resource centre Visit the Online Resource Centre for more information and useful weblinks. **www.oxfordtextbooks.co.uk/orc/foundations17_18/**

5 Income tax

5.1 Chapter outline

This chapter focuses on income tax and is organised into the following sections:

- Introduction to income tax;
- Sources of income tax law;
- Collection and payment of income tax;
- Rates of income tax and allowances;
- Calculation of income tax;
- Sources of taxable income;
- Charitable giving;
- Summary; and
- Full income tax calculation.

5.2 Introduction to income tax

Income tax considerations arise across the range of professional advice and services provided by lawyers to their clients. Income tax considerations cross the different areas of legal practice as well as the boundaries between the professions such as law, accountancy, and financial services. Income tax considerations will arise in work undertaken on behalf of corporate clients as well as work undertaken on behalf of private clients.

Lawyers must know about income tax whether they are advising clients of its potential consequences in pursuing a course of action in a case, having income tax deducted from their salary as an employee of a firm, deducting it from employees as a partner, director, or member of a firm, paying it directly when self-employed, or advising clients who are in need of assistance with welfare benefits.

Income tax is, therefore, an essential part of a lawyer's professional knowledge and training. Whilst it is not always necessary to have knowledge to the extent that a specialist tax lawyer would have, it is necessary to have knowledge and understanding sufficient to recognise its implications as they arise and affect the client.

Everyone should understand how income tax works and when they enter the legal profession they will be expected to know. Everyone is affected by income tax be they man, woman, or child. It is best, therefore, to put aside preconceptions that income tax is too difficult or complex or even that it should just be paid and instead read on. The role of the lawyer is to help clients solve problems and to do that a lawyer must understand the subjects which cause the problems.

The way to understand legal subjects is to view the subject matter in context, then in outline, and then to work through the detail. The detail can be broken up into stages using the outline as a guide through the problem. Income tax is no different. Once the context and overview are clear, the detail can be broken into stages and understanding should follow.

The context in which income tax is raised and collected, tax codes, the self-assessment process, and rates of income tax now follow.

5.3   Sources of income tax law

Income tax is an annual tax which Parliament renews each year by legislation.

In the annual budget speech, the Chancellor of the Exchequer delivers the Government's annual financial statement and review of taxation including income tax rates, allowances, and reliefs for the financial year. This leads to a finance bill because as the House of Commons is the only tax raising body for the whole of the UK, it must approve the Government's proposals delivered in the budget speech.

The Finance Bill presented to Parliament following the budget speech on 8 March 2017 set out the details of the Government's tax policy measures.

The Finance Bill 2017, when it becomes an Act of Parliament, will amend existing income tax legislation including the Income Tax Act 2007 ('ITA 2007'), the Income Tax (Trading and Other Income Act) 2005 ('ITTOIA'), and the Income Tax (Earnings and Pensions) Act 2003 ('ITEPA').

5.4   Collection and payment of income tax

Her Majesty's Revenue and Customs ('HMRC') is responsible for the collection of income tax. The vast majority of income tax is collected by employers from their employees through the Pay As You Earn System ('PAYE') and sent to HMRC.

Income tax is normally paid by people, not companies.

- People may be individual employees, self-employed, or persons who do not work at all;
- A person may fall into one or more categories at the same time;
- There is no lower or upper age limit for paying income tax;
- Income tax is also payable by trusts and estates and ss 11,14, and 15 of ITA 2007 provide for these situations. Even after death, any outstanding income tax which is owed is not extinguished and must be paid from the estate by the deceased's personal representatives. In this respect income tax is no respecter of people.

5.4.1   What is 'income'?

Income may be generated in different ways as well as through employment.

This means that when a person's income sources, or income streams as they are sometimes called, are added together this will result in:

- more income tax becoming payable than may have been deducted from the separate sources; or
- no further tax becoming payable; or
- a rebate of income tax being claimed.

5.4.2   Tax codes and the self-assessment process

5.4.2.1   Tax codes

Each year HMRC issues employees and people in receipt of income with an individual tax code. The tax code is made up of letters and numbers which represent the amount of tax free allowance and the tax rate applicable to the employee's or individual's income. If a person has employment, the tax code is also sent to the employer who then deducts income tax and class 1 national insurance contributions from the employee's wages in accordance with the tax code notification and sends them to HMRC. People who no longer work for their income, such as someone who is retired and in receipt of an occupational pension, should also receive an individual tax code.

5.4.2.2   Self-assessment

A person will have to pay more income tax than has been deducted from their employment if their total income from different sources such as salary, income from self-employment, savings, dividends, pension, annuities, and any other source of taxable income exceeds the threshold for paying basic rate income tax dictated by their tax code or they have untaxed income over £2,500. Some people have more than one paid employment due to the increase in part time jobs and complications of obtaining full time permanent employment. Others may be in receipt of an occupational pension and paid employment arising out of phased retirement or part time work.

As a consequence of people's working lives growing longer, traditional patterns of work changing, and the increased use of computer technology many more people are required to complete an annual tax return.

It is a legal requirement that a person registers for self-assessment with HMRC and completes an annual tax return when that person has income from different sources some of which is untaxed. Completing a self-assessment tax return enables all sources of income to be brought together and the person's liability to pay income tax to be assessed.

To summarise, a self-assessment tax return, SA100 or SA200, must be submitted when any of the following apply to a person:

- self-employed, a business partner, or a director of a limited company; or
- untaxed income of £2,500 or more; or
- an annual income of £100,000 or more; or
- savings or investment income of £10,000 or more; or
- dividends from shares and a higher rate or additional taxpayer; or
- income over £50,000 or living with a person with income over £50,000 and claiming Child Benefit; or
- assets have been sold giving rise to a Capital Gains Tax charge; or
- living abroad with UK income; or
- living in the UK with income from abroad; or
- a trustee or representative of someone who has died; or
- a trustee of a trust or registered pension scheme.

5.4.3   Deadlines for submitting tax returns

The deadline for submitting a completed self-assessment tax return is 31 October for a paper return or where HMRC is asked to calculate the amount of income tax payable. The deadline for submitting online returns is 31 January. There are penalties for submitting a late tax return together with interest and surcharges on any tax that is owed.

A system of online digital accounts is planned to be fully operational by 2020 to bring together individual and business tax information into one place. Businesses will be moving towards digital records and from April 2018, larger businesses will need to send quarterly tax information to HMRC.

5.4.4   Informing HMRC of changes

If a person's circumstances change, usually because they are in receipt of new income during the tax year, HMRC must be informed by 5 October following the end of the tax year in which the change of circumstances arose.

5.4.5   Income generated by trust funds

There are special rules for the payment of income tax on income generated by trust funds and arising during the administration of an estate which are not covered in this chapter.

5.4.6 Tax year and collection of tax

The tax year runs from 6 April to 5 April in the following year.

Tax payable on employment income is deducted through the PAYE system.

From 6 April 2016, the treatment of taxable savings accounts changed. From that date, banks or building societies no longer deduct basic rate tax from savings income. A new Personal Savings Allowance came into force based on the individual taxpayer's status as a basic, higher, or additional rate taxpayer. This is in addition to other tax free savings accounts like Individual Savings Accounts (ISAs) which a taxpayer may have.

A basic rate taxpayer automatically receives a £1,000 annual tax free Personal Savings Allowance and a higher rate taxpayer a £500 annual tax free Personal Savings Allowance. An additional rate taxpayer does not have a Personal Savings Allowance. Any tax due on savings income above the taxpayer's Personal Savings Allowance is collected via a self-assessment tax return or by adjusting the taxpayer's PAYE code.

Additionally, from 6 April 2016, the treatment of dividend income for income tax purposes changed. From 6 April 2016, taxpayers in receipt of dividends automatically receive an annual £5,000 tax free Dividend Allowance. Dividend income above the Dividend Allowance is taxed at 7.5 per cent for basic rate taxpayers, 32.5 per cent for higher rate taxpayers, and 38.1 per cent for additional rate taxpayers.

HMRC provides guidance on how the Personal Savings and Dividend Allowances work on its website http://www.hmrc.gov.uk with worked examples.

5.5 Allowances and rates of income tax

5.5.1 Personal allowances

Tables 5.1 and 5.2 set out the personal allowances and income tax rates which are provided for in ITA 2007, Part Two, Chapter 2:

Table 5.1 **Income tax allowances for 2017–2018**

Personal allowance	£11,500
Not every taxpayer receives the full personal allowance. There is a reduction in the personal allowance for those with 'net adjusted income' over £100,000. In 2017–2018 there will be no personal allowance available where adjusted net income exceeds £123,000.	
Marriage allowance	£1,150
Maximum amount of married couple's allowance including civil partnerships where one partner was born before 6 April 1935	£8,445
Minimum amount of married couple's allowance including civil partnerships where one partner was born before 6 April 1935	£3,260
Blind person's allowance	£2,320

5.5.2 Income tax heads and calculation

Section **5.6** which follows gives an overview of the heads of income and the procedural steps to calculate income tax.

5.6 Calculation of income tax

Income tax is a tax paid on income. All sources of taxable earnings must be brought into the calculation.

Table 5.2 **Income tax rates and bands for individuals in 2017–2018**

Income tax rate	Income bands
Basic rate 20%	£0–£33,500
Higher rate 40%	£33,500–£150,000
Additional rate of 45%	over £150,000
	(additional rate taxpayers do not receive the personal allowance)
Savings income	
Starting rate for savings	£0–£5,000
Basic rate Personal Savings Allowance	£1,000
Savings basic rate 20%	£0–£33,500
Higher rate Personal Savings Allowance	£500
Savings higher rate 40%	£32,000–£150,000
Savings additional rate 45%	over £150,000
(no Personal Savings Allowance for additional rate taxpayers)	
Dividend income	
Tax free Dividend Allowance	£5,000
Basic rate 7.5%	£0–£33,500
Higher rate 32.5%	£33,500–£150,000
Additional rate 38.1%	over £150,000

5.6.1   Income liable to tax

The different types of income liable to tax are set out in **Table 5.3**.

5.6.2   A simple method to calculate income tax

A simple way to calculate how much income tax a person is liable to pay in a tax year is by adding together all the sources of taxable income, deducting any relevant tax reliefs and the relevant personal allowances, applying the correct income tax rate to the taxable income and giving credit for any tax which has been paid already. The result will be the income tax payable for the tax year.

Table 5.3 **Heads of income listed under ITA 2007, s 3**

Amounts charged to tax under ITEPA 2003 Part 2	Employment income
Amounts charged to tax under ITEPA 2003 Part 9	Pension income
Amounts charged to tax under ITEPA 2003 Part 10	Social security income
Amounts charged to tax under ITTOIA 2005 Part 2	Trading income
Amounts charged to tax under ITTOIA 2005 Part 3	Property income
Amounts charged to tax under ITTOIA 2005 Part 4	Savings and investment income
Amounts charged to tax under ITTOIA 2005 Part 5	Miscellaneous income such as annual payments and income arising under some types of settlement and income which belongs to an estate beneficiary
Other heads, including ITA 2007 Parts 10, 12, and 13	Charities, accrued income profits, and tax avoidance

Table 5.4 sets out the procedural steps to calculate income tax. It may be helpful to keep the table visible when calculating income tax.

Table 5.4 **Procedural steps to calculate income tax**

Step 1   Add together all sources of taxable income including:

- salary
- profits from self-employment
- rental income
- savings income above savings allowance from taxable savings accounts
- dividend income above the dividend allowance
- pension and taxable annuity payments
- trust fund income
- taxable welfare benefits

Step 2   Exclude any non-taxable income including:

- housing benefit
- pension credit
- attendance allowance
- maternity allowance
- tax credits
- disability living allowance
- tax free savings accounts and premium bond prizes
- free TV licence for the over 75s
- winter fuel payments and Christmas bonus
- war widow's pension

Step 3   Deduct allowable tax reliefs on expenditure including:

- professional body or trade union subscriptions
- charges on income

This has the effect of reducing the amount of income on which tax is paid.

Step 4   Deduct the relevant personal allowances including:

- personal allowance
- blind person's allowance if applicable
- any other applicable allowances

Step 5   This leaves the taxable income.

Step 6   Separate the non-savings income from the savings income and any dividend income and calculate the tax payable on the non-savings income first by applying the basic rate to income falling within the basic rate band.

Step 7   This is expressed as a percentage of the taxable income left after deducting personal allowance

• basic rate tax is paid at 20% on taxable income	£0 – £33,500
• higher rate tax is paid at 40% on taxable income	£33,500 – £150,000
• additional rate tax is paid at 45% on taxable income	over £150,000

It is often the case that a person pays tax at 20% basic rate on part of their income and the balance over the basic rate threshold at the 40% higher rate. Taxpayers pay the balance of their income over the higher rate at the 45% additional rate.

Step 8   Apply the Personal Savings Allowance to any taxable savings income

Starting rate for savings	£0 – £5,000 tax free but subject to income limits
Basic rate taxpayer	£1,000 tax free Personal Savings Allowance
Higher rate taxpayer	£500 tax free Personal Savings Allowance
Additional rate taxpayer	No tax free Personal Savings Allowance

(continued)

Table 5.4 **Procedural steps to calculate income tax (*continued*)**

Step 9   Calculate the tax payable on taxable savings income not covered by Personal Savings Allowance.

Basic rate	20%	£0 – £33,500
Higher rate	40%	£33,500 – £150,000
Additional rate	45%	over £150,000

Step 10   Step 10 Apply the Dividend Allowance to any dividend income.

      The first £5,000 of any dividend income is tax free regardless of any other income.

Step 11   Calculate the tax payable on any dividend income over the Dividend Allowance.

Basic rate	7.5%	£0 – £33,500
Higher rate	32.5%	£33,500 – £150,000
Additional rate	38.1%	over £150,000

Step 12   Add together the tax due on the different sources of income which gives the total amount of income tax payable by the taxpayer.

Note

Not every taxpayer has savings income and or dividend income, therefore, the steps relating to the calculation of tax due on savings and dividends income should be omitted as necessary.

5.6.3   Examples

The following practical examples illustrate the procedural steps.

EXAMPLE 1 A simple income tax calculation for a basic rate taxpayer

Mary's annual income from her self-employment is £15,500. She has no other sources of income. She receives no welfare benefits and has no allowable expenditure against which she can set her income. She is entitled to a personal allowance of £11,500

Add together all sources of her income	£15,500
Deduct her personal allowance	(£11,500)
Mary's taxable income is	£4,000

Now calculate the income tax payable by Mary. Mary is a basic rate taxpayer. All her income falls within the basic rate band. Mary pays income tax at 20%.

£4,000 × 20% = £800 income tax payable

If Mary had been an employee, her employer would have received notification of Mary's tax code from HMRC instructing how much income tax to deduct from her monthly salary under the PAYE system.

EXAMPLE 2 A simple income tax calculation for a higher rate taxpayer who is a registered blind person

Samson's annual salary from his employment is £85,000. He has no other sources of income. He receives no welfare benefits and has no allowable expenditure which he can set against his income. He is entitled to a personal allowance of £11,500 and blind person's allowance of £2,320.

Add together all sources of his income	£85,000
Deduct his personal allowance	(£11,500)
Deduct his blind person's allowance	(£2,320)
Taxable income	£71,180

Now calculate the tax payable by Samson. Samson's taxable income falls between two tax thresholds and must be apportioned between the basic rate and higher rate bands. This is sometimes referred to as top slicing income because the top slice of income above £33,500 is taxed at the higher rate.

Taxable income		£71,180
Taxed at basic rate of 20%	£33,500	
Balance taxed at higher rate of 40%	£37,680	£71,180

This means that Samson will pay £33,500 @ 20% basic rate which is £6,700 and the balance of £37,680 @ 40% higher rate which is £15,072

Total amount of income tax payable by Samson is £6,700

£15,072   £21,772

However, because Samson is an employee, under the PAYE system, his employer will have received a coding notice from HMRC instructing the employer how much income tax to deduct from Samson's salary each month. Providing the tax code is correct and Samson has no other sources of income he will have no further liability to pay income tax in the tax year.

If there had been an underpayment or overpayment of tax by Samson, then normally this would be collected by HMRC adjusting his tax code.

5.7   Sources of taxable income

Sections **5.7** and **5.8** describe in more detail the sources of taxable income and how they are to be treated in an income tax calculation.

The following sources of income have to be included in the taxable income calculation:

- Salary or wages;
- Bonuses;
- Commission and tips;
- Benefits in kind;
- Pensions and annuities;
- Profits from self-employment;
- Income from taxable savings accounts;
- Dividend income;
- Rent from property;
- Earnings from abroad;
- Child benefit;
- Taxable social security benefits.

5.7.1   Salary or wages

This is relatively straightforward to identify. It is a legal requirement that an employer provides an employee with a written statement of the main terms and conditions of their employment. This should include salary or the method of its calculation and the payment intervals.

An employer is under a legal duty to provide an employee with an itemised pay statement and a P60 for each financial year of employment and a P45 if the employee leaves that employment. Both forms state the gross salary that has been paid in the tax year to that employee as well as the amount of income tax that has been deducted and the national insurance contributions that have been made by the employee and employer. This information is essential for calculating the taxable income.

If a person has more than one source of income including employment, the gross salary is brought into account for the purposes of calculating taxable income.

This is because once the income from the different sources has been added together it may bring the person into a higher tax band. Consider **Example 3** which follows.

EXAMPLE 3 Income tax calculation for a taxpayer with different sources of income and top slicing at the higher rate

Deborah has been appointed as a part-time District Judge and receives an annual salary of £60,000. She also receives a pension of £15,000 payable to her under the terms of her late husband's pension scheme. She has no other sources of income. She is entitled to a personal allowance of £11,500. She has no further allowances or reliefs.

Add together all sources of her taxable income.

District judge's salary	£60,000	
Pension	£15,000	£75,000
Deduct her personal allowance		(£11,500)
Deborah's taxable income is		£63,500

Now calculate the tax payable by Deborah.

Deborah's taxable income falls between two tax thresholds and must be apportioned between the basic rate and higher rate bands. The top slice of income above £33,500 is taxed at the higher rate.

Taxable income		£63,500
Income taxed at basic rate of 20%	£33,500	
Income taxed at higher rate of 40%	£30,000	£63,500

This means that Deborah will pay £33,500 of her taxable income @ 20% basic rate which is £6,700 tax and the balance of her taxable income being £30,000 @ the 40% higher rate which is £12,000 tax.

Total income tax payable by Deborah is £18,700.

5.7.2 Bonuses

In some employment situations, it is common for an employee to receive a contractual bonus which is payable according to the profitability of the employer's business. This provides a performance incentive for the employee who then has a stake in the success of his employer's business. Any bonus that is paid must be detailed in the employee's itemised pay statement and this information will feed into the employee's P60.

5.7.3 Commission and tips

Some jobs which are sales driven carry a contractual right to commission payable on the number or volume of sales achieved by the individual.

This provides the individual with financial targets. The formula for calculating the commission should be clearly drafted and incorporated into the contract of employment if the person is an employee or into the contract for services if the person is engaged on a self-employment basis. In this way, the commission entitlement and the tax liability which arises can be calculated. Any commission that is paid to an employee must be detailed in an itemised pay statement which will then be fed into the employee's P60. If the commission is paid under a contract for services an invoice should be raised by the person receiving the commission giving details of the required payment.

Some jobs which provide personal service to customers and which may be performed either by an employee or a person who has self-employed status, carry with them an expectation of receiving an additional payment from the customer when good service has been provided. This kind of payment is known as a gratuity or tip. The payment has to be freely given by the customer and not part of any contractual obligation. Table waiters, taxi drivers, and hairdressers are examples of people who may expect to receive such additional payments from a customer.

Tips must be brought into the calculation of taxable income. Tips and gratuities automatically added to bills in the form of a service charge and then paid to employees will be dealt with by the employer through the PAYE system. Tips paid directly to employees or to the self-employed must be declared by the person receiving them on their tax return.

5.7.4   Benefits in kind

These are contractual benefits given to employees as part of their remuneration package. The benefits are not directly financial in nature but have a taxable value. They include such things as company vehicles which an employee may use for purposes unrelated to work, fuel for a vehicle being used privately, healthcare insurance, living accommodation which is not a requirement of the job, and loans at a low interest rate.

Many benefits in kind are taxed at the cash equivalent value which means the cost to the employer of providing the benefit. However, there are some exceptions such as company cars to which special rules apply. HMRC sets the guidelines for dealing with benefits in kind.

5.7.5   Pensions and annuities

Pension income received from an occupational or private pension scheme is taxable and must be included in the taxable income calculation.

An annuity is an insurance product which provides a consistent source of income over a specific time period. It is often used as a way of planning for retirement and therefore may supplement pension income and in most cases the income is taxable.

5.7.6   Profits from self-employment

One of the advantages of being self-employed is that a greater number of expenses and allowances can be claimed to offset income tax liability compared with employee status.

So, for example, consumable items like vehicle running costs and mobile phone expenses, a solicitor's professional fees, heating and lighting expenses can be set against profits. Capital expenses on items such as computers, cars, tools, and equipment can also be set against profits.

Expenses for self-employment must be 'wholly and exclusively' incurred to run the business and if part of the expenditure relates to self-employment and part to personal use the expenditure has to be apportioned so that only the part which relates to the business can be claimed.

It is increasingly common to find people who are both employees working for an employer and self-employed working on their account during the same tax year. A solicitor in practice may be self-employed as a partner of a firm and a university lecturer teaching law to students. In this example, the solicitor would have to include both sources of income on his tax return to determine his total income from all sources.

5.7.7   Interest from taxable savings accounts

From 6 April 2016, savings income is credited gross to savings accounts ie without any tax being deducted. Prior to this date banks and building societies were required to deduct basic rate income tax from the interest payable on taxable savings accounts.

Income from taxable savings accounts must be added to any other sources of income to determine a taxpayer's total income, tax band, and the relevant Personal Savings Allowance. If the Personal Savings Allowance and personal allowance do not cover taxable savings income, it must be taxed after any non-savings income. This is an important point to remember because a taxpayer's basic rate band will be applied firstly to non-savings income, for example salary, which may use up the basic rate band so that any savings income not covered by the Personal Savings Allowance will be taxed at the higher rate.

There is also the 0 per cent starting rate band of £5,000 to assist people on low incomes in 2017–2018. The band remains the same as last year with its availability restricted by non-savings taxable income, excluding dividends. If non-savings income is within the £11,500 personal allowance plus the £5,000 starting rate, it is available. Then if any savings income is still not covered, the £1,000 basic rate Personal Savings Allowance is applied to the savings income.

Generally, no tax will be due on savings income when the total taxable income is below £17,000.

Table 5.5 **Personal Savings Allowance examples**

Example 1: Basic rate taxpayer	A taxpayer has income of £20,000 and £250 in savings income	No tax is payable on the savings income. As a basic rate taxpayer, the savings income is covered by the taxpayer's £1,000 Personal Savings Allowance.
Example 2: Basic rate taxpayer	A taxpayer has income of £20,000 and £1,500 in savings income.	No tax is payable on the savings income up to £1,000, but tax will be payable at 20% basic rate on the £500 savings income over the £1,000 Personal Savings Allowance.
Example 3: Higher rate taxpayer	A taxpayer has income of £60,000 a year and £250 in savings income.	No tax is payable pay on the savings income. A higher rate taxpayer has a £500 Personal Savings Allowance which covers the savings income.
Example 4: Higher rate taxpayer	A taxpayer has income of £60,000 and £1,000 in savings income.	No tax is payable on the first £500 of the savings income, but tax will be payable on the £500 over the £500 higher rate Personal Savings Allowance.
Additional rate taxpayer	A taxpayer has income of £150,000 and £2,000 in savings income.	The £2,000 savings income is taxable. Additional rate taxpayers do not receive a Personal Savings Allowance.

HMRC has produced guidelines on how the Personal Savings Allowance works and the table above is adapted from the guidelines to be found at https://www.gov.uk/government/publications/personal-savings-allowance-factsheet/.

The procedure to calculate the income tax payable including taxable savings income follows:

1. Add the savings income to the non-savings income
2. Deduct the personal allowance
3. Separate the savings income from the non-savings income and calculate the tax payable on the non-savings income first
4. Apply the relevant Personal Savings Allowance to the savings income
5. Calculate the tax on any savings income not covered by the Personal Savings Allowance at the applicable basic, higher, or additional tax rate
6. Add together the tax payable on the non-savings income and the savings income.

Sometimes, interest credited to a savings account may lead to additional tax becoming payable by the taxpayer. Consider **Example 4** which follows.

EXAMPLE 4 Income tax calculation for James for the year ended 2017–2018

Information

Salary gross	£75,500
Savings income	£15,000

Income Tax Calculation

Step 1	Add the savings income to the non-savings income	Savings income	£15,000	Taxable income
		Salary	£75,500	£90,500
		Total income =	£90,500	
Step 2	Deduct personal allowance	Total income	£90,500	Taxable income less personal allowance
		Less		£79,000
		Personal allowance (£11,500) = £79,000		
Step 3	Separate the non-savings income from the savings income and calculate tax on non-savings income first	Taxable income	£79,000	Tax due on non-savings income
		Less savings income	(£15,000)	£18,900
		Non-savings income	£64,000	
		James' non-savings income falls between the basic rate band and the higher rate band and must be apportioned between them.		
		Non-savings income totals £64,000		
		Non-savings income taxed at basic rate		
		£33,500 × 20% = £6,700		
		Non-savings income taxed at higher rate		
		£30,500 × 40% = £12,200		
		Tax due on non-savings income £18,900		
Step 4	Apply Personal Savings Allowance and calculate any further tax payable on savings income	Add together salary and savings income to establish James' Personal Savings Allowance. Ignore any dividend income for this purpose.		Tax payable on savings income
		Salary	£75,500	£5,800
		Savings income	£15,000	
			£90,500	
		James is a higher rate taxpayer and has a tax free Personal Savings Allowance of £500. The balance of his savings income of £14,500 is taxed at 40% higher rate = £5,800		
Step 5	Add up the income tax payable from all sources of income	Tax on non-savings income	£18,900	Tax payable from all sources of income
		Tax on savings income	£5,800	£24,700
		Total tax payable	£24,700	

5.7.8 Savings income tax rates

The rates are outlined in **Table 5.6**.

Table 5.6 **Savings income tax rates after deduction of Personal Savings Allowance**

Starting rate Subject to income limits	0%	£0–£5,000
Basic rate	20%	£0–£33,500
Higher rate	40%	£33,500–£150,000
Additional rate	45%	over £150,000

5.7.9 Dividend income

Dividends are paid out of company profits to shareholders. Company directors are not obliged to recommend a dividend be paid each year and normally cannot do so if the company has not made a profit. In this respect dividend income is different to savings income paid by banks and building societies where the payment of interest forms part of the agreement when the account is opened.

From 6 April 2016, dividends are paid gross to shareholders, ie without deduction of tax. Prior to this date dividends were paid net of 10 per cent basic rate dividend income tax.

The procedure for dealing with dividend income in a tax calculation follows.

1. Add the dividend income to any non-savings income

2. Deduct the personal allowance and applicable reliefs

3. Separate the non-savings income from the dividend income and calculate the tax payable on the non-savings income first

4. Apply the Dividend Allowance of £5,000 to the dividend income and calculate the tax payable on any dividend income above the Dividend Allowance at the applicable basic, higher, or additional tax rate.

5. Add together the tax payable on all sources of income. This leaves the tax payable by the taxpayer.

The dividend income tax rates are outlined in **Table 5.7**.

Table 5.7 **Dividend income tax rates 2016–2017 after deduction of the Dividend Allowance**

Basic rate	7.5%	£0–£33,500
Higher rate	32.5%	£33,500–£150,000
Additional rate	38.1%	over £150,000

Consider **Example 5** which follows and shows how dividend income may lead to more income tax becoming payable.

EXAMPLE 5 Income tax calculation for Miriam for the year ended 2017–2018

Information

Profit from self-employment	£25,000
Dividend income	£20,000

Income Tax Calculation

Step 1	Add up total income	Internet business profit	£25,000	Total income
		Dividend income	£20,000 = £45,000	£45,000
Step 3	Deduct personal allowance from total income	Total income	£45,000	Taxable income less personal allowance
		Less personal allowance	(£11,500) = £33,500	
				£33,500
Step 4	Separate the non-savings income from the dividend income and calculate tax on non-savings income first	Taxable income	£33,500	Tax due on non-savings income
		Less dividend income	(£20,000)	£2,700
		Non-savings income	£13,500	
		Miriam's non-savings income falls within the basic rate band and is taxed at 20%.		
		£13,500 x 20% = £2,700		

Information

Step 5	Apply Dividend Allowance and calculate tax payable on remainder of dividend.	Dividend income	£20,000	Tax payable on dividend income
		Less Dividend Allowance	(£5,000)	£1,125
		Amount be taxed	£15,000	
		The remainder of the dividend falls within Miriam's basic rate band and is taxed at 7.5%		
		£15,000 x 7.5% = £1,125		
Step 6	Add together the income tax payable on all sources of income	Tax on non-savings income	£2,700	Tax payable on all sources of income
		Tax on dividend income	£1,125	£3,825
			£3,825	

5.7.10 Rent from property

If a person lets out rooms or property then the profits should be brought into the calculation for income tax purposes.

The Rent-a-Room scheme was introduced by the Housing Benefit (Amendment) Regulations 2012 and provides that up to £7,500 per year may be earned tax free under the provisions of this scheme. Expenses cannot be set against rent which is a factor in advising whether to take advantage of the scheme.

5.7.11 Earnings from abroad

Income from abroad must be included in the taxable income calculation.

5.7.12 Child benefit

This was a tax free payment which can be made to either parent for each child under 16 and children under 20 in full time education. It is now linked to income and the taxpayer with an income over £50,000 may have to pay a high-income child benefit charge.

5.7.13 Social security benefits

The benefits which are taxable include Bereavement Allowance, Carer's Allowance, Employment and Support Allowance, Incapacity Benefit, Jobseeker's Allowance, State Pension, Widowed Mother's Allowance, Widowed Parent's Allowance, and Widow's Pension.

The Citizens Advice Bureau website http://www.adviceguide.org.uk provides clear information and guidance on taxable and non-taxable benefits.

5.8 Charitable giving

This section explains how giving to charity may provide tax relief for higher and additional rate taxpayers.

On the self-assessment tax return, there is a section which asks the taxpayer to provide details of any gifts made to charity. Giving to a registered charity is not only good for charities but is helpful to higher and additional rate taxpayers.

If the gift is accompanied by a Gift Aid declaration the charity can reclaim basic rate tax on the gift provided the individual pays at least basic rate income tax. This means that a gift of £100 can be worth £125 to the charity if Gift Aided. From the higher and additional rate taxpayers' perspective gifts to charity are helpful for income tax purposes because they provide higher and additional rate tax relief.

For example, a higher rate taxpayer can claim back the difference between the basic and higher rate of income tax on gifts to charity in their self-Assessment tax return. This means that on a gift of £100 the higher rate taxpayer could claim back tax of £20.00. It is important that the taxpayer keeps records of their charitable gifting.

5.9 Summary

In this chapter, the basic principles of income tax have been described.

After studying this chapter, a student should have a clear understanding of:

- how income tax is collected;
- tax codes and the self-assessment process;
- payment and the rates of income tax;
- the calculation of income tax;
- the main sources of taxable income and how they are dealt with in an income tax calculation; and
- the way tax relief is afforded to higher and additional rate taxpayers through gifts to charity.

This chapter concludes with **Example 6**, the example of a full income tax calculation for a taxpayer, Sophie Latham, for the year ended 5 April 2018 illustrating the procedural steps involved in an income tax calculation.

EXAMPLE 6 Full income tax calculation for Sophie Latham for the year ending 5 April 2018

Information

Salary gross	£45,000
Savings income from a taxable savings account	£2,000
Dividend income	£5,000

In April 2017 Sophie Latham took out a personal loan of £20,000. She pays interest at a fixed rate of 5% per annum. She loaned this money, as an interest free loan, to Green & Co LLP in order to become a salaried partner.

Income Tax Calculation

Step 1	Add together all sources of total income	Salary gross	£45,000	Total income
		Savings income	£2,000	£52,000
		Dividend income	£5,000	
Step 2	Deduct charge on income and personal allowance from total income	Taxable income	£52,000	Total income less allowances and reliefs
		Less		
		Charge on income 5% interest on loan (£1,000)		£39,500
		Personal allowance	(£11,500)	
			£39,500	
Step 3	Separate non-savings income from savings income and dividend income and tax non-savings income first	Taxable income	£39,500	Tax due on non-savings income
		Less savings income and dividend income	(£2,000)	£6,500
			(£5,000)	
		Leaves non-savings income of £32,500 to be taxed		
		£32,500 × 20% basic rate = £6,500		
		Tax due on non-savings income £6,500		

Information

Step 4	Apply Personal Savings Allowance and calculate further tax payable on savings income	Add together salary and savings income to establish Sophie's Personal Savings Allowance. Ignore dividend income for this purpose. Salary £45,000 Savings income £2,000 £47,000 Sophie is a higher rate taxpayer and has a tax free Personal Savings Allowance of £500. The balance of her savings income of £1,500 is taxed at 40% higher rate. £1,500 x 40% = £600	Tax due on savings income £600
Step 5	Apply Dividend Allowance and calculate any further tax payable.	The dividend income of £5,000 is covered by the tax free £5,000 Dividend Allowance. No further tax is payable.	No tax payable on dividend income
Step 6	Add up income tax payable from different sources of income	Tax due on non-savings income £6,500 + tax due on savings income £600 = £7,100	Tax payable from all different sources of income £7,100

online resource centre   Visit the Online Resource Centre for more information and useful weblinks.
www.oxfordtextbooks.co.uk/orc/foundations17_18/

6

Capital gains tax

6.1 Introduction

This chapter covers the area of capital gains tax ('CGT') and looks at the following:

- Who is liable for CGT?
- Disposal of assets;
- What are chargeable assets?
- How is a chargeable gain calculated?
- What are capital losses?
- Exemptions and reliefs.

6.2 The principles of CGT

CGT is charged on the gain (or increase in value) which is realised when a chargeable asset is disposed of. The statute which sets out all the rules relating to this is the Taxation of Chargeable Gains Tax Act 1992 ('TCGA').

6.3 Who is liable for capital gains tax?

The following are all potentially liable for CGT: individuals, partners in a partnership, personal representatives managing the estate of a deceased, and trustees administering a trust. Note that companies do not pay capital gains tax, although they do pay corporation tax on any capital profits they make. See **Chapter 8** for the details of this. Charities are not eligible for the payment of CGT.

6.4 Disposal of assets

How can a capital asset be disposed of? It may be sold (a disposal) or given away (a deemed disposal).

6.4.1 Disposals between spouses/civil partners

Note that spouses and civil partners can dispose of assets to each other without any CGT consequences (e.g. one spouse or civil partner makes a gift to their partner), if the spouse/civil partner then makes disposal to someone else). The base value of the asset for calculating capital gains is the value when it was acquired by the first spouse or civil partner. Hold-over relief can be used when the asset is ultimately disposed of, see **6.10.1.1**.

6.5   What are chargeable assets?

These are more or less any assets except those which are exempt from CGT and examples of some of these are the following:

1. Wasting assets: these are assets with a lifespan of less than 50 years. Examples would be a television, washing machine, or cars.

2. Main residence (provided it is classed as the taxpayer's main residence during the period of ownership).

3. Personal chattels worth less than £6,000.

4. Tax advantages investment schemes, such as ISAs.

5. Shares in Venture Capital Trusts and Enterprise Investment Schemes ('EIS') as long as these are held for a minimum amount of time.

6. British Government Bonds and sterling based corporate bonds.

7. Compensation awarded by a court following defamation and injury claims.

6.6   How is the capital gain calculated?

CGT is payable on the gain made on disposal of the asset after the relevant exemptions and reliefs have been deducted. The first step in ascertaining how much CGT is payable is to calculate the gain on the disposal of a chargeable asset.

The capital gain is:

The sale price (or market value if the asset is given away or sold at less than the market price) *Deduct from this:*

- The cost of the asset.
- Acquisition costs such as professional fees (eg those of a surveyor or solicitor).
- Expenses wholly and exclusively incurred in increasing the value of the asset (however note that this does not include insurance or maintenance costs).
- Disposal costs such as legal or estate agency fees.
- The annual exemption (see **6.10**), if it has not already been used in that tax year.

EXAMPLE 1

Peter has bought a piece of land for £20,000 in the current tax year and sold it for £132,000 in the same year. Legal fees on both transactions amounted to £2,500 in to-tal. What is the capital gain?

		£
Sale proceeds		132,000
Less		
Cost price	(20,000)	
Legal Fees	(2,500)	(22,500)
Capital Gain		109,500

6.7   The rate of CGT

The onus is on the individual to notify HMRC that he/she is liable for tax on a chargeable gain, and this is subject to the self-assessment regime in the same way as income tax. See **Chapter 5** for the details on the self-assessment regime.

Each individual has an allowance (annual exemption) in a tax year, for the tax year 2017/18 it is £11,300 which means the first £11,300 of any gain on a disposal made is tax free.

If there is still a gain after the deduction of the annual exemption, then the rate is dictated by the amount which is left over from the basic rate tax band (in 2017/18 this band is £33,500). If the gain falls within the basic rate tax band, it is taxed at 10 per cent. If the gain falls over the basic tax band (ie over £33,500) then the rate of tax payable on the gain is 20 per cent. (Note: except for chargeable gains on residential property that does not qualify for private residence relief, when the rates are 18 and 28%.)

Note: The basic rate tax band is used against income first and then against the capital gain.

EXAMPLE 2

Agnetha bought a painting for £10,000 during the current tax year and sold it for £28,200 in the same year. Professional fees on the transaction amounted to £1,000. She had no other taxable income for the year.

CGT calculation

	£
Sale proceeds	28,200
Less cost price	(10,000)
Professional fees	(1,000)
Annual exemption	(11,300)
Chargeable gain	5,900
CGT payable is:	
5,900 at 10%	590

EXAMPLE 3

Assad earns £31,210 net of all relevant allowances. His annual exemption has not been used so far this year. He has gains of £60,000 from the sale of shares. He does not qualify for any reliefs. He has £2,290 of the basic rate band remaining.

	£
CGT calculation	60,000
Annual Exemption	(11,300)
	48,700 gain
1st 2,290 of the gain taxed at 10%	229
Remainder of the gain 46,610 taxed at 20%	9,282
	9,511 CGT to pay

6.8 Capital losses

When a chargeable asset is sold or given away its market value may be in fact less than the market value of the asset at the time of acquisition.

In this situation a capital loss is realised. This loss can be used to be set off against capital gains made in the same tax year, or it can be carried forward and be set off against capital gains made in future tax years, indefinitely.

EXAMPLE 4

Frederick has made a capital gain, after all relevant reliefs have been applied, of £40,000. He has also made a capital loss earlier in the year of £8,000. Frederick's income is £8,000.

Solution:

	£
Capital Gain	40,000
Annual exemption	(11,300)
	28,700
Capital Loss	(8,000)
	20,700

£20,700 × 10% = £2,070 CGT to pay.

6.9 More than one disposal in a tax year

If an individual makes several capital gains in one year the gain(s) and/or losses are calculated separately; they are added together to ascertain the total value of the gains and the annual exemption is then deducted before calculating the tax due.

6.10 Exemptions and reliefs

There is an annual exemption available for each individual on the first £11,300 of the gains in the tax year 2017/18. Note that any unused portion cannot be carried forward into the following year.

6.10.1 Reliefs

The following reliefs are available:

6.10.1.1 Hold-over relief

This relief applies to transfers between spouses and civil partners, and it applies to a gift or sale at an undervalue.

Spouses and civil partners who are living together can dispose of assets to each other without any capital gains tax consequences and hold-over relief will be used when the asset is ultimately disposed of to someone else. The base value of the asset for calculating capital gains is the value when it was acquired by the first spouse or civil partner.

Note that the transferee is charged to tax on his/her own gain in addition to the transferor's gain.

EXAMPLE 5

Peter bought a painting and gave it to his wife Liz when it was valued at £20,000. There would be no tax to pay as a result of this transfer.

Liz then gives the painting to her daughter Simone, when it is valued at £50,000. This disposal *will* have CGT consequences.

Liz ultimately will be assessed to CGT on the gain made since the painting was purchased by her husband Peter, ie on the £30,000 gain. Simone is not liable for the tax payable as there was no election for hold-over relief.

To claim hold-over relief both the transferor and the transferee must make a joint election.

In **Example 5**, if both Liz and Simone had elected to use hold-over relief, then no CGT would be payable when Liz transfers the painting to Simone. However, when Simone eventually disposes of the painting there will be a CGT liability for Simone. CGT will be applied to the gain realised by the sale or disposal value minus the original acquisition value of £20,000.

In a business context this relief can be used against 'business assets'. These assets are:

- assets used for the purposes of a trade profession or vocation carried on by the transferor or his personal company; and
- shares used in an unquoted company or in the transferor's personal company.

Note that a 'personal company' is a company in which the transferor holds at least 5 per cent of the voting rights.

Note also that to use this relief the *whole* gain must be held over and cannot be reduced by the transferor's annual exemption.

EXAMPLE 6

Randolph purchased shares in an unquoted company when the shares were worth £50,000.

He later gave them to Alexander when they were worth £70,000.

At the time of the gift Randolph and Alexander elected to hold over any gain. Alexander later sold the shares for £90,000.

What is the gain that will be charged to CGT when Alexander sells the shares and who will be liable for the tax?

The gain charged to CGT will be £40,000 on Alexander's sale and Alexander will be liable for the CGT due.

6.10.1.2   Roll-over relief

This relief is available in several different circumstances which include:

- replacement of a business asset (including land, buildings, plant and machinery); and
- the replacement asset must be purchased 12 months before or within three years of the disposal of the original asset.

(NB: The whole proceeds must be reinvested.)

This relief usefully applies when a sole trader or partnership transfers the business to a limited company. The business must be transferred as a going concern in exchange for shares.

The gain can be 'rolled over' into the shares, so in effect for CGT purposes the shares were acquired for the same value as the asset transferred.

Under this relief any amount reinvested will qualify for a deferral of CGT.

6.10.2   Entrepreneur's relief ('ER')

ER has been available from 6 April 2008 for individuals making a capital gain on the disposal of whole or part of a trading business or a partnership or in shares in a trading company in which they have a qualifying interest.

ER applies if the pre-conditions are complied with as set out below; gains liable to CGT are taxed at the rate of 10 per cent up to an individual lifetime limit of £10 million. Gains in excess of the lifetime limit of £10 million are charged at 20 per cent.

For the purposes of ER, the individual making the claim in respect of a trading company must, during the one-year qualifying period:

- be an officer or employee of the company during one year prior to disposal; *and*
- hold at least 5 per cent of the ordinary share capital (and therefore be able to exercise at least 5 per cent of the voting rights)—the 'qualifying interest'.

Note that a commercial property letting business does not qualify for ER, and neither does disposal of let residential property, however disposal of furnished holiday letting property does qualify as it is considered to be a trading business.

The relief is on the whole or part disposal of a trading business, not on the disposal of an asset in isolation (ie part disposal of farm land will not qualify for relief).

EXAMPLE 7

For the tax year 2017/18 Xavier made a capital gain of £521,010 on the sale of her share in a business in which she was a partner..

1.	ER is applied as follows:
	Capital Gain £521,010
2.	Deduct any capital losses: no capital losses.
3.	Deduct annual exemption £521,010
	£(11,300)
	£509,710

Calculate the CGT due: £509,710 @ 10% = **£50,971 CGT due**.

6.11 Death of a taxpayer

When an individual dies, their estate is subject to Inheritance Tax. CGT is not a tax on death because dying is not treated as a disposal.

The Personal Representatives ('PRs') are treated as acquiring the assets at the market value at the date of death. This means that all of the capital gains on those assets made before death are wiped out.

EXAMPLE 8

Alfie dies owning a painting valued at £300,000. He had bought this painting for £50,000.
When Alfie dies:

- What value will his PR's acquire the painting for?
  Answer: £300,000
- Is the gain of £250,000 subject to CGT?
  Answer: No as there is a CGT uplift of £250,000

6.11.1 CGT and PRs

If an asset increases in value during the administration period (ie after the death of the taxpayer, and before it has been transferred to a beneficiary) administrators must pay CGT out of the estate.

If the PRs sell an asset at less than the value at the date of death, a CGT loss will have been incurred. This can only be used against the gains made during the administration period. If the capital loss relief is not used by the PRs during the administration period it is extinguished.

PRs have one annual exemption to use against the estate of £11,300 and they pay CGT at the rate of 20 per cent for any gain made during the period of administration.

6.12 Case study: Arthur Pickering Deceased

6.12.1 Scenario

You are a trainee solicitor with LPC and Co. You receive the following note from your Supervising Partner:

To: Trainee solicitor
From: Nancy Williams
Re: Arthur Pickering Deceased

An elderly client of mine died last week. His son Jason Pickering is coming to see me early next week to discuss the continuing administration of his late father's estate. Jason Pickering is the sole executor of his father's will.

Jason needs advice about the payment of a legacy in his father's will. Arthur Pickering left his stock exchange investments to be divided equally between his god-daughter Sarah Travers and his nephew Jerry Edwards. Since Arthur's death the shares have substantially increased in value. Neither of the beneficiaries wants to keep the shares, and would like them to be sold. The shares were valued at £120,000 at the date of his death and they are now worth £308,000. No other gains have been made during the seven-month administration period, all of which is within the current tax year.

Sarah Travers is a student nurse and she has no other chargeable gains in the current tax year. Sarah has a taxable income of £26,000.

Jerry Edwards has used £6,000 of his CGT annual exemption in the current tax year. Jerry has a taxable income of £56,000.

Look at the relevant calculations in the following scenarios:

1. The shares are sold by the executor, Jason Pickering, and the cash is transferred to beneficiaries; or

2. The shares are transferred to the beneficiaries who then sell them themselves.

6.12.2 Solution

Solution to (1)

The executor pays the CGT at the flat rate of 20% and has one annual exemption for the year.

Gain £308,000 – £120,000 = £188,000 capital gain

Less the annual exemption of (£11,300) = £176,700

£176,900 × 20% = £35,340 CGT payable by the executors out of the estate and divided by 2 to represent the split between the two beneficiaries = £17,670 payable by both Sarah and Jerry.

Solution to (2)

Sarah:

£94,000 gain (£188,000 gain ÷ 2) – £11,300 annual exemption = £82,700 taxable gain

£32,500 – £26,000 salary = £7,500, remaining of the basic rate band, capital gain taxed at 10% = £750

Deducting £7,500 from the gain of £82,700, there is still £75,200 of the gain to be taxed. This will be at the higher CGT rate of 20% tax as Sarah has used up all of her basic rate band.

Total CGT payable by Sarah

£75,200 × 20% = £15,040

= £15,040 + £750 = £15,790.

Jerry:

£94,000 – £5,300 (used £6,000 of his annual exemption) = £88,700 taxable gain

Total CGT payable by Jerry £88,700 × 20% = £17,740

Jerry pays CGT at the higher rate of 20% as he is already a 40% taxpayer in respect of his income.

If the shares are transferred to the beneficiaries and they sell them, Sarah will have £1,880 less CGT to pay, but Jerry will have slightly more CGT to pay (£70 extra).

Consider the situation if the shares had decreased in value to £50,000 during the administration period and were sold by the executor:

A CGT loss would arise. This can only be set against gains made by the estate during the administration period. When the administration period ends the loss is extinguished.

If the shares are transferred to the beneficiaries who sell them for themselves the beneficiaries would themselves have made a loss which they could retain to set against their own future gains.

6.13 Conclusion: checkpoints

You should now be able to:

- Establish who is liable for CGT;
- Understand what a chargeable asset is;
- Calculate the gain on disposal of a chargeable asset;
- Apply the annual exemption, and any necessary reliefs;
- Apply the correct rate of tax;
- Identify when PRs are liable to pay CGT and the rate of tax to be applied.

 online resource centre

Visit the Online Resource Centre for more information and useful weblinks.
www.oxfordtextbooks.co.uk/orc/foundations17_18

7

Inheritance tax

7.1 Introduction: basic structure of inheritance tax

This chapter deals with the charge to inheritance tax ('IHT'). In the chapter we explain in particular:

- the charge to inheritance tax (**7.2**);
- potentially exempt transfers ('PETs') (**7.3**); and
- the occasions to tax (**7.5**) and the basic steps to follow to calculate the liability to inheritance tax (**7.5.1** to **7.5.4**).

As the charge to IHT depends on what happened in the preceding seven years there are examples to show how the inheritance tax is calculated in the following circumstances:

- the charge to tax and a lifetime chargeable transfer ('LCT') (**7.6**);
- the charge to tax and an LCT where the transferor dies within seven years of the LCT (**7.7**);
- the charge to tax and a PET (**7.8**); and
- the charge to tax and death (**7.9**).

IHT is commonly thought of as a tax paid only on death. Certainly, liability to the tax is triggered by death, but it is also triggered when a person (the 'transferor') transfers money or property into certain types of trust during their lifetime. A lifetime transfer which triggers a liability to IHT is known as a lifetime chargeable transfer.

There are currently (tax year 2017/18) two rates and bands of tax: £1–£325,000, where IHT is payable at 0 per cent—this is referred to as the nil rate band ('NRB')—and £325,001 and over, where IHT is payable at 40 per cent. For deaths on or after 6 April 2017 an additional nil rate band was introduced by the Finance (No 2) Act 2015. This is termed the residential nil rate band (RNRB). Further details of this can be found on the Online Resource Centre.

Any liability to IHT on an LCT at the time of making the transfer (ie during the lifetime of the transferor) is charged at one half of the rates applicable on death, so 0 per cent and 20 per cent.

These rates of IHT have applied since 6 April 2009 and will apply to the end of the 2020/21 tax year. Where there is a liability to IHT, the amount of IHT payable is linked to the value of any gifts of money or property ('transfers of value') made by the transferor in the seven years preceding the transferor's death or the date of the LCT. This seven-year period is known as the cumulation period and is an important consideration in calculating the charge to IHT. The fact that the amount of tax is calculated by reference to the cumulative total of the person dying or making the LCT, as opposed to the person inheriting the estate or gift, means that, to an extent, the name 'inheritance tax' could be considered to be a misnomer.

After reading this chapter you should be able to identify the occasions on which IHT is charged, and also calculate the liability to tax. There are five basic steps to follow to calculate the liability and at **7.5** the points common to all occasions are set out. The charge to IHT on each of the specific occasions identified at **7.5** are dealt with at **7.6** to **7.9**, and any additional points that need to be taken into consideration are identified. The worked examples illustrate the calculation on each of the occasions. If you use the examples to help you to calculate an IHT liability on a different scenario, you should ensure that you are using the relevant worked example to fit the circumstances of your scenario.

7.1.1   Sources of inheritance tax law

Sources of IHT law are:

(a) Statute: the principal charging Act is the Inheritance Tax Act 1984 ('IHTA 1984'). The true name of the statute is the Capital Transfer Tax Act 1984 but the Finance Act 1986, s 100 provides that it may be known as the Inheritance Tax Act 1984 and it is by this title that it is generally referred to. However, as for income and capital gains tax, annual Finance Acts have made changes to the Act.

(b) Case law and HMRC statements. Again, as for income and capital gains tax, these may be relevant as sources of IHT law.

7.1.2   Administration

IHT is a direct tax and is administered in the same way as income and capital gains tax.

7.1.3   Collection of tax

7.1.3.1   Lifetime transfers

Tax due in respect of lifetime transfers liable to IHT is collected by direct assessment.

7.1.3.2   Death

Tax due on the death of a person is also collected by direct assessment. A form of self-assessment is used.

7.1.4   Appeals

There is a right of appeal should the taxpayer not agree with an HMRC decision. The appeal must be made in writing, usually within 30 days of the date of the decision. On sending an appeal the taxpayer can apply to postpone paying the tax that is the subject of the appeal. Interest will still accrue on any tax that has to be paid at the determination of the appeal. Most appeals are resolved by agreement with HMRC. If agreement is not reached the taxpayer can request a review of HMRC's decision or request that a tribunal consider the appeal.

7.2   The charge to inheritance tax

Section 1 of the IHTA 1984 states that 'Inheritance tax shall be charged on the value transferred by a chargeable transfer'. This raises two questions: what is a *chargeable transfer* and how is the *value transferred* calculated?

7.2.1   Chargeable transfers

7.2.1.1   The legislation

Section 2 of the IHTA 1984 expands on s 1 and explains that 'A chargeable transfer is a *transfer of value* which is made by an individual but is not ... an *exempt transfer*'. The Act then goes on to expand this further, stating what is meant by a transfer of value (IHTA 1984, s 3) and what is meant by an exempt transfer (see **7.5.2** and **7.6.3**).

A transfer of value:

is a disposition made by a person (the transferor) as a result of which the value of the transferor's estate immediately after the disposition is less than it would be but for the disposition; and the amount by which it is less is the value transferred by the transfer. (IHTA 1984, s 1(3))

The Act excludes some assets from the charge to tax and also details dispositions which are not transfers of value.

7.2.1.2   Excluded assets

Categories of excluded property are set out in IHTA 1984, ss 6, 47, and 48. Section 6 includes property situated outside the UK where the person beneficially entitled to it is domiciled outside the UK. Sections 47 and 48 deal with reversionary interests in settled property. The term 'reversionary interest' is used to describe the situation where X leaves some property in a settlement so that Y enjoys the income from that settlement during his lifetime, but, on Y's death, the property goes to Z absolutely. Prior to Y's death, Z's interest in the settled fund is referred to as a 'reversionary interest'. This interest is excluded property so far as Z is concerned. In some cases the reversionary interest will not be excluded property. One example would be if it was purchased for money or money's worth.

7.2.1.3   Dispositions which are not transfers of value

7.2.1.3.1   *Gratuitous benefit*

A disposition is not a transfer of value if the transferor had no intention to confer a gratuitous benefit. This principle is relevant where there has been a sale at an undervalue. If the transferor can prove that he made a bad bargain (eg through not recognising how much the asset was really worth) and had no intention of conferring a gratuitous benefit on the transferee, then the loss resulting to the transferor's estate arising from the bad bargain will not have any IHT implications.

7.2.1.3.2   *Dispositions for family maintenance (IHTA 1984, s 11)*

Payments by a transferor to spouses, civil partners, children, and dependent relations which result in a loss to the transferor's estate are not chargeable in the following circumstances:

(a) if the payment is by one spouse or civil partner for the maintenance of the other (this provision includes any disposition for maintenance made on the occasion of a divorce); or

(b) if the payment is for the maintenance, education, or training of a child of the marriage or civil partnership (or of any other child not in the care of its parents); or

(c) if the payment represents reasonable provision for the care and maintenance of a dependent relative.

7.3   Potentially exempt transfers

In addition to excluded assets and dispositions which are not transfers of value, some transfers of value made during a person's lifetime are classified by the Act as 'potentially exempt transfers' ('PETs') (IHTA 1984, s 3A). If a transfer of value is a PET, then if it is made seven years or more before the transferor dies it is an exempt transfer, otherwise—that is, if the transferor dies within seven years of making the transfer—it is a chargeable transfer. While the transferor is alive, it is thus potentially exempt.

Currently, a PET is a *lifetime* transfer of value made on or after 22 March 2006 to one of the following:

(a) another individual; or

(b) the trustees of a trust for the benefit of the disabled.

Whereas before the Finance Act 2006 the majority of lifetime transfers were PETs, this is no longer the case. An outright gift by an individual to another individual is the PET you are most likely to come across.

With the exception of a gift into a disabled trust, gifts made during a person's lifetime into trust will be lifetime chargeable transfers. Such examples of transfers are:

(a) a lifetime transfer to a discretionary trust; and

(b) a lifetime transfer giving a beneficiary an interest in possession.

Lifetime chargeable transfers are subject to a different charging regime during the lifetime of the trust. The regime comprises a periodic charge and an 'exit charge'. The regime is referred to in **Chapter 11**, but the detail of the regime is not needed for this part of the course.

7.4 The transfer of value on death

There is a deemed transfer of value on death. This means that when a person dies they are treated as if immediately before their death they made a transfer of value.

7.5 The occasions to tax

There are, then, three occasions on which IHT is charged:

(a) on a chargeable transfer made during a person's lifetime (a lifetime chargeable transfer, LCT);

(b) on a PET or LCT when the transferor does not survive seven years from the date of the transfer; and

(c) on death.

Having identified that there has been a chargeable transfer, to calculate the IHT payable on a chargeable transfer there are five basic steps to follow:

(1) Calculate the value transferred.

(2) Identify any available exemptions and deduct them from the value transferred.

(3) Identify any available reliefs and deduct them from the value transferred.

(4) Calculate the transferor's cumulative total as at the date of the transfer and the amount of the nil rate band remaining.

(5) Calculate the IHT payable by applying the appropriate rate (or rates) of tax to the value of the transfer for IHT purposes. The rate (or rates) will depend on whether the tax is being paid on the date of the transfer or on the death of the transferor.

The five basic steps remain the same regardless of the occasion on which the tax is being charged. Depending on which occasion is the relevant one, there are additional steps to go through. These are set out later when examples of calculating the tax are worked through for each of the three occasions on which IHT is charged.

Points which are common to all three occasions are discussed at each step.

7.5.1 Step 1: calculate the value transferred

The value transferred is usually the market value of the asset at the date of the transfer. Two provisos to this are set out at **7.5.1.1.** and **7.5.1.2.** There are other provisos to this which are set out when each occasion is looked at individually.

7.5.1.1 Related property

Some assets are worth more when valued together, as a set for example, than they would be if they were owned by more than one person. Six dining chairs could be worth £3,600 as a set, giving an individual value of £600. However, if they are not kept as a set the value of each chair would be only £200, giving a total value of only £1,200. A transferor could use this to his advantage. For example, Mr Evans owns a pair of antique side tables. The market value of the pair is £50,000 but if they were separated they would each be worth only £15,000. Mr Evans wants to give the side tables to his daughter. If he made a gift to her of the pair then he would have made a PET of £50,000 (ignoring any exemptions or reliefs). However, if Mr Evans were to give away one of the side tables to his wife the loss to his estate would be £35,000 (£50,000 less £15,000 being the value of the side table he retained). As the gift was to his wife it would be exempt for IHT purposes (see **7.5.2.1**). Mr Evans could then gift the remaining side table to his daughter; this would be a PET of £15,000 as the side table is no longer one of a pair and so has a lower value. His wife could gift the side table she received to their daughter, also making a PET of £15,000. The potential liability to IHT is therefore smaller than it would have been had Mr Evans made the gift to his daughter of both of the side tables.

Section 161 of the IHTA 1984 prevents transferors from avoiding IHT in this way. Property in one spouse's estate is related to property in the other spouse's estate. Where any property in one spouse's estate would be worth more if valued together with related property in the other spouse's estate, the property is valued as a proportion of the related property valued together.

This means that, on the facts of Mr Evans above, when he makes the gift of one side table to his daughter the side table is valued with the side table in his wife's estate, as the related property rules apply, and so the loss to his estate is $1/2 \times £50,000 = £25,000$, rather than £15,000.

Shareholdings are a good example of assets affected by the related property rules. The related property rules apply mainly to property in the estates of spouses but the rules do cover other situations where the transferor makes gifts to other exempt transferees, for example charities, and stands to benefit from a similar tax advantage.

7.5.1.2 Joint property

When an individual has only a share in an asset it is more difficult to sell the share than it would be to sell the whole. To take account of this difficulty the value of the individual's share in the asset is reduced by between 10 per cent and 15 per cent. For example, Joan and Ruth own a house as tenants in common, in equal shares. The house has a market value of £64,000. The value of Joan's share in the property for IHT purposes is in the region of £28,800 (one half of the property is worth £32,000; 10 per cent of this is £3,200, and so the discount leaves a value of £28,800). This can be an advantage to the transferor if the transferor's share in a property is gifted to another, or the transferor dies; the loss to the transferor's estate is smaller because of the discount. However, if a transferor owns an asset outright and chooses to gift a share in the asset, the loss to the transferor's estate is higher as the value of the share of the asset retained must be discounted before ascertaining the loss to the estate. For example, if Joan owned the house outright and chose to gift a half share to Ruth, the loss to Joan's estate would not be £32,000, one half of the value of the house. It would be £35,200, as the value of the share she has retained is worth only £28,800, after taking into account the discount.

When the joint owner is the transferor's spouse or civil partner the related property rules apply and no discount is given.

7.5.2 Step 2: identify any available exemptions and deduct them from the value transferred

A transfer of value made by an individual will not be a chargeable transfer if it is an exempt transfer. There are a number of exemptions available; some cause the whole transfer to be exempt, others cause part of the transfer to be exempt with the remainder of the transfer being a chargeable transfer or a PET.

The transfer of value may qualify for exemption by virtue of the fact that it is a disposition to an exempt transferee (these are applicable on lifetime dispositions *and* on death) or because it comes within one of a number of limited *lifetime* transfers which qualify for exemption.

7.5.2.1 Exemptions available on lifetime transfers and on death

The main exemptions available both on lifetime dispositions and on death are listed here. The statutory reference is given for the exemptions and the relevant section should be consulted for the full conditions applicable.

Exemptions available on lifetime dispositions only are set out at **7.6.3**.

(a) *Transfers between spouses or civil partners* (IHTA 1984, s 18): transfers between spouses or civil partners are exempt provided that the gift is immediate, ie the gift takes effect immediately. However, it is common for a spouse or civil partner to state in his will that his estate will pass to the other spouse or civil partner only if the other spouse or civil partner survives for a specified period. As long as the specified period does not exceed 12 months the spouse or civil partner exemption will still apply. Provided both the transferor and the spouse or civil partner are domiciled in the UK there is no limit on the amount of the exemption. However, the exemption is limited if the transferor was domiciled in the UK but the spouse or civil partner was not. Currently the exemption is limited to the nil rate band that applies at the date of the transfer.

(b) *Gifts to charities* (IHTA 1984, s 23).

(c) *Gifts to political parties* (IHTA 1984, s 24).

(d) *Gifts for national purposes* (eg to the British Museum or National Trust) (IHTA 1984, s 25).

7.5.3   Step 3: identify any available reliefs and deduct them from the value transferred

Applicable reliefs available both on lifetime transfers and deemed transfers of value on death are business property relief ('BPR') and agricultural property relief ('APR'). Generally, any exemption is deducted before any available relief. However, if the disposition is a lifetime disposition and BPR or APR is available at 50 per cent, the relief is given before deducting the annual and other exemptions. This ensures that the exemptions are maximised.

7.5.3.1   Business property relief

BPR relief operates to reduce the value transferred by a transfer of relevant business property by either 100 per cent (ie no charge to IHT) or 50 per cent. To qualify for the relief the transferor must have owned the relevant business property for two years prior to the transfer. However, if the relevant business property is a replacement for other relevant business property, then the relief will be available if the combined period of ownership is two years or more.

7.5.3.2   Relevant business property

The following categories of property qualify for BPR:

(a) a business or interest in a business, for example the business of a sole proprietor or a partner's interest in a business;

(b) shares in an unquoted company;

(c) shares in a quoted company which give the transferor control of the company; or

(d) land or building, machinery, or plant used for the purposes of a business carried on either:

(i) by a company (unquoted or quoted) of which the transferor has control; or

(ii) by a partnership of which the transferor was a partner.

The reduction in the value transferred is 100 per cent for business property coming within categories (a) and (b) and 50 per cent for business property coming within categories (c) and (d).

7.5.3.3   Related property

Under the related property rules (see **7.5.1.1**), holdings of spouses or civil partners are treated as one holding and if their total holding gives control then either will have control for the purposes of the relief. See **Example 3**.

7.5.3.4   Additional rule for lifetime transfers

Where a lifetime transfer is made (either a lifetime chargeable transfer or a PET where the transferor does not survive by seven years) and IHT (or additional IHT) becomes payable because the transferor dies within seven years, then the relief is not available unless the property originally transferred (or replacement property which qualifies as relevant business property) is still owned by the transferee at the date of the transferor's death (or transferee's death, if earlier).

EXAMPLE 1

William has shares in a quoted company giving him control of the voting. The other shares are held by unrelated parties. He gives his holding away. It is valued at £240,000. William dies one year after the gift.

The gift is a PET when it is made. As William dies within seven years of making the gift it becomes a chargeable transfer. Provided the share holding originally transferred (or replacement property which qualifies as relevant business property) is still owned by the transferee at the date of the transferor's death the shares are relevant property for the purposes of BPR (category (c) at **7.5.3.2**) and so BPR is available. The value transferred is reduced by 50 per cent. Ignoring other exemptions which may be available, the value transferred is 50 per cent of the value of the shares at the date of the transfer: 50% × £240,000 = £120,000.

EXAMPLE 2

At the time of his death Mr Slater was the owner of a building used by an unquoted company in which he had a controlling shareholding. The value of the land at the date of his death is £350,000. The shareholding in the company has a value of £450,000.

On his death there is a deemed transfer of value. The shares are relevant property for the purposes of BPR (category (b) at **7.5.3.2**) and so BPR is available. Their value transferred is reduced by 100 per cent. The value transferred is nil.

As Mr Slater has a controlling interest in the company, the building is also relevant property for the purposes of BPR (category (d) at **7.5.3.2**) and so BPR is available. The value transferred is reduced by 50 per cent. The value transferred is 50 per cent × the value of the buildings at the date of death: 50% × £350,000 = £175,000.

EXAMPLE 3

Mr Exton holds 40 per cent of the shares in a quoted trading company. His wife holds 20 per cent of the shares in the same company. Mr Exton gives his holding to his son.

This gift is a PET. Should Mr Exton die within seven years of making the gift then the PET will become a chargeable transfer. Due to the related property rules Mr and Mrs Exton's shareholdings are treated as one. Mr Exton is deemed to have a holding of 60 per cent and so has control of the company. The shares are relevant property for the purposes of BPR (category (c) at **7.5.3.2**) and so BPR is available. Their value transferred is reduced by 50 per cent.

7.5.3.5 Agricultural property relief

This relief operates in a similar way to BPR. It reduces the value transferred by a transfer of agricultural property by either 100 per cent (ie no charge to IHT) or 50 per cent. Agricultural property is defined in the IHTA 1984 and, basically, is agricultural land or pasture and farm buildings situated in the UK, the Channel Islands, or the Isle of Man. The agricultural value of the property is taken as the value at which the property would be valued if it was subject to a perpetual covenant prohibiting its use otherwise than as agricultural property.

To qualify as agricultural property, the property must have been:

(a) occupied by the transferor for agriculture throughout the two years immediately before the transfer (there is no condition on the time of ownership: the transferor may have rented the property initially and only purchased the property shortly before selling it—the transferor will still qualify for APR provided the total period of occupation was at least two years); or

(b) owned by the transferor for seven years before the transfer and occupied by someone for agriculture throughout that seven-year period.

Relief at 100 per cent is available for transfers on or after 10 March 1992 if:

(i) the transferor was the owner or tenant in possession; or

(ii) the transferor had the right to obtain possession within 12 months (by concession, if the transferor has the right to obtain vacant possession within 24 months, relief at 100 per cent is also given); or

(iii) where the transfer is after 1 September 1995, the transferor's interest fails to come within either of classes (i) or (ii) because of a new tenancy granted on or after 1 September 1995.

There are also rules governing the position where a tenancy is inherited.

Relief at 50 per cent is available on any other qualifying agricultural property.

7.5.3.6 Additional rule for lifetime transfers

Where a lifetime transfer is made (either a lifetime chargeable transfer or a PET where the transferor does not survive by seven years) and IHT (or additional IHT) becomes payable because the transferor dies within seven years, then the relief is not available unless the property originally transferred (or replacement property which qualifies as relevant agricultural property) is still owned by the transferee at the date of the transferor's death (or transferee's death, if earlier) and the property qualifies for the relief at the date of the transferor's death.

EXAMPLE 4

Joe owns his farm, which he works, and has done so for many years. The agricultural value of his farm is £160,000. If Joe were to gift the farm, or on his death, agricultural property relief at 100 per cent is available. The agricultural value of the farm in Joe's estate is reduced to nil.

EXAMPLE 5

Alistair owns a farm which has been let to a tenant farmer for the past 12 years. The agricultural value of the farm subject to the tenancy is £200,000. If there were to be a disposal by Alistair, agricultural relief would be available at 50 per cent and the value of the property would be reduced to £100,000 for IHT purposes.

7.5.4 Steps 4 and 5

Step 4: calculate the cumulative total of the transfers at the date of the transfer and the amount of the nil rate band remaining.

Step 5: calculate the IHT payable by applying the rate (or rates) of tax to the value of the transfer for IHT purposes.

These two steps require some further explanation.

7.5.4.1 The rates of IHT

IHT is currently charged at two rates. For the tax year 2017/18 the first £325,000 is taxed at 0 per cent, the nil rate band ('NRB'); the amount above £325,000 is taxed at 40 per cent (see the example on an LCT for the rate which applies to LCTs at the time they are made).

All calculations shown here have assumed that the current rates have always applied. This is not the case. The rates usually alter with each tax year, following an announcement in the budget by the Chancellor. Tax tables should be consulted to determine the rates of tax which were applicable at any given date.

Section 209 of the Finance Act 2012 provides for a lower rate of IHT to apply in certain circumstances. These are for deaths on or after 6 April 2012 where a reduced rate of tax (36 per cent instead of 40 per cent) may apply if 10 per cent of the estate is left to charity (see **7.9.6**).

7.5.4.2 The principle of cumulation

IHT operates on a cumulative basis, the cumulation period being seven years. The rate (or rates) of tax applicable to a chargeable transfer depends on the cumulative total of all chargeable transfers made by the transferor in the seven years preceding the transfer currently being charged. As a consequence of the cumulation principle, the transfer is taxed as the top slice of the aggregate of the cumulative total and the transfer. The cumulative total eats into the NRB. To calculate the rate (or rates) of tax at which the chargeable transfer is to be taxed, the cumulative total is deducted from the NRB. If, after deducting the cumulative total from the NRB, there is some NRB remaining then the amount of the transfer equal to the NRB remaining is taxed at 0 per cent and the remainder of the transfer is taxed at the rate applicable to the occasion of the charge.

It is important to emphasise that the cumulative total is relevant only in determining the rate (or rates) of tax. Once this has been determined, the rate(s) is then applied only to the value transferred by the current chargeable transfer. It is not applied to the cumulative total.

To calculate the transferor's cumulative total at the date of the current transfer it is necessary to look back over the seven years preceding the date of the transfer and identify the chargeable transfers, if any, which the transferor made during that period. Having identified the chargeable transfers the next step is to calculate the net value of those transfers for IHT purposes. This is achieved by following Steps 1 to 3 inclusive.

Examples 6 and **7** both assume that current rates apply.

EXAMPLE 6 (Calculating IHT on estate where the deceased made a transfer within seven years of death)

Isabelle dies; her estate is valued at £360,000 for IHT purposes. Three to four years before she died she gifted cash of £120,000 to her daughter, Jasmine. She made no other gifts.

When made, the gift to Jasmine was a PET. As Isabelle has died within seven years of making the gift it is a chargeable transfer. There are no other chargeable transfers within the seven years preceding Isabelle's death.

Ignoring any exemptions and reliefs which may be available on the gift to Jasmine the value transferred was £120,000. Isabelle's cumulative total at the date of her death is £120,000.

Deducting the cumulative total from the NRB, ie subtracting £120,000 from £325,000, leaves an amount of £205,000 of the NRB remaining. When the rate(s) of tax are applied to the value of the estate on Isabelle's death, there is £205,000 of the NRB available.

The rates of tax applied to the estate will be £205,000 taxed at 0 per cent and the remaining £155,000 of the estate (total £360,000) taxed at 40 per cent giving a total of £62,000 of IHT to pay.

EXAMPLE 7 (Calculating IHT on an LCT where: (a) the transferor had made no other lifetime gifts; and (b) the transferor made an LCT within seven years of the later LCT)

Ignoring exemptions and reliefs:

(a) Philip makes a gift to a discretionary trust of £375,000. This is an LCT and is chargeable to IHT. If this is the only gift Philip has made in the last seven years, Philip's cumulative total at the time of making the gift is nil, meaning that all of the NRB is available. The rates of tax applied will be £325,000 taxed at 0 per cent and the remaining £50,000 taxed at 20 per cent, giving a total of £10,000 of IHT to pay when the gift is made (see **7.6.1**).

(b) However, if, in the previous seven years, Philip has made chargeable transfers of £160,000, then the IHT payable is different. Philip's cumulative total is £160,000. Deducting this from the NRB leaves an amount of £165,000 of the NRB remaining. The rates of tax applied to the £375,000 will be £165,000 taxed at 0 per cent and the remaining £210,000 taxed at 20 per cent, giving a total of £42,000 IHT to pay.

7.5.4.3 Summary

Steps 4 and 5 can be summarised as the following sub-steps:

(a) Identify any chargeable transfers in the seven years preceding the current transfer.

(b) Calculate the value of each of those chargeable transfers for IHT purposes, ie find their net value for IHT. This is done by following Steps 1, 2, and 3 for each chargeable transfer.

(c) Calculate the transferor's cumulative total at the date of the current transfer, by adding together the net value of all chargeable transfers made in the preceding seven years.

(d) Calculate the balance of the NRB remaining, if any, by deducting the cumulative total from the NRB.

(e) Apply the rates of tax to the current transfer.

7.6 The charge to tax and a lifetime chargeable transfer

In addition to the points mentioned at **7.5.4.3**, when following the five steps to calculate the IHT payable on a chargeable transfer, some additional points should also be taken into account when the occasion is a lifetime chargeable transfer. These are identified as each step is considered.

7.6.1 The rates of tax

One matter which is best dealt with at this point is a mention of the rates of IHT charged on an LCT. Provided the transferor survives seven years from the date of the transfer then the rates of tax applicable to the transfer are one half of the usual rates; that is 0 per cent on the NRB and 20 per cent on values exceeding the NRB. However, should the transferor fail to survive the seven-year period, then the usual rates of tax apply to the transfer; that is the NRB at 0 per cent and 40 per cent on values exceeding the NRB. The way this works in practice is that at the time of the LCT, IHT is paid at the reduced rates. If the transferor then dies within the seven-year period, the additional tax is paid. The five basic steps are applied to an LCT at the time of the transfer.

7.6.2 Step 1: calculate the value transferred

For lifetime dispositions the value transferred is the amount by which the value of the transferor's estate is reduced by the disposition. That is the loss to the transferor's estate. The value transferred is normally determined by reference to market value. In the case of a gift, the loss will usually be the market value of the asset transferred. In the case of a sale at an undervalue, the loss will usually be the market value of the asset less the consideration received on the sale.

It is important to note that the loss to the transferor's estate will not always equal the gain to the transferee's estate.

EXAMPLE 8

Peter owns 51 per cent of the issued share capital of Crookesmoor Ltd. The total issued share capital amounts to 10,000 shares. Peter is able to pass an ordinary resolution at a shareholders' meeting on his own (an ordinary resolution is arranged by 51 per cent of the vote) and, because of this, his holding is deemed to carry control of the company and is valued accordingly. Peter's 51 per cent holding in the company is valued at £11 per share.

Peter wishes to give 200 of his shares (ie 2 per cent of the company), to his son, David. A stake of that size, being a very small minority holding in the company (ie one which does not carry control), is worth only £3 per share.

Assume that a 49 per cent holding in Crookesmoor Ltd, because it no longer carries control, is only worth £7 per share.

The diminution in Peter's estate is:

	£
Value of estate before gift (5,100 @ £11)	56,100
Less value of estate after gift (4,900 @ £7)	34,300
	21,800

This is a very different result from the £600, which is the value to David of the shares actually gifted (200 @ £3).

7.6.2.1 Related property

Do not overlook the effect of the related property rules (see **7.5.1.1**).

7.6.2.2 Grossing up

As mentioned earlier, the value transferred is the amount by which the transferor's estate is reduced by the disposition. The transferor is primarily liable for any IHT due on an LCT, but the transferee can pay. Usually it is the transferee who pays the IHT. This means that the loss to the transferor's estate is limited to the value of the gift itself. However, if the transferor pays the IHT due on a lifetime chargeable transfer then the loss to the transferor's estate will be the total of the gift and the IHT due on the transfer. The value of the gift must be grossed up to find the value transferred. If the transferor is paying the IHT, then the property gifted is generally described as the *net chargeable transfer* and the loss to the transferor's estate is described as the *gross chargeable transfer*, being the net chargeable transfer plus the attributable tax. The steps to follow when grossing up a transfer are:

(a) Calculate the net chargeable transfer (NCT); ie from the chargeable transfer deduct any exemptions or reliefs which may be available, for example the annual exemption, spouse exemption, BPR, or APR.

(b) Calculate the amount of the NCT exceeding the transferor's NRB at the date of the transfer. To do this calculate how much of the transferor's NRB is available by calculating the transferor's cumulative total at the date of the transfer and deducting it from the full NRB. This will give the amount of the NRB available. Subtracting this amount from the NCT will leave the amount of the NCT exceeding the NRB.

(c) Calculate the IHT payable. The formula to use is:

$$IHT = 1/4 \times amount\ of\ NCT\ exceeding\ NRB$$

This formula applies when the lifetime rate of IHT is 20 per cent. For periods when the rate of tax differed, consult tax tables.

(d) Calculate the gross chargeable transfer ('GCT'). This is done by adding the net chargeable transfer to the IHT payable: $GCT = NCT + IHT$. This is the loss to the transferor's estate.

EXAMPLE 9 (Grossing up—assumes that the current rates apply)

Mr Teal transfers £160,000 into a discretionary settlement. He is to pay the IHT. He has made chargeable transfers in the last seven years amounting to £340,000 for IHT purposes.

Working through the steps:

(a) Calculate the NCT. On the facts given here the only exemption or relief available is the annual exemption for the tax year in which the gift is made (see **7.6.3.1**). *Assume that the previous year's annual exemption was used elsewhere.* The NCT is £157,000 (ie £160,000 – £3,000 annual exemption).

(b) Calculate the amount of the NCT exceeding Mr Teal's NRB. Mr Teal has a cumulative total of £340,000. His NRB is used up and this means that all of the current chargeable transfer exceeds the NRB.

(c) Calculate the IHT payable. Applying the formula: $IHT = 1/4 \times £157,000 = £39,250$.

(d) Calculate the GCT. The GCT is the total of the NCT and IHT, which is £196,250, ie (£157,000 + £39,250).

The loss to Mr Teal's estate is the amount of the GCT, £196,250.

EXAMPLE 10 (Grossing up—assumes that the current rates of tax apply)

Mrs Francis transfers £350,000 into a discretionary settlement. She is also to pay the IHT. She has made no chargeable transfers in the last seven years.

(a) Calculate the NCT. On the facts given here the only exemption or relief available is the annual exemption for the tax year in which gift is made. *Assume that the previous year's annual exemption was used elsewhere.* The NCT is £347,000 (ie £350,000 – £3,000 annual exemption).

(b) Calculate the amount of the NCT exceeding Mrs Francis's NRB. Subtracting the full NRB of £325,000 from the NCT leaves an amount of £22,000 exceeding the NRB.

(c) Calculate the IHT payable. Applying the formula: $IHT = 1/4 \times £22,000 = £5,500$.

(d) Calculate the GCT. The GCT is the total of the NCT and IHT, which is £352,500, ie (£347,000 + £5,500).

The loss to Mrs Francis's estate is the amount of the GCT, £352,500.

EXAMPLE 11 (Grossing up—assumes that the current rates of tax apply)

Mr Frost transfers £270,000 into a discretionary settlement. He is to pay the IHT. He has made chargeable transfers in the last seven years amounting to £124,000 for IHT purposes.

(a) Calculate the NCT. On the facts given here the only exemption or relief available is the annual exemption for the tax year in which gift is made. *Assume that the previous year's annual exemption was used elsewhere.* The NCT is £267,000 (ie £270,000 – £3,000 annual exemption).

(b) Calculate the amount of the NCT exceeding Mr Frost's NRB. To do this, calculate how much of the transferor's NRB is available by calculating the transferor's cumulative total at the date of the transfer and deducting it from the full NRB. This will give the amount of the NRB available. Subtracting this amount from the NCT will leave the amount of the NCT exceeding the NRB.

Mr Frost has a cumulative total of £124,000. This leaves £201,000 of his NRB available for this transfer. Subtracting the £201,000 from the NCT leaves an amount of £66,000 exceeding the NRB.

(c) Calculate the IHT payable. Applying the formula: *IHT* = 1/4 × £66,000 = £16,500.

(d) Calculate the GCT. The GCT is the total of the NCT and IHT, which is £283,500 (ie £267,000 + £16,500).

The loss to Mr Frost's estate is the amount of the GCT, £283,500.

Note: if the transferor pays the tax, and should the transferor make other gifts or die within the next seven years, the *gross* figure must be brought forward as part of the cumulative total.

7.6.2.3 Incidental expenses of transfer and capital gains tax

There may be expenses incurred in connection with the gift, or a sale at an undervalue (eg legal costs, stamp duty, etc). There may also be a liability to capital gains tax ('CGT') as well as to IHT. The rules for deduction of expenses or CGT from the value transferred are as follows:

(a) If the expenses or CGT are paid by the transferor, they do not reduce the value transferred;

(b) If they are paid by the transferee, they reduce the value transferred.

7.6.3 Step 2: identify any available exemptions and deduct them from the value transferred

In addition to the exemptions detailed at **7.5.2** there are additional exemptions to be taken into account. These are available for lifetime dispositions only.

7.6.3.1 The annual exemption

The first £3,000 of transfers made by a transferor in any one tax year are exempt. Where the transfers of value exceed £3,000, the first £3,000 is taken to be exempt. If the total transfers fall short of £3,000, the unused part of the exemption may be carried forward to the following tax year. However, in the following tax year the £3,000 exemption for that year must be used before the amount brought forward. There is no further carry forward if the amount brought forward cannot be used in the following tax year. The exemption is applied chronologically if there is more than one transfer of value in a tax year. If there are several gifts on one day, the exemption is apportioned among them in proportion to the values transferred.

EXAMPLE 12

In the tax year 2012/13 Maria makes transfers of value of £1,800. In the tax year 2013/14 she makes transfers of value of £3,500. In the tax year 2014/15 she makes transfers of value of £6,000. She has not made any other gifts. The transfers of value made in the tax year 2012/13 fall within the annual exemption for that year and so are exempt for IHT purposes. Maria has used £1,800 of the annual exemption for that tax year; she has £1,200 of the annual exemption unused.

In the tax year 2013/14 she will have to use the annual exemption for that year, 2013/14. If some of the transfers are unrelieved after applying the annual exemption, she can utilise the unused exemption from 2012/13:

Tax year 2013/14

	£
Transfers of value	3,500
Less exemption (2013/14)	(3,000)
Chargeable transfers	500
Less balance of unused AE 2012/13	500
Total chargeable transfers	Nil

In 2014/15 Maria can only use the annual exemption for that year. £3,000 of the transfers of value made in that year will be chargeable transfers and will form Maria's cumulative total.

Tax year 2014/15	£
Transfers of value	6,000
Less exemption (2014/15)	(3,000)
Chargeable transfers	3,000

The unused balance of the annual exemption from the tax year 2012/13 (£700) will be lost.

EXAMPLE 13

On 15 June 2014 Emily makes a gift of £325,000 to her daughter on trust for life (an LCT). On 7 September 2014 Emily makes a gift of £50,000 to a discretionary settlement (LCT). She had also made earlier gifts, using her annual exemptions for the years 2012/13 and 2013/14.

The annual exemption for the tax year 2013/14 is applied against the gift made on 15 June 2014, reducing the value transferred to £322,000.

There is no annual exemption to apply against the gift made on 7 September 2014; its value transferred remains at £50,000.

7.6.3.2 Small gifts exemption

A transferor is allowed to make any number of gifts of up to £250 provided they are to different people, without affecting the cumulative total (IHTA 1984, s 20). The gifts must be outright and not by way of settlement. The gift itself must be no more than £250—the exemption cannot be used to cover the first £250 of a larger gift, ie if the gift is greater than £250, it is not an exempt transfer.

7.6.3.3 Gifts in consideration of marriage or civil partnership

Gifts in consideration of marriage or civil partnership are exempt up to certain limits (IHTA 1984, s 22). The limits are dependent on the relationship of the donor to the parties to the marriage or civil partnership. If the value of the gift exceeds the limit, the excess is chargeable. The limits are:

(a) £5,000 if the gift is by a parent of one of the parties to the marriage or civil partnership;

(b) £2,500 if the gift is by a remoter ancestor of one of the parties to the marriage or civil partnership (eg a grandparent or great-grandparent);

(c) £2,500 if the gift is by one of the parties to the marriage or civil partnership; or

(d) £1,000 if the gift is by any other person (eg a guest).

The gift must be:

(a) before a specific marriage or civil partnership and conditional on it, ie the donor must have a right to recover the gift if the marriage or civil partnership does not take place; or

(b) on or contemporaneously with the marriage or civil partnership; or

(c) after the marriage or civil partnership provided it was given in satisfaction of a prior legal obligation.

The gift must also be an outright gift to either of the parties to the marriage or civil partnership or, if settled, it must comply with the conditions set out in IHTA 1984, s 22.

Where the marriage or civil partnership exemption is available, it should be deducted before the annual exemption, so that the annual exemption can be used elsewhere, if required.

7.6.3.4   Normal expenditure out of income

Transfers of value are exempt if they can be proved to be part of the normal expenditure of the transferor, made out of income, and of such a size that, after allowing for all such transfers, the transferor is left with sufficient income to maintain the standard of living which the transferor is used to (IHTA 1984, s 21).

7.6.3.4.1   *Life policy written in trust*

The most likely example of expenditure which falls into this exemption is where the transferor takes out a policy which assures the transferor's own life for the benefit of, say, the transferor's children. When the policy matures (on the death of the transferor), the proceeds of the life policy do not pass through the transferor's estate (and thus do not attract IHT), but instead they go directly to the children. The transferor is deemed to make a gift to the children every time a premium on the policy is paid. However, the transferor will frequently be able to establish that such a gift does not represent a transfer of value because it can be exempted under the 'normal expenditure out of income' provisions. The transferor is paying the premiums out of income and is left with sufficient income to maintain the transferor's usual standard of living. As the premiums are paid regularly the payments are part of the transferor's normal expenditure.

7.6.4   **Step 3: identify any available reliefs and deduct them from the value transferred**

The only reliefs available are those set out at **7.5.3**. Do not forget the additional rules applicable to lifetime transfers for both BPR (**7.5.3.4**) and APR (**7.5.3.6**).

7.6.5   **Steps 4 and 5**

Calculate the transferor's cumulative total as at the date of the transfer and the amount of the NRB remaining and calculate the IHT payable by applying the rate (or rates) of tax to the value of the transfer for IHT purposes.

As stated at **7.6.1**, lifetime chargeable transfers are initially charged at half the rates in force at the time of the transfer. The 2015/16 rates of tax are 0 per cent for the first £325,000 and 20 per cent for the balance over that amount. As before, the rate or rates of tax applicable will depend on the cumulative total of all previous chargeable transfers made in the last seven years. When a transferor makes an LCT the amount of IHT payable is calculated by following the five steps. The position if the transferor dies within seven years of making the transfer, with the result that the full rates of IHT are chargeable, is discussed at **7.7**.

EXAMPLE 14 (Assumes that the current rates of tax apply)

On 5 June 2015 Zac transfers a cash payment of £340,000 into a discretionary settlement. He has made no previous lifetime transfers. Any IHT is to be paid by the trustees of the settlement. Calculate the IHT payable on the transfer.

Zac has made an LCT. Following the five steps:

Step 1: the value transferred is the amount of the cash payment, £340,000.

Step 2: one exemption available is the annual exemption for the tax year in which the gift is made, 2015/16. This means that the transfer is reduced by £3,000 to £337,000. As this is the first chargeable transfer Zac has made he also has available his annual exemption for the previous tax year, 2014/15. This reduces the transfer to £334,000.

Step 3: there are no reliefs which are available to Zac.

Step 4: Zac's cumulative total is nil as he has made no chargeable transfers in the seven years preceding the transfer on 5 June 2015. The whole of his NRB remains (£325,000).

Step 5: as this is an LCT the rates of tax are one half of the death rates, the NRB at 0 per cent and the balance of the transfer at 20 per cent. Applying the rates of tax, the first £325,000 is taxed at 0 per cent and the remaining £9,000 is taxed at 20 per cent. The trustees of the discretionary settlement have £1,800 of IHT to pay.

EXAMPLE 15 (Assumes that the current rates of tax apply)

*Revisiting **Example 7(b)** but without ignoring exemptions and reliefs*:

Philip makes a gift to a discretionary trust of £375,000 on 29 April 2015. On 1 May 2013 Philip made LCTs totalling £160,000. Any IHT is to be paid by the trustees of the settlement. Calculate the IHT payable on the gift made on 29 April 2015.

Philip has made a lifetime chargeable transfer.

As you are aware that Philip made LCTs before the LCT on 29 April 2015, you may find it useful to draw a timeline to establish what events occurred within the seven years before the LCT on 29 April 2015.

Figure 7.1 Timeline

The timeline should help you to establish Philip's cumulative total immediately before he made the gift on 29 April 2015.

Following the five steps:

Step 1: the value transferred is the amount of the cash payment, £375,000.

Step 2: one exemption available is the annual exemption for the tax year in which the gift is made, 2015/16. This means that the transfer is reduced by £3,000 to £372,000. As Philip made no lifetime gifts in the preceding tax year, 2014/15, the annual exemption for that year is also available. This reduces the transfer to £369,000.

Step 3: there are no reliefs which are available to Philip.

Step 4: looking at the timeline above, Philip made a LCT of £160,000 within seven years of the gift on 29 April 2015. To calculate his cumulative total, we can apply Steps 1 to 3 to the LCT on 1 May 2013.

Step 1: *the value transferred is the amount of the cash payment, £160,000.*

Step 2: *one exemption available is the annual exemption for the tax year in which the gift is made, 2013/14. This means that the transfer is reduced by £3,000 to £157,000. As Philip made no lifetime gifts in the preceding tax year, 2012/13, the annual exemption for that year is also available. This reduces the transfer to £154,000.*

Step 3: *there are no reliefs which are available to Philip.*

The value of the transfer made on 1 May 2013 for IHT purposes is £154,000.

Philip's cumulative total on 29 April 2015, immediately before he made the gift to the discretionary trust, was £154,000.

Step 5: Philip has £171,000 of his NRB available to him (£325,000 – £154,000). As this is an LCT, the rates of tax are one half of the death rates, the NRB at 0 per cent, and the balance of the transfer at 20 per cent. Applying the rates of tax to the £369,000, the first £171,000 is taxed at 0 per cent and the remaining £198,000 is taxed at 20 per cent. The trustees of the discretionary settlement have £39,600 of IHT to pay.

Exercise 1

> Exercise 1 illustrates the charge to IHT when a transferor makes an LCT where he has made other LCTs in the preceding seven years.
>
> Work through this example to ensure that you understand the steps to be followed and that you can apply them correctly.
>
> There is a commentary on the exercise at the end of the chapter.
>
> On 28 May 2016 Mr Martin transfers a cash sum of £211,000 into a discretionary settlement and the trustees are to pay any IHT due as a result of the transfer.
>
> Mr Martin had made a transfer into the settlement of £160,000 on 17 February 2009, just over seven years prior to the present gift.
>
> He also made a cash payment into the settlement of £134,000 on 9 August 2009, between six and seven years prior to the present gift. The tax on each of those transfers was paid by the trustees of the settlement.
>
> In addition to these LCTs Mr Martin also made a gift of £70,000 cash to his daughter on 1 June 2015. He made no other lifetime transfers. Any IHT is to be paid by the trustees of the settlement. Assuming that the current rates of tax apply, calculate the IHT payable on the transfer Mr Martin made on 28 May 2016.
>
> Follow the five steps.
>
> You may find it useful to refer to earlier examples to remind yourself of the steps. You may find **Example 14** useful for the basic calculation; **Examples 12** and **13** useful for the application of annual exemptions; and **Examples 6** and **15** useful for the situation where the transferor has a cumulative total at the date of the current transfer.

7.7   The charge to tax and an LCT where the transferor dies within seven years of the LCT

At **7.6.1** it was pointed out that, provided a transferor survived seven years from the date of making an LCT, the rate of IHT charged on values exceeding the NRB was reduced to 20 per cent. If the transferor failed to survive the seven-year period, IHT is charged at the full rate, 40 per cent. IHT at the reduced rate is paid at the time of the transfer and any additional liability is paid at the time of the transferor's death. In practice this means that if a transferor dies within the seven-year period there has to be a second calculation of IHT. The full calculation needs to be carried out as not only is the IHT payable at the full rates but also, due to the transferor's death, the transferor's cumulative total at the date of the LCT may have changed and so the amount of the NRB available may have altered. This would be the case if the transferor had made a PET within the seven years preceding the date of the LCT which was not included in the transferor's cumulative total at the time of the LCT because it was, at that time, a PET. If the PET was made within seven years of the transferor's death, then it will now be a chargeable transfer and so its value will be included in the transferor's cumulative total at the date of the LCT (see **Example 16**).

On occasions the value of the property gifted by the LCT may go down between the date of the gift and the date of the transferor's death. If this is the case then, usually, the lower (date of death) value is used to calculate the additional tax payable (IHTA 1984, s 131). The lower value is not used if the property gifted was a lease with less than 50 years unexpired, or if the gift was of tangible moveable property which was a wasting asset (see **Example 18**).

The lower value is only used to calculate the additional charge to IHT as a result of the donor's death. The original date of gift value is used in all other calculations, for example the calculation of the donor's cumulative total.

In addition to the five basic steps there are two other steps which may be relevant.

7.7.1   Step 6: taper relief

Although IHT is charged at the full rates if the transferor dies within the seven-year period, there is some relief so long as the transferor survived at least three years from the date of the gift. The relief is given by only a percentage of the IHT calculated being payable. The amount of the relief depends on how long the transferor survived after making the LCT.

If the transfer is made within three to four years of the transferor's death, only 80 per cent of the IHT calculated is payable. If the period between the transfer and the death is four to five years, 60 per cent of the IHT is payable; five to six years, 40 per cent; and six to seven years, only 20 per cent. This relief is known as taper relief, or tapering relief, as the amount of IHT payable tapers off the longer the transferor survives (see **Example 17**).

It is important to understand that taper relief reduces the IHT attributable to the transfer; it does not reduce the value transferred.

7.7.2   Step 7: taking into account any IHT paid at the date of the LCT

After applying taper relief, account is taken of any IHT that was paid at the date of the transfer. Full credit is given for tax paid at the time of the transfer. However, if the amount of tax paid at the date of the transfer exceeds the amount of IHT payable due to the death of the transferor within the seven-year period then the balance of IHT payable is reduced to nil. There will be no refund of tax.

EXAMPLE 16 (Effect of death on an LCT made within seven years of the transferor's death assuming that the current rates of tax apply throughout)

Mr Martin dies on 10 October 2011.

On 28 May 2011 Mr Martin transferred a cash sum of £211,000 into a discretionary settlement and the trustees were to pay any IHT due as a result of the transfer.

Mr Martin had made a transfer into the settlement of £160,000 on 17 February 2004, just over seven years prior to the gift made on 28 May 2011.

He also made a cash payment into the settlement of £134,000 on 9 August 2004, between six and seven years prior to the gift made on 28 May 2011. The tax on each of those transfers was paid by the trustees of the settlement.

In addition to these LCTs Mr Martin also made a gift of £70,000 cash to his daughter on 1 June 2010. He made no other lifetime transfers. Any IHT was to be paid by the trustees of the settlement. Assuming that the current rates of tax apply, calculate the IHT payable on the transfer Mr Martin made on 28 May 2011 as a result of Mr Martin's death.

The LCT made by Mr Martin on 28 May 2011 was within the seven years preceding his death. IHT is now chargeable on the LCT at the full rates. The full calculation needs to be repeated.

Following the five steps:

Step 1: the value transferred is the amount of the cash payment, £211,000.

Step 2: one exemption available is the annual exemption for the tax year in which the gift is made, 2011/12. This means that the transfer is reduced by £3,000 to £208,000. The annual exemption for the previous tax year, 2010/11, is not available as it is applied against the PET made on 1 June 2010. The PET is now chargeable due to Mr Martin's death within seven years of the gift.

Step 3: there are no reliefs which are available to Mr Martin (as before).

Step 4: going back for seven years from 28 May 2011 Mr Martin made one chargeable transfer, the transfer to the settlement on 9 August 2004. (The transfer on 17 February 2004 was made more than seven years before the transfer in 2011.) In addition, as Mr Martin has died within seven years of the gift to his daughter on 1 June 2010, the gift is no longer a PET; it becomes chargeable.

The value of the transfer made on 9 August 2004 was £134,000. The only exemption available will be the annual exemption for the tax year in which the gift was made. This reduces the transfer to £131,000. The annual exemption for the previous tax year will not be available to Mr Martin as it will have been used on the gift made on 17 February 2004. There are no reliefs which are available to this transfer. The value of the transfer for IHT purposes is £131,000.

The value of the transfer made on 1 June 2010 was £70,000.

One exemption available is the annual exemption for the tax year in which the gift is made, 2010/11. This means that the transfer is reduced by £3,000 to £67,000. The annual exemption for the previous tax year, 2009/10, is also available. The transfer is reduced by £3,000 to £64,000.

Mr Martin's cumulative total on 28 May 2011 is £195,000 (ie £131,000 + £64,000).

Step 5: Mr Martin has £130,000 of the NRB available to him (£325,000 – £195,000). The first £130,000 of the transfer is taxed at 0 per cent. The remainder £78,000 (£208,000 – £130,000) is taxed at 40 per cent. There is IHT of £31,200 for the trustees to pay.

Step 6: as Mr Martin died within three years of the LCT, taper relief is not available.

Step 7: IHT of £2,200 was paid at the time of the transfer. Credit is given for this payment. The amount of IHT payable by the trustee of the settlement due to Mr Martin's death within the seven-year period is £29,000 (£31,200 – £2,200).

EXAMPLE 17 (With taper relief)

On the same facts as **Example 16**, Mr Martin dies on 9 July 2015. The steps up to and including Step 5 remain as in **Example 16**. At Step 6, as the LCT was made within four to five years of his death taper relief is available. Only 60 per cent of the IHT is payable, 60 per cent of £31,200, giving an amount due of £18,720.

Step 7: IHT of £2,200 was paid at the time of the transfer. Credit is given for this payment. The amount of IHT payable by the trustees of the settlement due to Mr Martin's death within the seven-year period is £16,520 (£18,720 – £2,200).

Exercise 2

Exercise 2 illustrates the effect of death on the charge to IHT when a transferor makes an LCT where he has made other LCTs in the preceding seven years, and where the transferor subsequently dies within seven years.

Work through this example to ensure that you understand the steps to be followed and that you can apply them correctly.

There is a commentary on the exercise at the end of the chapter.

Mr Martin dies on 9 July 2016.

On 28 May 2011 Mr Martin transferred a cash sum of £211,000 into a discretionary settlement and the trustees were to pay any IHT due as a result of the transfer.

Mr Martin had made a transfer into the settlement of £160,000 on 17 February 2004, just over seven years prior to the gift made on 28 May 2011.

He also made a cash payment into the settlement of £134,000 on 9 August 2004, between six and seven years prior to the gift made on 28 May 2011. The tax on each of those transfers was paid by the trustees of the settlement.

In addition to these LCTs Mr Martin also made a gift of £70,000 cash to his daughter on 1 June 2010. He made no other lifetime transfers. Any IHT was to be paid by the trustees of the settlement. Assuming that the current rates of tax apply, calculate the IHT payable on the transfer Mr Martin made on 28 May 2011 as a result of Mr Martin's death.

You may find it useful to refer to earlier examples to remind yourself of the steps. You may find **Examples 14** and **16** useful for the basic calculation; **Example 12** useful for the application of annual exemptions; **Examples 6** and **15** useful for the situation where the transferor has a cumulative total at the date of the current transfer; and **Example 17** useful for the application of taper relief.

EXAMPLE 18 (Effect of death on an LCT made within seven years of the transferor's death where the value of the property gifted has fallen and assuming that the current rates of tax apply throughout)

On 15 November 2010 Jason makes a gift of a freehold property worth £472,000 to a discretionary settlement and the trustees are to pay any IHT due as a result of the transfer. He has made no previous lifetime transfers.

Jason dies on 10 February 2015. On that date the property has a value of only £412,000.

A: IHT on the occasion of the LCT

Following the five steps:

Step 1: the value transferred is the value of the property on the date of the transfer, £472,000.

Step 2: one exemption available is the annual exemption for the tax year in which the gift is made, 2010/11. This means that the transfer is reduced by £3,000 to £469,000. As this is the first chargeable transfer Jason has made he also has available his annual exemption for the previous tax year, 2009/10. This reduces the transfer to £466,000.

Step 3: there are no reliefs which are available to Jason.

Step 4: Jason's cumulative total is nil as he has made no chargeable transfers in the seven years preceding the transfer on the 15 November.

Step 5: as this is an LCT the rates of tax are one half of the official rates, the NRB at 0 per cent and the balance of the transfer at 20 per cent. Applying the rates of tax, the first £325,000 is taxed at 0 per cent and the remaining £141,000 at 20 per cent. The trustees of the discretionary settlement have £28,200 of IHT to pay.

B: Supplementary charge

As the transfer was within the seven years preceding his death IHT is now chargeable on the LCT at the full rates. The full calculation needs to be repeated.

Following the five steps:

Step 1: the value transferred is the value of the property on the date of the transfer, £472,000. However, as the value of the property has fallen, the date of death value can be used to calculate the additional tax payable (IHTA 1984, s 131). The value of the property is £412,000.

Step 2: one exemption available is the annual exemption for the tax year in which the gift is made, 2010/11. This means that the transfer is reduced by £3,000 to £409,000. As this is the first chargeable transfer Jason has made he also has available his annual exemption for the previous tax year, 2009/10. This reduces the transfer to £406,000.

Step 3: there are no reliefs which are available to Jason.

Step 4: Jason's cumulative total is nil as he has made no chargeable transfers in the seven years preceding transfer on 15 November.

Step 5: Jason has available to him the full NRB; the balance of the transfer is taxed at 40 per cent. Applying the rates of tax, the first £325,000 is taxed at 0 per cent and the remaining £81,000 at 40 per cent. There is IHT of £32,400 for the trustees to pay.

Step 6: as Jason died within four to five years of the LCT, taper relief is available. Only 60 per cent of the IHT is payable, 60 per cent of £32,400, giving an amount due of £19,440.

Step 7: IHT of £28,200 was paid at the time of the transfer. Credit is given for this payment. The amount of IHT payable by the trustees of the settlement due to Jason's death within the seven-year period is reduced to nil. There will be no repayment of the additional tax paid at the time of the transfer.

NB: the lower value of the property is used only to calculate the additional IHT payable by the trustee as a result of the donor's death. The original value is used when calculating the donor's cumulative total at the date of death (which in this case will be £466,000).

NB: similar principles apply when calculating the IHT payable by the donee of a PET when the donor dies within seven years of the gift. Thus, if in **Example 18** Jason's original transfer had been a PET rather than an LCT, there would have been no charge to tax at the time of the gift. On his death within seven years, the PET would have become chargeable. The calculation described in Steps 1–6 of paragraph B would be undertaken to establish the donee's liability to tax on the former PET. Jason's cumulative total of lifetime transfers, however, would remain at £466,000.

7.8   The charge to tax and a PET

IHT is charged on a PET when the transferor does not survive for a period of seven years from the date of the PET. If the transferor dies within that period, the transfer becomes a chargeable transfer and IHT is payable at the full rates at the date of death.

If a PET becomes a chargeable transfer, then the steps to follow to calculate the IHT payable are the five basic steps, taking note of the matters mentioned when the charge to IHT and an LCT was considered, and, in addition, Step 6, set out at **7.7.1** (Step 7 is not applicable as there will have been no IHT payable at the time of the PET). Sections **7.8.1** to **7.8.4** look at the steps as applicable to a PET which becomes chargeable.

7.8.1   Step 1: calculate the value transferred

The comments made when looking at Step 1 in the charge to tax and an LCT (**7.6.2**), the related property rules (**7.5.1.1**), and the comments on incidental expenses of transfer and CGT (**7.6.2.3**) are all relevant here. Also relevant are the comments at **7.7** on a fall in value of the gifted property between the date of the gift and the date of the transferor's death. The lower value, subject to the exceptions set out at **7.7**, is used in the calculation of IHT payable as a result of the donor's death within seven years of the date of the gift.

7.8.2   Step 2: identify any available exemptions and deduct them from the value transferred

As with LCTs, in addition to the exemptions set out at **7.5.2.1**, the exemptions available for lifetime dispositions, set out at **7.6.3**, are all available to reduce the value transferred by a PET.

7.8.3   Step 3: identify any available reliefs and deduct them from the value transferred

Only business property relief and agricultural relief are available. Again, do not overlook the additional rules applicable to lifetime transfers at **7.5.3.4** and **7.5.3.6** respectively.

7.8.4   Steps 4 and 5

Calculate the transferor's cumulative total as at the date of the transfer and the amount of the NRB remaining and calculate the IHT payable by applying the rate (or rates) of tax at the date of death to the value of the transfer for IHT purposes.

If a PET becomes a chargeable transfer, then IHT is charged at the full rates of tax. The transferor's cumulative total at the date the PET was made must be calculated to determine the applicable rate or rates of tax.

EXAMPLE 19 (Assumes that the current rates of tax apply throughout)

Isabelle dies on 15 June 2014. Her estate is valued at £360,000 for IHT purposes. She gifted cash of £120,000 to her daughter, Jasmine, on 21 December 2010. This was in addition to a gift of cash of £218,000 she made on 5 November 2005 to the trustees of a discretionary settlement. The trustees paid any IHT. She made no other gifts.

When made, the gift to Jasmine was a PET. As Isabelle has died within seven years of making the gift it is a chargeable transfer. There are no other chargeable transfers within the seven years preceding Isabelle's death.

Step 1: calculate the value transferred. As the gift was of cash the value transferred is £120,000.

Step 2: identify any exemptions and deduct them from the value transferred. One exemption available is the annual exemption for the tax year in which the gift is made, 2010/11. This reduces the transfer to £117,000. As Isabelle had made no lifetime gifts in the previous tax year, 2009/10, the annual exemption for that year is also available. This reduces the transfer to £114,000.

Step 3: identify any reliefs and deduct them from the value transferred. There are no reliefs available as the gift is cash.

Step 4: calculate the transferor's cumulative total at the date the gift is made and the amount of the NRB remaining. Going back seven years from 21 December 2010, the date of the PET which has become chargeable, Isabelle made one chargeable transfer, the gift to the settlement. This was an LCT. (Although the LCT has to be taken into account when calculating Isabelle's cumulative total in December 2010, no additional tax is payable on it as it was made more than seven years before her death.) To calculate Isabelle's cumulative total Steps 1 to 3 have to be applied to the LCT. The value transferred was £218,000. The exemptions available will be the annual exemption for the tax year in which the gift was made, 2005/6. This reduces the value transferred to £215,000. As she had made no transfers during the previous tax year, 2004/5, that year's annual exemption is also available reducing the value transferred to £212,000. No other exemptions are available and there are no reliefs available. The value of the LCT for IHT purposes is £212,000. Isabelle's cumulative total on 21 December 2010 is £212,000. She has £113,000 of the NRB available to her.

Step 5: calculate the IHT payable by applying the rate (or rates) of tax to the value of the transfer for IHT purposes. £113,000 of the transfer falls within the NRB. The remainder of the transfer, £1,000, will be taxed at 40 per cent. There will be IHT of £400 to pay on the transfer. See **7.8.5.1** for the final step in the calculation.

7.8.5   Step 6: taper relief

The final step to be taken is to apply taper relief, if applicable. This applies to PETs which become chargeable in exactly the same way as the additional charge to IHT on LCT where the transferor dies within seven years of the transfer (see **7.7.1**).

7.8.5.1   Continuing Example 19

As the gift was made three to four years before Isabelle's death, only 80 per cent of the tax is payable. The amount of tax to pay is £320.

Exercise 3

Exercise 3 illustrates the effect of death on the charge to IHT when a transferor makes a PET, and where the transferor subsequently dies within seven years.

Work through this example to ensure that you understood the steps to be followed and that you can apply them correctly.

There is a commentary on the exercise at the end of the chapter.

You may find it useful to refer to earlier examples to remind yourself of the steps. You may find **Examples 14** and **16** useful for the basic calculation. In addition, you may find **Exercise 2** and **Example 19** useful for cumulative total.

On 1 March 2011 Vinny makes a cash gift of £175,000 to her daughter. On 23 April 2014 she makes a cash gift of £180,000 to her god-daughter. Vinny dies on 3 August 2017.

Assuming that the current rates of tax apply, calculate the IHT due on the gift made on 23 April 2014 as a result of Vinny's death.

7.9   The charge to tax and death

As stated at **7.4**, there is a deemed transfer of value on death. Again the five basic steps need to be gone through to calculate the IHT payable on the occasion of a person's death. There are some additional points to be taken into account and these are mentioned as the five steps are considered.

7.9.1   Step 1: calculate the value transferred

On death, the value transferred is the value of the deceased's *estate* immediately *before* the deceased's death (IHTA 1984, s 4).

7.9.1.1 The estate

The deceased's estate is the aggregate of all property to which, immediately prior to death, the deceased was beneficially entitled, other than excluded property. This includes not only assets which the deceased owned as sole owner, but also the deceased's share of any property owned jointly, either as beneficial joint tenants or as tenants in common.

The deceased's estate also includes the value of any interest which the deceased had in settled property. Only property in which the deceased had an interest in possession is included. An example of a deceased having an interest in possession is where the deceased was the sole life tenant of a will trust. The value of the interest is included where either (a) the trust was set up before 22 March 2006, or (b) the trust was set up on or after 22 March 2006 and was an immediate post-death interest trust. The capital value of the trust fund will be aggregated with the deceased's estate for the purposes of calculating any liability to IHT.

Also included in the value of the deceased's estate will be the value of any property subject to a reservation of a benefit (see **7.10**).

7.9.1.2 Liabilities

The value of the estate is the total value of the assets which make up the estate, less any liabilities of the estate.

7.9.1.3 Excluded property

As mentioned at **7.2.1.2**, some assets are excluded for IHT purposes. Do not forget that a reversionary interest in settled property is excluded property.

7.9.1.4 The value of the estate

The general rule is that assets are to be valued at their market value immediately before death. The date-of-death value is usually referred to as the probate valuation. There are exceptions to the market value rule and these are explained in **7.9.1.5** to **7.9.1.8**.

7.9.1.5 Related property

Do not overlook the effect of the related property rules (see **7.5.1.1**). A provision which should not be overlooked is the provision contained in s 176 of the IHTA 1984. This gives some relief to the related property rules. If property in the deceased's estate is valued as related property and is sold within three years of the date of death, then, provided the sale meets the conditions set out in the section, s 176 of IHTA 1984 allows the property to be revalued without it being treated as related property. This means that the lower value can be substituted for IHT purposes.

7.9.1.6 Value immediately before death

Section 4 of the IHTA 1984 states that 'the value transferred is the value of the deceased's estate immediately *before* death'. However, some assets are valued immediately *after* death in order that any changes in the value of the asset by reason of the death can be taken into account. One example would be a life policy. Where the deceased has taken out a life policy and the proceeds to be paid out on death form part of the estate, it is the policy proceeds which are taxable even though the proceeds are not due immediately before death; they are only due as a result of the death and the insurance company does not in fact pay out until after death! Another example is the loss of goodwill. Where the deceased was a proprietor of a business it will frequently be the case that the business will suffer as a result of the deceased's death through loss of goodwill and, consequently, the value of the business will fall. The legislation permits this factor to be taken into account when valuing the business at the date of death, even though the goodwill is not in fact lost until some time later.

7.9.1.7 Sale of land within four years of death

The usual market value rules apply to land held in a deceased's estate. However, if an interest in land is sold within four years of the date of death for less than the probate value the lower value can, in certain circumstances, be substituted for the probate value (IHTA 1984, ss 190–8).

7.9.1.8   Sale of qualifying shares within 12 months of death

Again, the usual market value rules apply to shares held in a deceased's estate. If the shares are shares in a company which is quoted on a recognised stock exchange or holdings in an authorised unit trust (qualifying shares) and are sold within 12 months of the date of death for less than the probate value, the lower value can, in certain circumstances, be substituted for the probate value (IHTA 1984, ss 178–89). When calculating the overall loss to the estate by virtue of the qualifying shares being sold for less than the probate value, it is the aggregate, or net, loss to the estate taking into account the proceeds of sale of all qualifying shares sold during the 12 months.

7.9.2   Step 2

Identify any available exemptions and deduct them from the value transferred.

The only exemptions available are the ones set out at **7.5.2.1**. Do not forget that the ones set out when looking at an LCT are *not* available on death.

7.9.3   Step 3

Identify any available reliefs and deduct them from the value transferred.

In addition to the reliefs set out at **7.5.3** there are two other reliefs available on death.

7.9.3.1   Woodlands relief

If the deceased's estate included land in the UK which was not eligible for agricultural property relief but on which trees and underwood are growing, woodlands relief may be available (IHTA 1984, s 125). The deceased must have been beneficially entitled to the land throughout the five years preceding the date of death or must have been beneficially entitled to the land otherwise than for consideration in money or money's worth (ie had been given or inherited the land on the death of another).

The relief operates in a different way to BPR and APR. Those reliefs operate by including the value of the asset in the value of the estate and applying a relief calculated as a percentage of the value of the asset. Woodlands relief operates by excluding the value of the woodlands from the estate. Any liability to IHT is deferred until there is a disposal of the woodlands.

For the relief to operate the beneficiary of the woodlands must elect to HMRC for the relief.

7.9.3.2   Quick succession relief

Quick succession relief ('QSR') offers some relief where a person dies within five years of receiving a chargeable transfer (IHTA 1984, s 141). For it to apply, the deceased's estate must have been increased by a chargeable transfer (either a lifetime gift or one which occurred on death) made to the deceased within five years of the deceased's death ('the first transfer'). In addition, IHT must have been paid on the first transfer. For the relief to be applicable there is *no* requirement that the property the deceased received as a result of the first transfer still forms part of the deceased's estate at the date of death.

The relief operates by giving a tax credit which then reduces the IHT payable on death ('the second transfer').

There are two stages to calculating the tax credit. First the calculation:

$$\frac{(G - T)}{G} \times T$$

where G is the gross amount of the first transfer and T is the amount of IHT paid on the first transfer.

A percentage of the figure arrived at is allowed as the tax credit, the percentage depending on the amount of time which has elapsed between the two transfers. The percentages are:

100 per cent if the first transfer was one year or less before death.
80 per cent if the first transfer was one to two years before death.

60 per cent if the first transfer was two to three years before death.

40 per cent if the first transfer was three to four years before death.

20 per cent if the first transfer was four to five years before death.

The amount of the tax credit cannot result in a refund of IHT.

EXAMPLE 20 (Assume that the current rates of tax apply throughout)

Ignoring exemptions and reliefs:

Gladys dies in August 2015. She leaves her estate, valued at £500,000, to her daughter, Barbara. Gladys made no lifetime gifts. The IHT payable on Gladys's estate is £70,000 (ie £325,000 @ 0% and £175,000 @ 40%). Barbara dies suddenly in October 2016. She has made no lifetime gifts. Her estate is valued at £750,000 and she leaves this to her sister. As Barbara dies within five years of inheriting her mother's estate QSR is available.

The amount of the QSR is:

Stage One:

$$\frac{(G - T)}{G} \times T \frac{(500,000 - 70,000)}{500,000} \times 70,000 = 60,200$$

Stage Two:

As Gladys died one to two years before Barbara's death 80 per cent of this figure is available: 80% = 60,200 = £48,160.

The IHT payable on Barbara's estate is £170,000 (£325,000 @ 0% and £425,000 @ 40%) less the QSR of £48,160, leaving IHT to pay of £121,840.

7.9.4   Steps 4 and 5

Calculate the transferor's cumulative total as at the date of the transfer and the amount of the NRB remaining and calculate the IHT payable by applying the rate (or rates) of tax to the value of the transfer for IHT purposes.

On death, the transferor's estate is liable to IHT. The rate or rates of tax will depend on the cumulative total of all chargeable transfers made by the transferor in the seven years before death. It must be remembered that the cumulative total will include all PETs which have now become chargeable transfers as a result of the transferor's death within seven years.

EXAMPLE 21 (Assumes that the current rates of tax apply throughout)

James dies on 31 May 2015. The value of his estate is £75,000; there are no exemptions or reliefs available to his estate. During his lifetime James made only one gift. He made a gift, on 1 April 2010, of £160,000 cash into a discretionary settlement with the trustees paying any IHT due as a result of the transfer.

Following the five steps to calculate the IHT payable on the estate:

Step 1: the value transferred is the value of the estate, £75,000.

Step 2: there are no exemptions available.

Step 3: there are no reliefs available.

Step 4: there is one transfer made in the seven years preceding his death which will make up his cumulative total. The value of the transfer made on 1 April 2010 was £160,000. One exemption available will be the annual exemption for the tax year in which the gift was made, 2009/10. This will reduce the value of the gift to £157,000. The annual exemption for the previous year, 2008/9, is also available and will reduce the value of the gift to £154,000. There are no reliefs which are available to this transfer.

James's cumulative total on the date of his death is £154,000.

Step 5: there is £171,000 of James's NRB remaining (£325,000 − £154,000). All the estate, £75,000, will be taxed at 0 per cent. There is no IHT to pay.

Exercise 4

> Exercise 4 illustrates the charge to IHT on a transferor's estate on the death of the transferor, when the transferor has made transfers of value during the preceding seven years.
>
> Work through this example to ensure that you understand the steps to be followed and that you can apply them correctly.
>
> There is a commentary on the exercise at the end of the chapter.
>
> You may find it useful to refer to earlier examples to remind yourself of the steps. You may find **Examples 14** and **16** useful for the basic calculation. In addition, you may find **Exercise 3** and **Example 21** useful.
>
> James dies on 31 May 2015. The value of his estate is £60,000; there are no exemptions or reliefs available to his estate. During his lifetime James made several gifts. He made a gift, on 1 April 2010, of £157,000 cash into a discretionary settlement with the trustees paying any IHT due as a result of the transfer.
>
> On 25 June 2011 he made a gift of £100,000, cash, to his daughter.
>
> The only other gift he made was a gift of £45,000 cash on 4 July 2012 to his son. Assuming that the current rates of tax apply, calculate the IHT due on James's estate.

7.9.5 Transfer of unused NRB

For deaths on or after 9 October 2007 a claim can be made for the part of the NRB unused on the death of a spouse or civil partner (IHTA 1984, s 8A, as amended).

The effect of this is that where the first to die used none of the NRB available on the first death, the surviving spouse/civil partner has double the NRB available on the second death. If part of the NRB had been used on the first death, a proportion of the NRB at the date of the second death is available on the second death.

EXAMPLE 22 (Assumes that the current rates of tax apply throughout)

George died in May 2012. By his will he left all his estate to John, his civil partner. George had made no lifetime gifts. His cumulative total at the date of his death was nil.

John dies in October 2014. His estate has a net value after deduction of liabilities of £800,000. In his will he leaves his estate to his brother and sisters.

On George's death no IHT was payable as his estate passed to an exempt beneficiary, his civil partner, John. As George's cumulative total was nil, the full amount of his NRB at the date of his death was unused.

Following the five steps to calculate the IHT payable on John's estate:

Step 1: the value transferred is the value of the estate, £800,000.

Step 2: there are no exemptions available.

Step 3: there are no reliefs available.

Step 4: John's cumulative total at the date of death is nil as he has made no chargeable transfers in the seven years preceding his death.

Step 5: the full NRB is available to John's estate, £325,000. As George did not use his NRB at the date of his death, there is a further 100 per cent of the NRB available to John's estate. Applying the rates of tax, the first £650,000 is taxed at 0 per cent and the remaining £150,000 at 40 per cent. There is IHT of £60,000 for the personal representatives to pay.

EXAMPLE 23 (Using the rates of tax for 2008/9 and 2014/15)

George died in May 2008. By his will he left £156,000 to his nephew. He left the remainder of his estate, with a net value of £500,000, to John, his civil partner. George had made no lifetime gifts. His cumulative total at the date of his death was nil.

John dies in October 2014. His estate has a net value after deduction of liabilities of £800,000. In his will he leaves his estate to his brother and sisters.

Following the five steps to calculate the IHT payable on the estate on George's death:

Step 1: the value transferred is the value of the estate, £656,000.

Step 2: there is one exemption available. The civil partner exemption is available on the £500,000 passing to John. The value is reduced to £156,000.

Step 3: there are no reliefs available.

Step 4: George's cumulative total at the date of death is nil as he has made no chargeable transfers in the seven years preceding his death.

Step 5: the full NRB, £312,000 in 2008/9, is available to George's estate. Applying the rates of tax, the £156,000 is all taxed at 0 per cent. There is no IHT to pay. George has used 50 per cent of his NRB.

On **John's** death his net estate is valued at £800,000.

Following the five steps to calculate the IHT payable on John's estate:

Step 1: the value transferred is the value of the estate, £800,000.

Step 2: there are no exemptions available.

Step 3: there are no reliefs available.

Step 4: John's cumulative total at the date of death is nil as he has made no chargeable transfers in the seven years preceding his death.

Step 5: the full NRB is available to John's estate, £325,000. As George used 50 per cent of his NRB at the date of his death, there is a further 50 per cent of the NRB at the date of John's death (50 per cent of £325,000) available to John's estate. Applying the rates of tax, the first £487,500 (£325,000 + £162,500) is taxed at 0 per cent and the remaining £312,500 at 40 per cent. There is IHT of £125,000, for the personal representatives to pay.

Where on the death of a surviving spouse or civil partner there are two, or more, unused NRBs available for a transfer, the maximum that can be transferred is 100 per cent of the NRB at the date of death of the surviving spouse or civil partner. There are rules which set out how the amount available for transfer is calculated, but this is beyond the scope of this chapter.

7.9.6   The residence nil rate band (RNRB)

For deaths on or after 6 April 2017 an individual will be entitled to an additional NRB, termed the residence nil rate band ('RNRB'). This will be available if the:

- individual owned a home, or a share of one, and it is included in their estate;
- individual's direct descendants such as children or grandchildren inherit the home, or a share of it; and
- value of the individual's estate is not more than £2 million.

An estate will also be entitled to the RNRB when an individual has downsized to a less valuable home or sold or given away their home after 7 July 2015.

The maximum available amount of the RNRB is being phased in over three tax years to 2020/21.

For deaths in the tax year 2017/18 the RNRB is £100,000. The RNRB will increase to £125,000 in 2018/19; £150,000 in 2019/20; and £175,000 in 2020/21. For later years the RNRB will increase yearly in line with inflation (based on the Consumer Prices Index).

As is the case with the transfer of unused NRB (see **7.9.5**), any unused RNRB when some-one dies can be transferred to the deceased's spouse or civil partner's estate. This can also be done if the first of the couple died before 6 April 2017, even though the RNRB wasn't available at that time.

For estates valued at more than £2 million, the RNRB (and any transferred RNRB) will be gradually withdrawn or tapered away.

7.9.7 Giving to charity and the reduction of the rate of IHT from 40 per cent to 36 per cent

For deaths on or after 6 April 2012 there is a reduction of the rate of IHT from 40 per cent to 36 per cent where at least 10 per cent of the estate goes to charity. For the purposes of calculating the percentage of the estate that passes to charity the estate is divided into three components. The components reflect the different ways in which assets can be owned and are:

(1) The survivorship component—joint assets passing by survivorship.

(2) The settled property component—assets in trust.

(3) The general component—assets owned outright or as tenants in common.

Each component can be looked at separately with the reduced rate being applied to the assets falling into the component, provided at least 10 per cent of the total value of the component passes to charity. It is also possible to merge components to maximise the benefit of the 36 per cent rate.

For more detailed information about this, and for worked examples, please refer to the HMRC website at http://www.hmrc.gov.uk/inheritancetax/pass-money-property/charity-reduce.htm.

7.9.8 LCTs and PETs made in the seven years preceding the date of death

Do not overlook the fact that when a person dies not only may there be a charge to IHT on the deceased's estate; there may also be additional IHT to pay on any LCT made in the seven years preceding the date of death. This is because, at the time of the LCT, IHT is paid at half the rates applicable on death, with the balance of any IHT being due if the transferor dies within seven years of the date of the transfer.

There may also be a liability to IHT on any PET made in the seven years preceding the date of death. This is due to the fact that a PET is treated as an exempt transfer at the time it is made and only becomes a chargeable transfer if the transferor dies within seven years of making the PET.

EXAMPLE 24 (Assumes that the current rates of tax apply throughout)

Jonathon dies on 17 February 2014. His estate comprises a house he owns jointly, in equal shares, with his sister. The market value of the house is £90,000. He also owned at the date of his death an interest in a partnership, his interest having a market value of £100,000. The other assets in his estate have a value of £100,000. By his will he has left a legacy of £10,000 to the Royal National Institute for the Blind (a registered charity) and the remainder of his estate passes to his sister.

During his lifetime he made the following gifts: on 24 September 2005 a gift of £50,000 cash to one of his nieces, Jane; on 15 May 2007 a gift of £130,000 cash to his nephew, Mark, on the occasion of Mark's wedding; and on 10 November 2008 a gift of £218,000 cash to the trustees of a discretionary settlement, on which he agreed to pay any IHT due. In addition to these gifts, on 2 June 2011 he gifted a building which was used by the partnership to his nephew, Andrew. The building was owned solely by Jonathon and had a market value of £100,000. Andrew still owned the building at the date of his uncle's death. What IHT was payable during Jonathon's lifetime and what IHT is payable on his death?

During his lifetime only one of the gifts made was an LCT, the gift to the discretionary settlement. The other gifts were made to individuals and so were PETs.

Following the five steps to calculate the IHT payable when the LCT was made on 10 November 2008:

Step 1: the value transferred is the amount of the cash payment, £218,000.

Step 2: one exemption is available, the annual exemption. Jonathon has available the annual exemption for the tax year in which the gift is made, 2008/9; this reduces the value of the gift to £215,000. The annual exemption for the previous tax year, 2007/8, is not available as it is applied against the PET made on 15 May 2007.

Step 3: there are no reliefs available.

Step 4: Jonathon's cumulative total is nil as he has made no chargeable transfers in the seven years preceding this transfer. (The gifts on 24 September 2005 and 15 May 2007 are PETs.)

Step 5: the whole of Jonathon's NRB is available. The value transferred, £215,000, falls within the NRB: there is no IHT payable when the gift is made.

When Jonathon dies not only will there be a charge to IHT on his estate; there may also be additional IHT to pay on any LCT made in the seven years preceding his death and a charge to IHT on any PETs made in the seven years preceding his death. The gift made on 15 May 2007 was made in the seven years preceding his death, as was the LCT on 10 November 2008 and the PET on 2 June 2011.

Following the five steps, beginning with the earliest gift:

Step 1: the value transferred was the value of the cash gift, £130,000.

Step 2: the gift was made in consideration of Mark's marriage. The first £1,000 is exempt, reducing the value transferred to £129,000. One exemption available is the annual exemption for the tax year in which the gift is made, 2007/8. This means that the transfer is reduced by £3,000 to £126,000. As Jonathon had made no lifetime gifts in the previous tax year, 2006/7, the annual exemption that tax year is also available. This reduces the transfer by £3,000 to £123,000.

Step 3: there are no reliefs available.

Step 4: Jonathon's cumulative total on 15 May 2007 was nil. The gift made on 24 September 2005 was a PET. As it was made more than seven years before Jonathon died it is not chargeable.

Step 5: all the NRB is available and so there is no IHT to pay on the occasion of Jonathon's death on the gift made on 15 May 2007.

Looking next at the LCT made on 10 November 2008: repeating the steps taken above when calculating the IHT payable at the time the gift was made:

Step 1: the value transferred is the amount of the cash payment, £218,000.

Step 2: one exemption is available, the annual exemption. Jonathon has available the annual exemption for the tax year in which the gift is made, 2008/9; this reduces the value of the gift to £215,000. The annual exemption for the previous tax year, 2007/8, is not available as it is applied against the PET made on the 15 May 2007.

Step 3: there are no reliefs available.

Step 4: Jonathon's cumulative total is £123,000, which is the value of the transfer made on 15 May 2007.

Step 5: £202,000 of Jonathon's NRB is available. £202,000 of the value transferred is taxed at 0 per cent; the remainder, £13,000, is taxed at 40 per cent, giving a total of £5,200 IHT.

As this is a calculation of the additional IHT due on an LCT due to the death of the transferor within seven years of the making of the gift:

Step 6: this provides for taper relief to be applied, if appropriate. The gift was made within five to six years of Jonathon's death and so only 40 per cent of the IHT is payable, £2,080.

Step 7: there was no IHT payable at the time the transfer was made and so the IHT due on the LCT as a result of Jonathon's death within seven years of the transfer is £2,080.

Following the steps for the transfer made on 2 June 2011: Step 1: the value transferred is the market value of the building, £100,000. Step 2: the annual exemption for the tax year in which the gift was made, 2011/12, is available, as is the annual exemption for the preceding tax year, 2010/11. However, Step 3: as the building was used for the purpose of the business carried out by the partnership of which Jonathon was a partner, the building qualifies for BPR at 50 per cent (**7.5.3.2**). The BPR is given before deducting the annual exemptions (**7.5.3**), leaving a value transferred of £44,000. Step 4: Jonathon's cumulative total on 2 June 2011 was £338,000 (£123,000 + £215,000). There is no NRB remaining and the whole £44,000 will be taxed at 40 per cent, making IHT of £17,600. Step 6: as the gift was made within two to three years of Jonathon's death there is no taper relief. Step 7 is not applicable as the transfer was a PET when originally made and so there will have been no IHT paid at the time of the gift.

The liability to IHT on the estate remains to be calculated.

Step 1: the value of the estate is the value of Jonathon's share in the house, which, as it was jointly owned, will have the joint owner's discount applied, giving a value of £45,000 – (10 per cent *of* £45,000) = £40,500. The remainder of the estate was valued at £200,000. The value of the estate is £240,500.

Step 2: there is one exemption, the gift to the charity of £10,000 is exempt, reducing the value transferred to £230,500.

Step 3: the interest in a partnership qualifies for BPR at 100 per cent, reducing the value of the estate to £130,500.

Step 4: the total value for IHT purposes of each of the chargeable transfers made in the seven years preceding the date of death will form Jonathon's cumulative total. At the date of his death this total is £382,000 (£123,000 + £215,000 + £44,000).

Step 5: all Jonathon's NRB has been used; all the estate, £130,500, will be taxed at 40 per cent, giving IHT of £52,200 to pay.

The IHT due on the gift made on 10 November 2008 to the discretionary settlement, £2,080, is payable by the trustees of the settlement, out of the trust monies.

The IHT due on the gift made on 2 June 2011 to Andrew, £17,600, is payable by Andrew.

The IHT due on the estate, £52,200, is payable by Jonathon's personal representatives from the monies in his estate.

7.10   Gifts subject to a reservation

A gift of property is subject to a reservation if, after gifting the property, some benefit is still enjoyed or retained by the transferor. It would be tempting under the IHT legislation for the transferor to give away property to another individual but to continue to retain an interest in it. That way, the property would not form part of the transferor's estate liable to IHT on death. Also, provided the transferor survived seven years from the date of the gift the property would escape IHT altogether. (Even if the transferor died within seven years of making the gift then, provided the value of the gift fell within the transferor's NRB at the date the gift was made, and the rates of IHT remain the same, no more IHT would be payable on the death than would have been paid had the gift not been made and the asset still formed part of the deceased's estate. If the transferor died within the seven-year period and the value of the property transferred exceeded the available NRB, then taper relief would operate to reduce the amount of IHT payable.) A good example of a gift where a benefit is retained would be a parent who makes a gift of a holiday home to a child but continues to use the holiday home frequently throughout the year without paying any rent to the child.

There is legislation to prevent taxpayers trying to avoid IHT in this way (Finance Act 1986, s 102).

The original gift of the asset will be a lifetime transfer, an LCT, or a PET, depending on the recipient of the gift. In addition, if the property is still subject to a reservation at the transferor's death, then the property, at its value at the date of death, will be included in the transferor's estate and will be taxed as part of the transferor's estate on death. If the original gift was made in the seven years preceding the transferor's death, IHT or additional IHT may be payable on the original gift as a result of the death.

If, in the earlier example of the gift of a holiday home, the parent was still enjoying visits to the property at the time of death, which was six years after the original gift, the original PET would become chargeable as a result of the death. In addition, the value of the property would also be included in the value of the parent's estate at the date of death. There would be a double charge to IHT.

If the reservation ceases before death, then the transferor will be treated as making a PET on the date the reservation ceases. In the earlier example, if the parent ceased using the property five years after having made the original gift, there would be a PET at the date the parent stopped using it. The value of the PET would be the value of the property at that date. If the parent died one year after ceasing to use the property, both PETs would become chargeable as they would have been made in the seven years preceding the parent's death.

As the making of a gift with a reservation can result in a double charge to IHT there are provisions giving some relief for this.

Care should be taken to avoid giving advice to a client which could result in a gift with a reservation being made.

7.11   Liability, burden, and payment of tax

The question of *liability* is concerned with who will actually be required to send to HMRC any IHT that is due: *burden* is concerned with who ultimately bears the tax (a matter of no concern to HMRC but of considerable interest to, for example, the beneficiaries of a deceased's estate).

7.11.1 LCTs

7.11.1.1 Due date for payment

IHT due on the value transferred by an LCT normally falls due six months after the end of the month in which the transfer takes place. However, if the LCT occurs between 6 April and 30 September (inclusive) in the tax year, then the IHT is due on 30 April in the following year.

Overdue IHT attracts interest.

7.11.1.2 Liability and burden

The primary liability for (and burden of) IHT due in respect of an LCT lies with the transferor. The majority of LCTs will involve the transferor transferring property to trustees. If the tax is not paid by the transferor by the due date, then the trustees become liable. If the trustees are unable to pay the tax, then HMRC have power to seek payment from persons who have an interest in the settlement.

It is possible for the transferee to agree to pay the tax instead of the transferor in this instance.

7.11.1.3 Additional tax due on death

Where a person dies within seven years of making a LCT, additional tax may become payable. If so, then this is due six months after the end of the month in which death occurred.

The primary liability for this additional tax lies with the transferee (ie the trustees). However, if the tax remains unpaid after the due date, HMRC can seek payment from persons who have an interest in the settlement and, as a final recourse, from the personal representatives of the transferor's estate.

7.11.2 PETs which become chargeable

7.11.2.1 Due date for payment

IHT falls due six months after the end of the month in which the transferor's death occurs.

Overdue tax attracts interest.

7.11.2.2 Liability and burden

The transferee is primarily liable (and bears the burden of the tax). In the case of a trust, the transferee will be the trustees and the burden will fall on the trust property (effectively on the beneficiaries). If the tax remains unpaid 12 months after the date of death, then the personal representatives of the deceased's estate are liable, leaving them to try to recover the tax from those who have primary liability.

7.11.3 Death

7.11.3.1 Due date for payment

IHT on death is due six months after the end of the month in which death occurs.

Overdue tax attracts interest.

7.11.3.2 Liability and burden

This depends on the property bearing the IHT.

7.11.3.3 Deceased's free estate

The personal representatives ('PRs') are liable for the IHT on the deceased's free estate. If the will is silent as to burden, tax on the free estate in the UK is normally borne by the residue (in the case of foreign property, by that property itself). If the testator has specifically provided that particular gifts in the will are to bear their own tax, that direction will normally prevail.

7.11.3.4   Settled property in which the deceased had an interest

If IHT is due, as a result of the death, on assets in a trust fund in which the deceased had an interest, then the trustees of the settlement are liable for the IHT due. The burden falls on the trust property.

7.11.3.5   Property passing other than under the deceased's will or intestacy

If property passed outside the will, for example the deceased's share of a house owned as beneficial joint tenants with the deceased's sister, then the beneficiary of the asset, the sister, bears the burden for the IHT attributable to it although the liability falls on the PRs.

7.11.4   Instalment option

In certain cases, IHT may be paid by ten equal annual instalments, the first instalment due on the normal due date for payment.

Only certain assets qualify for the instalment option. These are:

(a)   land and buildings;

(b)   shares or securities giving control immediately before the transfer;

(c)   unquoted shares or securities of a company which did not give the transferor control provided HMRC are satisfied that the sum attributable to their value cannot be paid in one sum without undue hardship;

(d)   unquoted shares (but not securities) of a company which did not give the transferor control where the value transferred attributable to the shares exceeds £20,000 *and* either the nominal value of the shares is not less than 10 per cent of the nominal value of all the shares of the company at the time of the transfer, *or* the shares are ordinary shares and their nominal value is not less than 10 per cent of the nominal value of all ordinary shares of the company at that time;

(e)   (where the transfer is on death) unquoted shares or securities of a company which did not give the transferor control where the tax on the holding and on any other shares or securities qualifying for the instalment option comprises at least 20 per cent of the tax payable by a particular person;

(f)   a business or interest in a business.

7.11.5   Entitlement

The instalment facility is available in respect of:

(a)   transfers on death;

(b)   LCTs where the transferee pays the IHT (the transferor is primarily liable); or

(c)   a PET which becomes chargeable, provided the transferee pays the IHT and still owns the property at the date of the transferor's death. If the property is sold, then the whole amount of IHT remaining becomes payable immediately.

EXAMPLE 25

Colin dies on 20 November 2014. Part of his estate comprises 20,000 shares in a quoted company which gave Colin control of the company. The shareholding is valued at £75,000 at the date of Colin's death. The IHT payable in respect of shares is, say, £27,400.

If the instalment option is not opted for, IHT falls due on 31 May 2015.

However, if the instalment option is opted for, £2,740 (1/10 × £27,400) is payable on each 31 May from 31 May 2015 until 31 May 2024.

7.11.6   Interest

Where land is concerned (other than land on which agricultural property relief is available), interest accrues on the balance of IHT outstanding from the date when the first instalment becomes due for payment.

However, in respect of the other categories of property qualifying for the instalment option, the general rule is that no interest is payable provided that each instalment is paid by the due date.

7.12 Tax planning

7.12.1 Lifetime gifts and taper relief

As a general principle, tax will be saved by making a transfer during one's lifetime rather than on death. This is due to the seven-year cumulation period.

If the transferor survives seven years after making the gift, then no tax will be payable on the gift if it was a PET and tax at only half the official rates will have been paid if it was an LCT.

Even if death occurs within seven years, the full charge to IHT may be mitigated by taper relief. However, it is important to understand that taper relief reduces the *IHT* attributable to the chargeable transfer, *not* the value of the chargeable transfer itself. Therefore, taper relief is only applicable if IHT is payable on the chargeable transfer.

IHT will only be payable on the chargeable transfer if the value of the transfer, taking into account the transferor's cumulative total at the date the transfer was made, exceeds the transferor's NRB. If the chargeable transfer (taking into account the cumulative total at the date of the gift) does not exceed the NRB available at the date of chargeable transfer, no IHT is payable and so taper relief is inapplicable.

7.12.2 Appreciating assets

An asset which has potential for capital appreciation should be considered before other assets if the transferor is thinking of making lifetime gifts. This is because the value of the asset at the *date of transfer* is taken for IHT purposes. Should the asset remain in the estate its value at the date of death will have been higher (it is an appreciating asset) and a higher liability to IHT could result.

The instalment option may be available to reduce the burden of any IHT on lifetime gifts (and hold-over relief may be available to hold over any CGT).

However, it may be not within the taxpayer's means to give away his assets several years before his death.

7.12.3 Utilising exemptions

7.12.3.1 Exemptions generally

Full use should be made of the available exemptions, of which the annual exemption is the most important. It allows property to be handed down tax-free over a period of time.

7.12.3.2 Spouse or civil partnership exemption

Each spouse or civil partner is liable for IHT. It may be worthwhile for the wealthier spouse or civil partner to transfer property to the other spouse or civil partner to enable both spouses or civil partners to make full use of their annual exemptions and NRB. For example, if the estates are of sufficient size, it may be beneficial for spouses or civil partners to arrange their estates such that each has an estate at least equal to the NRB. This will mean that they will each be able to give away the maximum amount without paying tax.

7.13 Conclusion: checkpoints

You should now be able to:

- identify the occasions when a charge to IHT arises (**7.5**);
- calculate the IHT liability on an LCT (**7.6**);

- calculate the IHT liability on an LCT where the transferor dies within seven years of the LCT (**7.7**);
- calculate the IHT liability on a PET where the transferor dies within seven years of the PET (**7.8**); and
- calculate the IHT liability of death (**7.9**).

7.14 Commentary to exercises

Exercise 1

This exercise illustrates the charge to IHT when a transferor makes an LCT where he has made other LCTs in the preceding seven years.

Following the five steps:

Step 1: the value transferred is the amount of the cash payment, £211,000.

Step 2: one exemption available is the annual exemption for the tax year in which the gift is made, 2016/17. This means that the transfer is reduced by £3,000 to £208,000. As he had made no chargeable transfers during the previous tax year, 2015/16, that year's annual exemption is also available, reducing the value transferred to £205,000. (The PET on 1 June 2015 is ignored for the purposes of the annual exemption (IHTA 1984, s 19(3A)).)

Step 3: there are no reliefs which are available to Mr Martin.

Step 4: going back for seven years from 28 May 2016 Mr Martin made one chargeable transfer, the transfer to the settlement on 9 August 2009. (The transfer on 17 February 2009 was made more than seven years before the transfer in 2016. The gift to his daughter on 1 June 2015 was a PET. As Mr Martin is still alive the PET is treated as (potentially) exempt and so can be ignored for the purposes of calculating his NRB.) The value of the transfer made on 9 August 2009 was £134,000. The only exemption available will be the annual exemption for the tax year in which the gift was made (2009/10). This reduces the transfer to £131,000. (The annual exemption for the previous tax year (2008/9) will not be available to Mr Martin as it will have been used on the gift made on 17 February 2009.) There are no reliefs which are available to this transfer. The value of the transfer for IHT purposes is £131,000. Mr Martin's cumulative total on 28 May 2016 is £131,000.

Step 5: Mr Martin has £194,000 of the NRB available to him (£325,000 – £131,000). The first £194,000 of the transfer is taxed at 0 per cent. The remainder, £11,000 (£205,000 – £194,000), is taxed at 20 per cent. There is IHT of £2,200 for the trustees to pay.

Exercise 2

Exercise 2 illustrates the effect of death on the charge to IHT when a transferor makes an LCT where he has made other LCTs in the preceding seven years, and where the transferor subsequently dies within seven years.

Following the steps:

Step 1: the value transferred is the amount of the cash payment, £211,000.

Step 2: one exemption available is the annual exemption for the tax year in which the gift is made, 2011/12. This means that the transfer is reduced by £3,000 to £208,000. The annual exemption for the previous tax year, 2010/11, is not available as it is applied against the PET made on 1 June 2010. The PET is now chargeable due to Mr Martin's death within seven years of the gift.

Step 3: there are no reliefs which are available to Mr Martin (as before).

Step 4: going back for seven years from 28 May 2011 Mr Martin made one chargeable transfer, the transfer to the settlement on 9 August 2004. (The transfer on 17 February 2004 was made more than seven years before the transfer in 2010.) In addition, as Mr Martin has died within seven years of the gift to his daughter on 1 June 2010 the gift is no longer a PET; it becomes chargeable.

The value of the transfer made on 9 August 2004 was £134,000. The only exemption available will be the annual exemption for the tax year in which the gift was made. This reduces the transfer to £131,000. The annual exemption for the previous tax year will not be available to Mr Martin as it will have been used on the gift made on 17 February 2004. There are no reliefs which are available to this transfer. The value of the transfer for IHT purposes is £131,000.

The value of the transfer made on 1 June 2010 was £70,000. One exemption available is the annual exemption for the tax year in which the gift is made, 2010/11. This means that the transfer is reduced by £3,000 to £67,000. The annual exemption for the previous tax year, 2009/10, is also available. The transfer is reduced by £3,000 to £64,000.

Mr Martin's cumulative total on 28 May 2011 is £195,000 (ie £131,000 + £64,000).

Step 5: Mr Martin has £130,000 of the NRB available to him (£325,000 – £195,000). The first £130,000 of the transfer is taxed at 0 per cent. The remainder £78,000 (£208,000 – £130,000) is taxed at 40 per cent. There is IHT of £31,200 for the trustees to pay.

Step 6: as the LCT was made within five to six years of his death, taper relief is available. Only 40 per cent of the IHT is payable, 40 per cent of £31,200, giving an amount due of £12,480.

Step 7: IHT of £2,200 was paid at the time of the transfer. Credit is given for this payment. The amount of IHT payable by the trustee of the settlement due to Mr Martin's death within the seven-year period is £10,280 (£12,480 – £2,200).

Had the amount of the IHT paid by the trustees at the time of the transfer exceeded the liability to IHT due to Mr Martin's death within the seven-year period then the amount payable as the result of his death would be reduced to nil. There would be no repayment of the additional tax paid at the time of the transfer.

Exercise 3

Exercise 3 illustrates the effect of death on the charge to IHT when a transferor makes a PET, and where the transferor subsequently dies within seven years.

Following the steps:

Step 1: calculate the value transferred. As the gift was cash the value transferred was £180,000.

Step 2: identify any exemptions and deduct them from the value transferred. One exemption available is the annual exemption for the tax year in which the gift is made, 2014/15. This reduces the transfer to £177,000. As Vinny had made no lifetime gifts in the previous tax year, 2013/14, the annual exemption for that year is also available. This reduces the transfer to £174,000.

Step 3: identify any reliefs and deduct them from the value transferred. There are no reliefs available as the gift is cash.

Step 4: calculate the transferor's cumulative total at the date the gift is made and the amount of the NRB remaining. Going back seven years from 23 April 2014, the date of the PET which has become chargeable, Vinny made one PET, the gift of £175,000, to her daughter on 1 March 2011. Although this was a PET, it was made within seven years of Vinny's death and so is now taken into account when calculating her cumulative total. To calculate Vinny's cumulative total **Steps 1** to **3** have to be applied to the gift made on 1 March 2011. The value transferred was £175,000. The exemptions available will be the annual exemption for the tax year in which the gift was made, 2010/11. This reduces the value transferred to £172,000. As she had made no transfers during the previous tax year, 2009/10, that year's annual exemption is also available, reducing the value transferred to £169,000. No other exemptions are available and there are no reliefs available. The value of the gift made on 1 March 2011 is £169,000. Vinny has £156,000 of the NRB available to her (£325,000 – £169,000).

Step 5: calculate the IHT payable by applying the rate (or rates) of tax to the value of the transfer for IHT purposes. £156,000 of the transfer falls within the NRB. The remainder of the transfer (£18,000) will be taxed at 40 per cent. There will be IHT of £7,200 to pay on the transfer.

Step 6: as the gift was made three to four years before Vinny's death, taper relief is available. Only 80 per cent of the tax is payable. The amount of tax to pay is £5,760.

Exercise 4

Exercise 4 illustrates the charge to IHT on a transferor's estate on death of the transferor, when the transferor has made transfers of value during the preceding seven years.

Following the steps:

Step 1: the value transferred is the value of the estate, £60,000.

Step 2: there are no exemptions available.

Step 3: there are no reliefs available.

Step 4: there are three transfers made in the seven years preceding James's death. James's cumulative total will equal the total of the value for IHT purposes of each of the three transfers.

The value of the transfer made on 1 April 2010 was £157,000. One exemption available will be the annual exemption for the tax year in which the gift was made, 2009/10. This will reduce the value of the gift to £154,000. The annual exemption for the previous year, 2008/9, is also available and will reduce the value of the gift to £151,000. There are no reliefs which are available to this transfer.

The value of the gift made on 25 June 2011 was £100,000. Again, one exemption available will be the annual exemption for the tax year in which the gift was made, 2011/12. This will reduce the value of the gift to £97,000. The annual exemption for the previous year, 2010/11, is also available and will reduce the value of the gift to £94,000. There are no reliefs which are available to this transfer.

The value of the gift made on 4 July 2012 was £45,000. Again one exemption available will be the annual exemption for the tax year in which the gift was made, 2012/13. This will reduce the value of the gift to £42,000. The annual exemption for the previous year, 2011/12, has already been used. There are no reliefs which are available to this transfer.

James's cumulative total on the date of his death is £287,000 (£151,000 + £94,000 + £42,000).

James has £38,000 of the NRB available to him (£325,000 – £287,000).

Step 5: calculate the IHT payable by applying the rate (or rates) of tax to the value of the estate (£60,000). The first £38,000 of his estate is taxed at 0 per cent. The remainder £22,000 (£60,000 – £38,000) is taxed at 40 per cent. There is IHT of £8,800 for the trustees to pay.

online resource centre   Visit the Online Resource Centre for more information and useful weblinks.
www.oxfordtextbooks.co.uk/orc/foundations17_18/

Corporation tax

8.1 Introduction to corporation tax

All companies incorporated in the UK which actively carry on business are liable to pay corporation tax ('CT') on their taxable profits. This chapter considers the charge to CT with particular focus on:

- Calculating chargeable income profits and allowable deductions;
- The treatment of company capital gains and capital losses;
- Trading loss relief;
- Capital allowances;
- Close companies;
- A complete CT calculation.

A company will be taxed on both income profits and capital gains made during each financial year, both of which are calculated in a very similar way to those of an individual. Sole traders, partnerships, and limited liability partnerships all pay income tax and capital gains tax ('CGT'). They do not pay CT.

When a company makes a capital gain the chargeable gain is calculated in broadly the same way it would be for an individual. However a company does not pay CGT on the capital gain, it pays CT on both income profits and capital gains.

8.2 Calculating the income profits of a limited company

The chargeable trading income of a company is calculated in accordance with the principles laid down in the Income Tax (Trading and Other Income) Act 2005 ('ITTOIA 2005'), particularly Part 2 relating to 'profits of a trade', and the Corporation Tax Acts ('CTA') of 2009 and 2010.

8.2.1 Allowable deductions from trading income

A company is liable to pay CT on its chargeable trading income. The company can deduct allowable expenses from this income provided those expenses are of an 'income nature' and were incurred 'wholly and exclusively' in the company's business.

The phrase 'income nature' usually relates to an expense which recurs throughout the trading year so a 'one-off' expense, for example the purchase of capital assets such as plant and machinery, is not an expense of an income nature and therefore not an allowable deduction. The basic rule is to be able to distinguish between an expense incurred on an ongoing basis, which is deductible, and an expense in acquiring a capital asset, which is not deductible.

Many companies are not always clear as to which expenses are deductible from their trading income and which are not deductible.

Typical examples of expenses which are allowable deductions:

- Directors' salaries and fees;
- Staff wages and salaries;

- Bank charges and bank interest on a business loan or overdraft;
- Office expenses incurred in the running of the business such as telephone bills, heating, or postage costs;
- Travel expenses incurred on behalf of the company;
- Subscriptions to professional journals;
- Insurance of business assets;
- Legal fees incurred on advising the company.

Typical examples of expenses which are not allowable deductions:

- Entertaining for customers;
- Purchase of cars;
- Purchase of computers;
- Travel between home and place of business;
- Legal fees relating to the purchase of company assets;
- Dividends paid to shareholders;
- Improvements to company assets.

8.3   Calculating the capital gains of a limited company

The company may make a capital gain when it disposes of all or part of a business asset, regardless of whether the asset is sold or given away.

Capital gains are most likely to arise on the disposal of land or buildings owned by the company. Typical examples of capital business assets are:

- Plant and machinery;
- Land and buildings used by the business;
- Fixtures and fittings;
- A franchise;
- The goodwill of the business.

The principles used to calculate the capital gain made by a company are very similar to the calculation of an individual's capital gain. The differences between the two are:

1. A company does not have the benefit of an annual exemption as a company is not an individual; and
2. A company has the benefit of an indexation allowance to account for an element of inflation in the gain.

Companies, but not individuals, can claim indexation allowance. The indexation allowance is an allowance from HMRC acknowledging that part of the capital gain results from inflation and should be deducted from the gain. The relevant allowance can be calculated from tables published by HMRC. These tables use a formula based on inflation from the date of purchase (or March 1982 if held then) and the date of disposal.

The capital gain is calculated in accordance with CGT rules. It is important to remember that any capital gains made by a company are not liable for CGT, they are liable for CT.

In summary, a company's capital gain involves the following calculation: the sale price or market value, less:

- Purchase price or acquisition value price;
- Relevant expenditure (for example including professional fees which relate to the purchase and sale of the asset);

- Indexation allowance calculated up to the date of disposal of the asset;
- Any relevant reliefs—the most commonly used relief is roll-over relief on the replacement of a qualifying business asset.

EXAMPLE 1 Calculating a company's capital gain

Clear Optics Ltd sold the land adjoining the company premises for £400,000 during the current financial year. The company purchased the land three years ago for £150,000.

Legal and professional fees in respect of the purchase and sale of the land total £18,000 and the indexation allowance is £15,600.

The company has not made any other capital gains or any losses and has decided not to make an election for roll-over relief.

Calculation of the capital gain on the sale of land by Clear Optics Ltd.

£	£
Sale price	400,000
Less	
Purchase price	(150,000)
Professional fees incurred in the purchase and sale	(18,000)
Indexation allowance	(15,600) **(183,600)**
Gain subject to CT	**216,400**

8.4 Roll-over relief

Roll-over relief is discussed in more detail in **Chapter 6** on Capital Gains Tax (see **6.10.1.2**).

Briefly, the relief allows a company to postpone the payment of any CT due on the disposal of a 'qualifying asset', until that replacement asset is itself disposed of, provided a replacement asset is acquired within the required period of time. The required period is within one year before, or three years after the disposal of the asset.

The most common types of 'qualifying assets' are buildings or parts of buildings (which must be occupied and used for the purposes of the business), interests in land, and fixed plant or machinery.

EXAMPLE 2 Roll-over relief

Mansell Fibres Ltd bought some freehold business premises for £85,000. The company sold the premises a few years later for £110,000, making a chargeable capital gain of £25,000. All the sale proceeds were reinvested in new freehold business premises which cost £120,000.

Payment of CGT on the capital gain of £25,000 can be postponed as the entire proceeds of sale were reinvested. The cost of the new premises will be treated as £95,000 for CGT purposes when they are eventually sold (£120,000 less the capital gain of £25,000).

8.5 Capital losses

A company, like an individual, does not always make a gain on the disposal of an asset. A company which makes a capital loss can deduct that loss from any capital gain it has made in the same year or in future years.

Using the Clear Optics Ltd example in **8.3**:

EXAMPLE 3

Clear Optics Ltd made a capital loss of £10,000 in the preceding year. There are no capital gains made in the same year against which it could set that capital loss.

How Clear Optics Ltd can use the capital loss of £10,000:

	£
Capital gain (as above)	216,400
Capital loss carried forward	(10,000)
Capital gain subject to CT	**206,400**

8.6 Trading losses

A company does not make a trading profit every year. Sometimes a trading loss will be made, in which case the company can offset this trading loss against other gains or profits of the business in the same accounting period. Trading loss relief is provided by CTA 2010.

Applying the rules:

1. Under ss 37–38 CTA 2010 a company can set the trading loss against any other trading profits from any source and/or capital gains the company has made during the same financial year in which the trading loss was made.

   If all the trading loss cannot be used against trading profits or capital gains in the same financial year then the balance of the loss can be:

2. Carried back and set against any trading profits and/or capital gain for the previous financial year. Any CT paid already in this year will be re-calculated in respect to the adjusted profit and a claim for repayment of CT made if appropriate.

   Any remaining trading losses which are not used can be:

3. Carried forward and set against total taxable profits of a company or other companies within a group. As from 1 April 2017 a company will only be able to set trading losses carried forward against no more than 50 per cent of the company's profits above £5 million.

It is worth noting that a company making a capital loss cannot set that loss against trading profits. A capital loss can only be set against a capital gain in the same or future financial years.

EXAMPLE 4   Applying the trading loss rules

Greenbank Builders Ltd produced the following trading figures for the last four financial years:

	£
Year 1	
Trading profit	25,000
Year 2	
Trading loss	**100,000**
Capital gain	10,000
Year 3	
Trading profit	30,000
Year 4	
Trading profit	10,000
Rental income	5,000

EXAMPLE 5 How Greenbank Builders Ltd can use the trading loss of £100,000 made in Year 2

	£
1. There is no trading profit in Year 2 against which the trading loss of £100,000 can be offset. Therefore set the trading loss of £100,000 against the capital gain of £10,000 made in the same year.	100,000 – 10,000 capital gain = 90,000 trading loss unused
2. Carry the unused trading loss of £90,000 back to Year 1 and set this unused loss against the trading profit of £25,000 for that year. Reclaim any CT paid.	90,000 loss – 25,000 trading profit = 65,000 trading loss unused
3. Carry the unused trading loss of £65,000 to Year 3 of trading and set against the trading profit of £30,000 for that year.	65,000 loss – 30,000 trading profit = 35,000 trading loss unused
4. Carry the unused trading loss of £35,000 forward to Year 4 of trading and set against the trading profit of £10,000 for that year. The remaining £25,000 trading loss can also be set against the rental income of £5,000, leaving a trading loss of £20,000 unused to be carried forward and set against future income of the company.	35,000 loss – 10,000 trading profit = 25,000 trading loss unused £25,000 unused trading loss also set against rental income of £5,000 = £20,000 trading loss to be carried forward.

8.7 Capital Allowances ('CA')

The purchase of capital assets, such as plant and machinery, are not a deductible expense which can be set against company trading profits. There is no current legislation available which permits any allowance to take account of the depreciation of such assets.

To alleviate the potential cash flow problems of a company which wishes to invest in new capital assets, the Capital Allowances Act 2001 ('CAA') allows a company to deduct a fixed percentage of the cost of capital assets against the company's chargeable trading income. These agreed deductions are known as capital allowances ('CAs').

A company is not allowed to claim CAs for the cost of assets it buys and sells as part of its trade. These are deducted from the company trading profits.

The CA most commonly used relates to plant and machinery, for example manufacturing equipment and computers.

8.7.1 Plant and machinery

For plant and machinery to 'qualify' for a capital allowance the following must apply:

- the plant and machinery must be used wholly or partly for the purpose of that business;
- the asset is not bought and sold as part of the business; and
- the asset has a life of more than two years but up to a maximum of 25 years (Note here that long life assets have a life of more than 25 years. See **8.7.5**).

8.7.2 Writing-down allowances ('WDAs')

WDAs are available to a business each year. They reduce, or 'write down', any balance of capital expenditure on plant and machinery for which either the annual investment allowance (see **8.7.4**) or the first-year allowance (see **8.7.3**) cannot be claimed. The business can also claim a WDA against the cost of assets carried forward from the previous accounting period.

There are two rates of WDA for plant and machinery (18 per cent and 8 per cent, see below):

- most plant and machinery has a capital allowance of 18 per cent (referred to as the 'main rate' pool of assets);
- long-life assets, integral features, certain thermal insulation, and some cars have a capital allowance of 8 per cent (referred to as the 'special rate' pool of assets).

A company owning assets in the main pool, usually plant and machinery, has a WDA of 18 per cent of the cost of the asset (the cost of which are usually pooled together) which it can set against the company's trading profit.

After applying the WDA at the end of each financial year the value of the asset is gradually reduced. This is referred to as the 'written down value' of that asset.

EXAMPLE 6

Canine Products Ltd bought a new fork lift truck for £140,000 this year. It is not a long life asset. No further purchases were made in the same financial year. The annual investment allowance has already been used in full against another new asset (see **8.7.4**) therefore the CA which applies to the new fork lift truck is:

£	£
Year 1	25,200 WDA (deductible from trading profit) – written down value of truck is 114,800
140,000 × 18%	
Year 2	20,664 WDA (deductible from trading profit) – written down value of truck is 94,136
114,800 × 18%	
Year 3	16,945 WDA (deductible from trading profit) – written down value of truck is 77,191
94,136 × 18%	
Year 4	13,894 WDA (to deduct from trading profit) – written down value of truck is 63,297
77,191 × 18%	

This process continues for the following years.

8.7.3   First-year allowances (also known as 'enhanced capital allowances' or 'ECAs')

There are 100 per cent first-year allowances available for the cost of certain types of asset. A business can deduct the full cost of these assets against its trading profits.

The main assets that qualify for ECAs are:

- new cars bought after April 2018 with low CO_2 emissions less than 50gm/km or that are electrically powered;
- energy saving equipment on the energy technology product list, eg certain motors;
- water saving equipment on the water efficient technologies product list, eg meters, efficient toilets and taps;
- plant and machinery for gas refuelling stations, eg storage tanks, pumps;
- gas, biogas, and hydrogen refuelling equipment;
- carbon efficient biofuels plant;
- new zero-emission goods vehicles.

8.7.4   Annual Investment Allowance ('AIA')

Businesses can claim an AIA for capital expenditure on most plant and machinery, other than expenditure on cars. The AIA is available for most businesses that purchase plant and machinery, including long life assets, during their financial year.

The current AIA, introduced in 1 January 2016, is £200,000 per annum and is scheduled to continue at the sum for the indefinite future. If the company expenditure exceeds the AIA limit of £200,000 the amount of that excess qualifies for the usual WDA on plant and machinery of 18 per cent per annum.

If the asset is a long life asset with a life of more than 25 years, the excess over the available AIA of £200,000 has a WDA of 8 per cent per annum.

8.7.5 Long life assets and integral features

Long life assets are assets that have a useful working life of more than 25 years. They have a CA of 8 per cent and are eligible for the AIA of £200,000.

Integral features belong to a specific category of plant and machinery which are integral to a building (such as escalators, air conditioning systems, and lifts).

Integral features have a WDA of 8 per cent and are also eligible for the AIA.

8.7.6 Pooling

A company will usually have several assets in the same category which attract capital allowances. To simplify the calculation of the allowance all the assets with the same rate of allowance are 'pooled'. The relevant WDA is then applied to that pool.

EXAMPLE 7

Crystal Lee buys a new laser cutting machine to use in her manufacturing business, Lee & Ware Ltd, during the current financial year. The machine costs £550,000.

The business already has a pool of plant and machinery from the previous accounting period now valued at £100,000. It also owns a long life asset now valued at £40,000.

The company will be entitled to the following capital allowances in the current financial year which runs from 1 April 2017 to 31 March 2018:

CAPITAL ALLOWANCES	£
Annual Investment Allowance	
AIA on new machinery	200,000
On remaining value of new machinery £550,000 − £200,000 = £350,000 × 18%	63,000
The pool from the previous accounting period	
£100,000 × 18%	18,000
Long life asset	
£40,000 × 8%	3,200
Total capital allowances for the period	**284,200**

The total capital allowance of £284,200 will be deducted from the trading profit for the current financial year.

8.7.7 Balancing charge allowance

A company can dispose of an asset for more than the written down value ('WDV') of that asset. In this case, there is a balancing charge on the difference between the sale price and the WDV. This difference is added to the trading profits of the company and is chargeable to CT.

EXAMPLE 8

Lee & Ware Ltd decide to sell a machine originally purchased for £100,000 three years previously.

	£
Sale price of machine	55,000
The written down value	(30,000)
Gain	25,000

The gain of £25,000 is added to the trading profits of Lee & Ware Ltd and charged to corporation tax.

8.7.8   Cars

The CA for cars is complex and is related to the car's carbon dioxide emissions. This is beyond the scope of this chapter.

8.8   Calculating corporation tax

8.8.1   The financial year

The 'financial year' or 'fiscal year' for a company runs from the 1 April to 31 March in each year whereas for individuals, the tax year runs from 6 April to 5 April.

The Chancellor announces the rates of CT and the various allowances and reliefs in the Budget each year. Any changes are announced one or more financial years ahead of the year in which they will come into effect.

Company accounting periods are not always the same as the financial year. Where the company's financial accounting period covers two financial years and the rates of CT change on the 1 April during that time, the company will need to complete two calculations. It will need to apportion the profits according to the number of days in each accounting period which falls into each of the two financial years. The company also has to apply the appropriate CT rates for each of the financial years if the rates have changed.

8.8.2   Corporation tax rates

For the financial year beginning on 1 April 2017 the main rate of corporation tax is 19 per cent of a company's taxable profits. In future years this main rate of corporation tax will then be reduced as follows:

- 19 per cent for the financial years beginning on 1 April 2018, and 1 April 2019;
- 17 per cent for the financial year beginning on 1 April 2020.

EXAMPLE 9 (for the current financial year)

A company with taxable profits of £190,000 in the year 1 April 2017 to 31 March 2018 will be liable for corporation tax of £190,000 × 19% = £36,100.

A company with taxable profits of £5,190,000 in the year 1 April 2017 to 31 March 2018 will be liable for corporation tax of £5,190,000 × 19% = £986,100

8.9   Payment of CT

A company which is liable to pay CT is required to fulfil various obligations to HM Revenue and Customs ('HMRC') under s 55 Finance Act 2005. Currently HMRC has strict deadlines within which the company must declare it is liable for CT, pay the correct CT due on time, and electronically file a self-assessment Company Tax Return and supporting documentation online.

A company has to pay the CT for which it is liable before submitting the Company Tax Return, unlike income tax payments when the deadlines are the same for filing the tax return and the payment of the tax due.

The company is liable to pay any CT due nine months and one day after the end of its financial accounting period and to file the Company Tax Return within 12 months of the end of its financial accounting period. Any CT which is either underpaid or overdue is subject to interest and penalties.

EXAMPLE 10

The financial year of Gateway Chemical Ltd is 1 April 2017 to 31 March 2018 as is the corporation tax accounting period.

To comply with current HMRC deadlines the company must:

- pay the CT due by 1 January 2019; and
- file the Company Tax Return by 31 March 2019.

However it is important to note that extensive changes in respect of the recording and reporting of income to HMRC are being introduced as part of a project; Making Tax Digital for Business ('MTDfB').

From April 2020, under the proposed MTDfB requirements, businesses which pay corporation tax will be required to:

- maintain digital records;
- report summary information to HMRC every quarter via their digital tax accounts (DTAs); and
- make an 'End of Year Declaration' through their DTAs.

This End of Year declaration will be similar to submitting a self-assessment tax return online although it may need to be submitted earlier than a tax return. Businesses will have ten months from the end of their accounting period (or 31 January following their tax year if this is sooner).

Businesses with a turnover of under £10,000 will be exempt from these requirements.

8.10 The payment of dividends

A company which makes a profit can decide either to retain the profits within the company, which will increase the value of the shares, or to pay a dividend to its shareholders.

The payment of a dividend is not an expense which can be deducted from the company profits. If the company chooses to pay a dividend to its shareholders this is a distribution of profit on which CT has already been paid.

8.11 Close companies

Most of the small businesses in the UK are close companies. This is because they are often owned by family members and the company tends to be relatively small, with usually only one or two shareholders or people with controlling interests.

It is important to be able to identify whether a company is a close company. The main reason is that any company controlled by a small number of people could arrange its affairs to enable some or all of that group to avoid income tax, particularly in respect of loans from the company. Legislation to prevent such tax avoidance was introduced many years ago but more recently provisions have been created to enable a close company to be clearly identified.

8.11.1   Identifying a close company

A close company is, generally speaking, a company which is controlled by:

1. five or fewer participators; or
2. any number of participators if those participators are also directors.

8.11.1.1   Meaning of 'control'

Generally speaking a company is controlled by a person who:

1. owns (or has the right to acquire) over 50 per cent of the shares or 50 per cent of the voting shares of the company; or
2. holds over 50 per cent of the share capital of the company.

In assessing whether a particular person does have 'control' it is not only their shares and rights which are taken into account but also the shares and rights of their 'associates'. These may be attributed to him or her and can count as his or her shares or rights in identifying who does control a company.

'Associates' for this purpose are a person's:

1. Husband, wife, or civil partner;
2. Parent or remoter ancestor;
3. Child or remoter issue;
4. Brother or sister;
5. Partner.

8.11.1.2   Meaning of 'participator'

A participator includes anyone who has a share or interest in the capital or income of the company and specifically includes:

1. A person who has share capital or voting rights in the company;
2. A person who is a loan creditor of the company;
3. A person who possesses or is entitled to acquire a right to receive or participate in distributions of the company.

8.11.1.3   Meaning of 'director'

The term 'director' is applied in the broadest sense and includes those who are, in reality, 'shadow directors' and who occupy the position of director within the company, regardless of their title, and at whose directions the directors and employees are accustomed to act.

The term 'director' also includes anyone who is a manager of the company or concerned in the management of the company's business.

8.12   Taxation of close companies

Close companies have specific tax rules as they could be used as a vehicle to obtain tax advantages because they are usually owned by family members.

The main area of concern is that of loans to a participator who could make him/herself an interest free loan through the company. As there is usually no tax on loans, when a loan is made to a participator there are no tax consequences for the participator provided it remains a loan. Additionally, there is no charge to income tax as the loan would not be part of the participator's income.

8.12.1 Loan to a participator in a close company

A close company which makes a loan to a participator must also pay HMRC an amount equal to 32.5 per cent of a loan made after 6 April 2016 (this was previously 25 per cent of the loan).

EXAMPLE 11

Midway Pottery Ltd is a close company which agreed to lend £40,000 to a participator. In addition to this loan the company will also have to deposit the sum of £13,000 (£40,000 x 32.5 per cent) with HMRC, thereby costing the company £53,000 in total.

8.12.2 Exceptions to the rule

The rule at **8.12.1** is not applicable and the 32.5 per cent deposit does not have to be paid to HMRC where:

1. The loan is made to a participator in the ordinary course of the close company's business which includes lending money; or

2. The loan (together with any other loans to that person):
    - does not exceed £15,000; and
    - the participator works full time for the company; and
    - the participator owns less than 5 per cent of the shares.

When the participator repays the loan or the loan is waived or written off, HMRC then refunds the 32.5 per cent value of the loan paid to them.

This additional 32.5 per cent payment to HMRC is neither deductible as an expense from the trading profits of the company nor can it be deducted from the corporation tax due.

8.12.3 Writing off the loan

If the loan to the participator is written off it is treated as if it were dividend income in the hands of the participator, grossed up (see **Chapter 5** on income tax) and added to the participator's income, with the participator having a 10 per cent tax credit (ie as if the participator received the dividend income less 10 per cent tax).

EXAMPLE 12 Close company

Simple Food Ltd has issued share capital of 60,000 ordinary shares of £1 each.

Name		Number of shares
Andrew	Chairman	5,000
Ben	Director	2,800
Charles	Director	2,400
David	Director	4,400
Emma	Director	2,200
Fiona	Andrew's daughter	1,800
George	Sales manager	3,600
Haseeb	George's father	3,000
Indira	George's brother	3,000
Jasmine	George's sister	2,400
Miscellaneous shareholders		29,400
Total shares		**60,000**

In order to assess whether or not Simple Food Ltd is a close company, apply the following tests:

1. Identify the five participators with the largest shareholdings and, if this is insufficient to give control; then
2. Look at the directors' shareholdings.

1. The five participators with the largest shareholdings

Participator	Shareholding
Andrew	5,000
Add associates:	
Fiona	1,800
David	4,400
George	3,600 (treated as shadow director)
Add associates:	
Haseeb	3,000
Indira	3,000
Jasmine	2,400
Ben	2,800
Charles	2,400
Total shares	**28,400**

Total shareholding of the five participators with the largest shareholdings is 28,400. This is not a controlling interest and so, using this test, Simple Food Ltd is not a close company.

The first test, identifying the five participators with the largest shareholding, does not result in their holding a controlling interest. However it is necessary to apply the second test whereby the number of shares held by the directors is calculated.

2. The Director's shareholdings

Participator	Shareholding
Andrew	5,000
Add associates:	
Fiona	1,800
David	4,400
George	3,600
Add associates:	
Haseeb	3,000
Indira	3,000
Jasmine	2,400
Ben	2,800
Charles	2,400
Emma	2,200
Total shares	**30,600**

Total shareholding of the directors is 30,600. This is a controlling interest in Simple Food Ltd and it is therefore a close company.

8.13 Steps to a complete CT calculation

It is useful to approach a full CT calculation by applying a series of steps to include all the varying elements, as shown in **Table 8.1**:

Table 8.1 **Steps to complete a full CT calculation**

Step 1	
Calculate the company income profits from all sources	Deduct allowable expenses to give the net income profit
Step 2	
Calculate capital allowances	Deduct capital allowances from the net income profit
Step 3	
Calculate chargeable capital gains and add to total from Step 2	Deduct acquisition price, professional fees, costs of any improvements, indexation allowance
Step 4	
Identify any available capital losses for the current and any previous financial years	Deduct these capital losses from any available capital gains
Step 5	
Identify any available trading losses for the current and any previous financial years	Deduct these trading losses from the taxable trading profit
Step 6	
Calculate the CT due applying the current tax rates	

EXAMPLE 13 Example of a CT calculation

Key Engineers Ltd, a national manufacturing company for the building trade, is forecast to make a gross income profit of £5,600,000 in the current financial year which runs from 1 April 2017 to 31 March 2018.

The financial statements for the company show the following outgoings for the year:

	£	Notes
Wages and salaries	900,000	
General expenses	80,000	
Advertising expenses	20,000	
Dividend paid out	40,000	
Purchase of new manufacturing equipment	570,000	This equipment has a life expectancy of 17 years.

Further information

• Existing plant and machinery

The company has existing plant and machinery (with a useful life of less than 25 years) with a written down value of £48,000 at the beginning of this financial year.

• Factory

The company sold a factory and made a gain of £90,000 earlier this year. The professional costs on the sale and purchase total £20,000.

The indexation allowance is £5,600.

Previous trading years—losses and gains

2015/16: The company made a trading profit of £40,000 and a capital gain of £3,000.
2016/17: The company made a trading loss of £68,000 and a capital loss of £7,000.
Calculating the CT payable by Key Engineers Ltd for the current financial year

Step 1	£	£
Trading profit		
Gross income profit		5,600,000
Deduct		
Wages and salaries	(900,000)	
General expenses	(80,000)	
Advertising expenses	(20,000)	(1,000,000)
Net income profit		4,600,000
Step 2		
Capital Allowances		
New manufacturing equipment—AIA	(200,000)	
Balance of manufacturing equipment AIA £570,000 − £200,000 = £370,000 × 18%	(66,600)	
1. Pool of existing plant & machinery £48,000 × 18%	(8,640)	(275,240)
		4,324,760
Step 3		
Capital Gains		
Gain on sale	90,000	
Less professional fees	(20,000)	
Less indexation allowance	(5,600)	64,400
		4,389,160
Step 4		
Capital losses		
The CL of £7,000 from 2016/17 is c/f and deducted from the CG of £64,400 for the current year.		(7,000)
Step 5		
Trading losses		
The 2016/17 trading loss (TL) of £68,000 cannot be set against the capital loss (CL) of £7,000 and is therefore carried back to 2015/16.		
The TL of £68,000 from 2016/17 can be set against the £40,000 trading profit (TP) and against the capital gain (CG) of £3,000 both made in 2015/16.		
This leaves a TL of £25,000 to c/f to set against (deduct from) chargeable profits in the current year.		(25,000)
Step 6		
To calculate CT due on the taxable profit		4,357,160
£4,357,160 × 19% = £827,860.4 CT due		

Note:

- Dividends are not an allowable deduction as they are paid from taxed profit.

8.14   Conclusion: checkpoints

You should now be able to:

1. Calculate the income profits of a company and identify allowable deductions;
2. Identify a close company;
3. Apply trading losses and any capital gains and losses;
4. Calculate the appropriate capital allowances;
5. Complete a full CT calculation.

 online resource centre   Visit the Online Resource Centre for more information and useful weblinks.
www.oxfordtextbooks.co.uk/orc/foundations17_18/

9

Value added tax

9.1 Introduction

This chapter covers value added tax ('VAT'). In particular, this chapter will cover:

- the circumstances in which VAT is charged;
- the rates of VAT;
- when VAT can be reclaimed;
- accounting for VAT; and
- doing VAT calculations.

VAT is a tax charged on supplies of goods and services made by businesses that have (or should have) registered for VAT. Effectively, the suppliers of goods and services act as a tax collector by charging VAT on supplies made and then pay this over to HM Revenue & Customs ('HMRC'). However, these businesses will also be charged VAT on goods and services that are supplied to the business and will usually be able to reclaim this from HMRC.

For example, a clothing shop called India Closet buys dresses from a wholesaler and then sells these dresses on to individual consumers. The wholesaler would add VAT to the price it charges India Closet for the dresses supplied. India Closet would add VAT to the price it charges the individual consumer for a dress. India Closet would be able to set off the amount of VAT received from the consumer against the VAT charged by the wholesaler (see **9.5**).

9.2 Sources of VAT law

VAT was introduced in 1973 to bring UK law into line with the EU. As a result, it is governed by various EU directives, in particular the Principal VAT Directive (2006/112). These directives are given effect in the UK mainly by the Value Added Tax Act 1994 ('VATA'), as amended by various Finance Acts, and this is the main source of UK VAT law. Many of the detailed rules of the scheme are contained in various statutory instruments.

HMRC also issues 'VAT Notices'. These do not have legal force but provide invaluable guidance on the detail of the VAT scheme. They are available on the Government's website at https://www.gov.uk/topic/business-tax/vat, along with lots of other useful information about the operation of VAT.

Overall, the scheme is complex with many detailed rules that apply to specific situations. Considerably more research would be needed in order to advise about VAT in practice. This chapter will provide a basic summary of principles of VAT that are of general application.

9.3 When is VAT charged?

Most business transactions involve the supply of goods and/or services. VAT is only charged on 'taxable supplies' of goods and/or services. A supply is taxable if it meets all of these conditions:

- It was made in the UK (for VAT purposes, the UK includes the Isle of Man);
- It was made by a 'taxable person' (see **9.3.1**);

- It was made in the course of a business (see **9.3.2**); and
- It is not exempt from the scope of VAT (see **9.4.4**).

VAT is charged on the full value of the goods and services, even if the supplier accepts goods in part exchange. If there is a part exchange, the monetary equivalent of the goods exchanged will be used to calculate the VAT payable.

This section will go on to consider what is meant by some essential terms.

9.3.1   Who is a 'taxable person'?

A taxable person is a person who is acting in the course of a business and has or should have registered for VAT (see **9.6** for further details about registration). The business will often be an individual, a partnership, or a company. Other types of organisation can be a taxable person, for example a club, an association, or a charity.

The taxable person registers for VAT and this registration covers all of the taxable supplies made by that person, even if the registered person runs several businesses that make taxable supplies. For ease of explanation, this chapter will refer to 'the business' even though it is the person who is registered rather than the business.

9.3.2   What is a 'business'?

For these purposes, a business is mainly concerned with making supplies of goods and/or services in exchange for consideration. This must be a frequent occurrence on a sufficient scale and it must be ongoing. Occasionally receiving income from sources such as leisure activities or hobbies and other isolated transactions do not count as a business for these purposes.

A business will often consist of someone earning an income through a trade, vocation, or profession, either as a self-employed individual or through an entity such as a limited company. Other types of activity will count as business activity such as a club that charges a membership fee in return for membership benefits or an organisation that charges admission to premises.

A body whose activities are mainly non-business may perform some business activities. For example, the maintenance of a museum is a non-business activity. If the museum charges an entry fee or sells merchandise to raise money, these would be business activities. If the body's taxable turnover from the business activities reaches the VAT threshold (see **9.6**), it will have to register for VAT even though most of its activities are non-business activities that are not taxable to VAT.

9.4   What are the rates of VAT?

Most transactions are charged at the standard rate of VAT, which is currently 20 per cent. There is also a 'reduced' rate and a 'zero' rate, each of which applies to specific categories of supply. Some goods and services are outside the scope of VAT altogether.

There is detailed guidance in VAT Notices about how different categories of supply are rated. It is beyond the scope of this book to set out in detail how supplies are rated but this section will provide a summary.

9.4.1   Standard rate of VAT

The standard rate (currently 20 per cent) is the default rate. VAT is charged at the standard rate where another rate does not apply and the goods or services are not exempt from VAT. The supply of legal services by solicitors is charged at the standard rate. The effect of this is that, for each £100 invoiced to the client, the firm must charge the client £20 VAT.

9.4.2   Reduced rate of VAT

The goods and services that are charged at the reduced rate (currently 5 per cent) are set out in Schedule 7 VATA. Some examples of goods and services that are currently charged at the reduced rate are:

- domestic fuel or power;
- children's car seats;
- contraceptive products;
- smoking cessation products; and
- installation of energy-saving materials in residential or charitable buildings.

9.4.3   Zero rate of VAT

The goods and services that are charged at the zero rate (0 per cent) are set out in Schedule 8 VATA. Some examples of goods and services that are currently charged at the zero rate are:

- water and sewerage services;
- books and newspapers;
- children's clothes and shoes;
- public transport; and
- most food—the provisions are fairly complicated as not all food is charged at the zero rate; for example it does not include meals in restaurants or hot takeaways.

These supplies are taxable to VAT, but they are charged at 0 per cent so no VAT will actually be payable. They will be included in the supplying business's VAT account and the supplying business will be able to reclaim VAT it has paid on related business expenditure (see **9.5**).

9.4.4   Exempt from VAT

Some supplies of goods and services are exempt from VAT, as set out in Schedule 9 VATA. Some examples of supplies that are exempt from VAT are:

- insurance, finance, and credit services;
- education and training;
- health services;
- burial and cremation services;
- fund raising events by charities; and
- subscriptions to membership organisations.

Exempt supplies are not subject to VAT at all and so will not appear in the supplying business's VAT account. The business will not be able to reclaim VAT on related expenditure.

If a business only supplies exempt goods and services, the business itself cannot register for VAT at all.

9.4.5   Outside the scope of VAT

Some activities are outside the scope of VAT altogether (as opposed to being exempt from VAT). These activities cannot be taxable supplies for the purposes of VAT. Matters outside the scope of VAT include non-business activities, for example selling an item from a personal hobby collection such as a stamp collection. Fees that are fixed by statute are also outside the scope of VAT, for example the charge for a vehicle MOT test.

9.5 Input and output VAT

As we have already seen, as well as charging VAT on the supplies it makes, a business will also be charged VAT by its suppliers.

The VAT that the business adds to the price of the supplies it makes is known as 'output' VAT (charged on the business's output—that is the goods and/or services that it supplies). The supplier must account to HMRC for the output VAT that it has collected from customers so output VAT is also known as VAT payable.

On the other hand, the VAT that a business pays to its suppliers for goods and services received is known as 'input' VAT (charged on goods and services coming *in* to the business).

9.5.1 Reclaiming VAT

The business can normally reclaim its input VAT from HMRC. Generally, the business can only reclaim VAT paid for goods and services received that relate to taxable supplies made by the business. The business cannot reclaim VAT on supplies made to the business that relate to any non-business activity or to any exempt supplies the supplier makes in turn.

The business will reclaim its input VAT by deducting it from the amount of output VAT it has collected and paying the balance of output VAT to HMRC. For this reason, input VAT is also known as VAT deductible. If the input VAT exceeds the output VAT, the supplier can reclaim the difference from HMRC (see **Table 9.1**).

If an item is used for both business and pleasure, for example a computer, VAT can only be reclaimed in the proportion that the item is used for business. It is worth noting that, as a general rule, input VAT paid by a business on the purchase of a car cannot be reclaimed. The exceptions are very limited and include cars intended to be used exclusively for business purposes or intended primarily to be used in a taxi business or in a driving school.

VAT on business entertainment expenses cannot be reclaimed either.

EXAMPLE 1 Input and output VAT

Let's return to the example of the clothes shop, India Closet, from the introduction and consider the VAT position on a couple of transactions from the perspective of the shop. India Closet buys 20 dresses worth £200 in total from a wholesaler. The wholesaler will add VAT at the standard rate of 20 per cent, so India Closet will pay £40 input VAT. India Closet pays £240 in total to the wholesaler, including the VAT.

India Closet sells each dress for £40. It will charge the customer output VAT at the standard rate of 20 per cent, so £8 VAT will be charged to the customer for each dress, meaning that the customer pays a total of £48 for each dress. If India Closet sells 10 dresses for this price in the same accounting period in which it bought the dresses, it will have charged a total of £8 × 10 = £80 output VAT to the customers in that period.

At the end of the accounting period, India Closet will account to HMRC for its VAT by setting off the £80 output VAT collected against the £40 input VAT paid out, as shown in **Table 9.2**.

India Closet would, of course, have had considerably more input and output VAT to account for in reality. There is a more detailed example at the end of this chapter.

Table 9.1 **Input and output VAT**

If	Calculation	Equals
Input tax > output tax	Input tax – output tax	Amount to reclaim from HMRC
Output tax > input tax	Output tax – input tax	Amount due to HMRC

Table 9.2 **Calculation of VAT due**

	£80 (output VAT payable to HMRC)
Less	£40 (input VAT deductible)
Leaves	£40 (due to HMRC)

9.6 Registration

As we have seen, any business that is registered for VAT will add VAT to the price of goods and services that it supplies in the UK.

A business must register for VAT if it has turnover of taxable supplies that exceeds the 'VAT threshold', which is currently £85,000 per year. (Turnover means all of the business's income from taxable supplies before any expenses are deducted.) A business can choose to register for VAT even if its turnover is below the VAT threshold.

9.6.1 Voluntary registration

A business that is not registered does not charge VAT on its supplies of goods and services but will still be charged VAT by its suppliers. A business may choose to register for VAT even if its turnover is below the threshold. There are advantages and disadvantages to voluntary registration.

The main advantage is that the business will be able to reclaim from HMRC the VAT that it pays to its suppliers. This will be particularly advantageous if the business makes mostly zero rated supplies: it would be able to reclaim standard rate VAT that it has paid out to its suppliers without having to charge its customers any VAT because the supplies made by the business are zero rated.

The main disadvantage is that the business will have to charge its customers VAT. This is not a problem if the customers are themselves registered for VAT because the customers will be able to reclaim the VAT that they pay to the business. If the business tends to supply to non-registered customers, not registering voluntarily may provide a competitive advantage as the business would be able to charge a lower price than its VAT-registered competitors because it would not have to charge customers VAT.

The other important disadvantage of voluntary registration is that the business would have to take on the administrative burden of accounting for VAT (see **9.8**).

9.7 The tax point

The VAT on the supply of goods or services becomes chargeable on an identifiable date that is known as the 'tax point'. This is important because the rate of VAT chargeable will be the rate that was in force at the tax point. The supplier will need to account to HMRC at the end of the accounting period in which the tax point falls (see **9.8.3**).

For the supply of goods, the basic rule is that the tax point is the date when the goods were sent to the customer or taken away by the customer. If the goods are not sent or taken away, the tax point will be the date on which they were made available for the customer to use.

For the supply of services, the basic rule is that the tax point is the date on which the service is performed. This will usually be the date when all work is completed, apart from invoicing the customer.

The 'basic' tax points can be overridden by the actual arrangements in two situations:

- If the supplier issues a VAT invoice (see **9.8.1**) or payment is made before the basic tax point, the actual tax point will be the date of the invoice or the payment, whichever was earlier.

- If the supplier issues a VAT invoice up to 14 days after the basic tax point, the actual tax point will be the date of the invoice. This rule can be amended on application to HMRC, for example because the business issues its invoices monthly.

9.8 Accounting for VAT

Registration for VAT brings with it various accounting requirements. The business must:

- issue VAT invoices to its VAT-registered customers;
- keep proper VAT records, including a VAT account; and
- submit a VAT return to HMRC at the end of each accounting period.

This section will briefly consider each of these requirements, as well as the penalties for non-compliance.

9.8.1   VAT invoices

When a person who is registered for VAT supplies goods or services charged at the standard or reduced rate to another registered person, he must also supply a VAT invoice. This invoice should usually include certain information, including the name, address and VAT number of the supplier, the tax point (see **9.7**), and a description of the goods/services that includes the amount charged before VAT, the amount of VAT, and the total including VAT.

There is no requirement to issue VAT invoices to customers who are not themselves registered for VAT. There is no practical way to check whether the customer is registered for VAT so most suppliers will issue a VAT invoice to any customer that requests one.

9.8.2   The business's VAT records

A business that is registered for VAT must keep records and accounts of all taxable goods and services that it receives or supplies in the course of its business. This is true whatever rate of VAT applies, including the zero rate. The business must also keep a record of any exempt supplies that it makes but is not required to record exempt supplies received. Examples of the sorts of records a business might keep include:

- the business's annual accounts;
- bank statements;
- paying-in slips;
- invoices for purchases and sales;
- daily records of takings, such as till rolls; and
- relevant correspondence.

A record that *must* be kept is a 'VAT account'. This is a summary of the input and output VAT of the business for each tax period. This can be created by adding up the VAT totals in the business's day-to-day records at convenient intervals, say once a month, and recording the totals of input (deductible) and output (payable) tax in the VAT account. At the end of the VAT accounting period (see **9.8.3**), each side of the VAT account can be totalled. The smaller figure can be taken away from the larger figure to calculate how much tax to pay to or reclaim from HMRC. If the output (payable) is higher, the business will be paying to HMRC but if the input (deductible) is higher, the business will be reclaiming.

All records must be kept up to date and contain enough detail to allow the business to calculate how much VAT to pay to or reclaim from HMRC. There is no set way to keep these records. The business must be able to make the records easily available to HMRC on request and the records must allow HMRC easily to check that the figures in the VAT return (see **9.8.3**) are accurate.

The business must also keep a copy of all VAT invoices that it issues.

9.8.3   VAT returns

VAT-registered persons must submit a VAT return to HMRC online and pay any VAT owed to HMRC electronically. (There are extremely limited exceptions where the taxable person can submit a paper return instead but virtually all VAT returns are now required to be submitted online.) A VAT return must be submitted by a registered person in each accounting period. If he has not traded at all during the relevant period, he will submit a 'nil return'.

VAT returns must be made at pre-determined intervals. The period covered by the VAT return is known as the 'tax period'. The standard tax period is three months. When a person registers for VAT, he is allocated the four tax periods each year in which he must submit his VAT return, for example he might have to submit at the end of the months of February, May, August, and November. This is so that the returns received by HMRC from registered persons will be spread evenly throughout the year.

It is possible to apply to change the length of tax period to monthly or yearly in some circumstances.

Essentially, in the VAT return, the business will subtract its VAT deductible (input VAT) from its VAT payable (output VAT), giving the net amount of VAT that the business must pay to HMRC. If the deductible VAT exceeds the payable VAT, the business can reclaim the difference from HMRC.

9.8.4 Penalties

HMRC's principal method of enforcing the VAT regime is by charging penalties for non-compliance. Penalties can be charged in a variety of situations that will be briefly summarised in this section. The details of enforcement are beyond the scope of this text.

As described at **9.6**, there is a requirement to register for VAT if a person's turnover of taxable supplies exceeds the VAT threshold. Failure to register when required will cause a penalty charge. This will be a percentage of the VAT due from the date when the person should have registered, with the percentage increasing if the failure continues.

If the business fails to submit a VAT return, HMRC will assess the tax due to the best of its judgement. If the business repeatedly pays the amount assessed by HMRC instead of making a proper VAT return, HMRC will increase the amount assessed each time.

If the business submits its return late or does not pay the VAT due on time, HMRC can make a surcharge on the VAT due. This surcharge will be a percentage of the VAT due and will keep increasing as the default continues.

If the amount of VAT due is under declared due to a significant or repeated lack of care in submitting the return then a penalty can be charged; this will be a percentage of the tax that should have been paid. Interest may also be charged on mis-declarations from the date when the correct tax should have been paid.

If the return is made dishonestly with an intention to evade paying VAT, the penalties are more serious with a maximum penalty of the total amount of VAT evaded. Tax evasion may also give rise to criminal charges.

9.9 Doing VAT calculations

Calculating the amount of VAT due on a supply is relatively straightforward—just multiply the value of the supply by the relevant percentage, as shown in **Table 9.3**.

You will frequently know the amount paid for the supply including the VAT and will need to calculate how much of the amount paid consists of VAT. HMRC provides 'VAT fractions' to enable this calculation to be made easily. To calculate how much of a VAT-inclusive sum consists of VAT, simply multiply the VAT-inclusive sum by the relevant VAT fraction, as shown in **Table 9.4**.

Table 9.3 **VAT percentages**

VAT rate	Multiply by
0%	0 (VAT will always be £0)
5%	0.05
20%	0.2

Table 9.4 **VAT fractions**

VAT rate	Multiply by
0%	0 (VAT will always be £0)
5%	1/21
20%	1/6

So, if a solicitor sends a bill totalling £240 including VAT charged at the standard rate, we can calculate how much of the amount billed is VAT:

£240 × 1/6 = £40 (meaning that £40 of the £240 billed is VAT).

EXAMPLE 2 VAT calculation

Let's have a closer look at the VAT affairs of India Closet. As well as buying clothes from wholesalers, the shop has also started to manufacture some of its own clothing. In the accounting period that has just ended, the shop has paid the following totals, including VAT, on supplies of goods from VAT-registered suppliers:

Adult clothing	£30,000
Children's clothing	£10,000
Textiles	£21,000
Machinery	£6,000

The shop has made the following sales, excluding VAT:

Adult clothing	£250,000
Children's clothing	£80,000

In addition, India Closet purchased a company car for the use of its employees. The car is occasionally used for domestic purposes by employees, outside the shop's opening hours.

Last month, India Closet put on a lavish lunch in store to try to attract new business. The lunch cost £500.

The task is to calculate how much VAT India Closet must pay to HMRC for this accounting period.

First, calculate how much input VAT India Closet has paid on supplies received.

We know the VAT-inclusive amounts that India Closet has paid for each type of supply and must calculate the amount of VAT:

Item	VAT rate	Calculation	Input VAT
Adult clothing	Standard 20%	30,000 × 1/6	5,000
Children's clothing	Zero 0%	10,000 × 0	0
Textiles	Standard 20%	21,000 × 1/6	3,500
Machinery	Standard 20%	6,000 × 1/6	1,000
Total input VAT			9,500

The car is not exclusively for business purposes so the VAT paid by India Closet cannot be reclaimed, nor can the VAT on the business entertainment expense of the lunch.

Next, calculate how much output VAT India Closet has charged on supplies made.

This time the figures are exclusive of VAT so we will apply the relevant rate of VAT to each type of supply:

Item	VAT rate	Calculation	Output VAT
Adult clothing	Standard 20%	250,000 × 0.2	50,000
Children's clothing	Zero 0%	80,000 × 0	0
Total output VAT			50,000

Finally, we can calculate the VAT due to HMRC. As the output figure is higher than the input figure, India Closet will make a payment of the difference to HMRC:

Output VAT total	50,000
Less Input VAT total	9,500
equals tax due to HMRC	40,500

9.10 Conclusion: checkpoints

You should now be able to:

- identify the sources of VAT law;
- understand when VAT is charged;
- understand the rates of VAT in outline;
- understand the distinction between input and output VAT, including the circumstances in which VAT is reclaimable;
- identify the registration and accounting requirements for VAT; and
- perform a simple VAT calculation.

online resource centre   Visit the Online Resource Centre for more information and useful weblinks. **www.oxfordtextbooks.co.uk/orc/foundations17_18/**

Taxation of sole proprietors and partnerships

10.1 Introduction

This chapter deals with the taxation of sole proprietors (known as sole traders) and partnerships with particular consideration given to:

- Income tax liability of sole traders and partners;
- Calculating the trading profits;
- Capital gains and capital losses;
- Trading losses;
- Basis of assessment;
- Capital allowances;
- Changes in a partnership.

Unlike companies who pay corporation tax, sole traders and partners are liable to pay income tax on their income in accordance with the Income Tax (Trading and Other Income) Act 2005 ('ITTOIA').

The starting point is for the sole trader or partner to work out their statutory income. Statutory income is the total amount of all the income a sole trader or partner receives. This income can be from several different sources in addition to their income for their business or partnership; for example they could also have bank and building society interest, rent due from properties they own, or dividends from their shareholdings. The taxpayer can then deduct their personal allowance and any charge on income to give the net amount of income on which they are liable to pay income tax.

The term 'business' used throughout this chapter refers to both sole traders and to partners.

Further details about the calculation of income tax for a sole trader and a partner are contained in **Chapter 5**.

10.2 Sole trader liability to income tax and VAT

A sole trader has to register him/herself as self-employed with HMRC within three months of becoming self-employed.

A sole trader may also need to register for VAT if the sales or turnover of the business exceed the annual stated minimum. This will mean the business will have to charge VAT on invoices but can claim back VAT on purchases made for the business. However some supplies may be exempt or zero rated.

See **9.6** on VAT for more detailed information.

10.3   Partners' liability to income tax

Each partner is taxed on their own share of the partnership income. The partnership itself is not liable for income tax. The partnership nominates one partner who is responsible for completing and submitting the Partnership Tax Return and who is the main contact within the partnership.

The nominated partner is responsible for filing the tax return each year to HMRC. This tax return declares the partnership's income, expenses, and deductions, clearly showing the net income of the partnership and how much income each partner has allocated to them under the terms of the partnership agreement. This is filed alongside the partner's personal income tax return so that each partner will pay income tax on their partnership income, in addition to any other income, at that partner's relevant tax rate for the year.

Each partner has an individual liability for his own tax and does not have any liability for the income tax of the other partners.

10.3.1   Partnership accounts

Each partner is allocated a share of the partnership profits and it is this share which is included in each partner's individual tax return.

EXAMPLE 1

Ahmed, Ben, and Cora are the three partners in The Fresh Cordial Partnership. The accounts for the partnership at the end of the current year show a net profit of £200,000 for the year. The partnership agreement shows that the partners share this profit as follows:

Salaries

Ahmed	£18,000
Ben	£20,000
Cora	£20,000

The partners are entitled to interest on their capital at 10 per cent per annum, each receiving

Ahmed	£10,000
Ben	£5,000
Cora	£5,000

The profits after payment of salaries and interest on capital are shared in the following proportions

Ahmed	Ben	Cora
50%	25%	25%

Each partner is entitled to:

	£	£	£	£
Net profit				**200,000**
	Ahmed	**Ben**	**Cora**	**Total**
Salary	18,000	20,000	20,000	58,000
Interest on cap	10,000	5,000	5,000	20,000
Profit share	61,000	30,500	30,500	122,000
	89,000	55,500	55,500	**200,000**

Note: the profit share of each partner is calculated as follows:

Net profit		200,000
Less:		
Total salaries	(58,000)	
Total interest on capital	(20,000)	(78,000)
Available to profit share		122,000

Ahmed will receive 50 per cent of the £122,000 available for profit sharing (£61,000), Ben will receive 25 per cent (£30,500), and Cora will receive 25 per cent (£30,500).

Ahmed will include his income from the partnership of £89,000 in his income tax return, Ben will include £55,500 in his tax return, and Cora will include £55,500 in her tax return.

For details as to when any income tax payable is due see **Chapter 5**.

10.4 Calculating the trading profit of sole traders and partners

The trading profits of sole traders and partnerships are calculated on a similar basis in accordance with the basic rules of income tax set out in the Income Tax Act 2007 (ITA 2007) and applying the following steps:

1. Calculate the statutory income—see **10.1** for a brief summary and **Chapter 5** for a detailed explanation of 'statutory income'.
2. Apply allowable deductible expenses.
3. Deduct any capital allowances.
4. Deduct the relevant personal allowance.

10.4.1 Allowable deductible expenses

A deductible expense has to be of an 'income nature' and incurred 'wholly and exclusively' in the business of the sole trader or the partner.

Expenses of an 'income nature' usually recur throughout the year on an ongoing basis. They are not a 'one-off' expense, for example the purchase of an asset such as business or partnership premises. It is important to distinguish between an expense incurred on an ongoing basis (which is an allowable deduction) and an expense incurred in the purchase of a capital asset (which is not an allowable deduction).

It is usually clear whether or not an expense has been incurred 'wholly and exclusively' in the business; for example the purchase of a car for the private use of the sole trader or partner, as opposed to use in the business, does not meet this criterion.

10.4.2 Capital allowances

Other than capital allowances there are no other allowances available which take account of the depreciation of capital assets, such as plant and machinery, that can be set against the trading profits of a sole trader or partnership.

The Capital Allowances Act 2001 ('CAA 2001') allows a business to deduct a fixed percentage of the cost of capital assets against its profits. These agreed deductions are known as capital allowances ('CAs'). CAs are available for all businesses and are used as a deduction from the profits in each accounting period.

The sole trader/partner is not allowed to claim capital allowances for the cost of assets it buys and sells as part of the business as these are treated as expenses and deducted from the trading profits.

The most relevant capital allowance relates to plant and machinery, for example computers, with an allowance of 18 per cent each year which the sole trader/partner can set against trading profits.

It is worth noting that there is a specific category of long life assets. These are assets with a useful working life of more than 25 years and they have a capital allowance of 8 per cent.

Additionally, there are 100 per cent first-year allowances available, which can be deducted from trading profits, for the cost of certain types of asset such as energy-saving equipment and cars with very low carbon dioxide emissions.

The Annual Investment Allowance ('AIA') is available each year for most businesses which purchase plant and machinery or long life assets in that year. The AIA available from 1 January 2016 onwards is £200,000. See **Chapter 8 (8.7.4)** for further details.

10.4.2.1   Writing-down allowances

Writing-down allowances ('WDAs') are an annual allowance that can be claimed to reduce or 'write down' any remaining balance of capital expenditure on plant and machinery in respect of which a capital allowance has not been claimed. A business buying plant and machinery is entitled to a WDA in respect of the cost of those assets on a reducing basis. See **8.7.2** for a detailed explanation.

10.4.2.2   Balancing charges

When a sole trader or partnership decides to sell one of its assets HMRC ensures that no more tax relief is available than it is entitled to in respect of the written down value ('WDV') of that asset.

Should the business sell the asset for more than the WDV, the difference between the WDV and the sale price (the 'balancing charge') is added to the trading profits and so increases the amount chargeable to tax.

EXAMPLE 2 Balancing charge

The Field and Warren Partnership purchased some laser cutting equipment for £80,000 three years ago.
The written down value of the cutting equipment is £35,000.
The partnership decides to sell this equipment for £40,000.

	£
Sale price of laser equipment	40,000
The written down value	(35,000)
Gain	5,000

The gain of £5,000 is added to the Field and Warren Partnership taxable profits.

If the asset is sold for less than the WDV the difference between the WDV and the sale price is set against the profits for the year thereby reducing the amount chargeable to tax.

For a more detailed discussion of CAs and worked examples, see **Chapter 8**.

10.5   Charge on income

When a partner or a sole trader takes out a loan and invests the entire loan in their business, for example to buy an interest in a partnership, he/she can set off the interest payable on that loan against their income. This approach is designed to encourage investment in business.

EXAMPLE 3

Julie Harvey, a partner in Design for Living, borrows £50,000 from High Bank to invest in the partnership.
She pays 6 per cent interest per annum on the loan.

Julie can set off the interest payments of £3,000 against her statutory income each year.

10.6 Capital gains and capital losses

Sole traders and partners can make a capital gain and/or a capital loss when they dispose of assets, in the same way that an individual can. Neither sole traders nor partners are likely to give away capital assets so any disposal most probably results from the sale of an asset. The capital gains tax ('CGT') reliefs of roll-over relief, hold-over relief, and entrepreneur's relief may be available depending on the circumstances of each individual.

See **Chapter 6** on CGT for further information.

10.6.1 Capital gains

The calculation of any capital gains incurred by a business on the sale of assets is worked out by applying the same principles used in calculating the capital gain for an individual. The same rates of CGT of 10 per cent and/or 20 per cent apply, depending on the individual's income.

10.6.1.1 Capital gains of a partner in a partnership

The proceeds of sale realised from the disposal of a partnership asset are normally divided between the partners in accordance with the terms of their partnership agreement.

EXAMPLE 4

The four partners in The Natural Food Partnership sell their factory on which they make a capital gain of £100,000.

The partnership agreement states that capital gains are to be divided between the partners equally. In this case the partners will therefore be treated as receiving 25 per cent each of the capital gain. Each partner will also share the allowable deductions in the same percentage.

10.6.2 Capital losses

The calculation of a capital loss incurred by a business is worked out by applying the same principles as for individuals. Capital losses made by a business can be set against any capital gains made by the business in the same financial year. Any unused capital losses can be carried forward indefinitely to set against capital gains made in the future.

See **Chapter 6** for a detailed discussion and worked examples of both capital gains and capital losses.

10.7 Trading losses

A sole trader or partnership does not always make a trading profit each year and it may well be that in some years the accounts of the business show that a trading loss has been incurred. If this is the case, relief in respect of a trading loss is available under ss 37–38 CTA 2010 as follows:

1. A business can set the trading loss incurred against any other trading profits and/or capital gains made during the same year of the trading loss.

If it is not possible to use all the trading loss against trading profits and/or capital gains in the same year then the balance of the loss can be:

2. Carried back against any trading profits and/or capital gains for the previous year.

Any remaining trading losses which are not used can be:

3. Carried forward indefinitely and set against trading profits.

Unused trading loss(es) cannot be set against any capital gains when the unused loss is being carried forward.

EXAMPLE 5

Creative Concepts, a small business specialising in web design, incurred a trading loss of £80,000 in their 2016/2017 tax year. They estimate their trading profit will be £90,000 in their 2017/2018 tax year.

The trading profits/losses and capital gains/losses incurred by the business for the preceding two years are as follows:

Tax year 2015/16	Trading profit £20,000 Capital gain £10,000
Tax year 2016/17	**Trading loss £80,000** Rental income £1,000 Capital gain £2,000
Tax year 2017/18	Estimated profit of £90,000 Capital gain of £6,000

EXAMPLE 6 How Creative Concepts can use the 2016/2017 £80,000 trading loss

Tax year 2015/16	Trading loss of £80,000 can be set against the rental income of £1,000 and the capital gain of £2,000 for 2016/2017. This leaves unused trading loss of £77,000.
Tax year 2016/17	Carry back the unused £77,000 trading loss and set against the trading profit of £20,000 and the capital gain of £10,000 in 2015/16. This leaves an unused trading loss of £47,000.
Tax year 2017/18	Carry forward the unused trading loss of £47,000 and set against the current year's estimated trading profit of £90,000.

The estimated trading profit of £90,000 in the tax year 2017/18 will be reduced to £43,000 and the trading loss has been utilised in full. If the trading loss had not been completely utilised it could not be set against the capital gain of £6,000 in the tax year 2017/18 and would need to be carried forward to be used against any trading profits in the following year.

A further discussion of the application of trading losses with worked examples is contained in **Chapter 8**.

10.8 The basis of assessment of trading profits

Business accounts are drawn up on an earnings basis which takes into account all the income generated in the accounting period even though invoices may not have been submitted and expenses incurred may not have been paid.

A business can choose an accounting period of 12 months in which to make up the accounts, for example 1 February to 31 January. The accounting period need not be the same as the tax year ending on 5 April. Many businesses opt for 31 March as the end of their accounting period.

A business is taxed on the profits made during its accounting period and ending in the tax year to 5 April; this is referred to as the 'basis period' or 'basis of assessment period'.

10.8.1 First year rules—a new business

In the initial opening years of a new business there are specific rules for calculating the profits on which tax is payable.

EXAMPLE 7

Year 1 of trading: **Tax year 2016/17** (6 April 2016 to 5 April 2017)	Tax will be assessed on the profits made from the date of commencement of the business to the following 5 April. Example—Carr Parts started their business on 1 February 2017. The business will be assessed on their trading profits from 1 February to 5 April 2017.
Year 2 of trading: **Tax year 2017/18** (6 April 2017 to 5 April 2018)	Tax will be assessed on the trading profits for the first full 12-month accounting period ending in the second tax year. Example—Carr Parts will be assessed on their trading profits from 1 February 2017 to 31 January 2018.
Year 3 of trading onwards: **Tax year 2018/19** (6 April 2018 to 5 April 2019)	Tax is assessed on the current year or 'normal' basis (ie on the profits of the 12-month accounting period ending in the current tax year). In this example Carr Parts will be assessed on their trading profit for their accounting year ending 31 January 2019.

10.8.2   The rules on the closing of a business

In the final trading year of a business the trading income is assessed to tax on the profits earned from the end of the last accounting period up to the date the business stops trading. However overlap relief must be taken into account—see **10.9**.

10.9   Overlap relief

Under the opening year rules a business which makes up its accounts to a year-end other than 5 April will have some of its profits taxed twice during the first couple of years of trading.

In view of this, HMRC permit 'overlap relief' which allows profits taxed twice in the opening years of a business to be deducted from profits in the year the business stops trading. This ensures that the amount of profits assessed to income tax is equivalent to the actual total profits made during the life of the business.

EXAMPLE 8

The Organic Seed Partnership commenced business on 1 February 2014 and make up their accounts to 31 January in each tax year. Due to an unprecedented rent increase which the partners cannot afford, they decide they will cease trading on 31 January 2022.

The business makes a trading profit of £30,000 in their first year of trading ending on 31 January 2015.

First year of trading

Tax year 2013/14 (6 April 2013 to 5 April 2014).
Assessed on the actual profits for the two-month period from 1 February 2014 – 5 April 2014:
$2/12 \times £30,000$ profits = £5,000 subject to income tax.

Second year of trading

Tax year 2014/15 (6 April 2014 to 5 April 2015).
Assessed on the actual profits made for the full 12 months from 1 February 2014 – 31 January 2015—(the 'opening year basis') ie assessed on £30,000.

Third year of trading

Tax year 2015/16 (6 April 2015 to 5 April 2016).
Assessed on the actual profits made for the full 12 months from 1 February 2015 – 31 January 2016.

So for the period 1 February to 5 April 2014 the business will be assessed to tax twice; once in the tax year 2013/14 and again in the tax year 2014/15. Therefore, when the business ceases to trade it will be entitled to deduct £5,000 from the trading profits made in the final year of assessment—this is 'overlap relief'.

10.10   A change in the membership of a partnership

A new partner joining an existing partnership, where at least one partner is continuing as a partner, will be assessed to income tax as if this was a new business. This basis of assessment does not apply to continuing partners.

10.10.1   New partners joining the existing partnership

A new partner joining an existing partnership will be subject to the opening year rules—see **10.8.1** for details. The new partner will be assessed to income tax from the date when he/she entered the partnership until the end of the tax year.

As with other partners, the partnership profits allocated to the new partner will be on the basis of the division of profits contained in the partnership agreement.

EXAMPLE 9

James and Mandy Ashton are the two partners in The Calico Curtain Partnership. They make up their accounts to 31 December each year and agreed a profit sharing ratio of 50:50.

The partners decided to make their designer, Josh Mason, a partner from 1 January 2018 and they will then share the profits between the three partners on an equal basis.

The partnership profits are:

Year ending	Profits £
31 December 2017	10,000
31 December 2018	15,000
31 December 2019	30,000
31 December 2020	40,000

Tax year 2017/18 (6 April 2017 to 5 April 2018)

James and Mandy will be assessed on the profits of £10,000 from 1 January 2017 to 31 December 2017:
- James will receive 50 per cent of the profits (ie £5,000)
- Mandy will receive 50 per cent of the profits (ie £5,000)

Josh will be assessed to tax on the profits from 1 January 2018 (his date of admission to the partnership) to 5 April 2018:

Profits for the first 3 months (January to March) are £15,000 x 3/12 = £3,750.

Josh will be assessed on 1/3rd of these profits (ie £3,750 x 1/3 = £1,250).

Tax year 2018/19

The partners will be assessed on the profits of £15,000 from 1 January 2018 to 31 December 2018:
- James will receive 1/3rd of the profits (ie £5,000)
- Mandy will receive 1/3rd of the profits (ie £5,000)

Josh will be assessed on the full 12-month trading period and will receive 1/3rd share of the total profits for that year (ie £5,000).

Tax year 2019/20

The partners will be assessed on the profits of £30,000 from 1 January 2019 to 31 December 2019:
- James will receive 1/3rd of the profits (ie £10,000)
- Mandy will receive 1/3rd of the profits (ie £10,000)
- Josh will receive 1/3rd of the profits (ie £10,000)

10.10.2   When a partner leaves the partnership

A partner leaving the partnership for any reason, such as retirement, expulsion, or death, is assessed to income tax in the tax year in which he/she leaves on the basis of the closing year rules. The partner leaving will be assessed on the profits from the day after the last basis period to the date they leave the partnership on the same basis as if the partnership had just stopped trading.

A partner leaving the partnership for any reason, whether it be due to retirement, expulsion, or death, is assessed to income tax in the tax year in which they leave on the basis of the closing year rules. The partner leaving will be assessed on the profits from the day after the last basis period to the date they leave the partnership on the same basis as if they had just stopped trading.

The division of profits will remain in the usual profit sharing ratios.

EXAMPLE 10

The Mediterranean Herbs Partnership has four partners: Sharma, Aled, Fiona, and Donal. The partners share the profits on an equal basis of ¼ each. The end of the partnership accounting year is 31 December.

Sharma died on 30 June 2017 (during the 2017/18 tax year). After her death the remaining three partners agreed to share the partnership profits equally.

Year ended	Profits (£)
31 December 2016	40,000
31 December 2017	48,000

Sharma will be assessed to tax on the following basis:

Tax year 2016/17

The profits of £40,000 are shared equally between the four partners.

Sharma will be assessed on her ¼ share of the profits (ie on £10,000).

Tax year 2017/18

Sharma will be assessed to tax on the profits from 1 January 2017 to 30 June 2017 (the date of death).

If Sharma was still alive she would have been entitled to receive ¼ share of the £48,000 profits (ie £12,000). Sharma's estate will receive 6/12 of her share calculated from 1 January 2017 to 30 June 2017 (ie 6/12 × £12,000 = £6,000).

She will receive the benefit of any overlap relief she was entitled to from the opening years of the partnership.

10.11 Division of profits and losses between partners

The profits and losses are divided between the partners according to the profit sharing ratio; it is on this income allocation that the partners will pay their tax bill for that year.

10.12 Terminal loss relief

Where a business suffers a loss in the final 12 months of trading, this loss can be utilised against the profits of the same trade for the previous three years prior to cessation of trading. The loss has to be set against earlier years first before it can be carried forward and set against later years (s 89 ITA 2007).

Under s 89 there is no relief against non-trading income or capital gains, or indeed any income other than the trade which produced the loss.

The business must claim the relief within four years of the end of the tax year in which the loss arose.

EXAMPLE 11

A partnership which has been operating for ten years has an annual accounting period ending 31 October. The business ceases trading on 30 June 2017. The accounts for the last two years of trading are as follows:

1 November 2015 – 31 October 2016: a trading profit of £10,000
1 November 2016 – 30 June 2017 (eight months): a trading loss of £7,000

The trading loss of £7,000 incurred in 2017 can be set against the trading profit of £10,000 in the final accounting period.

10.13 Start-up loss relief

Under ITA 2007 s 72, any losses incurred in the first four years of a new business can be carried back and used against the income of the taxpayer, for the three years prior to the tax year in which the loss was made. Income from earlier years should be used first.

These losses can only be set against a taxpayer's income and not against any capital gains the taxpayer may have.

10.14 Carry forward relief on incorporation of a business

When a sole proprietor or partner transfers the business to a company and receives an allotment of shares in the company for the sale of that business, the individual can set off any unused trading losses against income (by way of salary or dividend payments on the shares) received from the company for any year in which they own those shares (ITA 2007, s 86).

10.15 Conclusion: checkpoints

You should now be able to:

- Understand the income tax liability of sole traders and partners;
- Apply the rules relating to trading losses;
- Apply capital allowances correctly;
- Understand the opening/closing year rules;
- Appreciate when overlap relief is available;
- Understand the tax consequences of a change in membership in a partnership;
- Apply the loss relief rules.

online resource centre   Visit the Online Resource Centre for more information and useful weblinks.
www.oxfordtextbooks.co.uk/orc/foundations17_18/

Taxation of trusts and settlements

11.1 Introduction and background

11.1.1 Introduction

This chapter is an introduction to the taxation regimes of the main types of trusts and settlements.

Each of the three main taxes is considered separately:

- inheritance tax;
- capital gains tax; and
- income tax.

11.1.2 Background

Settlements may be created by settlors in their lifetime, or by will, or they may arise under the intestacy rules. It is our purpose here to consider the tax implications of such settlements from the viewpoint of both the trustees and the beneficiaries.

Each tax must initially be considered separately as, although the Finance Act 2006 gives a common definition of 'settled property', 'settlement', and 'settlor' for capital gains tax and income tax, there is no overall integrated approach to the taxation of trusts.

There is some consistency in the method of taxing the trust. However, as mentioned at **11.5**, you may find it a useful exercise, to aid your understanding, to draw up and complete a grid detailing the different types of trust and the taxation treatment they are subject to.

Examples of the main types of trust include:

(a) Those which can be created both during the settlor's lifetime or on death:

- Discretionary trust. This is a trust where no beneficiary has the immediate right to receive any income (etc) from the property: for example, where the settlor settles the property on trust for a class of beneficiaries and gives the trustees the discretion as to which of the beneficiaries, if any, receives any of the income from the trust property, or any of the capital.

- Interest in possession trust. Here a beneficiary has the immediate right to the income from, or the use or enjoyment of, the property: for example, David, in his will, leaves his residuary estate to his wife, Susan, for life, and on her death to his children equally. On David's death Susan has an interest in possession in the residuary estate.

- Contingent interest trust. Under such a trust the beneficiary does not have the immediate right to receive any income (etc) from the property. The beneficiary has the right when the contingency is fulfilled: for example, during his lifetime, Gordon settles £250,000 on trust for such of his grandchildren, alive at the date of the settlement, who attain the age of 18 years and if more than one then in equal shares. If at the time the settlement is created Gordon's grandchildren are seven, nine, and 11 none of them will have the immediate right to receive the income from the property. Once the eldest reaches 18 then that grandchild will have the right to receive the income from a one-third share of the property.

(b) Those created only on death, either in the settlor's will or on intestacy:

- Trusts for bereaved minors;
- Trusts for bereaved young persons;
- Trusts with an immediate post-death interest.

These types of trust were created by the amendments made to the Inheritance Tax Act 1984 by the Finance Act 2006. The trusts are described in more detail at **11.2.3.2**. They enjoy a more favourable, or different, taxation for inheritance tax ('IHT') purposes than other types of trust.

11.2   Inheritance tax

On 22 March 2006 the Chancellor announced major changes to the inheritance tax regime for trusts and settlements. These changes were embodied in the Finance Act 2006. As a result of the changes it is useful to distinguish between those trusts and settlements created during the settlor's lifetime and those created on death, either under a will or on an intestacy.

It is not the place of this chapter to reflect the inheritance taxation treatment before 22 March 2006, merely to record the position as it now stands.

Statutory references in this section are to the Inheritance Tax Act 1984 ('IHTA') (as amended) unless otherwise indicated.

11.2.1   Definition of 'settlement'

For the purposes of inheritance tax, the term 'settlement' is defined by s 43(2). It includes a disposition whereby property is for the time being:

(a) held in trust for persons in succession (eg 'to Lesley for life, remainder to Rosalind');

(b) held for a person subject to a contingency (eg 'to Charles provided he attains the age of 25');

(c) held on trust to accumulate the whole or part of the income, or to make payments from income at the discretion of the trustees or some other person;

(d) charged or burdened with the payment of an annuity.

There is no settlement for inheritance tax purposes where property is held behind a trust for sale as beneficial joint tenants or tenants in common, nor where it is held in a bare trust.

Where chargeable events occur, the primary liability for the payment of the tax lies with the trustees—the burden falling upon the trust property. In appropriate cases, the instalment option will be available if the charge arises on a death or, in other situations, if qualifying property remains settled.

11.2.2   Creation of a settlement

When a settlement is created it constitutes a transfer of value by the settlor and its chargeability will be determined in the normal way. As mentioned at **11.2**, it is useful to distinguish between those trusts and settlements created during the settlor's lifetime and those created on death, either under a will or on an intestacy. For the purposes of considering the taxation of the various types of trust and settlements for inheritance tax purposes this chapter considers the various types under those two headings.

11.2.2.1   Created during the settlor's lifetime

See **11.1.2** for examples of the types of trust and settlements that can be created during the settlor's lifetime.

A transfer into one of these constitutes a transfer of value by the settlor and, unless covered by an exemption, it is a lifetime chargeable transfer ('LCT').

As we saw (in **7.3** and **7.6**) the *inter vivos* creation of a settlement is an LCT, chargeable at half the rate(s) which would have applied on a death at that time, with the possibility of a supplementary charge should the settlor then die within seven years. Grossing up will apply on creation, unless the settled fund pays the tax. There are special rules which apply where a settlor creates 'related settlements' (basically, several settlements on the same day) and where property is subsequently added to the settlement.

11.2.2.2   Created on death

See **11.1.2** for examples of the types of trust and settlements that can be created on death, either under the deceased's will, or on intestacy.

Whether the trust is created by the settlor's will or the operation of the intestacy rules the property involved is part of the transfer deemed to take place on death and so chargeable (unless, again, covered by an exemption).

11.2.3   Liability of the trustees during the continuance of the trust

11.2.3.1   Created during the settlor's lifetime

For the purposes of this chapter, all trusts and settlements created during a settlor's lifetime are subject to the same inheritance tax treatment. The exception, being gifts into a disabled trust, is beyond the scope of this chapter.

Property in the trust is defined in s 58 of IHTA 1984 as 'relevant property', and so the phrase 'relevant property regime' has been coined to describe the regime applied.

Under the relevant property regime the property in the trust or settlement is subject to two categories of chargeable events:

(a) The periodic charge. This is imposed at ten-yearly intervals, the first occasion of the charge normally being the tenth anniversary of the creation of the trust. Basically, the charge is upon the value of 'relevant property' in the settlement at the time.

(b) The exit charge. This is imposed when capital 'leaves' the settlement during the first ten years or between periodic charges (eg because the trustees exercise a discretion to distribute capital; or a beneficiary fulfils a contingency and becomes absolutely entitled; or the trustees appoint out capital in the fund to a beneficiary). The value to be charged is the value leaving the settlement. However, no exit charge will apply where the capital leaves the settlement within three months of the creation of the trust or of a periodic charge (s 65), or if it does so within two years of the creation of the settlement where this happened on death (s 144).

11.2.3.1.1   Rates of tax and cumulation

The periodic charge is levied at 30 per cent of the lifetime rate of inheritance tax—that is, at a maximum rate of 6 per cent (30 per cent of 20 per cent). The exit charge is levied at a proportion of the charge which would have been levied on a periodic charge had it occurred at the time—the precise method of calculation depending upon whether the exit charge arises before the trust's first ten-year anniversary or subsequently.

In all cases, in calculating the tax payable the settlor's cumulative total of chargeable lifetime transfers in the seven years prior to the creation of the settlement is the starting point of the settlement's cumulative total. This is so however long the settlement has been in existence.

11.2.3.2   Created on death

Again, generally, trusts created on the death of the settlor are subject to taxation under the relevant property regime. See **11.2.3.1**.

However, the following trusts are not subject to the relevant property regime, but are taxed in a more favourable, or different, way. They are considered separately.

11.2.3.2.1   Trusts for bereaved minors

This type of trust is excluded from the relevant property regime provided various conditions are met. These are set out in s 71A of the IHTA 1984, inserted by the Finance Act 2006. A bereaved minor is defined as a minor of whom at least one parent has died. The conditions are that:

(a) the trust must be created by the will of a deceased parent of the bereaved minor, arise on intestacy, or be established under the Criminal Injuries Compensation Scheme;

(b) the beneficiary will, on attaining the age of 18 years, or before, become absolutely entitled to the settled property and the income arising from it; and

(c) whilst the beneficiary is alive and under 18 any income from the trust is applied for the benefit of the bereaved minor.

Provided these conditions are met, then, when the settled property vests in the beneficiary on attaining the age of 18, or earlier, no exit charge applies. In addition, no matter how long the period between the commencement of the trust and the date the beneficiary attains a vested interest, no periodic charges shall apply (IHTA 1984, ss 71A–C, as amended).

11.2.3.2.2   Trusts for bereaved young persons/Age 18 to 25 trusts

This type of trust is covered by ss 71D–F of the IHTA 1984, as amended. A trust to which s 71D of the IHTA 1984, as amended, applies falls under a 'light touch' relevant property regime. Provided the conditions of the section are met then no periodic charges apply and the basis for the exit charge when the beneficiary attains a vested interest is limited. The conditions are that:

(a) the beneficiary has not attained the age of 25 years;

(b) at least one parent of the beneficiary has died; and

(c) the trust is established under the will of a deceased parent or the Criminal Injuries Compensation Scheme.

In fact, if the beneficiary attains an absolute interest on or before attaining 18 then there is no exit charge. If the beneficiary attains the absolute interest after 18 but no later than his/her 25th birthday then the period over which the exit charge is calculated is limited to the period commencing on the beneficiary's 18th birthday, ceasing on the date the beneficiary is entitled to an absolute interest, which will be on or before reaching 25 years.

There is also no exit charge should the beneficiary die before attaining an absolute interest or on any advancements made before attaining an absolute interest.

11.2.3.2.3   Trusts with an immediate post-death interest

Where, under a will or on intestacy, a beneficial entitlement in the trust property arises on the death of the settlor (and where s 71A does not apply and it is not a disabled person's trust) s 49A of the IHTA 1984, inserted by the Finance Act 2006, provides that the charging basis set out in s 49 applies. The trust will not be taxed under the relevant property regime. The charging basis is set out at **11.2.3.2.4**. This type of trust is an interest in possession trust, but when the beneficial entitlement arises on the death of the transferor it is taxed in a different way for IHT purposes.

11.2.3.2.4   Charging basis (s 49)

A beneficiary who has an immediate post-death interest is treated as if beneficially entitled to the property in which that interest subsists. In other words, if under a trust created by Toby's will, Laurence is the life tenant entitled to the income from a trust fund whose capital is valued at £500,000, that capital value is treated as part of Laurence's estate for tax purposes. If he were entitled to half of the income from the fund then £250,000 would be deemed to be part of his estate.

11.2.3.2.5 *Chargeable events for the s 49 charging basis of trusts with an immediate post-death interest*
Chargeable events occur whenever, and to the extent that, the interest in possession termi-nates—since this will (effectively) be treated as a disposition of the property by the person with the interest in possession. The chargeable events will be:

(a) Death of the life tenant—a chargeable event
Thus, the deemed transfer on the death of the life tenant includes the trust property. The trustees are primarily liable for the tax attributable to this part of the estate, and the burden of that tax will fall upon the trust property. However, the tax payable on both the unsettled and settled estate will be affected by the need to cumulate both with any chargeable lifetime transfers made by the life tenant in the seven years prior to the death to fix the rate(s) of tax payable.

(b) Termination during the lifetime of the life tenant—chargeable events
The termination may occur during the lifetime of the life tenant—for example, on the sale, gift, or surrender of the life interest, or the consent by the life tenant to the advancement of the remainderman. Normally, unless exempt, such lifetime terminations will be treated as potentially exempt transfers ('PETs') made by the life tenant and thus only actually charge-able to tax if the life tenant dies within the next seven years.

Notice that a tax charge may arise on a sale of the life tenant's interest. A transfer of value will occur even if the sale has been for the full market value of the life tenant's interest—because the life tenant has been treated as 'owning' the property, whereas the value of the life interest will be determined on an actuarial basis.

EXAMPLE 1

Lisa is the life tenant of a fund of £100,000 and she sells her life interest to Penelope for £25,000 (its full actuarial value). There will be a transfer of value (normally a PET) of the amount by which her estate goes down in value—£75,000. This demonstrates the fact that inheritance tax is not merely a tax on gifts or transactions at an undervalue.

(c) Termination during the lifetime of the life tenant—no chargeable event
If on the termination of the interest in possession the life tenant becomes absolutely entitled to the settled property, no charge will arise. This is because the value of the life tenant's estate does not change, and so there can be no transfer of value. Thus suppose that trustees advance £10,000 from capital to the life tenant under a power given to them by the trust instrument (this would not, of course, be possible under the general law). Prior to the advancement, this sum would have been deemed to be part of the life tenant's estate; it is now the life tenant's absolutely.

Again, no charge will arise on a partition of the settled property to the extent of the prop-erty taken by the life tenant under the arrangement.

EXAMPLE 2

Lucas is the life tenant and Roger the remainderman of a settled fund worth £500,000, and they agree to break the settlement on terms that Lucas will take £100,000 absolutely and Roger the remaining £400,000. The amount taken by Lucas does not affect the value of his estate; however, there is a transfer of value (normally a PET) by Lucas of the amount taken by Roger.

However, if the life tenant purchases a reversionary interest, special rules apply to prevent avoidance of tax.

EXAMPLE 3

Lois is the life tenant under a settlement of £500,000. Ronald is the remainderman, and Lois agrees to purchase his reversion for its full actuarial value of (say) £100,000. Her estate both before and after the transaction includes the value of the settled property, but the estate of Lois has now been depleted by the £100,000 paid to Ronald. She has, in effect, bought something which was already regarded as hers for tax purposes and reduced the value of her estate in the process. By s 55 she is prevented from gaining any tax advantage from such a deal: she will be deemed under this provision to have made a transfer of value (normally a PET) of the amount paid to Ronald.

11.2.3.3   Charitable and similar trusts

Trusts for charitable and similar purposes and those for the benefit of mentally disabled persons and those in receipt of an attendance allowance are not subject to the rules described at **11.2.3.1** and **11.2.3.2**. Nor are pension fund trusts (s 151), employee trusts (s 86), or protective trusts even after forfeiture (ss 73 and 88).

11.2.3.4   Survivorship clauses

These are commonly included in wills for a variety of tax and succession reasons. A standard provision of this kind is: 'To Benedict provided he survives me for 28 days but if he fails to do so then to Clarissa'.

Because Benedict's interest is contingent, a settlement with no interest in possession arises on the death of the testator. At the end of the survivorship period (or on Benedict's earlier death) this will come to an end because Benedict (or Clarissa should Benedict fail to survive) becomes absolutely entitled to the property. In principle, therefore, an exit charge should then arise. However, provided the survivorship period does not exceed six months, this will not happen (s 92).

11.3   Capital gains tax

Statutory references in this section are to the Taxation of Chargeable Gains Act 1992 (as amended) unless otherwise stated.

11.3.1   The basic position

As we shall see, the creation of a settlement is a disposal for the purposes of the tax. Thereafter, so long as the property remains within the definition of 'settled property'—with the possibility of an 'exit charge' when it ceases to do so—it is subject to a special charging regime. Disposals (actual or notional) by the trustees of the trust property may trigger a charge to tax; disposals by the beneficiaries of their beneficial interests generally do not.

11.3.2   Definition of 'settled property'

'Settled property', is defined (s 68) as 'any property held in trust' except in those situations excepted from the definition by s 60. This excludes from the definition property held by a person:

(a) as nominee for another person; or

(b) as trustee for another person who is absolutely entitled as against the trustee (ie someone who has the exclusive right—subject only to the payment of trust expenses—to direct how the property should be dealt with). Such a situation (sometimes called a 'bare trust') might arise where a remainderman has become absolutely entitled on the death of the life tenant, or a beneficiary has fulfilled a contingency; or

(c) as trustee for any person who would be absolutely entitled as against the trustees but for infancy or other disability. This must be the only reason why the person concerned is not able to call immediately for the property to be 'handed over'—that is, that person's interest must be vested. If a contingency (eg attaining 18) still has to be fulfilled, the property remains settled property.

Where one of the three exceptions applies, the trust property is for tax purposes dealt with as if it were vested in the beneficiary concerned, and acts of the nominee or trustee are treated as those of the beneficiary.

If two or more persons hold property as joint tenants or tenants in common, the property is not 'settled property' for the purposes of capital gains tax provided they are together absolutely entitled to the property.

11.3.3 Settlor's liability

This will depend upon whether the settlement is created in the lifetime or on death.

11.3.3.1 Lifetime settlement

Whenever property is transferred to trustees, there is a disposal for capital gains tax purposes by the settlor to the trustees. This is so whether the settlement is revocable or irrevocable, and even if the settlor (or the settlor's spouse or civil partner) is a trustee (even the sole trustee) or a beneficiary.

The disposal (and corresponding acquisition by the trustees) is at the then market value of the property concerned. Any gain or loss will essentially be computed in the ordinary way. However, as the settlor and the trustees are connected persons (s 18(3)) any loss can only be relieved by setting it against gains made on subsequent disposal(s) to the trustees. If hold-over relief is available (either because the assets are put into the trust by a transfer which is an LCT for inheritance tax purposes (s 260) or are business assets (s 165)), it may be claimed by the election of the settlor alone.

11.3.3.2 Settlement created on death

Here, there will be no disposal (in line with the general scheme of the Act that death is not a chargeable event for capital gains tax purposes). The deceased's personal representatives will be deemed to acquire the assets concerned at their market value at the date of death, and this will also be the value at which the trustees will be deemed to have acquired them.

11.3.4 Liability of trustees

As in the case of income tax, trustees are a single and continuing body for tax purposes; thus a change of trustees is not a chargeable event for capital gains tax ('CGT') purposes. For the tax year 2017/18 the main rate of CGT that trustees pay is 20 per cent. However, as is the situation with individual taxpayers, any gains on residential property not being a main residence (**11.3.4.1 (b)**) are subject to tax at 28 per cent.

11.3.4.1 Actual disposals

Where the trustees sell trust assets, any chargeable gain or allowable loss is calculated in the normal way. The exemptions and reliefs to which they may be entitled include:

(a) *Annual exempt amount* (s 3 and Sch 1). This is available normally at half the rate to which an individual is entitled in the year in question (for the tax year 2017/18 it is £5,650). However, where the same settlor has created more than one settlement, the available exempt amount is divided equally between them—subject to the proviso that each trust is entitled to a minimum exemption of 10 per cent of the exemption available to individuals (for the tax year 2017/18, therefore, £1,130).

(b) *Private residence relief* (s 225). Trustees may claim this exemption on the disposal of a property which has been the only or main residence of a person entitled to occupy it under the terms of the settlement.

(c) *Roll-over relief* (s 152). This will be available only if the trustees are carrying on an unincorporated business.

Where trustees incur a loss on the disposal, it can be relieved against any gains which they have in the same tax year, with any surplus being carried forward to future years.

11.3.4.2   Notional disposals (s 71)

When someone becomes absolutely entitled to (any part of) the trust property as against the trustees (or would become so entitled but for infancy or other disability) such property (or part) ceases to be 'settled property'. This may occur, for example: where the trustees exercise a power of advancement—though not where cash is advanced, since sterling is an exempt asset for tax purposes; when a beneficiary obtains a vested interest on fulfilling a contingency; where the remainderman becomes absolutely entitled on the *inter vivos* termination of a life interest (eg on the surrender of the life tenant's interest).

On the happening of any such event, the trustees are deemed to dispose of the property concerned and immediately reacquire it (as nominee of the beneficiary) at its then market value. Any chargeable gain or allowable loss is calculated in (essentially) the ordinary way. Hold-over relief may be claimed in appropriate circumstances on a joint election by the trustees and the beneficiary.

If the trustees incur an allowable loss for which they are unable to obtain relief, the loss may effectively be transferred to the beneficiary who becomes absolutely entitled.

Where the event causing the property to cease to be 'settled property' is the death of the life tenant, there is no chargeable disposal; but (as is generally the case for capital gains tax purposes on death) there is nonetheless a deemed disposal and reacquisition by the trustees at the then market value of the property (s 73). The effect is that the remainderman acquires the property at this value. However, tax must now be paid on any gain held over when the property was put into the settlement.

If on the death of the life tenant the property remains settled property (eg because another life tenant becomes entitled, or because a remainderman is only contingently entitled), the position is governed by s 72. There is again no chargeable disposal, but there is a deemed disposal and reacquisition of the property by the trustees which will form the basis of any future charge. However, tax will again be payable on any gain held over when the property was put into the settlement.

11.3.5   The beneficiaries

The tax position of the beneficiaries will depend upon whether or not the trust property is within the definition of 'settled property'.

11.3.5.1   Settled property (s 76)

On the disposal by a beneficiary of the beneficial interest there is no chargeable event—unless that beneficial interest was acquired by the beneficiary or a predecessor in title for consideration in money or money's worth (other than consideration consisting of another interest under the settlement).

11.3.5.2   Bare trust

If the property has ceased to be 'settled property', the beneficiary is effectively treated as already the 'owner' of the property. The result is that any subsequent disposals by the trustees are treated and taxed as if made by the beneficiary.

11.4   Income tax

11.4.1   The basic position

As we will see, income arising under a trust will normally suffer tax in the hands of the trustees in a manner not dissimilar (in general terms) to that applicable to personal representatives. Beneficiaries under the trust may have to include trust income in their tax returns, thus perhaps (according to their circumstances) enabling them to make a repayment claim or causing them to be liable to higher rate tax.

However, in relation to certain *inter vivos* trusts there are anti-avoidance provisions which effectively require the income from the settlement still to be taxed as part of the settlor's income. These provisions affect (broadly) the following categories of settlement, a term which is for these purposes very widely defined:

(a) where the settlor has made a settlement under which the settlor's minor children benefit;

(b) where the settlor or the settlor's spouse or civil partner has retained an interest in the settlement, whether or not actual benefits are received by them;

(c) where the settlor, the settlor's spouse or civil partner, or minor child has received a capital payment or benefit from the settlement.

These provisions, which do not apply to trusts arising on death, are complex and are not further discussed in this book.

11.4.2   Liability of trustees

11.4.2.1   Generally

Trustees (who are for tax purposes a single and continuing body) are liable to income tax at the basic rate (tax year 2017/18 20 per cent) on all of the income arising to the trust (other than dividends where the rate is 7.5 per cent), without any deduction for any trust expenses. Their statutory income is calculated in essentially the same way as that of individual taxpayers; they cannot, however, claim personal reliefs—but are not liable to higher rate tax.

11.4.2.2   Dividend trust rate and trust rate

For the tax year 2017/18 this is 38.1 per cent for dividend income and 45 per cent on other income and is payable on all income which (under Trustee Act 1925, s 31 or the trust instrument) is to be accumulated, or is payable at the discretion of the trustees or some other person—and (in either case) is not to be treated (before distribution) as the income of either the settlor (see **11.4.1**) or a beneficiary.

In practice, the liability to pay tax at this special rate applies to most cases where there is a settlement without an interest in possession.

The special rate is in effect only levied on the amount of trust income actually available for accumulation or for the exercise of the discretion, since the trustees are able to deduct expenses 'properly' chargeable to income under the general law (whatever the trust instrument may actually provide). Such expenses must, however, be claimed against dividends in priority to other income.

The trust rate is not applied to all income.

The first £1,000 of income received net of tax or with a tax credit will be liable at only the basic rate depending on the type of income (7.5 per cent for dividends, 20 per cent for other income). This first £1,000 is termed the standard rate band.

Any income in excess of the £1,000 is taxed at the dividend trust rate and trust rate (38.1 per cent for dividend income and 45 per cent on other income).

Where any of the net income of the trust is paid to, or applied for the benefit of, a beneficiary, the trustees must provide a tax deduction certificate for the tax paid by them.

11.4.3   Beneficiaries with a right to trust income

In cases where beneficiaries have a vested interest in the income of the trust it will be taxed as part of their income when it arises, whether it is accumulated, applied for their benefit, or distributed to them.

A beneficiary who has a vested interest in the capital will (unless the trust instrument otherwise provides) normally also have a vested interest in the income—even if under 18. A beneficiary whose right to capital is contingent on attaining an age greater than 18 will (unless Trustee Act 1925, s 31 has been excluded or modified by the trust instrument) effectively receive a vested interest in the income at 18. From that age until either the capital vests or the interest fails (eg because the beneficiary dies before fulfilling the contingency), the trustees (under s 31) must pay the income to the beneficiary. It must be returned, therefore, as part of the beneficiary's statutory income.

Where beneficiaries have vested interests, it is their share of the income (after trustees' expenses have been met) grossed up at basic rate which must be included in their returns. They have tax credits for the tax paid by the trustees.

Capital payments by the trustees will, in principle, not be liable to income tax. However, where the beneficiary is entitled to have income augmented from capital such 'topping-up' payments will be taxed in the hands of the beneficiary—*Brodie's Will Trustees v IRC* (1933) 17 TC 432; *Cunard's Trustees v IRC* [1946] 1 All ER 159.

11.4.4   Beneficiaries with no right to trust income

This situation arises where the beneficiary's entitlement to the income depends upon the fulfilment of a contingency, or the exercise of a discretion in the beneficiary's favour.

In these cases, the trust income will be taxed at the trust rate, in the hands of the trustees as it arises (**11.4.2.2**). If such income is simply accumulated, it is not taxable as part of the beneficiary's income; and the accumulations, when finally paid over to the beneficiary, are effectively capital and therefore not then liable to income tax. However, if any of the income is advanced to, or applied for the benefit of, the beneficiary the amounts so paid or applied (grossed up at the rate paid by the trustees) are then treated as part of the beneficiary's income for tax purposes—with the benefit of a tax credit for the total tax effectively already paid by the trustees.

11.5   Conclusion: checkpoints

You should now be able to explain to a client:

- inheritance tax;
- capital gains tax; and
- income tax;

and treatment of the following types of trusts and settlements:

- discretionary;
- interest in possession;
- bereaved minors;
- bereaved young persons;
- immediate post-death interest; and
- bare.

You may find it useful to draw up and complete a grid, as shown **Table 11.1**, with the taxation treatment of the various trusts as a useful exercise and revision tool.

Table 11.1 **Taxation of various trusts**

	Discretionary	Interest in possession	Bereaved minors	Bereaved young persons	Immediate post-death interest	Bare
Inheritance tax—settlor	11.2.2.1/ 11.2.2.2	11.2.2.1/ 11.2.2.2	11.2.3.2.1	11.2.3.2.2	11.2.3.2.3	11.3.2
Inheritance tax—during life of trust	11.2.3.1/ 11.2.3.2	11.2.3.1/ 11.2.3.2	11.2.3.2	11.2.3.2	11.2.3.2	11.2.3
Capital gains tax—settlor	11.3.3	11.3.3	11.3.3	11.3.3	11.3.3	11.3.3
Capital gains tax—during life of trust	11.3.4	11.3.4	11.3.4	11.3.4	11.3.4	11.3.5.2
Income tax—during life of trust	11.4.4	11.4.3	11.4.4	11.4.4	11.4.3	11.4.3

online resource centre

Visit the Online Resource Centre for more information and useful weblinks.
www.oxfordtextbooks.co.uk/orc/foundations17_18/

Part 3

Wills and administration of estates

12 Introduction to wills and administration of estates   173
13 Entitlement to the estate   174
14 Application for a grant of representation   209
15 Post-grant practice   249

Introduction to wills and administration of estates

12.1 Introduction

The aim of this part of the book is to provide you with a basis for understanding the practice and procedure of obtaining a grant of representation and the administration of an estate.

When someone dies, their relatives or friends will usually have dealt with the most pressing matters—registering the death and arranging the funeral—before consulting a solicitor. In simple cases, or where the deceased has left little property, it may well be that a solicitor is not consulted at all. Commonly, however, the advice of a solicitor will be sought as to who is entitled to the deceased's property, as to the liability of the estate to tax, and generally as to 'what has to be done' in order to pass the deceased's property to those now entitled to it.

12.2 Breakdown of the task

- *Chapter 13 Entitlement to the estate:* to a large extent, who is entitled to the deceased's property will depend upon whether or not there is a valid will (**13.2**). To the extent that there is not, the intestacy rules apply (**13.10**). Some property, however, passes independently of the will or the operation of the intestacy rules (**13.18**). Sometimes, relatives or dependants may be able to make a claim for provision to be made for them which if successful would have the effect of 'varying' the dispositions made in the deceased's will or taking effect under the intestacy rules (**13.23**).

- *Chapter 14 Application for a grant of representation:* we begin this chapter with a consideration of the nature and effect of grants of representation (**14.2**) and a summary of the practice involved in obtaining a grant (**14.12**). This chapter ends with a more detailed consideration of the court's requirements (**14.19**) followed by those of HMRC (**14.26**).

- *Chapter 15 Post-grant practice:* the duties and powers of personal representatives are considered first (**15.2**). The administration of the estate begins in earnest with the collection/realisation of the assets, following which the debts and other liabilities must be discharged (**15.6**). The final steps involve the distribution of the estate to those entitled (**15.14**).

online resource centre

Visit the Online Resource Centre for more information and useful weblinks.
www.oxfordtextbooks.co.uk/orc/foundations17_18/

Entitlement to the estate

13.1 Basic structure of entitlement to the estate

In this chapter, we will be discussing the law underlying the entitlement to a person's property on his or her death. To do this, we shall need to consider aspects of:

- the law of 'testate succession' where the deceased has left a will (**13.2** to **13.9**);
- the law of 'intestate succession' if there is no will, or if any will left by the deceased is not wholly effective to dispose of their estate (**13.10** to **13.17**);
- the law governing devolution of property not passing under the terms of the deceased's will or the operation of the intestacy rules (**13.18** to **13.22**); and
- the law enabling members of the family or dependants of the deceased to make claims for provision against the estate (**13.23** to **13.31**).

13.2 Wills

In the following paragraphs we are assuming that a person has died leaving a will. You may have been instructed by a relative or friend of the deceased who has been appointed as executor by the will, or your firm may have been appointed. The role of executors is, in effect, to manage the deceased's estate until it can be distributed to those entitled. Normally, these entitlements will be determined by the deceased's will, but this is subject to a number of important provisos, namely that:

(a) the will is valid (**13.3**), ie that the deceased (the testator) was both capable of and had the intention to make this will, and that it was properly executed. If the will is invalid it will be wholly ineffective, and the deceased's property will pass to those entitled under the intestacy rules (see **13.10** to **13.15**);

(b) the will has not been revoked (**13.4**). If so, again the deceased's property will pass to those entitled on intestacy;

(c) where the will has been altered, whether such alterations are effective (**13.5**);

(d) if the will refers to any other documents, whether these documents have been 'incorporated' and thus become part of the will (**13.6**);

(e) the will effectively deals with the whole of the deceased's estate capable of passing by will. Any such property that does not pass under the will, because, for example, the clause dealing with the residue of the deceased's estate fails (**13.7**), again passes under the intestacy rules;

(f) certain of the deceased's property may not have been capable of being disposed of by will, but will pass as of right to those entitled (**13.18** to **13.22**); and

(g) the will has not been varied after the testator's death. This may seem a surprising concept, but it is possible for the court to vary entitlements under a will if a successful claim is made under the Inheritance (Provision for Family and Dependants) Act 1975 (**13.23** to **13.30**). It is also possible for beneficiaries under a will (and those entitled under the intestacy rules) to vary their entitlements by consent, and indeed to reject outright gifts which would otherwise pass to them (**15.12**).

13.3 Validity of wills

13.3.1 Generally

English law will generally recognise a will as valid (Wills Act 1963) if it accords with the internal law of either:

(a) the country in which it was executed; or

(b) the country in which the deceased was domiciled or of which he was a national—either at the time of its execution or of the deceased's death.

So far as English domestic law is concerned, a valid will requires that the testator should have the *capacity* and *intention* to make the will, and compliance with the prescribed *formalities*.

13.3.2 Capacity

At the date of making the will, the testator must not (normally) have been under the age of 18 (being of age is, however, not a requirement if the testator was in a position to make a 'privileged' will as a soldier on actual military service or a seaman at sea). Additionally, the testator must have had the necessary mental capacity. The common law position has been somewhat altered by the Mental Capacity Act 2005.

13.3.2.1 The common law test

The traditional test for mental capacity to make a will was laid down in *Banks v Goodfellow* (1870) LR 5; (1870) QB 549. Testators must have understood three things:

(a) the nature of the act (ie the making of a will) and its effects;

(b) the extent of their property; and

(c) the claims to which they ought to give effect.

Generally, it had to be shown that the requisite understanding existed at the date of execution of the will. However, the rule in *Parker v Felgate* (1883) 8 PD 171 laid down an acceptable alternative where that could not be done. Under this rule, it was sufficient to show that:

(a) the requisite capacity existed at the date of giving instructions for the preparation of the will;

(b) the will was prepared in accordance with those instructions; and

(c) at the time of execution the testator understood that he was signing a will for which instructions had previously been given (though it is not necessary for the testator at that time to be able either to remember what those instructions were, or to understand the will if read over to him).

13.3.2.2 Position under the Mental Capacity Act 2005

The Mental Capacity Act 2005 was fully implemented in October 2007. The Act provides a new single test of capacity and reforms the law and procedures relating to decision-making on behalf of people who are unable to make decisions for themselves. A Code of Practice was issued in April 2007 giving further guidance on the Act.

Section 1 of the Act provides, among other things, for a statutory presumption of capacity, ie it is assumed that a person has capacity until the contrary is proved.

Section 2 sets out a single test of capacity, ie that a person lacks capacity in relation to a matter if at the material time he is unable to make a decision for himself in relation to the matter because of an impairment of, or a disturbance in the functioning of, the mind or brain.

Section 3 defines when a person is unable to make decision for the purposes of s 2—for example, that a person is unable to understand the information relevant to the decision.

How does the statutory test of capacity relate to the common law test of capacity to make a will as set out in *Banks v Goodfellow*? According to the Code of Practice, the Act's definition of capacity is in line with the common law tests and the Act does not replace them. Such post-2007 case law as we have also indicates that s 3 is largely a restatement of the *Banks v Goodfellow* test.

It also seems likely that the rule in *Parker v Felgate* has survived the Mental Capacity Act 2005.

13.3.2.3 Proof of capacity

At common law the onus of proving the existence of the necessary mental capacity lay with the person seeking to prove the will, ie to have it accepted by the court as valid. Two rebuttable presumptions were of assistance here, namely that capacity was assumed where the will appeared to be rational and that mental states continued.

As noted at **13.3.2.2**, under the Mental Capacity Act 2005, it is to be assumed that a person has capacity until the contrary is proved (s 1). The burden of proof is thus now on the person who challenges the will.

EXAMPLE 1

Ann, aged 80, made a will shortly before her death. She was known to be suffering from Alzheimer's disease. Ann's solicitor obtained her consent to consult her doctor who confirmed that Ann was only suffering from a mild form of the disease, and that there were times when Ann would have the necessary mental capacity to make a will. The doctor agreed to be present when the will was executed, and supplied the solicitor with a short note confirming that (at that time) Ann was capable of understanding the nature and effect of the will. The solicitor also kept an attendance note of the circumstances at the time of execution. If a person wished to challenge the will on the basis of Ann's lack of testamentary capacity, then the burden of proof would rest with them. In the light of the evidence gathered by Ann's solicitors, it looks unlikely that they would succeed.

13.3.2.4 Lack of capacity

Where capacity is not presumed or proven, the will cannot be admitted to probate.

For completeness, you should note that where a person lacks the necessary mental capacity to make a valid will for him or herself, the Court of Protection is able (under the provisions of s 16 of the Mental Capacity Act 2005) to make a 'statutory will' on behalf of that person.

13.3.3 Intention

13.3.3.1 The requirement

The testator must have had a general intention to make a will, and a specific intention to make the particular will. Put another way, the testator must know and approve the contents of the will. To the extent that such knowledge and approval are lacking, the will cannot be admitted to probate.

The necessary knowledge and approval must normally have existed at the date of the execution of the will: however, the rule in *Parker v Felgate* (**13.3.2.1**) also applies in this context.

13.3.3.2 Proof

The onus of proof lies on the propounder of the will. There is generally a rebuttable presumption that a testator with the necessary mental capacity executed the will with the requisite knowledge and approval of its contents. Those who seek to challenge the will would have to prove that the testator made the will (or perhaps a particular provision in it) as a result of force, fear, fraud, or undue influence; or that the necessary knowledge and approval were lacking because of a mistake.

There is no such presumption of knowledge and approval in two situations:

(a) if the testator is blind or illiterate, or someone has signed the will on the testator's behalf. As we will see (**13.3.4.2**) a suitably drafted attestation clause will assist in supplying the necessary evidence of knowledge and approval;

(b) if there are suspicious circumstances—in particular where the will substantially benefits the person who prepared it (or a close relative of that person). In such cases, evidence will be required of the testator's knowledge and approval of the contents of the will: otherwise, the gift will fail.

13.3.4   Formalities

13.3.4.1   Section 9 of the Wills Act 1837 (as substituted by s 17 of the Administration of Justice Act 1982)

This section provides that:
No will shall be valid unless—

(a) it is in writing, and signed by the testator, or by some other person in his presence and by his direction; and

(b) it appears that the testator intended by his signature to give effect to the will; and

(c) the signature is made or acknowledged by the testator in the presence of two or more witnesses present at the same time; and

(d) each witness either—

(i) attests and signs the will; or

(ii) acknowledges his signature in the presence of the testator (but not necessarily in the presence of any other witness), but no form of attestation shall be necessary.

The section does not apply to privileged wills, which can be made informally—even orally. Nor does it apply to statutory wills under the Mental Health Act 1983, for which that Act lays down special rules.

13.3.4.2   Attestation clause

Most wills will contain an attestation clause (it is to be hoped that all those professionally drawn will do so), although it is not a requirement for validity. If so, your task in proving the formal validity of the will is straightforward, as it will be presumed that the will has been executed in accordance with s 9 of the Wills Act 1837, ie there is a presumption of due execution.

There are a number of different forms of attestation clauses in common use, but all should show (as a minimum) compliance with the statutory requirements.

EXAMPLE 2

Hugh Jones has died. At the end of his typewritten will there is an attestation clause; the signatures are in ink.

SIGNED by Hugh Jones as his
last will in our joint presence   *Hugh Jones*
and then by us in his

Jean Fredericks
18, Westway, Barchester
Alan Price
2, The Grove, Barchester

Unless there is evidence to the contrary, the will is presumed to be formally valid.

Where the testator was blind or illiterate, or someone else signed on behalf of the testator, we saw (in **13.3.3.2**) that there is no presumption of knowledge and approval and that this will have to be established if the will is to be admitted to probate. The simplest way of doing this is by the inclusion of a special attestation clause showing that:

(a) the will was read over to the testator in the presence of the witnesses;

(b) the testator understood and approved the will;

(c) the testator then signed the will or it was signed by another in the testator's presence and at his direction; and

(d) the witnesses attested the will as before.

If the will does not include an attestation clause (or only an inadequate one) compliance with the requirements of s 9 will have to be proved. This will also be necessary if there is something on the face of the will, for example the testator's signature is not complete, to show that there were unusual circumstances at the time of execution. The 'mechanics' of how this is done are discussed at **14.24**, but it is convenient to consider later in this chapter the requirements of s 9 in greater detail.

13.3.4.3   In writing

A will may be typed or handwritten (in ink or pencil—though the use of both will raise a rebuttable presumption that the parts written in pencil are 'deliberative only' and they will only be admitted to probate if there is evidence that the testator intended them to be final). There is no restriction as to the material upon which a will may be written, nor as to the language used: it may even be written in code, provided there is evidence available enabling it to be deciphered.

13.3.4.4   Signature

The testator's usual signature is ideal, but any mark (eg a thumbprint or rubber stamp) made by the testator and intended to be a signature will suffice. One of the leading cases on this point is *In the Goods of Chalcraft* [1948] P 222; [1948] 1 All ER 700, where a dying testatrix managed to sign 'E. Chal' but was unable to complete her full signature. It was held that this was sufficient; the testatrix intended what she had written (as much as she could manage in the circumstances) to be her signature. In another case, *In the Estate of Cook* [1960] 1 WLR 353; [1960] 1 All ER 689, the will began with the name of the testatrix and ended with the words 'Your loving mother'. The court accepted that the testatrix intended this to be her signature.

However, testators do not need to sign their own wills; the Act allows signature by another—at the testator's direction and in the testator's presence. The person so signing (who may be one of the witnesses) may sign their own name or that of the testator.

Barrett v Bem [2012] EWCA Civ 52 is the first case to rule on what it means for the will to be 'signed at the testator's direction'. After eight years of litigation the Court of Appeal decided that a deathbed will signed by the dying man's sister (the sole beneficiary under the will) at his direction was invalid. Lewinson LJ (delivering the judgment of the court) said that a court should not find that a will had been signed at the testator's direction 'unless there is positive and discernible communication (which may be verbal or non-verbal) by the testator that he wished the will to be signed on his behalf by the third party'. In the court's judgment the evidence in the present case did not establish that the will had been properly executed. The court also confirmed as good practice in such cases that the attestation clause should show that the will had been signed by the third party at the testator's direction—see **13.3.4.2**.

13.3.4.5   With intent to give effect to the will

It is usual (and logical) for the signature to appear at the end of the will, but this need not necessarily be the case. In *Wood v Smith* [1993] Ch 90, the testator had made his signature at the beginning of the will, intending this to give effect to his will, but written before he had made any provisions disposing of his estate. The Court of Appeal held that this could constitute a valid execution of the will provided the signing and the subsequently written dispositions all formed part of one transaction.

13.3.4.6   Signature made/acknowledged in the presence of two or more
witnesses present at the same time

Where the testator is (as is usually the case) signing the will, the signature must be completed in the presence of at least two witnesses, present at the same time. The witnesses do not need to be able to see the contents of the will, or even to know that the testator is signing a will. They must, however, be able to see the testator writing the signature (for this reason a blind person cannot act as a witness), though it is not necessary for them to see the signature itself. Alternatively, the testator may sign the will and then acknowledge that signature (by words or conduct) in the presence of the (two or more) witnesses, who must be present at the same time and be able to see the signature. Again, ideally, this will be recited in the attestation clause. There are no special rules as to the capacity of the witnesses, but they must be bodily and mentally present (not, eg drunk or asleep). Although, by s 15 of the Wills Act 1837, a beneficiary will normally lose a gift under a will where that beneficiary or their spouse has witnessed the will (**13.7.5**), this does not affect the formal validity of the will.

13.3.4.7   Witnesses attest and sign (or acknowledge their signatures)
in the presence of the testator

Attestation is, in effect, the validation of the testator's signature. The witnesses need not sign (or acknowledge) in each other's presence, though in practice this is what usually happens. However, the presence of the testator (bodily and mentally) is required when the signature/ acknowledgement is made.

13.3.5   Codicils

A codicil is used to add to, amend, or partially revoke the terms of an existing will. The requirements for a valid codicil are the same as those required for a valid will.

13.4   Revocation of a will

13.4.1   The general position

Provided a testator retains testamentary capacity, a will is revocable at any time during the testator's lifetime. This is so even if the testator has entered into a contract not to revoke the will (though if the will is revoked the estate may be liable for the breach of contract).

13.4.1.1   Circumstances in which revocation may occur

Revocation may occur:

(a) automatically by operation of law:

(i)   marriage (see **13.4.1.3**) or civil partnership (see **13.4.1.4**);

(ii) divorce, dissolution, or nullity (see **13.4.1.5** and **13.4.1.6**);

(b) by deliberate act of the testator:

(i)   later will or codicil (see **13.4.1.7**);

(ii) destruction (see **13.4.1.8**).

Sometimes, revocation is regarded as conditional only. This is considered in **13.4.2**.

The law relating to alterations is discussed in **13.5**.

13.4.1.2   Mutual wills

A qualification to the principle of revocability is the equitable doctrine of mutual wills. The law in this area was recently confirmed in *Charles v Fraser* [2010] EWHC 2154, including the following:

(a) Mutual wills are wills made by two or more persons, usually in substantially the same terms and conferring reciprocal benefits, following an agreement between them to make such wills and not to revoke them without the consent of the other.

(b) For the doctrine to apply there has to be what amounts to a contract between the two testators that both wills shall be irrevocable and remain unaltered. The agreement may be incorporated in the will or proved by extraneous evidence, which may be oral or in writing.

(c) The agreement is enforced in equity by the imposition of a constructive trust on the property which is the subject matter of the agreement. The beneficiaries under the will that was not to be revoked may apply to the court for an order that the estate is held on trust to give effect to the provisions of that will.

It should be noted that such wills can be problematic and are not 'popular' with practitioners.

13.4.1.3   Marriage (including marriages between same sex couples
taking place on/after 29 March 2014)

Until recently, marriage has only been possible between a man and a woman; same sex couples wishing to formalise their relationship could enter into a civil partnership (see **13.4.1.4**). As from 29 March 2014 same sex couples can also marry (s 1, Marriage (Same Sex Couples) Act 2014). Schedule 3 of the Act also provides that a reference to 'marriage' in existing legislation is to be read as including a reference to a marriage of a same sex couple, and a reference to a person who is 'married' will include a reference to a person who is married to someone of the same sex.

If the testator has married after executing a will, that marriage will generally revoke that will (Wills Act 1837, s 18 (both in its original form and as substituted by Administration of Justice Act 1982)).

The scope of the exceptions to this general rule depends upon whether the will was made before 1983 or after 1982. Normally wills are dated at the time of execution, and we shall only deal here with wills made after 1982. The principal exceptions are found in s 18(3) and (4) of the Wills Act 1837 (as substituted):

(a) Section 18(3) provides that where 'it appears from the will that at the time it was made the testator was expecting to be married to a particular person and that he intended that the will should not be revoked by the marriage, the will shall not be revoked by his marriage to that person'.

(b) Section 18(4) provides that where 'it appears from a will that at the time it was made the testator was expecting to be married to a particular person and that he intended that a disposition in the will should not be revoked by his marriage to that person ...' then that particular disposition will not be revoked by the marriage, and the rest of the dispositions will also be 'saved' unless the contrary appears from the will.

Only intrinsic evidence is admissible to establish the testator's expectation and intention, and an express declaration included in the will covering the points will prevent revocation.

EXAMPLE 3

John Kent married Avril Brown in September 2009, and died in April this year. His will, dated 8 August 2009, contained the following declaration:

'I DECLARE that I make this will in the expectation of my marriage to Avril Brown and that I intend that this will shall not be revoked by that marriage.'

John's will is effective despite his marriage.

It is possible for a testator to make a will conditional upon marriage, ie the will does not take effect unless and until the marriage takes place. Clearly, in such cases the question of revocation by subsequent marriage does not arise.

13.4.1.4 Civil partnerships

The Civil Partnership Act 2004 came into force on 5 December 2005, enabling same-sex couples to form an official 'civil partnership'. In broad terms, registered civil partners enjoy the same benefits as spouses. Civil partners, for example, have the same inheritance rights as married couples and enjoy the same benefits for taxation purposes. Changes of particular relevance to us are indicated at **13.4.1.6**, but civil partners also have similar rights to married couples for employment, welfare benefit, maintenance, and child support purposes, etc.

So far as the topic of revocation is concerned, the Act inserts a new s 18B into the Wills Act 1837. A civil partnership between a testator and another person will generally revoke the testator's existing will, just as we have seen a marriage does. There are similar exceptions to those set out in **13.4.1.3**, ie revocation will not occur if it appears from the will that the testator was expecting to form a civil partnership with a particular person and intended that the will, or a disposition in the will, should not be revoked by the formation of that civil partnership.

13.4.1.5 Divorce/nullity of marriage

Here, s 18A(1) of the Wills Act 1837 provides (subject to contrary intention in the will) for a sort of 'limited revocation' on a decree absolute of divorce or nullity. Any provisions in the will as to the appointment of the former spouse as executor or trustee take effect as if the former spouse had died on the date upon which the marriage is dissolved or annulled, and will thus be ineffective. Further, any property that is given by the will to the former spouse passes as if that spouse had died on that day, and will thus not pass to the former spouse.

Under s 6 of the Children Act 1989 (again, subject to expressed contrary intention) any appointment of the spouse as guardian of the testator's children is similarly 'revoked' on decree absolute of divorce.

Note that these provisions do not apply on separation, nor do they affect any provisions of the will other than those indicated.

13.4.1.6 Dissolution/nullity of civil partnerships

So far as civil partnerships are concerned, there is a court-based procedure for dissolving the civil partnership which is similar to the current divorce process for married couples. A new s 18C inserted into the Wills Act 1837 makes provision similar to that outlined in **13.4.1.5**. If the civil partnership is dissolved or nullified by the court, then the former civil partner will be treated as if they had died on the day upon which the dissolution or nullity takes effect, and, subject to a contrary intention in the will, any gift or appointment of them as an executor will be ineffective.

Any appointment of the former civil partner as guardian of the testator's children is also 'revoked'—see s 6 of the Children Act 1989.

13.4.1.7 Later will/codicil

By s 20 of the Wills Act 1837 a will is revoked (wholly or partially) by a later will or codicil; or 'by some writing declaring an intention to revoke the same and executed in the manner' of a will—as in *Re Spracklan's Estate* [1938] 2 All ER 345, where the Court of Appeal held that a letter (signed by the testatrix and duly attested) to her bank manager asking him to destroy the will which the bank was keeping for her satisfied this requirement.

A later will or codicil impliedly revokes an earlier testamentary disposition only to the extent that it is inconsistent with or merely repeats the terms of the earlier document. However, it is common—and helpful for the avoidance of doubt—for a will to contain an express revocation clause, such as, 'I hereby revoke all previous wills and codicils made by me'.

Clearly, a codicil to a will should not contain such a revocation clause!

The doctrine of conditional revocation may apply (see **13.4.2**).

13.4.1.8   Destruction

By s 20 of the Wills Act 1837 a will is also revoked by 'burning tearing or otherwise destroying the same by the testator or by some person in his presence and by his direction with the intention of revoking the same'.

There are thus two essential elements for an effective revocation:

(a) *An act of destruction.* An act of destruction is necessary; merely writing 'cancelled' or 'revoked' across the will is not enough. Nor is putting a line through parts of the will, or even the signature of the testator (though it will be otherwise if there has been an effective obliteration). In *Re Adams (Dec'd)* [1990] Ch 601, the testator's signature had been heavily scored through with a ball-point pen so as to render it illegible. The court held that a material part of the will had been destroyed with the intention to effect a revocation of the whole. Where part only of the will is destroyed, this may amount to a revocation of that part of the will only, or of the whole will if of a sufficiently substantial or vital part (eg the testator's or witnesses' signatures, *Hobbs v Knight* (1838) 1 Curt 769).

The court will admit extrinsic evidence of the testator's intention in determining the extent of any revocation, and may infer this from the state of the will at the date of death.

Destruction by someone other than the testator must, to be effective, be done in the testator's presence and at the testator's direction; if not, it is not possible for the testator subsequently to 'ratify' the act.

(b) *An intention to revoke.* The testator must have the intention to revoke at the time of the will's destruction. The necessary mental capacity is the same as that required for the making of a will (see **13.3.2**). Accidental revocation is, therefore, an impossibility; so is one based upon a mistaken belief that the will is invalid or has already been revoked. If a will is found mutilated at the date of death, this will be rebuttably presumed to have been done by the testator with the intention of revoking it (wholly or partially, depending upon the extent of the mutilation). There is a further rebuttable presumption that a will last known to have been in the testator's possession, but which cannot be found at the date of death, has been destroyed by the testator with the intention of revoking it.

The doctrine of conditional revocation may again apply (see **13.4.2**).

13.4.2   Conditional revocation

This topic is generally beyond the scope of this book. Suffice it to say that we consider at **13.4.1** the situation where a testator has an absolute intention to revoke an existing will, in which case the revocation is immediately effective (assuming the other essential elements are present). There may be evidence, however, that the intention to revoke is conditional only, when the revocation will not be effective unless and until the condition is met. The condition might be, for example, the validity of a new will. Difficult questions may arise in such cases, both as to admissibility of evidence and as to construction (especially where revocation clauses appear to have been mistakenly included in wills or codicils) and specialist practitioner's books should be consulted.

The doctrine of conditional revocation may also apply in the context of alterations (see **13.5.1.3**).

13.5   Alterations in wills

13.5.1   Section 21 of the Wills Act 1837

This lays down the basic rule, which is that:

no obliteration, interlineation, or other alteration made in any will after the execution thereof shall be valid or have any effect, except so far as the words or effect of the will before such alteration shall not be apparent, unless such alteration shall be executed in like manner as hereinbefore is required for the execution of a will …

13.5.1.1 Effective alterations

An alteration will be effective if:

(a) it is made (or is presumed to have been made without evidence to the contrary) before execution. An unattested alteration is rebuttably presumed to have been made after execution (except where the 'alteration' is the filling in of a blank space, when the rebuttable presumption is that this was done prior to execution). Either presumption is rebutted by intrinsic or extrinsic evidence to the contrary;

(b) it is made after the will but duly executed. In practice, it is sufficient if the testator and the witnesses initial the alteration; or

(c) the original wording or effect of the will is, as a result of the 'alteration', not apparent (ie is not decipherable by natural means, see **13.5.1.3**(b)).

13.5.1.2 Ineffective alterations

An alteration will be ineffective if:

(a) it is unattested and made by the testator after (or it cannot be established to have been made before) execution and does not amount to an obliteration;

(b) it is made by someone other than the testator and without his knowledge and approval; or

(c) it is made by the testator without an intention to revoke.

13.5.1.3 Consequences of invalid alteration

This will depend upon whether the original wording is 'apparent' or not. The wording is apparent if it can be deciphered by 'natural means' (such as holding up to the light or using a magnifying glass) without resort to 'forbidden' methods (such as the use of chemicals, infra-red photography, or extrinsic evidence):

(a) If the original wording is so apparent, it will be admitted to probate.

(b) If it is not so apparent, the will is prima facie admitted to probate with a blank space where the obliteration has occurred. However, where there has been an attempted substitution in place of what has been obliterated the doctrine of conditional revocation may apply; this will allow the courts to employ any of the forbidden methods mentioned above in an attempt to ascertain and give effect to the original wording.

13.5.2 Precautions

It is clearly sensible to have all alterations (even those made before execution of the will) initialled by the testator and the witnesses. Further, testators should be discouraged from attempting to make their own 'adjustments' to their wills.

13.6 Incorporation by reference

As we have seen (**13.3.4**), for a document to be admitted to probate it must be executed in accordance with the requirements of s 9 of the Wills Act 1837. However, a document not so executed may, in effect, become part of the will under the doctrine of incorporation by reference.

For this to happen, three conditions must be met:

(a) The document must be clearly identified in the will.

(b) The document must already exist at the date of the will. The onus of proving this fact lies with the person seeking incorporation of the document.

(c) The document must be referred to in the will as already in existence at the time of execution. If this is not the case (eg because the statement is equivocal or the reference is to a document to be prepared in the future) the document in question cannot be incorporated.

EXAMPLE 4

Clause 3 of a recently deceased testator's will (made in 2009) states 'I leave £10,000 to be held on the trusts set out in clause 5 of the Trust Deed dated 8 March 2005 and made between myself of the one part and Daniel Thomas and Ruth Brown of the other part'. The deceased's executor, Daniel Thomas, tells you that he has the trust deed mentioned in the will at home in his safe. It would seem that all the requirements for incorporation are satisfied; the gift under the will is prima facie valid and the trust deed would be admitted to probate with the will (see **14.24**).

13.7 Failure of gifts by will

There are a number of reasons why gifts contained in wills may fail. We shall only deal (at **13.7.3** to **13.7.5**) with three of those reasons, and with the consequences of failure at **13.7.6**. You should additionally note, however, that a gift will fail if the wording is uncertain, as will gifts contrary to public policy. In the last category, for example, a person convicted of murdering the testator is not permitted to take a benefit under the victim's will (or intestacy). Again, a beneficiary of a gift under a will is entitled to refuse that gift (ie to disclaim it), and a gift offending the rules against perpetuity and accumulation will also fail. None of these issues is considered further here.

First, a mention of terminology that you may encounter in wills. Technically, a 'legacy' is a gift of personalty (eg money, shares, chattels) and a devise is a gift of realty (eg freehold land). The term 'legacy' is commonly used to encompass both types of gift, as we will in the remainder of this chapter.

Legacies can further be classified as specific, general, demonstrative, or residuary (**13.7.2**), relevant when considering whether a legacy fails and the consequences of failure. Before considering the 'hallmarks' of these legacies, we should briefly note two rules of construction as to the date from which the will speaks.

13.7.1 Date from which the will speaks

Unless there is a contrary intention in the will, then:

(a) as to property, the will speaks and takes effect 'as if it had been executed immediately before the death of the testator' (Wills Act 1837, s 24). Thus a gift of the contents of the testator's house will prima facie be construed as a gift of the contents as at the date of death (rather than at the date of the will). The use of words such as 'my', 'now', or 'at present' in describing the gift may be sufficient to indicate a contrary intention. For example, a gift of 'my 500 shares in ABC plc' would probably be construed as a gift of the shares owned at the date of the will. On the other hand, a gift of 'all my shares in ABC plc' would prima facie pass the shares owned at the date of death; the subject matter of the gift here is generic and so described as to be capable of increase or decrease between the date of the will and the date of death.

(b) As to the objects of the gift (ie the beneficiaries), the will speaks from the date of execution. In other words, s 24 does not apply (unless a contrary intention appears from the will). As a result, a gift to 'the vicar of St Luke's Church Barchester' is prima facie a gift to the person fulfilling that description at the date of the will. This rule does not apply to 'class gifts' or to identified gifts to each member of a class (see further at **13.8.2**).

13.7.2 Legacies: specific, general, demonstrative, pecuniary, or residuary

13.7.2.1 Specific legacy

This is a gift of particular property owned by the deceased distinguished from any other property of the same kind which may be owned by the deceased, for example 'my 500 shares in XYZ plc', 'my freehold property Greenacre'. Such gifts are subject to the doctrine of ademption if the testator does not own the property concerned at the date of death (see **13.7.3**).

13.7.2.2 General legacy

This is a gift of property not distinguished by the testator from other similar property, for example '500 shares in XYZ plc'. This constitutes a gift of *any* 500 shares in the company (even if in fact that was the number which the testator owned at the date of the will). Such gifts are not subject to the doctrine of ademption, so that if in the example the testator did not own any XYZ plc shares at the date of death, the beneficiary is entitled to require estate funds (provided these are sufficient) to be used to buy 500 such shares.

13.7.2.3 Demonstrative legacy

Such legacies (not commonly encountered today) are essentially general in character, but a specific source is identified from which it is to be paid, for example '£1,000 to Ambrose to be paid from my Newtown Building Society Account'. Such legacies are not adeemed if the account has been closed during the testator's lifetime, or there is insufficient in the account at the date of death to pay the legacy in full. In such circumstances, the beneficiary is entitled to any balance at that time, and to have the deficiency paid as a general legacy.

13.7.2.4 Pecuniary legacy

This is a gift of money, and usually is general in character, for example a gift of '£5,000'. However, it may be specific (eg a gift of 'the £5,000 which I keep in my safe' or 'the £5,000 which Xavier owes me'); or demonstrative (eg '£5,000 payable from my current account at Newtown Bank').

13.7.2.5 Residuary legacy/devise

Residuary gifts embrace all the rest of the deceased's property (ie not disposed of by any specific, general, or demonstrative gifts).

13.7.3 Failure of legacies: ademption

To the extent that a testator no longer owns the property which is the subject of a specific legacy at the date of death, the gift is adeemed, ie it fails, and the disappointed beneficiary is not entitled to any compensation. Ademption may occur because the testator has sold the property, or given it away before death.

EXAMPLE 5

Clause 3 of Paul's will states, 'I give my 800 shares in PQR plc to my brother Robert'. It is likely that this will be construed as a specific gift of the 800 shares that Paul owned at the date of the will in PQR plc. If Paul sold 300 of those shares before he died, Robert would only take the remaining 500 shares.

Ademption can also occur where there has been a change in substance (ie in the very nature of the property) as opposed to a mere change in name or form. This distinction is not always easy to see.

EXAMPLE 6

Clause 4 of Paul's will provides, 'I give my 100 shares in BCD plc to my sister Susan'. Again this is likely to be construed as a specific gift. Suppose before Paul died BCD plc subdivided its shares so that one original share was represented by five new shares. It is likely that this would be construed as a mere change in the form of the shares, and Susan would take the 500 (new) shares in BCD plc. If, however, BCD plc were taken over by another company (say, FGH plc), and FGH plc issued shares in FGH plc to replace those held in the original company, it is likely that this would be seen as a change in substance (ie shares in an entirely different company) and the gift of the BCD plc shares to Susan would fail.

Note that ademption only applies to specific legacies; it has no application to general legacies (eg '500 shares in XYZ plc', see **13.7.2.2**) or where the subject matter of the gift is ascertained at the date of death (eg 'the contents of my house', see **13.7.1**).

13.7.4   Failure of legacies: lapse

13.7.4.1   Beneficiary dying before testator

As a general rule, a beneficiary must survive the testator in order to take a gift under that testator's will, otherwise the gift lapses—in which event (unless there is an effective substitutional provision, see **13.7.4.3**) the subject matter of the intended gift will fall into residue, or (if itself a share of residue) pass under the intestacy rules (see **13.7.6**).

We saw at **13.4.1** that if the testator's marriage/civil partnership has been dissolved, then, unless the will provides otherwise, gifts in the will to the former spouse/civil partner will in effect lapse.

A class gift (see **13.8.2**) only lapses if all members of the class predecease the testator: the rule is similar in the case of gifts to beneficial joint tenants.

13.7.4.2   *Commorientes*

Usually there is no problem in determining who died first—the testator or the beneficiary—and thus whether the gift has lapsed. What, however, if they die in a common accident (eg a plane crash), and the order of death is uncertain? Unless the will provides that the beneficiary must survive the testator for a certain period (28 days is common) the *commorientes* rule (Law of Property Act 1925, s 184) applies. Under this rule, where there is no evidence as to the order in which deaths have occurred then, for succession purposes, the younger is deemed to have survived the elder. Thus a gift in the younger's will to the elder would lapse, but not vice versa. The *commorientes* rule generally applies both where there is a will, and where there is no will so that the estate will be distributed under the intestacy rules (see **13.12**).

13.7.4.3   Substitutional gifts

Although it is not possible to prevent the operation of the doctrine of lapse, the will may specifically provide as to what is to happen to the gifted property if the original beneficiary dies before the testator. This is particularly common so far as residuary gifts are concerned.

EXAMPLE 7

Della's will leaves '£2,000 to my niece Jane and the rest of my estate to my husband Neil but if he fails to survive me then to my son Mark'. Only Della's son Mark survives her; the gifts to Jane and Neil therefore lapse. Jane's gift will thus fall into residue, and Mark will take Della's entire estate.

13.7.4.4   Substitution by statute

Section 33 of the Wills Act 1837 in effect provides a sort of statutory substitutional clause—but only where the original gift is to the testator's issue (ie child or remoter lineal descendant). This section applies where:

(a) a will contains a gift to the child or issue (ie grandchild, great-grandchild, etc) of the testator; and

(b) the intended beneficiary dies before the testator, leaving issue; and

(c) issue of the intended beneficiary are living (including *en ventre sa mère*) at the testator's death.

If these conditions are met then, in the absence of a contrary intention shown by the will, the gift takes effect as a gift to such issue, who take (in equal shares if more than one) the gift which their parent would have taken. It is not clear whether if the original gift is contingent the gift 'substituted' by s 33 is subject to the same contingency.

The section also applies (in the absence of a contrary intention in the will) to a class gift to the testator's children or remoter issue. It is important to appreciate that s 33 cannot prevent the failure of gifts in favour of beneficiaries who predecease but who are not issue of the testator. Thus in the example of Della's will at **13.7.4.3**, s 33 would not operate to save the gift of £2,000 for any of Jane's children who survived Della. However, if Mark had also predeceased but his two children survived Della, then under s 33, Della's entire estate would pass to those two children in equal shares.

13.7.5   Failure of gifts to witnesses

A gift in a will fails if the beneficiary or the beneficiary's spouse or civil partner witnesses the will, though the validity of the will as such is not affected (Wills Act 1837, s 15). However, the gift will not fail if, ignoring the attestation by the beneficiary or spouse or civil partner, the will is duly executed, ie because there are at least two other witnesses who are not beneficiaries or their spouses or civil partners. Further, a gift within the terms of s 15 may be 'saved' if the will is subsequently confirmed by a codicil which is independently witnessed.

If the will appoints solicitors (or other professionals) to act as executors, it will invariably also contain a charging clause, enabling them to be paid for their work in administering the estate. On a death prior to 1 February 2001, s 15 would cause the charging clause to fail if a member of the firm appointed was one of the (two) witnesses to the will. However, where the deceased died after 31 January 2001, by virtue of s 28(4)(a) of the Trustee Act 2000, such a provision is treated as remuneration for services (and not as a gift) so that the charging clause would not fail in such circumstances.

Where the beneficiary's spouse or civil partner has witnessed the will, s 15 applies only if the beneficiary and the witness were married or civil partners at the date of the execution of the will; there will be no problem where they married or entered into a civil partnership after that date.

13.7.6   Consequences of failure of legacies

If the gift fails then clearly the original intended beneficiary will not take. Who will take instead?

13.7.6.1   Alternative provision in will or by statute

First, it is necessary to consider whether the will itself has made alternative provision in the event of failure of the original gift. Thus, in the case of ademption, has the testator provided that the beneficiary is to receive alternative property if the original gifted property is no longer in the estate at death? In the case of lapse, does the will contain an effective substitutional clause (**13.7.4.3**)? Alternatively, is the gift saved by statute (see Wills Act 1837, s 33, **13.7.4.4**) or the saving provisions of s 15 of the Wills Act 1837 or s 28(4) of the Trustee Act 2000?

13.7.6.2   No alternative provision

Save where the gift has adeemed, the property which was the subject matter of the failed gift will form part of the deceased's estate. Who is now entitled to this property? The answer will depend on the type of gift which has failed. Unless the failed gift was a gift of residue, then (assuming there is an effective residuary gift) the gifted property will 'fall into residue', ie swell the property that would otherwise pass under the residuary legacy.

If a gift of residue wholly fails, the entire residuary estate will pass to those entitled under the intestacy rules (see **13.10** to **13.17**). If, however, the gift of residue only fails in part, there is a 'partial intestacy' as to the property comprised in the failed gift: this part will again pass to those entitled on the deceased's intestacy. A partial intestacy will also arise where the will contains effective non-residuary gifts, but either there is no gift of residue or it fails wholly or in part.

EXAMPLE 8

Jack's will contains the following gifts, '£1,000 to my godson Stephen Smith and the residue of my estate to be divided equally between my daughter Harriet and my late wife's son Keith Jones'. Both Stephen and Keith have predeceased Jack, but Harriet and Keith's daughter Rachel survive.

The pecuniary legacy lapses, and this sum will now form part of the residuary estate. Harriet will take one half of the residue in accordance with the will, but what will happen to Keith's lapsed one half share? It will not pass to Harriet as the gift was to Harriet and Keith as tenants in common in equal shares and the will does not provide what is to happen if one of them predeceases the testator. Section 33 of the Wills Act 1837 will not save the remaining one half share for Rachel (because Keith is not Jack's issue). Jack is thus partially intestate, and the failed gift will pass to those entitled on Jack's intestacy.

In this example, a partial intestacy would have been avoided if:

(a) the will had included an express substitutional gift in favour of Keith's issue in the event of the gift to Keith failing; or

(b) the will had provided that the residue was to be divided 'equally between such of my daughter Harriet and my late wife's son Keith Jones as survive me'. In this case, the effect would have been to pass the whole of the residuary estate to Harriet; or

(c) the will had left the residuary estate to Harriet and Keith 'jointly' (ie as joint tenants) rather than 'equally'. Here again the effect would have been that Harriet would take the whole of the residuary estate.

If Jack's daughter had also died before him leaving no children alive at the date of his death, then Jack's entire estate would pass under the intestacy rules.

13.8 Gifts to children in wills

We do not intend to cover the law on construction of wills—a major topic in itself. Gifts to children are so common in wills, however, that it is worth noting a few points of construction in relation to such gifts.

13.8.1 Meaning of 'children'

In the absence of contrary intention in the will, gifts to a person's 'children' (whether that person is the testator or anyone else) will include all children of that person (whether legitimate, illegitimate, or adopted by them). It will not include a natural child of that person who has been adopted by someone else. Relevant legislation includes the Legitimacy Act 1976, the Adoption Act 1976, and (for wills made after 3 April 1988) the Family Law Reform Act 1987.

13.8.2 Class gifts

Class gifts are particularly used in wills to leave property to children where it is not desired to name the children individually. Class gifts do raise a number of construction issues: we do not intend to explore the complex cases, but merely to explain briefly the basic rules and highlight points that may need further research.

13.8.2.1 How to recognise a class gift

A class gift is a gift of property to be divided among beneficiaries who fulfil a general description, for example '£50,000 to the children of Zoe', '£50,000 to the children of Zoe who attain the age of 18'. In such cases, the total value of the gift is clear: the problem is to know how to share it among those entitled. This will obviously depend upon how many people fit the description. In the examples given, it would not be possible to answer this question with certainty at least until the death of Zoe; in the meantime, no distribution would be possible.

A similar problem arises where the gift in the will takes the form of an individual gift to the members of a class, for example '£5,000 to each of the children of Zebedee'. Here, what the prospective beneficiaries are to take is identified but until the death of Zebedee it cannot be known how many children will qualify.

13.8.2.2 Class-closing rules

The courts have invented class-closing rules to overcome these problems and allow distribution at an earlier date. The various rules (which one applies to a given case depends upon the type of gift involved) determine when the class will close. In principle, this will generally happen when there is one person fitting the description who has a vested interest. At whatever point the class closes, it does so to the exclusion of any potential beneficiary not then 'living'—a term which includes a child conceived and subsequently born alive. This is obviously 'unfair' to those thus excluded from benefit, but this disadvantage is considered to be outweighed by the advantage of earlier distribution.

The class-closing rules may be excluded by a clear provision in the testator's will, such as 'to the children of Zoe living at my death', or 'to the children of Zebedee whenever born'.

As indicated earlier, the rules (if not so excluded) differ in detail according to the type of gift involved. We shall only mention here the types of class gift most commonly encountered:

(a) Immediate vested gift, for example '£5,000 to the children of Arthur'. The class closes at the date of the testator's death if there is any child of Arthur then living. If there are none, the class remains open until the death of Arthur.

(b) Immediate contingent gift, for example '£5,000 to the children of Arthur who attain the age of 18'. Here the class closes at the testator's death if any such child has already reached the age of 18. The class will include any of Arthur's children who are 18 plus any others then living who subsequently attain that age. If a 'class member' dies before 18, then they will not share in the gift. If at the date of the testator's death no child of Arthur has fulfilled the contingency (ie attained 18), the class remains open until one does; the class will then close around that child and any others then living who subsequently attain the age of 18.

(c) Individual gift to members of a class, for example '£5,000 to each of the children of Arthur' or '£5,000 to each of the children of Arthur who attain the age of 18'. In these cases, unless there is a contrary intention in the will, the class will close at the date of the testator's death. If there are no children of Arthur then living, the gift fails.

13.9 Wills: checkpoints

1. Formal validity:

    (a) Is the will signed by the testator and two witnesses (**13.3.4.1**)?

    (b) Does the will contain an appropriate attestation clause (**13.3.4.2**)?

    (c) If no/inadequate attestation clause, has s 9 of the Wills Act 1837 been complied with (**13.3.4.3** to **13.3.4.7**)?

    (d) Is there any suggestion that the testator lacked capacity (**13.3.2**)? Note that the burden of proving that the testator lacked capacity rests with the person(s) who challenged the will (**13.3.2.3**).

(e) Is there any suggestion that the testator did not know and approve of the contents of the will (**13.3.3**)? Note presumptions (**13.3.3.2**).

2. Revocation:

   (a) Is the will the most recent one (**13.4.1.7**)?

   (b) Does it contain a revocation clause (**13.4.1.7**)?

   (c) Has the testator married (**13.4.1.3**) or entered into a civil partnership (**13.4.1.4**) since the date of the will?

   (d) Has the marriage/civil partnership of the testator been dissolved/annulled (**13.4.1.5** and **13.4.1.6**)?

3. Alterations:

   (a) Are any alterations effective (**13.5.1.1**)?

   (b) Are any alterations ineffective (**13.5.1.2**)?

4. Incorporation:

   (a) If the will refers to another document, has that document been incorporated and is it available (**13.6**)?

5. Failure of gifts:

   (a) Does the testator's estate include property specifically gifted by the will (**13.7.2**)?

   (b) Have any named beneficiaries predeceased the testator (**13.7.4.1**)?

   (c) If so, is there an effective substitutional gift (**13.7.4.3**) or is the gift saved by s 33 of the Wills Act 1837 (**13.7.4.4**)?

   (d) Has a beneficiary or their spouse/civil partner acted as witness (**13.7.5**)?

6. Class gifts:

   (a) Does the will contain class gifts (**13.8.2.1**)?

   (b) If so, have the class-closing rules (**13.8.2.2**) been excluded by the terms of the will?

   (c) If not:

      (i) Does the will contain an immediate vested class gift and, if so, is any person within the class alive at the date of the testator's death?

      (ii) Does the will contain an immediate contingent class gift and, if so, has any person fulfilled the contingency at the date of the testator's death?

      (iii) Does the will contain an individual gift to members of a class and, if so, is any person within the class alive at the testator's death?

13.10 Intestacy

We have already made reference to the 'intestacy rules'. Distribution of a deceased's estate is governed by these rules when the deceased has died either:

(a) wholly (or totally) intestate, ie without having effectively disposed of any of their property by will. This may be because the deceased never made a will or the will is invalid; or

(b) partially intestate, ie having made a valid will but this does not dispose of the whole of the estate. This situation may arise where the will contains no residuary gift, or where there is a gift of residue but this has wholly or partly failed (eg because a residuary beneficiary has predeceased the testator, and there is no effective substitutional gift, either in the will or by the operation of s 33 of the Wills Act 1837—see **13.7**).

In the first case, the distribution of the whole of the deceased's succession estate will be in accordance with the intestacy rules: in the second, these rules will only apply to such of the deceased's property as does not pass under the will. In both cases, however, certain types of property will pass on death quite independently of the intestacy rules; for example, property held by the deceased as a beneficial joint tenant (see **13.19.1**).

The Inheritance and Trustees' Powers Act came into force on 1 October 2014. The Act implements some of the Law Commission's recommendations contained in its 2011 Report 'Intestacy and Family Provision Claims on Death'. The Act improves and clarifies various areas in the law of succession and trusts—including the intestacy rules, claims under the family provision legislation (see **13.23**), and trustees' powers of maintenance and advancement (see **15.4.10** and **15.4.11**).

13.11   Intestacy: the basic position

Where the deceased left a will, its effective provisions will be implemented. To the extent that the estate is not disposed of by will, its distribution is governed by the rules in Part IV of the Administration of Estates Act 1925 (as amended).

13.11.1   Section 33(1) of the Administration of Estates Act 1925 (as amended)

Section 33(1) provides that the personal representatives hold the intestate's estate not disposed of by will on trust with a power to sell. The personal representatives must pay the funeral, testamentary, and administration expenses, debts, and other liabilities of the deceased out of the intestate's ready money and from the net proceeds of any part of the estate which is sold.

The residuary estate (what is left after all the liabilities and expenses have been discharged) is then to be shared among those entitled according to the statutory rules.

13.11.2   Entitlement

As we will see, the position of a spouse (provided that spouse survives the intestate by 28 days) is considered first under the intestacy rules. The surviving spouse may take the whole of the intestate's estate. If not, or the spouse does not so survive, the rules then set out in order of entitlement categories of the deceased's blood relatives who are entitled to (or to a share in) the intestate's estate. Earlier classes take to the exclusion of later classes of relatives, and generally children of a predeceasing relative take their parent's share. If the deceased was partially intestate, the surviving spouse or some of these relatives may also benefit under the will, but this will not affect any entitlement that they may have under the intestacy rules. **Figures 13.1** and **13.2** immediately following **13.17** set out the various entitlements.

By virtue of the Civil Partnership Act 2004 a civil partner has similar rights to the intestate's estate as those enjoyed by a spouse—and of course by virtue of the Marriage (Same Sex Couples) Act 2014 a 'spouse' will include a party to a same sex marriage.

13.11.3   The statutory trusts

In the case of certain classes of relatives—namely, issue (children, grandchildren, etc), brothers and sisters, uncles and aunts—it will be seen that the class takes on 'the statutory trusts'. Section 47 of the Administration of Estates Act 1925 defines this expression as meaning:

(a) equally for all members of the class of relatives concerned living or *en ventre sa mère* (ie conceived) at the date of the intestate's death who attain the age of 18 or marry or enter into a civil partnership under that age;

(b) the issue of any class members who predecease take *per stirpes* their parent's share provided they (ie the issue) attain 18 or marry or enter into a civil partnership earlier.

Where the potential beneficiary dies before the intestate (regardless of whether that person had attained the age of 18 or was married or had entered into a civil partnership), but leaves issue, then the substitution referred to in (b) above applies (see **Example 9**—Andrew, David, and Ethan).

Where, however, the potential beneficiary *is living at the date of the intestate's death* but subsequently dies before attaining a vested interest (ie before attaining the age of 18 or earlier marriage or entry into a civil partnership), then in relation to a death on/after 1 February 2012 it will depend upon whether that person was survived by their own issue. If not, the estate will be dealt with as if that person had never existed (see **Example 9**—Frances and Georgia).

If, however, that person is survived by issue (see **Example 9**—Henry) then such issue take their deceased parent's share on the statutory trusts—(see **Example 9**—Julia) by virtue of s 3 of the Estates of Deceased Persons (Forfeiture Rule and Law of Succession) Act 2011. (Prior to this Act taking effect such issue, somewhat anomalously, would not have been entitled.)

EXAMPLE 9

Ian's estate will pass to his issue on the statutory trusts. As he had three children it will prima facie be divided into three shares.

Ian has recently died intestate, leaving the following issue:

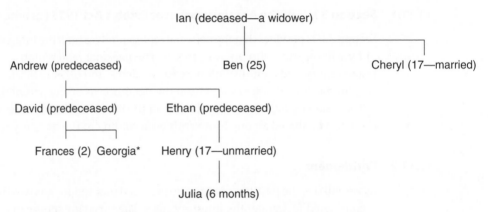

* Georgia was *en ventre sa mère* at the date of Ian's death.

Both Ben and Cheryl will take a vested one-third share each—they have satisfied the contingency. Note that Cheryl, although she has fulfilled the contingency, is under 18 and so will not be able to give an effective discharge to the personal representatives. The capital of her share will have to be held for her until she attains her majority. She will, however, be entitled to receive the income in the meantime, as a married infant can give a good receipt for income. Were she to die before attaining 18, her one-third share would pass as part of her estate to those entitled on her intestacy.

Andrew's share will pass under the statutory trusts to his issue, ie his one-third share will be subdivided into two equal shares. The (one-sixth) share which David would have inherited, had he survived Ian, will be held on the statutory trusts for Frances and Georgia; Ethan's one-sixth share will similarly be held for Henry (he does not obtain a vested interest because he is not married).

If both Frances and Georgia were to die before attaining vested interests (eg they both die aged 15) their one-sixth share would accrue to Henry, provided he in turn survives to attain a vested interest. If he fails to do so and Julia predeceased him, the estate will be distributed as if Frances, Georgia, and Henry had never existed. The whole of Andrew's share would therefore accrue to Ben and Cheryl, since these will be the only interests under the statutory trusts which vest. However, if his daughter Julia (or any other issue) were to survive him she/they would take his share on the statutory trusts.

13.12 Entitlement where there is a surviving spouse (or a surviving civil partner) of the intestate

To be entitled the spouse (ie a person to whom the intestate was lawfully married at the date of death) must survive the intestate by 28 days. There is no entitlement under the intestacy rules for a divorced spouse (ie after decree absolute) or one who is judicially separated.

Similar provisions apply where the deceased left a surviving civil partner—to be entitled the civil partner must survive by 28 days and there is no entitlement once the civil partnership is dissolved.

We noted in **13.7.4.2** that the *commorientes* rule (where the order of death is uncertain) relates also to cases where there is a total or partial intestacy. So far as intestate succession between spouses/civil partners is concerned, the spouse/civil partners must survive the deceased by 28 days, so that the point cannot arise. In the case of intestate succession between other relatives, the *commorientes* rule will apply in the usual way, as there is no requirement that they survive the deceased by 28 days in order to become entitled.

Assuming that the deceased's spouse or civil partner so survives, that spouse's or civil partner's entitlement will depend on whether the deceased's issue also survive (see **Figure 13.1**).

13.12.1   Spouse (or civil partner) alone

Where there are no issue the personal representatives hold the whole of the residuary estate for the surviving spouse (or civil partner) absolutely.

13.12.2   Spouse (or civil partner) and issue

13.12.2.1   The spouse (or civil partner)

The spouse (or civil partner) is entitled to:

(a) the personal chattels absolutely;

(b) the residuary estate of the intestate other than the personal chattels is charged with payment of a 'fixed net sum' (currently £250,000) free of duties and costs, to the surviving spouse or civil partner, together with simple interest from the date of death until payment; and

(c) one half of the residuary estate absolutely.

All property passing to the surviving spouse or civil partner under these rules passes tax-free as it enjoys the benefit of the inheritance tax spouse/civil partner exemption.

13.12.2.2   The issue

The issue are entitled (on the statutory trusts, see **13.11.3**) to the other one half of the residuary estate absolutely.

13.12.2.3   Personal chattels

The term 'personal chattels' is defined by s 55(1)(x) of the Administration of Estates Act 1925.

13.12.2.3.1   *For wills or codicils executed on or after 1 October 2014*

Section 3(1) Inheritance and Trustees' Powers Act 2014 substituted a new s 55(1)(x) of the 1925 Act. Under the Act, personal chattels are defined as 'tangible movable property', other than such property which:

- consists of money or security; or

- was used at the death of the intestate solely or mainly for business purposes; or

- was held at the death of the intestate as an investment.

13.12.2.3.2   *For wills or codicils executed before 1 October 2014*

Section 3(2) provides that if a will or codicil containing a reference to personal chattels by reference to s 55(1)(x) of the 1925 Act was executed prior to the new definition coming into effect (1 October 2014), then unless the contrary intention appears the new definition is to be disregarded in interpreting the reference to personal chattels.

The previous definition was defined as including:

carriages, horses, stable furniture and effects (not used for business purposes), motor cars and accessories (not used for business purposes), garden effects, domestic animals, plate, plated articles, linen, china, glass, books, pictures, prints, furniture, jewellery, articles of household or personal use or ornament, musical and scientific instruments and apparatus, wines, liquors and consumable stores, but do not include any chattels used at the death of the intestate for business purposes nor money or securities for money.

In spite of this definition showing signs of its age, it is clear that it is intended to cover items of personal and domestic use and ornament. In most cases there is unlikely to be much difficulty in determining whether a particular item, by its nature, falls within the definition. However, use is sometimes relevant: assets used for business purposes are excluded, so that it would appear that a car used for both business and private purposes falls outside the definition.

The phrase 'articles of household or personal use' has been held to include, for example:

(a) a 60-foot yacht used by the deceased for pleasure (*Re Chaplin* [1950] Ch 507; [1950] 2 All ER 155);

(b) a stamp collection made by the deceased as a hobby (*Re Reynold's Will Trusts* [1966] 1 WLR 19; [1966] 3 All ER 686); and

(c) a collection of watches worth some £50,000 out of an estate of approximately £80,000 (*Re Crispin's Will Trusts* [1975] Ch 245; [1974] 3 WLR 657; [1974] 3 All ER 772).

13.12.3   Special rule applying to spouses (or civil partners)

An election for appropriation of the matrimonial home may be open to the surviving spouse or civil partner which, if exercised, will affect the distribution described in the previous paragraphs of **13.12**.

Schedule 2 to the Intestates' Estates Act 1952 enables the surviving spouse/civil partner, in effect, to purchase the matrimonial home (or the deceased's interest in it where they were beneficial tenants in common). The election is not necessary where the deceased and the surviving spouse/civil partner were beneficial joint tenants because the deceased's interest accrues automatically to the survivor, independently of the intestacy rules.

The 'matrimonial home' is defined as that in which the surviving spouse/civil partner was resident at the date of death of the intestate; it does not matter whether the deceased was also so resident.

The Act gives the spouse/civil partner the right to require the personal representatives to appropriate the matrimonial home (at its value at the date of appropriation, see *Re Collins* [1975] 1 WLR 309; [1975] 1 All ER 321) in partial or total satisfaction of the spouse/civil partner's fixed net sum and/or absolute interest in the residuary estate. If these are not adequate to 'purchase' the deceased's interest, the spouse/civil partner may make up the deficiency out of their own resources.

This election too must be made in writing to the personal representatives within 12 months of the grant (the court having again a discretion to extend the time limit). Normally, during this period the personal representatives cannot sell the matrimonial home without the consent of the spouse/civil partner. If the spouse/civil partner is one of two or more personal representatives, the notice should be given to the others. The Schedule does not say what is to happen if the spouse/civil partner is the sole personal representative.

In four cases, the consent of the court is required before the election can be made. Broadly, this would be when the home was only part of a building owned by the deceased, or if the home was part of a farm or other business premises, and specialist texts should be consulted in these circumstances.

The general power of appropriation (**15.4.2.1**) is also available to the surviving spouse/civil partner if also the personal representative of the intestate—but note the 'self-dealing' rule mentioned in **15.4.2.3**.

13.13   Issue of the intestate

Subject to the entitlement of any surviving spouse/civil partner, the residuary estate is held for the issue of the intestate on the statutory trusts.

Effectively, children take to the exclusion of remoter issue, except where a child predeceases the intestate leaving issue, when, as we have seen, the issue take their parent's share on the statutory trusts.

An adopted child is treated as a legitimate child of its adoptive parent(s) and not as the child of its natural parents (Adoption Act 1976, s 39). A legitimated child is treated as if born legitimate (Legitimacy Act 1976, ss 5 and 10). Note, however, that stepchildren have no entitlement to the estate of their step-parent under the intestacy rules.

Section 18 of the Family Law Reform Act 1987 provides that (on a death on/after 4 April 1988) the distribution of assets on intestacy is to be determined without regard to whether the parents of a particular person were (or were not) married to each other. In other words, illegitimacy is ignored—and this applies not only to the intestate's issue but to all other relatives who may be entitled under the intestacy rules (on a death before 4 April 1988 different rules applied).

The Family Law Reform Act 1987 provides no special protection for personal representatives who distribute in ignorance of illegitimate claimants. However, under s 18(2) there is a presumption that an illegitimate child is not survived by its father, or any person related to that child only through its father, unless the contrary is shown. Section 5 of the 2014 Act restricts this outdated rule, which discriminates against unmarried fathers (and which may contravene the European Convention on Human Rights), by providing that this presumption of death does not apply if a person is recorded as the intestate's father, or as a parent (other than the mother), ie a second female parent, of the intestate on the deceased's birth certificate or other official birth record.

13.14 Other relatives of the intestate

If there are no surviving spouse/civil partner or issue, the order of entitlement to share in the estate is as follows:

(a) parents (equally if both alive); but if none then

(b) brothers and sisters of the whole blood (ie who share the same parents as the deceased) on the statutory trusts; but if none then

(c) brothers and sisters of the half blood (ie who share only one parent with the deceased) on the statutory trusts; but if none then

(d) grandparents (equally if more than one); but if none then

(e) uncles and aunts of the whole blood (ie brothers and sisters of the whole blood of one of the intestate's parents) on the statutory trusts; but if none then

(f) uncles and aunts of the half blood (ie brothers and sisters of the half blood of one of the intestate's parents) on the statutory trusts. It is blood relatives of the intestate who are entitled, not those related only by marriage.

Apart from parents or grandparents, members of each class take on the statutory trusts. For example, Harry (a bachelor) dies intestate. His only surviving relative is a niece, Isla, the daughter of his late sister Gwen. Isla will be entitled to all of Harry's estate provided she attains 18 (or marries under that age). Of course, if Gwen had survived Harry, Isla would have no entitlement.

13.15 The Crown

If the intestate is not survived by any relatives qualifying to share in the estate in any of the categories described at **13.14** then the Crown takes the residuary estate as *bona vacantia*. If the intestate died resident within the Duchy of Lancaster or in Cornwall, the Duchy or Duke of Cornwall respectively take as *bona vacantia*.

Section 46 of the Administration of Estates Act 1925 gives the Crown, etc a discretion in such cases to make provision for the intestate's dependants (who need not be related to the deceased) and for 'any other person for whom the intestate might reasonably have been expected to make provision'.

13.16 Inheritance tax and intestacy

It is not our purpose here to go into this topic in any detail, but merely to stress again that any property passing to the deceased's spouse/civil partner under the intestacy rules (even if only for life) will be wholly exempt from inheritance tax (as it will be covered by the spouse/civil partner exemption).

13.17 Intestacy: checkpoints

1. Does any of the deceased's estate pass by will (**13.11**)?
2. As to property undisposed of by any will and passing under the intestacy rules:
   (a) Has the deceased's spouse/civil partner survived by 28 days?
   (b) If so, see Figure **13.1** and **13.12**.
   (c) If the surviving spouse/civil partner does not take the entire residuary estate, is appropriation of the matrimonial home relevant or necessary (**13.12.3**)?
3. If the spouse/civil partner does not survive for 28 days:
   (a) Are there issue (**13.12** and **13.13**)? (NB: the statutory trusts (**13.11.3**).)
   (b) If not, are there other relatives qualifying to share in the estate (**13.14**)? (NB: the statutory trusts (**13.11.3**).)

Figure 13.1 Destination table where intestate's spouse/civil partner survives by 28 days

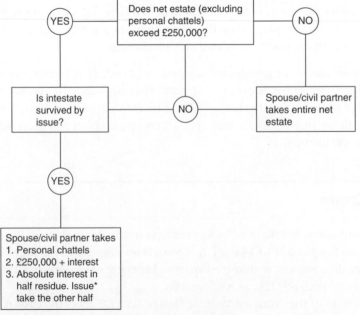

* On the statutory trusts (**13.11.3**).

Figure 13.2   Destination table where intestate's spouse/civil partner does not survive by 28 days

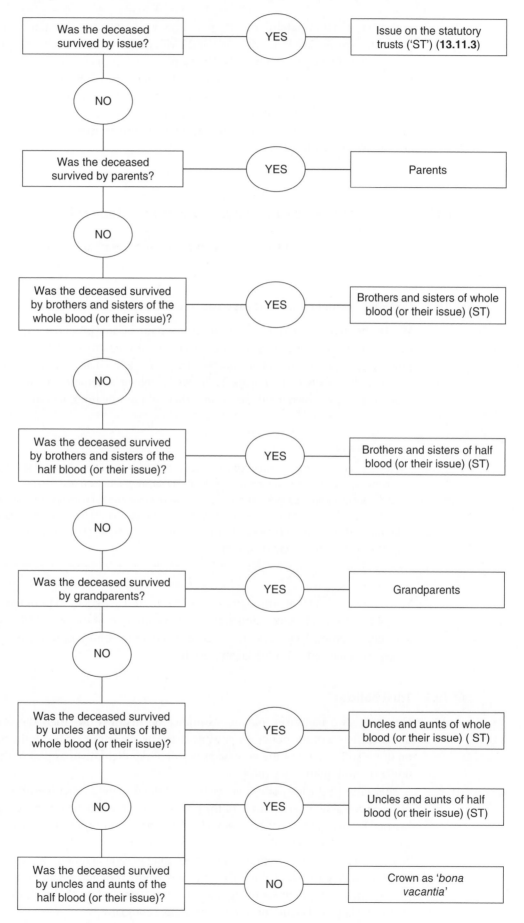

13.18   Property not passing under the will or the intestacy rules

We have noted that certain property passes on death quite independently of the will (if any) or intestacy rules. This is the case even if the will purports to gift such property, as it is simply not capable of being passed by will. The value of such property may well be significant, and knowledge of how such property passes will be relevant when advising on entitlements to property owned by the deceased. Depending on the type of property, it may or may not be part of the deceased's taxable estate chargeable to inheritance tax on death. Although not of immediate concern, for ease of reference, such property is listed at **13.20** and **13.21**—and see also **Figures** 13.1 and 13.2.

13.19   Property passing outside the will or intestacy rules

The property listed in **13.19.1** to **13.19.7** does not form part of the deceased's 'succession estate' and therefore is not payable to the deceased's personal representatives.

13.19.1   Property owned by the deceased as beneficial joint tenant

Where the deceased was a beneficial joint tenant of any property, the deceased's interest accrues automatically on death to the surviving joint tenant(s). This is the case whether the property is personalty (eg a bank account) or land (eg the matrimonial home).

Where the jointly owned property is held as beneficial tenants in common, however, the share of each joint owner will pass under their will (or the intestacy rules).

EXAMPLE 10

Joyce and John, who are not married, live together with their daughter Kelly (aged 18) who is Joyce's only child. Joyce has a joint bank account (beneficial joint tenancy) with John, and they jointly own their home as tenants in common. Joyce dies intestate, survived by John and Kelly. Joyce's share of the money in the bank account will pass by survivorship to John, and can be claimed by producing a copy of her death certificate to the bank. Her share in the home, however, will form part of her succession estate, which here passes under the intestacy rules to Kelly.

We will see at **13.20** that although a deceased's interest as beneficial joint tenant *does not* form part of the deceased's succession estate, it *does* form part of the deceased's estate for inheritance tax purposes. The deceased's interest as tenant in common, however, forms part of the succession estate and also the taxable estate.

13.19.2   Trust policies

If the deceased had taken out life assurance on his own life, then the sum assured may, under the terms of the policy, be payable to the deceased's estate. If so, the proceeds payable on death will be paid to the deceased's personal representatives as part of the estate passing under the will or intestacy rules.

Alternatively, the life policy may be held for the benefit of other person(s) either as a result of an express assignment or trust of the policy, or as a result of being written under s 11 of the Married Women's Property Act 1882. The latter case is only applicable if the intended beneficiaries are the life assured's spouse or, since the Civil Partnership Act 2004 came into force, civil partner and/or children; in other cases, an express assignment or trust of the policy will be required. In either case, the policy 'belongs' to the beneficiaries and the policy monies are payable directly to them (or trustees for them) on proof of death, by sending a death certificate and completed claim form to the insurance company.

EXAMPLE 11

Peter has taken out two policies of life assurance. The Eversure Assurance Co policy is written in trust for his wife, Pam. The other policy, which is with the Longlife Assurance Co, is payable to his estate. Peter's will leaves his estate to his wife and children in equal shares. Pam survives Peter and is able to obtain the proceeds of the Eversure policy shortly after Peter's death. She finds this sum a useful means of support, pending the distribution of her late husband's estate (which includes the proceeds of the Longlife policy) in accordance with the will.

13.19.3 Pension scheme benefits

Many occupational pension schemes are drafted in such a way that a lump sum payable on death 'in service' does not form part of the estate of the deceased member of the scheme. This is achieved by making any such sum payable to family members entirely at the discretion of the trustees of the scheme—though usually the member is allowed to make a (non-binding) 'nomination' of his preferred recipient—not to be confused with the sort of nomination discussed at **13.19.4**. The deceased has no interest in such lump sum (and thus it cannot form part of his succession estate). The trustees of the scheme only require proof of death to enable payment to be made.

Again, it must be stressed that not all pension schemes operate in this way; frequently, any 'death in service' benefit is part of the estate of the deceased passing under the terms of the will or the intestacy rules.

13.19.4 Statutory nominations

In the case of certain investments, a person who is aged 16 or over may pass the property concerned on death under a statutory nomination made in writing and attested by one witness. Such a nomination is revoked by subsequent marriage, a later nomination, or if the nominee predeceases the nominator; however, it is unaffected by any subsequent will.

It is now only possible to make such a nomination of monies deposited in friendly societies and industrial and provident societies up to a limit in each case of £5,000. It used to be possible to nominate funds in trustee savings banks (withdrawn 1 May 1979) and National Savings Certificates and the National Savings Bank (withdrawn 1 May 1981). However, nominations made before these dates remain effective (unless revoked).

If property capable of nomination in this way is not so nominated, it forms part of the property passing on death under the terms of the deceased's will or the intestacy rules.

13.19.5 *Donationes mortis causa*

You will no doubt have encountered this type of gift in earlier studies of trust law and you will recall that they are gifts made in contemplation of death. We do not intend to go into further detail here, but only to mention that property passing under a valid *donatio mortis causa* passes directly to the donee on death.

13.19.6 Life interests in trust property

Where the deceased was possessed of such an interest at the date of death, the trust property will pass in accordance with the terms of the trust instrument.

13.19.7 Gifts with the reservation of benefit

This is an inheritance tax concept—it basically means that the deceased has given away property in their lifetime, but has retained some benefit in the gifted property. Regardless of the tax position, if the property has been effectively gifted in their lifetime, it will no longer belong to the deceased for succession purposes.

13.20   Property not forming part of the succession estate but forming part of the deceased's estate for inheritance tax purposes

Although the following property is not payable to the deceased's personal representatives, it nevertheless must be included in calculating the value of property passing on death for inheritance tax purposes, ie it forms part of the deceased's taxable estate:

(a) Property held by the deceased as beneficial joint tenant—the value of the deceased's share only, not the whole value of the property. Thus in the example at **13.19.1**, the value of Joyce's share of money in the bank account (not the total amount in the account) would be included in her estate for tax purposes. The value of her interest in the house (part of her succession estate) would, of course, also form part of her taxable estate on death. If Joyce and John had been married, any property passing to John would, of course, enjoy the benefit of the spouse exemption for inheritance tax purposes. See also Table **13.1**.

(b) Nominated property (**13.19.4**).

(c) *Donationes mortis causa* (**13.19.5**).

(d) Life interests in trust property (**13.19.6**).

(e) Gifts with a reservation of benefit (**13.19.7**).

13.21   Property not forming part of the deceased's estate for succession or inheritance tax purposes

These are:

(a) Trust policies (**13.19.2**). Policies payable to the deceased's estate would, however, form part of the taxable estate.

(b) Pension scheme benefits payable at the discretion of the pension trustees (**13.19.3**). If the lump sum benefit is payable to the deceased's estate, again it will be included in the estate for inheritance tax.

Table 13.1 **Summary chart of commonly encountered property referred to in 13.20 and 13.21**

Asset	Does the asset form part of succession estate?	Does the asset form part of taxable estate?
Deceased's interests as beneficial joint tenant	No	Yes (but exempt if passing to spouse/civil partner)
Deceased's interests as tenant in common	Yes	Yes (but exempt if passing to spouse/civil partner)
Life policy not written in trust	Yes	Yes
Life policy written in trust	No	No
Pension benefits passing to estate	Yes	Yes
Discretionary pension benefits	No	No

13.22   Property not passing under the will or the intestacy rules: checkpoints

1. Is there property which does not pass as part of the deceased's succession estate (**13.19**)?

2. If so, does such property:

   (a) Form part of the deceased's taxable estate (**13.20**)?

   (b) Not form part of the deceased's taxable estate (**13.21**)?

13.23 Provision for family and dependants

In this section we will consider, in outline, how a successful claim under the Inheritance (Provision for Family and Dependants) Act 1975 may alter the distribution of property that would otherwise be in accordance with the deceased's will, the operation of the intestacy rules, or a combination of both in the case of partial intestacy. In some cases, orders can be made which affect certain types of property which pass outside the deceased's succession estate, or even property disposed of by the deceased in their lifetime.

The Act enables certain classes of persons to apply for provision from the deceased's estate on the basis that the deceased's will or intestacy fails to make adequate financial provision for them, and only applies if the deceased dies domiciled in England and Wales.

You may be asked to advise a potential applicant under the Act, or to advise the personal representatives about the merits of a claim made against the deceased's estate. In the latter case, any statements by the deceased (or, indeed, any other evidence) as to why no provision was made for the claimant should be carefully preserved; such statements will be relevant if the claim goes to court, and may be useful in negotiations with the claimant.

Schedule 2 of the 2014 Act contains a number of amendments to the family provision legislation. All statutory references in the remainder of this part of the chapter are to the Inheritance (Provision for Family and Dependants) Act 1975 unless otherwise stated.

13.24 The basis of the claim for provision

In order to succeed an applicant must:

(a) apply within the time limit (**13.25**);

(b) fall within one of the categories of applicant set out in s 1(1) (as amended) (**13.26**); and

(c) satisfy the court that the will or intestacy fails to make reasonable financial provision for the applicant (**13.27**).

The court may then order financial provision to be made out of the deceased's net estate (**13.30**). The deceased may have anticipated that a claim might be made under the Act and may have disposed of property prior to death in an attempt to defeat such a claim. The Act contains anti-avoidance provisions (ss 10 and 11) enabling an order to be made relating to such property in limited circumstances, although this is not further discussed here.

The Act also sets out certain guidelines which the court must take into account both when deciding whether reasonable financial provision has been made for the applicant and, if not, whether any order should be made (**13.28**).

13.25 The application

13.25.1 The time limit for making applications

Applications should normally be made within six months from the grant of representation (the document which confirms or grants authority to act as personal representatives) to the deceased's estate. A late application is only permitted if the court gives leave. Paragraph 6 of Sch 2 of the 2014 Act expressly permits an application to be made before a grant of representation has been made in respect of the estate.

13.25.2 Protection of personal representatives from personal liability

Linked to the six-month time limit is the protection against personal liability granted by the Act to the personal representatives. If no claim has been made within the time limit, then the personal representatives may distribute the deceased's estate, and will not be liable personally even if the court allows a late application. Until the time limit has expired, the personal representatives run the risk of personal liability if the claim is successful where property distributed to beneficiaries has been dissipated by them. As claims can only be made against the net estate, the deceased's debts can, however, safely be paid.

13.25.3   Ascertaining whether a grant of representation has been issued

A claimant under the Act will need to know whether, or when, a grant of representation has been issued to enable the application to be made within the time limit. There is a procedure, known as a standing search, which will enable an applicant to find this out, and to obtain a copy of the grant. Specialist texts should be consulted for details of the procedure.

13.26   The applicant

13.26.1   Categories of applicant

The onus is on applicants to show that they come within one of the categories set out in s 1(1) in order that they can apply for an order to be made in their favour.

Applications under the Act are personal actions. If the applicant dies before the matter is determined by the court, then the application cannot proceed.

13.26.1.1   The deceased's spouse (or civil partner) (s 1(1)(a))

The marriage (including now a same sex marriage—see **13.4.1.3**) or civil partnership must have subsisted at the time of the deceased's death. A judicially separated spouse can apply, unless an order has been made under s 15 by the matrimonial court, preventing an application under the Act.

13.26.1.2   The former spouse (or former civil partner) of the deceased who has not 'remarried' (s 1(1)(b))

The marriage may have ended by decree of divorce or nullity. Again, no claim can be made if the matrimonial court has barred an application under the Act (ss 15 and 15A) by the former spouse—commonly part of a 'clean break' order. Since 5 December 2005 former civil partners are included in this category, but similarly are not able to apply if the court has barred an application under the family provision legislation.

13.26.1.3   A cohabitant (s 1(1)(ba))

This provision enables a claim to be made by a person who has lived in the same household as the deceased, as their husband or wife, throughout the two-year period immediately prior to the deceased's death. Since 5 December 2005 this category is extended to include a person who had lived with the deceased in the same household throughout the two years prior to the death as part of a same-sex couple without a formal civil partnership being registered.

In *Gully v Dix* [2004] 1 FCR 453 the Court of Appeal considered whether a claimant could still be 'living in the same household as the deceased' at the time of his death—even though they were in fact living separately at that time. The couple had been living together for 27 years, but the deceased (who was an alcoholic) had become increasingly erratic in his behaviour and the claimant had been advised to move out temporarily for the sake of her health some three months before his death. It was held that they could still be living 'in the same household' if they were still 'tied by their relationship' and *neither* of them had 'demonstrated a settled acceptance or recognition that the relationship [was] ... at an end'. This was the case in this instance and the claimant was eligible to make an application under s 1(1)(ba).

13.26.1.4   A child of the deceased (s 1(1)(c))

Note that adult children can apply, but are unlikely to be successful if the applicant is able-bodied and in employment.

13.26.1.5   A person who has been treated as a child of the family of the deceased (s 1(1)(d))

The claimant has to have been treated by the deceased as a child of the family in relation to any marriage, civil partnership, or any other family in which the deceased stood in the role of a parent.

Paragraph 2(3) of Sch 2 of the 2014 Act effectively ensures that a 'single parent family' is included within the scope of this amended section.

Claims by adults are possible, but unlikely to be successful unless something more is shown.

13.26.1.6   A dependant (s 1(1)(e))

A dependant is any person (not included in the foregoing paragraphs) who immediately before the death of the deceased was being maintained, either wholly or partly, by the deceased.

In *Gully v Dix* (see **13.26.1.3**) the Court of Appeal held that Mrs Gully also had a claim under s 1(1)(e). Although the deceased was not actually maintaining her at the moment of his death, the 'settled basis' of maintenance by the deceased had not been terminated by the abnormal situation existing in the three months prior to his death.

Broadly, this category allows claims by those financially dependent on the deceased. The deceased must have been making a substantial contribution in money or money's worth towards the reasonable needs of the claimant. A contribution by the deceased made for full valuable consideration pursuant to an arrangement of a commercial nature is not included.

13.27   Reasonable financial provision

The Act (in s 1(2)) sets out a two-stage process:

(a) Has the will or the intestacy rules, or in appropriate cases a combination of the two, failed to make reasonable financial provision for the applicant?

(b) If so, the court considers what would amount to such reasonable financial provision.

What amounts to reasonable financial provision will depend on who is making the application, as the Act sets out two standards. One is applicable to an application by the surviving spouse, and the maintenance standard applies to other categories of applicant.

13.27.1   The surviving spouse/civil partner standard (s 1(2)(a))

13.27.1.1   The surviving spouse/civil partner

If the applicant is the surviving spouse/civil partner, the standard is such financial provision as would be reasonable in all the circumstances, whether or not that provision is required for maintenance.

This standard is thus more generous than the maintenance standard (see **13.27.2**). The intention is that the surviving spouse/civil partner will have a claim on the family assets at least equivalent to that of a divorced spouse, and the court is directed to have regard to the provision which would have been awarded in divorce proceedings (s 3(2), see **13.28.2.1**).

13.27.1.2   Discretion to apply surviving spouse standard to judicially separated spouses and former spouses or civil partners

By s 14 the court has a discretion to apply the surviving spouse standard to judicially separated and former spouses if the death occurs within 12 months of the final decree in the judicial separation or divorce proceedings—and no final order has been made (or refused) in those proceedings. A similar discretion will apply to applications by former civil partners.

13.27.2   The maintenance standard

The standard is such provision as would be reasonable in all the circumstances for the applicant to receive for maintenance (s 1(2)(b)). Case law establishes that reasonable provision for maintenance is such that enables the applicant to live decently and comfortably according to their situation.

13.27.3   The test

The question for the court, judged objectively on the basis of facts known at the time of the hearing (s 3(5)), is whether the will or intestacy makes reasonable financial provision for the applicant. The court is not bound by testators' views as to whether they felt they were acting reasonably in making no, or only limited, provision for the applicant.

13.27.3.1   Evidence of a testator's reasons

If there is evidence (including hearsay evidence) of the reasons why a testator has not made provision in the will for an applicant, however, this is admissible (Civil Evidence Act 1995, s 1 and see **13.28.1.5**). For instance, the testator may have placed a written statement with the will, giving reasons as to why no provision has been made for an adult child. The court will judge what weight should be given to this evidence. It will clearly be given more weight if it is considered judgement (eg 'my son has a well-paid job; my daughter's accident has prevented her earning her own living'), but the court will also take into account those children's circumstances at the time of the hearing.

The will, once admitted to probate, is a public document, and thus open to inspection. A written statement of reasons placed with the will and not referred to in it will not be admitted to probate, and thus remains confidential.

13.28   The guidelines

The court must take into account the guidelines in s 3(1), both when determining whether the applicant has established that no reasonable financial provision has been made (**13.27.3**), and in determining what order, if any, should be made under s 2 (**13.29**). It is entirely in the court's discretion as to whether any order should be made at all.

Some of the guidelines are relevant to all applicants; some only relate to a particular category of applicant.

13.28.1   Guidelines relevant to all applicants

13.28.1.1   Financial resources and needs of the applicant, any other applicant, and any beneficiary whether now or in the foreseeable future

The court will assess the relative financial position of persons with any claim on the estate. Thus a needy applicant will have greater prospects of success if the beneficiaries are well off. In *Re Collins* [1990] Fam 56, it was held that the fact that the applicant was in receipt of social security benefits did not preclude the court from making an order out of her mother's estate.

13.28.1.2   Any moral obligation of the deceased to any applicant or beneficiary

For example, in *Re Callaghan* [1984] Fam 1, a claim was made by an adult child of the family against his stepfather's estate. The stepfather died intestate and his estate passed to his three sisters whom he had not seen for ten years. The court held that the deceased's greatest obligation was owed to the applicant who had kept in close touch with him and looked after him in his last illness. The court also took into account that many of the assets of the estate came from the applicant's mother who had died some years previously, and ordered a lump-sum payment of £15,000 to the applicant to enable him to buy his council house outright.

13.28.1.3   The size and nature of the net estate of the deceased

The larger the estate, the easier it will be for the court to order reasonable provision for an applicant. Conversely, as costs will usually be awarded out of the estate, the court will discourage claims where the estate is small (*Re Coventry* [1980] Ch 461).

The source of the deceased's estate may be relevant, as in *Re Callaghan* (**13.28.1.2**).

13.28.1.4   Physical or mental disability

Any physical or mental disability of any applicant or beneficiary will be taken into account.

13.28.1.5   Any other relevant matter including the conduct of the applicant or any other person

Clearly the court has a wide discretion as to the matters it can take into account under this heading. As already mentioned, any statement (whether oral or written) by the deceased as to the reasons for the disposition of the estate can be considered (**13.27.3.1**). In *Re Callaghan* (**13.28.1.2**) the caring conduct of the applicant assisted his claim.

13.28.2   Guidelines relevant to particular categories of applicant

In addition to the factors set out at **13.28.1**, the court must also take into account the points covered in the following paragraphs.

13.28.2.1   Where the applicant is the surviving spouse (or civil partner) (s 3(2))

The following factors are relevant:

(a) the age of the applicant and the duration of the marriage;

(b) the applicant's contribution to the welfare of the deceased's family; and

(c) the provision which the applicant might reasonably have expected to receive if, at the date of death, the marriage had instead been terminated by divorce, or the civil partnership had been terminated by a dissolution order. Paragraph 5(2) of Sch 2 of the 2014 Act makes it clear that this is not to be taken as setting an upper or lower limit to the level of any award made under the family provision legislation.

However, the likely provision on divorce is only a starting point; a different award may be appropriate on a financial provision application. For instance, the divorce court will have to consider the future needs of both parties—clearly this will no longer be relevant.

Where the estate is significant, the decisions in the family law cases of *White v White* [2003] 3 WLR 1571 (HL), *Miller v Miller; McFarlane v McFarlane* [2006] UKHL 24, and *Charman v Charman (No 4)* [2007] 1 FLR 1246 (CA) may have the effect of increasing the size of the award to the surviving spouse. Principles emerging from those cases indicate that in allocating assets between the couple on divorce, the court needs to achieve a fair outcome, bearing in mind the concepts of need, sharing, and, on occasion, compensation. Any proposed financial order should be tested against the 'yardstick of equality': any departure from that yardstick should only be made for good reason.

Similar factors will apply where the application is made by the deceased's civil partner.

13.28.2.2   Where the applicant is a former spouse (or civil partner) (s 3(2))

The guidelines (a) and (b) set out at **13.28.2.1** apply. Guideline (c) (what the divorce court would order) only applies if the court exercises its discretion to apply the surviving spouse standard (see **13.27.1.2**). Again, para 5(2) of Sch 2 of the 2014 Act (see **13.28.2.1**) applies. Even if an application by a former spouse has not been barred by the matrimonial court (13.26.1.2), the Court of Appeal has indicated that only rarely would post-decree applications be successful. This is because the matrimonial court will have already considered the issues of maintenance and the allocation of assets between the parties.

Again, similar factors and principles will apply in the case of civil partnerships.

13.28.2.3 Where the applicant is a cohabitant (s 3(2A))

The following factors are relevant:

(a) the age of the applicant and how long they have lived in the same household as husband or wife of the deceased; and

(b) the applicant's contribution to the welfare of the family of the deceased, including by looking after the home or caring for the family.

13.28.2.4 Where the applicant is a child (s 3(3))

Here the court must consider the manner in which the applicant was being or might be expected to be educated or trained.

13.28.2.5 Where the applicant is a child of the family (s 3(3))

As well as considering the education guideline (in **13.28.2.4**), s 3(3) as amended by para 5(3) of Sch 2 of the 2014 Act directs the court to have regard to:

(a) whether the deceased maintained the applicant, and if so the duration of that maintenance, the basis upon which is was provided and how much maintenance the deceased contributed. A new para (aa) of s 3(3) requires the court also to have regard to whether the deceased assumed responsibility for the applicant's maintenance and, if so, to what extent;

(b) whether, if the deceased maintained or assumed responsibility for maintaining the applicant, the deceased did so knowing that the applicant was not his or her own child; and

(c) the liability of any other person to maintain the applicant.

13.28.2.6 Where the applicant was maintained by the deceased (s 3(4))

Here the court must, in addition to the general guidelines, consider the extent to which and the basis upon which the deceased assumed responsibility for the applicant.

13.29 Family provision orders

13.29.1 Types of financial provision orders

The court must take into account the guidelines set out in **13.28** in deciding whether to make an order under s 2 and, if so, the type of order. The most common order is for a lump-sum payment, either in cash or by way of a transfer of a particular asset, but periodical payment orders (eg £200 per month) can also be made. Interim periodical payment orders are possible pending the determination of the final order. Paragraph 4 of Sch 2 of the 2014 Act inserts a new s 2(1) into the 1975 Act giving the court an express power to vary, for the applicant's benefit, the trusts upon which the deceased's estate is held.

13.29.2 Inheritance tax

How is the inheritance tax position affected if the court makes an order varying the disposition of the deceased's estate? The Act provides (s 19(1)) that for all purposes, including inheritance tax, the variation is deemed to be effective as from the deceased's death. In effect, the order is 'read back', as if the deceased had made the provision ordered by the court. If, for example, the court orders that provision be made for a surviving spouse, the estate's liability for inheritance tax will be reduced. This is because the property passing to the surviving spouse will be exempt from inheritance tax.

If an award is made the court can direct whether any inheritance tax is to be borne by the applicant or the estate.

13.30 Property available for financial provision orders

The deceased's 'net estate' from which any order for financial provision orders is made is widely defined in s 25(1). It comprises the following:

(a) all property of the deceased owned at the date of death and which could have been disposed of by will, less:

   (i) funeral testamentary and administration expenses;

   (ii) debts and liabilities; and

   (iii) inheritance tax;

(b) the deceased's severable share of a joint tenancy (which normally passes by survivorship, see 13.19.1) even if the application is made outside the six-month time limit (**13.25.1**) and the court so orders (s 9 as amended by para 7 of Sch 2 of the 2014 Act). A further amendment effected by para 7 makes it clear that when considering how to value the deceased's severable share in a property, the court will, as a general rule, have regard to its value at the date the claim is heard, but that the court retains the discretion to choose a different date if appropriate;

(c) any property which the court has ordered under the anti-avoidance provisions to be available (under s 10 or 11, which are not further discussed here); and

(d) any property in respect of which the deceased made a statutory nomination (**13.19.4**), a *donatio mortis causa* (**13.19.5**), or which the deceased could have appointed in his/her lifetime under a general power of appointment which has not been exercised.

13.31 Family provision: checkpoints

1. Advising the personal representatives:

   (a) Has notice of any claim under the Act been received within the prescribed time limit (**13.25**)?

   (b) Does the claimant prima facie fall within any of the categories within s 1(1) of the Act (**13.26**)?

      (i) If so, do the dispositions taking effect on death make any provision for the claimant and could this be regarded as reasonable financial provision (**13.27**) to the relevant standard (**13.27.1** and **13.27.2**)?

      (ii) Is there any evidence as to why the deceased failed to make more generous provision for the claimant (**13.27.3.1**)?

      (iii) Do any of the general or special guidelines have any particular relevance to the claim (**13.28**)?

2. Advising the claimant:

   (a) Has a grant been issued and, if so, how long ago (see 13.25)?

   (b) Does the claimant prima facie fall within any of the categories within s 1(1) of the Act (**13.26**)?

   (c) If so, do the dispositions taking effect on death make any provision for the claimant and could this be regarded as reasonable financial provision (**13.27**) to the relevant standard (**13.27.1** and **13.27.2**)?

    (d) Is there any evidence as to why the deceased failed to make more generous provision for the claimant (**13.27.3.1**)?

    (e) Do any of the general or special guidelines have any particular relevance to the claim (**13.28**)?

Visit the Online Resource Centre for more information and useful weblinks.
www.oxfordtextbooks.co.uk/orc/foundations17_18/

Application for a grant of representation

14.1 Introduction

In this chapter we will be discussing the law and procedure relating to the issue of a grant of representation to the personal representatives of someone who has died. We will be considering:

- the nature, effect, and the principal types of grant; the position of the personal representatives; and the responsibilities of solicitors instructed to act in the administration of an estate (**14.2** to **14.11**);
- obtaining the grant—practice (**14.12** to **14.18**);
- the court's requirements; oaths for executors, for administrators with will annexed and for administrators; and further affidavit evidence that may be required (**14.19** to **14.25**); and
- HMRC's requirements; excepted estates; Form IHT 400 and its Schedules; and the calculation of inheritance tax ('IHT') (**14.26** to **14.31**).

Figure 14.2 sets out pre-grant procedures.

14.2 Grants of representation

In **14.2 to 14.18** we begin our consideration of the practice and procedure relating to the issue of a grant of representation. Such grants are court orders and are evidence of the personal representative's title to deal with the deceased's estate.

We will begin by examining briefly the court's jurisdiction in probate matters (**14.2.1**) and the responsibilities of solicitors instructed to act in the administration of an estate (**14.3**). We will then consider the effect of grants (**14.4**) and those cases where a grant is not necessary (**14.5**). The principal types of grant will then be examined (**14.6**). The following paragraphs (**14.7** to **14.11**) will look at various aspects of the position of personal representatives. Finally, in **14.12** to **14.18** we will deal with a number of practical issues involved in obtaining the grant.

14.2.1 Background

14.2.1.1 Probate jurisdiction

The probate jurisdiction of the court is concerned with three issues:

(a) whether a document may be admissible to probate;

(b) who is entitled to a grant of representation; and

(c) whether a grant already made should be revoked.

Most probate business is non-contentious (in the probate lawyer's jargon, 'common form') and is exclusively the province of the Family Division of the High Court. Where there is a dispute concerning any of these issues, the matter becomes contentious. Contentious (or 'solemn form') business is conducted in the Chancery Division, the County Court having a concurrent jurisdiction where the value of the estate is below the County Court limit at the date of death (£350,000 County Court Jurisdiction Order 2014 (SI 2014 No 503)). However, even in these cases, once the dispute is resolved the grant issues from the Family Division.

A grant is normally made by the English courts where the deceased left property situated in England and Wales (Administration of Justice Act 1932, s 2).

14.2.1.2 Non-contentious business

Common form business is mostly conducted in either the Principal Registry of the Family Division in London (headed by a senior district judge and a number of district judges) or in one of the District Probate Registries (or sub-Registries attached to most of them), each headed by a registrar. The jurisdiction of the Registries is not restricted to any geographical area. On the death of someone living (say) in Bristol there is no reason why the grant should not be applied for in Newcastle-upon-Tyne (or indeed anywhere else). However, it will normally in practice be more convenient to use the local Registry.

Application for a grant may be made by a personal representative in person or through a probate practitioner, the definition of which includes a practising solicitor.

Non-contentious business is regulated by the Non-Contentious Probate Rules 1987, as amended by the Non-Contentious Probate (Amendment) Rules 1991. For convenience, these are hereafter referred to as 'the Rules' or 'NCPR'.

The Ministry of Justice has conducted a consultation on amendments to the Rules, which ended on 29 August 2013. The results of this consultation have not (at the time of writing) been made public.

14.3 Responsibilities of solicitors instructed by personal representatives

It is not essential for personal representatives to instruct solicitors to act for them in obtaining a grant or in the administration of the estate. However, where a solicitor is instructed it is important to appreciate that the personal representatives are the solicitor's clients. Clearly, there is a potential for a conflict of interest if the solicitor also advises members of the family or the beneficiaries—especially if any hint of a dispute emerges.

It is also important to remember that the personal representatives will often be close relatives of the deceased and therefore (particularly initially) experiencing a degree of distress. The solicitor acting must be sensitive to this in dealings with the client, tempering efficiency with sympathy and understanding of the client's feelings.

14.3.1 Initial duties

On receiving instructions, the solicitor's first responsibilities will relate to the obtaining of the grant. There are basically three types of grant, which are discussed in more detail in **14.6**:

(a) *Probate*. This grant normally only issues to an executor duly appointed by the will or a codicil.

(b) *Letters of administration with will annexed*. This grant is appropriate where there is a will but for some reason it is not possible to make a grant of probate to an executor.

(c) *Letters of administration*. This grant, often called 'simple administration', is issued where the deceased died intestate.

Whichever is the appropriate grant, details will be required of the various assets and liabilities of the estate so that their value can be established. If there is a will, this will need to be obtained and its validity and admissibility to probate considered. Any application for a grant has to be supported by certain papers which will have to be prepared: these include the appropriate Oath (**14.19** to **14.23**) and in some cases other affidavit evidence (**14.24**); and either a return of estate information (**14.27**) or an inheritance tax account (**14.28** to **14.30**).

Once all the documentation is complete and any tax has been paid, application for the grant is made by lodging the various papers (including any will and codicils) at the selected

Registry, either in person or by post, together with a cheque for the appropriate court fees. On receipt by the Registry, the papers are examined to check that they are in order and any testamentary documents are photocopied. The court records are searched to check, inter alia, that no grant has already been made and that no application has been made to another Registry. If all is in order, the grant is prepared, signed by a duly authorised signatory, and sealed with the seal of the Family Division or of the District Registry. The grant is then sent, together with any office copies requested on making the application, to the 'extracting solicitor'—usually some 10 to 14 days after the application is lodged.

14.3.2   Later duties

Once the grant has been obtained, it will be necessary to advise the personal representatives as to their powers and duties. The various assets will need to be realised and the liabilities discharged. There may be a need to advise on a variety of matters, including beneficial entitlement, interim distribution, and possible changes in the disposition of the estate, before the estate can be finally wound up. These matters are considered in **Chapter 15**.

14.4   The effect of the issue of a grant

A grant of representation issued by the court is conclusive evidence as to the terms and due execution of any will (and codicil), or that the deceased died intestate.

From the viewpoint of the personal representatives, the effect of the grant depends upon whether they are executors or administrators.

14.4.1   Executors

An executor's title to act derives from the will (or codicil). The deceased's property vests in the executor on death, and the executor has full authority to deal with it without a grant. An executor may even commence court proceedings prior to the issue of a grant, though it may be necessary to obtain a grant before judgment.

The grant of probate, then, merely confirms the executor's title to act. However, a grant (or an office copy) is the only acceptable proof of the executor's title and, except in cases considered in **14.5**, will in practice always be required to enable the executor to deal with the deceased's property.

14.4.2   Administrators

Whether the grant is with will annexed or of simple administration, the issue of the grant actually confers authority to act upon the administrator; prior to this not even the person with the best right to a grant has any authority to act. It is only on the issue of the grant that the deceased's property vests in the administrator; in the interim it has been vested in the Public Trustee. What is more, the grant once made does not relate back to the date of death so as to confirm any action taken in the interim—except for the limited purpose of protecting the deceased's estate from wrongful injury in that period.

14.5   Grant not necessary

As we saw in **13.18** to **13.22** there are a number of situations where property passes on death directly to those entitled and not through the hands of the personal representatives; in these cases, since the personal representatives do not need to make title to the assets, a grant is not necessary.

It may also sometimes be possible for property which does pass to the personal representatives to be obtained or dealt with by them without the need for a grant.

14.5.1   Small sums due to the estate

Under the Administration of Estates (Small Payments) Act 1965, it may be possible for the personal representatives to obtain payment of sums due to the estate on production of a copy of the death certificate. However, where orders have been made under this Act, there is an upper limit (currently £5,000) in respect of each item—and if this is exceeded a grant will be necessary to establish title to the whole sum, not just the excess. The Act allows such payment to be made to the person appearing to be entitled to the grant or to be beneficially entitled to the asset concerned. The Act merely permits payment without a grant, however; it is not obligatory. Monies which are covered by orders under this Act include:

(a) money held in the National Savings Bank, National Savings Certificates, or Premium Savings Bonds (NB: small balances in accounts with the high street clearing banks are not covered by orders under the Act);

(b) monies payable on the death of a member of a trade union, industrial or provident society, or a friendly society;

(c) civil servants' salaries, wages, or superannuation benefits; and

(d) service, police, and firemen's pensions.

Similar provisions apply under the Building Societies Act 1986 to funds invested in a building society.

The Law Commission's Final Report on Intestacy and Family Provision Claims on Death (see **13.10**) made no recommendation that the £5,000 limit should be increased, but has recommended that the issue be further examined by the Government.

14.6   Types of grant

We have already identified the three types of grants. Entitlement to these will now be more fully considered, and is set out in diagrammatic form in **Figure 14.1**.

14.6.1   Probate

This grant can only be made to an executor, who is usually expressly appointed by the will or a codicil. If a firm of solicitors is appointed, unless the will clearly provides to the contrary (as it should), it will be the partners at the date of the will (or codicil containing the appointment) who are entitled to act. The appointment of an executor may be implied (in which case the appointee is described as 'executor according to the tenor of the will') where the will shows an intention that a particular person should perform the functions of an executor.

Appointments of executors are usually 'unlimited' as to property and time. However, it is possible for the appointment to be limited in either of these respects, for example 'I appoint X to be executor as to my business of …'; 'I appoint Y to be executor until my son Z attains his majority'. A grant issued to any such executor will be similarly limited.

14.6.2   Letters of administration with will annexed

This grant is appropriate where there is a valid will but it is not possible to make a grant of probate in favour of an executor. It may be that the will fails to appoint an executor, or that those appointed are dead or are unwilling or unable to act. Other situations where this grant will issue include cases where the appointed executors are minors or otherwise incapable of taking a grant (see **14.7**).

14.6.2.1   Rule 20 of the NCPR

This governs the order of entitlement to a grant where the deceased left a valid will. At the head of the list is an executor (who as we have seen is entitled to a grant of probate). Where such a grant is not possible, the rule lays down the order of entitlement to a grant of letters of administration with will annexed. For a person in a later category, to establish title to the grant it will be necessary to account satisfactorily for all those (including executors) who would have a better right (see **14.22.3**).

Under r 20 the full order is:

(a) an executor;

(b) a trustee of the residuary estate;

(c) any other residuary beneficiary (including one for life), or (where there is a partial intestacy because the residue is not wholly disposed of by the will) anyone entitled to share in the undisposed-of residue. Normally, a residuary beneficiary whose interest is vested will be preferred to one whose interest is contingent only;

(d) the personal representative of anyone in (c) other than a life tenant of residue;

(e) any other beneficiary (including a life tenant or one holding as a trustee) or a creditor. Again, a person with a vested interest is normally preferred to one whose interest is contingent only; and

(f) the personal representative of anyone in (e) other than a life tenant or person holding as a trustee.

As can be seen, the order mainly depends upon entitlement to the deceased's property under the terms of the will, with the residuary interest being treated as the principal interest, whatever its value in relation to the other gifts under the will.

14.6.2.2   Rule 21 of the NCPR

Where a gift in a will fails by virtue of s 15 of the Wills Act 1837 (because the beneficiary or the beneficiary's spouse/civil partner has witnessed the will, see **13.7.5**), that beneficiary loses the right to a grant under r 20 as a beneficiary named in the will—though may still claim in any other capacity (eg as a person entitled on intestacy or as a creditor).

14.6.3   **Letters of administration**

A grant of 'simple administration' is appropriate where there is no valid will.

The order of entitlement to the grant is governed by r 22 of the NCPR, which, as will be seen, broadly follows the order of entitlement to share in the estate of the intestate (discussed at **13.10** to **13.17**). Again, for anyone in a lower category to be able to establish title to the grant it will be necessary to satisfactorily account for all those with a better right (see **14.23.2**).

14.6.3.1   Rule 22 of the NCPR

The order under r 22 is:

(a) the surviving spouse (or civil partner);

(b) the children of the deceased and the issue of any child who has predeceased;

(c) the deceased's parents;

(d) the deceased's brothers and sisters of the whole blood and the issue of any who have predeceased;

(e) the deceased's brothers and sisters of the half blood and the issue of any who have predeceased;

(f) grandparents;

(g) uncles and aunts of the whole blood and the issue of any who have predeceased;

(h) uncles and aunts of the half blood and the issue of any who have predeceased;

(i) the Treasury Solicitor where the Crown claims *bona vacantia*; and

(j) a creditor of the deceased.

14.6.3.2   Personal representatives

Basically, the personal representatives of a person have the same right to a grant as the deceased whom they represent. This is subject to r 27 of the NCPR (**14.8**) and to r 22(4) which gives preference to persons within categories (b) to (h) in **14.6.3.1** over the personal representative of a surviving spouse who has died before obtaining a grant—unless the spouse was beneficially entitled to the whole estate.

14.6.4   Limited grants

There are a number of situations in which a limited grant may be appropriate. These include grants where the only person entitled to a grant is a minor or suffering from mental incapacity (**14.7**).

14.6.5   Special grants

The most commonly encountered special grant is administration *de bonis non*. Such a grant is made to allow the completion of the administration of the deceased's estate following the death of the sole, or last surviving, personal representative to whom a grant has been issued who has died leaving part of the estate unadministered. It is also the appropriate grant following the revocation of a previous grant.

A *de bonis non* grant is not necessary where one of several proving personal representatives has died; the remaining grantees have full authority to complete the administration of the estate. Nor is it appropriate on a death before a grant has been issued; a *de bonis non* grant is always a 'second grant'.

Further, it will not be necessary to obtain such a grant where the so-called 'chain of representation' exists. This occurs where a sole, or last surviving, proving executor (ie one to whom a grant of probate has been issued) dies and that executor's executor duly takes a grant of probate.

EXAMPLE 1

Suppose that Toby dies appointing Tabitha to be his executor. Tabitha proves the will but dies before completing the administration of Toby's estate, appointing Trevor to be her executor. By proving Tabitha's will, Trevor automatically becomes also the executor by representation of Toby and able to complete the administration of Toby's estate. The 'chain' only operates through proving executors. If, in the example, Tabitha had failed to appoint an executor, or if Trevor had renounced or died before taking a grant to Tabitha's estate, or either Toby or Tabitha had died intestate, there would have been no chain and a grant *de bonis non* would have been needed to complete the administration of Toby's estate.

The order of entitlement to a *de bonis non* grant is governed by r 20 (**14.6.2.1**) if the original grant was of probate or administration with will annexed; or r 22 (**14.6.3.1**) where it was a grant of simple administration.

14.7   Personal representatives: capacity

In principle, a testator is free to appoint anyone as executor. Equally, any person who under r 20 or r 22 of the NCPR has the right to a grant is entitled to apply for a grant of letters of administration. There is no rule automatically debarring (say) someone who is insolvent or who has a criminal record. However, there are a number of qualifications to this general principle, which are considered in the following paragraphs.

14.7.1   Minors

A minor cannot take a grant. If the minor is one of several executors or potential administrators, the practice is to make a grant immediately to the adult executors or administrators, with, in the case of a grant of probate, power being reserved to the minor to apply for a grant of 'double probate' on attaining 18. Where the minor is the only or last surviving executor or potential administrator, a grant of letters of administration (with will annexed if there is a will) is made (normally to the minor's parent or guardian) for the use and benefit of the minor until age 18, when it automatically terminates and a grant can then be made to the executor/administrator now entitled.

14.7.2   Mental incapacity

Where executors or potential administrators are suffering from mental incapacity such as to render them incapable of managing their own affairs, the position is broadly similar to that applying in the case of minors, and where it is the only executor/potential administrator who is so incapacitated a grant for the use and benefit of that person will be made to the persons specified in r 35 of the NCPR.

14.7.3   Section 116 of the Senior Courts Act 1981

Section 116 gives the court discretion, where it considers that 'by reason of any special circumstances' it is necessary or expedient, to issue a grant to someone other than the person who is prima facie entitled under the Rules. A grant in these circumstances may be issued to anyone (not necessarily the person with the 'next best right'), and may be general or limited in any way in which the court sees fit.

This power has been used, for example, to pass over a potential grantee shown to be unfit to administer the estate (eg because bankrupt) or otherwise unsuitable or unable to act (eg because in prison, or missing and whereabouts unknown).

14.7.4   Section 50 of the Administration of Justice Act 1985

This allows the court to remove any existing personal representative and appoint a substitute. Such substitute will be an executor if replacing an executor; otherwise the grantee will be an administrator.

14.8   Personal representatives: several claimants

14.8.1   Probate

On an application for a grant of probate, all the executors appointed by the will or any codicil (and whose appointments have not been revoked by a later codicil) must in some way be accounted for. How this is achieved will be discussed at **14.21**. Subject to this, the grant may issue to any one or more of them, up to the limit imposed by s 114 of the Senior Courts Act 1981 (**14.9**). Rule 27 of the NCPR requires that notice of the application shall normally be given to any executors to whom power is being reserved (see **14.10.2**).

14.8.2   Administration

When a grant of letters of administration with will annexed or simple administration is applied for, all those having a better right to a grant than the applicant(s) must be 'cleared off' (ie accounted for). We will consider how this should be done at **14.22** and **14.23**. Where there are several potential grantees in the same degree of priority, r 27 allows the grant to be made (again, subject to the limits imposed by s 114 of the Senior Courts Act 1981) to any one or more of them, but this time without any requirement for notice to the others entitled in the same degree.

However, r 27 further provides that preference should normally be given to:

(a) an adult rather than someone on behalf of a minor entitled in the same degree; and

(b) a living person rather than the personal representative of a deceased person who, if living, would have been entitled in the same degree.

14.9 Personal representatives: number

14.9.1 Executors

A sole executor always has full authority to act, even in cases where minority or life interests arise (contrast the position of administrators at **14.9.2**).

A testator can appoint any number of executors, but a grant of probate cannot issue to more than four (Senior Courts Act 1981, s 114). Those who have not predeceased the testator or renounced have 'power reserved' to them (see further **14.10.2**).

However, s 114 does not prevent the possibility of a grant to a maximum of four executors in respect of part of the deceased's estate and another grant to four different executors in respect of another part. Thus, if the deceased had appointed four executors to deal with his business and four further executors to deal with the rest of the estate, two grants in respect of the different parts of the estate can be made to them all.

14.9.2 Administrators

Here, whether the grant is with will annexed or simple administration, s 114 again provides for a maximum of four grantees. However, in certain cases, it also requires that there should normally be a minimum of two (or a trust corporation, such as the Public Trustee or a bank). This minimum requirement arises whenever, under any will or on the intestacy, a beneficiary is an infant, or, under any will, there is a life interest. However, if a grant is made to two grantees as a result of this requirement and one of them then dies, there is no requirement for a replacement to be appointed: the survivor has full authority to act henceforth alone (though the court may on application appoint a 'replacement').

14.9.3 Additional personal representatives

14.9.3.1 Rule 25 of the NCPR

A person entitled to a grant of administration may, without leave, apply for a grant together with a person entitled in a lower degree, provided there is no other person entitled in priority to the person to be joined—or, if there are any such persons, they have all renounced. If the person sought to be joined does not have any (or any immediate) right to a grant, an *ex parte* application to a district judge or registrar will normally be required.

14.10 Personal representatives: renunciation/power reserved

No one can be forced to accept office as an executor or administrator, though a person entitled to a grant can be forced to make up their mind whether to take a grant or not. Executors or administrators are free to renounce their rights to a grant provided they have not accepted office. As an alternative to renunciation, an executor who does not wish to act in the administration may have 'power reserved' (see **14.10.2**).

14.10.1 Executors: renunciation

An executor accepts office, thus losing the right to renounce, by taking a grant, or even before this by 'intermeddling' in the estate, ie by doing something which shows an intention to accept office. Acts of charity, humanity, or necessity are not sufficient to constitute such acceptance. Thus, for example, arranging the funeral will not be enough; but writing to request payment of monies due to the estate will.

A renunciation must be in writing, signed by the renouncing executor, and containing a statement that the executor has not intermeddled. It becomes effective on being filed at the Registry (usually with the papers to lead the grant to some other person).

An executor cannot generally renounce part of the office; it must be accepted in full, or renounced in full.

Under r 37 of the NCPR, a renunciation by an executor of the right to a grant of probate does not operate as the renunciation of any rights that person may have to a grant of letters of administration (whether as beneficiary or creditor), unless there is also an express renunciation of those rights.

14.10.2 Executors: power reserved

Rather than renounce, one of several executors appointed by the will/codicil who does not wish to act in the administration can instead have 'power reserved' (see further **14.21.7.3**). This, in effect, means that the executor concerned will not be involved in the application for the grant and thus will not be entitled/required to take part in the process of dealing with the testator's affairs. However, if circumstances change (eg a proving executor falls ill or dies, or the non-proving executor changes his mind) the executor to whom power has been reserved can apply for a grant at a later stage—and thereafter be involved with the administration.

14.10.3 Administrators: renunciation

An administrator accepts office only by taking a grant: no amount of 'intermeddling' prior to this will constitute acceptance. Renunciation is again effected in writing, signed by the renouncing 'administrator' (no declaration that there has been no intermeddling being required in this case), and this is filed (usually) with the other papers to lead the grant to someone else. Rule 37(2) provides that an administrator who has renounced in one capacity (eg as a residuary beneficiary) can claim a grant in another (eg as a creditor).

14.11 Grants of representation: checkpoints

1. Effect of the issue of a grant (**14.4**).
2. Is a grant necessary (**13.19** and **14.5**)?
3. If yes, which one is appropriate:
    (a) Is there a will?
        (i) If so, probate (**14.6.1**) or letters of administration with will annexed (**14.6.2**).
        (ii) Entitlement to grant governed by r 20 of the NCPR (**14.6.2.1**).
    (b) If no will:
        (i) Letters of administration (**14.6.3**).
        (ii) Entitlement to grant governed by r 22 of the NCPR (**14.6.3.1**).
4. Are any potential grantees:
    (a) Minors (**14.7.1**)?
    (b) Mentally incapable (**14.7.2**)?
5. Is more than one person entitled to the grant (**14.8**)?
6. How many may/must apply (**14.9** and **14.10**)?
7. May a potential applicant renounce (**14.10**)?

Figure 14.1   **Application for a grant of representation**

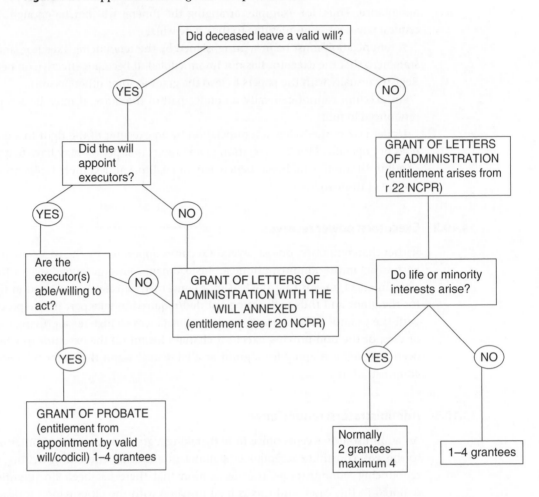

14.12   Obtaining the grant: practice overview

14.12.1   The early stages

We have already outlined some of the issues to be considered in the early stages of the administration of an estate. At **14.12.2** to **14.12.4** we will endeavour to put those matters in context and consider other practical issues which may arise in the pre-grant period of the matter.

14.12.2   Early stages: instructions

The personal representatives may (and frequently do) instruct a solicitor to act for them in the conduct of the administration. You may yourself be appointed an executor, or be a partner in a firm which has been appointed to act. In all of these cases you will have to ascertain the information you need to begin the task from the personal representatives or family members who may (especially initially) be in a distressed state. Whilst it is, of course, important that you perform your role efficiently, it is equally important that you conduct matters with sensitivity and with a proper concern for those who may not only be very upset but perhaps in temporary difficult financial circumstances resulting from the death.

14.12.2.1   What do you need to know?

Much of the information required to enable you to complete the first stage of the administration of the estate (obtaining the grant) will be apparent from the discussions in the previous sections of this chapter. In addition, you will also need to establish how and to whom the estate is to be distributed (**Chapter 13**), and whether any problems are likely to be encountered in this connection. There may, for example, be missing beneficiaries (see **15.7.2**) or the possibility of a claim under the Inheritance (Provision for Family and Dependants) Act 1975 (see **13.23** to **13.30**).

14.12.2.2   Checklists

The best way to ensure the efficient collection of the information you need from the personal representatives or family members is to use a suitable checklist. Most firms will have their own version of such a checklist, which should prompt you to discover the details appropriate to any given case relating to the following matters:

(a) full personal details relating to the deceased, the immediate family, and any dependants;

(b) full personal details relating to the proposed personal representative(s), and to beneficiaries entitled to share in the estate. In both cases, as we have seen, who these people are will very much depend upon whether or not there is a will;

(c) details of the various assets:

   (i)   in the deceased's succession estate (ie passing under the will or the intestacy rules);

   (ii) not in the succession estate but in the taxable estate (ie any property of which the deceased was a beneficial joint tenant, or in respect of which he/she had made a statutory nomination or a *donatio mortis causa*; any settled property of which the deceased had been a tenant for life);

   (iii) not forming part of the estate for either succession or taxation purposes (such as s 11 of the Married Women's Property Act 1882 and other trust policies, or certain lump sum pension scheme benefits);

(d) details of the various liabilities due from the estate or charged upon any of the assets listed above;

(e) details of any lifetime gifts within the seven years prior to the death (or at any time if a benefit was reserved).

14.12.3   **Early stages: what else will you need?**

In addition to the information identified at **14.12.2.2**, you will need (as appropriate) the following:

(a) The death certificate—you will need this to register the death (see **14.13**).

(b) The original will and any codicil(s). Your firm may already be holding these, or perhaps they have been lodged for safe keeping with the deceased's bank. Once obtained, it will be necessary to consider any issues of validity, etc which may arise (see **13.3** to **13.8**) and whether affidavit evidence may be required to support the application (see **14.24**).

(c) Any 'paperwork' associated with the various assets and liabilities. Thus, for example, you will need the title deeds relating to any land (or at least to discover their whereabouts). Similarly, such things as share certificates, insurance policies, bank and building society account details, outstanding bills, etc should be obtained.

(d) Details of any insurances (eg house and contents cover) effected by the deceased. Arrangements should be made, as soon as possible, either to have the interest of the personal representatives noted on any such policies, or for fresh cover in their name to be taken out. In the case of motor insurance, ensure (if needed) that appropriate cover is (or has been) arranged to enable family members to continue to use the vehicle.

14.12.4   **Early stages: financial difficulties?**

Always check at the first interview whether members of the deceased's family have any immediate financial needs as a result of the death. It will be some weeks (perhaps months) before significant funds will become available from the estate; do any surviving spouse/civil partner and children have access to adequate funds in the meantime?

What sources of funds might there be to assist here? Where the deceased had a joint bank or building society account with the surviving spouse/civil partner or the survivor has adequate funds of their own the problem may not be acute. Where there are funds which could be released without a grant (in particular, any s 11 of the Married Women's Property Act 1882 or other trust policies, or certain pension fund lump-sum benefits payable at the discretion of the trustees of the scheme) try to take the necessary steps to enable payment to be made as quickly as possible. Similarly, where a state- or employment-related 'pension' may be payable, deal with this as a matter of priority.

14.13   Registering the death

The first task upon receipt of instructions is to register the death with the various banks, building societies, insurance companies, etc in which the deceased had investments and to establish the amounts due to the estate as at the date of death.

This is done by sending a copy of the death certificate (solicitors may alternatively send a letter certifying the death) to the various institutions, with a request for information as to the amount due to the estate. The Law Society has agreed a protocol with the British Bankers' Association, the Building Societies Association, and the Association of British Insurers which allows solicitors to send instead a 'death certificate verification' form certifying that they have in their possession and inspected an original certificate. However, not all institutions accept this alternative procedure.

In the case of shareholdings, you should register the death with the various companies and ask them to confirm the extent of the deceased's holding; it may be that the personal representatives have not in fact located all the share certificates. You may then wish to instruct a stockbroker to prepare a valuation for you. Where the deceased owned land, the assistance of a surveyor may be required; it will be helpful in such a case if the surveyor can also give a valuation of the household and personal effects. Expert assistance in valuing the deceased's assets will also be necessary where, for example, the deceased was 'in business', whether as a sole trader or partner, or the business was conducted through the medium of a company.

The deceased's Inspector of Taxes should also be notified of the death. You will then usually receive a tax return to be completed in due course in respect of the pre-death period of the tax year in question and another relating to the post-death period; if the administration period stretches beyond the end of that tax year, further returns for the later years will be required.

At an early stage, you should also notify the various creditors of the death and that the estate is now responsible for the debts due to them. This should stop the family being further distressed by demands for payment.

If there is a will and there are beneficiaries other than those instructing you, you should inform them of their 'interest' under the will and that—subject to the will being admitted to probate and the needs of the administration—you will be contacting them again as soon as you are able to deal with their legacies. It will be helpful if you give them an estimate of the timescale involved, being as realistic as possible in this. It is important to be cautious in what you say because the will might prove not to be admissible and/or there might not be sufficient funds to enable payment in full of all the legacies after the various liabilities have been discharged.

14.14   Preparing the papers to lead the grant

As confirmation of the amounts due to the estate is received, the appropriate Oath (see further **14.21** to **14.23**) and inheritance tax forms (see further **14.27** to **14.30**) can be drafted, along with any other supporting evidence (such as affidavits and copy testamentary documents) which may be required in the particular case (see further **14.24**). Fair copies will have to be prepared for swearing or signature (as appropriate) before being lodged at the selected Registry.

14.15   Funds for payment of inheritance tax

In order to obtain the grant the personal representatives will have to pay any inheritance tax due on the delivery of the inheritance tax account. However, they normally need the grant as evidence of their title—without which those holding the deceased's funds will be unwilling to part with them! How can the deceased's personal representatives solve this 'circular' problem?

We saw in **14.5** that it is possible to obtain amounts due to the estate without production of a grant under the Administration of Estates (Small Payments) Act 1965 and any such funds could be used to help pay the tax bill.

However, it is likely in many cases that much more will be needed than can be raised in this way. HMRC have agreed a process with the British Bankers' Association and the Building Societies Association which allows personal representatives to draw on money held in bank/building society accounts in the deceased's sole name to pay the inheritance tax that is due on delivery of Form IHT 400. The scheme is voluntary on the part of the financial institutions, and where the deceased had a number of accounts with a bank/building society—including loan and credit card accounts—only the net balance is likely to be available.

If taking advantage of this scheme, a separate Schedule—IHT 423 (see **14.28.3.3**) must be completed and submitted to the bank or building society concerned in respect of each account from which it is sought to transfer funds in payment of the tax due.

Under a protocol agreed between the British Bankers' Association, the Law Society, and the Society of Trust and Estate Practitioners (STEP) the deceased's bank—subject to any right of set-off where there are debts due to it and certain other conditions—will allow the balance on the deceased's accounts to be used before production of a grant of representation for the payment of IHT and the funeral account. The bank may also allow these funds to be used to pay probate fees.

In the following paragraphs we consider other sources of funding which may be available to the personal representatives.

14.15.1   Bank loan

Either the deceased's or the personal representatives' bank will normally be happy to lend whatever is needed to pay the inheritance tax. The bank will usually insist upon an undertaking from the personal representatives to account to it from the first proceeds of the realisation of the estate assets once the grant has been obtained. An undertaking may also be required from the solicitor acting for the personal representatives, in which event the solicitors should first obtain an irrevocable authority from the personal representatives.

The bank will of course charge interest, so that, irrespective of the terms of any undertaking, the loan should be discharged as soon as possible. Provided the arrangement with the bank takes the form of a loan (rather than an overdraft facility) the personal representatives may be entitled to income tax relief for the interest payable.

14.15.2   Loan from beneficiary

A beneficiary may well be prepared (in order to mitigate or avoid the cost of bank borrowing) to lend money to help pay the inheritance tax (either interest-free or at a rate less than the commercial rate charged by the bank). If interest is paid, it will also qualify for income tax relief.

This approach will only work, of course, if the beneficiaries have money readily available—either from existing resources, or from monies passing to them on the death but outside of the will or the intestacy rules (such as the proceeds of a s 11 of the Married Women's Property Act 1882 or other trust policy, jointly held property accruing by survivorship, nominated property, or lump-sum benefits under a superannuation scheme payable at the discretion of the trustees of the scheme).

14.15.3   Sale of assets

We saw in **14.4.1** that an executor's authority derives from the will, the grant merely confirming this; administrators, on the other hand, actually have their authority conferred by the grant. In principle, therefore, it is possible for an executor (but not an administrator) to sell estate assets prior to the issue of the grant: in practice, however, purchasers may well wish to see confirmation of the vendor's title before parting with their money! In particular, although it is possible to enter into a contract to sell land 'subject to probate', the grant will be needed to make the executor's title before the sale can be completed.

However, it may be possible for an executor to sell some assets before grant. A grant is not needed to pass title to chattels; this is achieved by delivery coupled with the necessary intention. Further, under Stock Exchange rules an executor can sell quoted shares before the grant is issued, subject to an undertaking for its production being given.

14.15.4 Direct payment to HMRC

Where the deceased's assets include policies of life assurance whose proceeds are payable to the personal representatives, the insurance company may be prepared to release some/all the monies due to the estate direct to HMRC in payment of inheritance tax.

14.16 Swearing or affirming the Oath

This must be done before an independent solicitor (or Justice of the Peace), and it will be a necessary formality also for any other affidavit evidence required. The fees payable are currently £5 per deponent for each Oath or other affidavit, plus £2 per deponent for marking each will, codicil, or exhibit to any other affidavit.

14.17 Lodging the papers

When all is ready, it is necessary to lodge (by post or in person) at the selected Registry:

(a) the appropriate Oath;

(b) the will and codicil(s) (if any) plus *two* A4 copies of each such documents;

(c) if an excepted estate, Form IHT 205 (see **14.27.2**); otherwise the receipted probate summary (Schedule IHT 421—see **14.28.3.2**);

(d) any further supporting documents, such as further affidavits, copy testamentary documents (eg because the originals contain unattested alterations), and renunciations; and

(e) a cheque for the probate fees. Where the *net estate*—ie the amount remaining in the deceased's sole name after funeral expenses and debts have been deducted (joint assets passing automatically to the surviving joint owner are ignored for the purposes of the fee calculation)—does not exceed £5,000, no fee is payable. For larger estates, the fee is currently £155.

Normally, the issue of one or more office copies of the grant should be requested on lodging the application. This will (inter alia) help to speed up the process of registering the grant.

14.18 Obtaining the grant: practice overview: checkpoints

1. When taking instructions, what information/documentation, etc do you need (**14.12.2** and **14.12.3**)?

2. With whom do you need to register the death (**14.13**)?

3. How is any IHT payable on delivery of the account to be funded (**14.15**)?

4. What do you need to lodge at the selected Registry to lead the grant (**14.17**)?

See further **Figure 14.2**.

Figure 14.2   Estate administration—pre-grant procedure

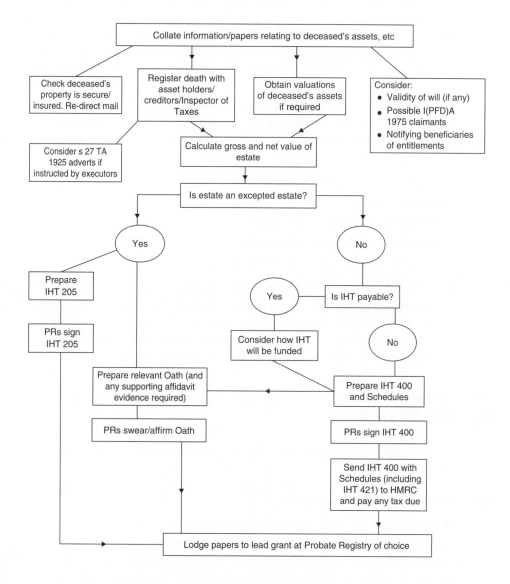

14.19   The court's requirements: Oaths

Every application for a grant of representation must be supported by an Oath—in effect, evidence in the form of an affidavit—sworn or affirmed by the personal representatives, usually before a solicitor holding a current practising certificate and who is not a partner or employee of the firm preparing the Oath.

The essential purposes of the Oath are:

(a) to identify the applicants and the deceased;

(b) (in the case of a grant of letters of administration) to account for those who have a better right to a grant under r 20 or 22 of the NCPR; and

(c) to establish the applicant's title to the grant sought.

14.20 The requirements generally

Increasingly, firms are now using commercial software packages to produce 'customised' Oaths for the particular case in which they may be acting. Alternatively, pre-printed forms are completed and adapted to meet the circumstances of the particular case. In this event, it is important to make sure that the 'finished document' reads as a piece, ie it should make proper sense in the same way as if it had been specifically drafted for the case concerned.

There are a number of different versions of pre-printed forms available from law stationers, which may vary slightly, for example in the order in which information is presented or in what is actually pre-printed, but whose basic structure is essentially similar. They all contain marginal notes to assist in their completion. In cases of doubt or difficulty the guidance of the court should be sought.

We will here consider the completion of Oaths for executors (**14.21**); for administrators with will annexed (**14.22**); and for administrators (**14.23**). In **14.24** we will consider some of the situations in which it may be necessary to provide the court with further affidavit evidence. In all cases, the heading will be the same:

IN THE HIGH COURT OF JUSTICE

FAMILY DIVISION

THE PRINCIPAL REGISTRY (or)

THE DISTRICT PROBATE REGISTRY AT

In the estate of deceased (See **14.21.1**)

The details of the extracting solicitor should also be given; the Registry will then address any correspondence or queries to the solicitor rather than the personal representatives. It will be convenient (especially in the case of larger firms) for the solicitor's reference also to be given. This will then appear on the grant when issued and thus make it easier to identify who is dealing with the matter when this is received in the extracting solicitor's office.

14.21 Oath for executors

This is the appropriate Oath where an executor appointed by the will or a codicil seeks a grant of probate. See **Form 14.1**.

14.21.1 'In the estate of … deceased'

This is, in effect, the final part of the heading. The true full name of the deceased should be entered here. In most cases, this will present no difficulty.

However, sometimes it may be necessary to include an alternative 'alias' name, for example because the will was not executed in the deceased's full name, because the deceased's name has changed since making the will, or because the deceased held property in different names.

The inclusion of an 'alternative' name will not, however, be necessary unless one of the indicated circumstances applies. Thus the fact that the deceased was named 'John' but was habitually called 'Jack' does not require any reference or explanation in the Oath, unless, for example, he made his will in the name of Jack, or held property in that name. Whenever an alias is necessary, the deceased (wherever his name is to be mentioned in the Oath) should be described by the true full name, followed by the alternative(s), for example 'John Edward Smith otherwise John Smith'. To comply with the requirements of r 9 of the NCPR it will also be necessary to furnish an explanation for the 'alias'.

14.21.1.1 The true full name

Normally, this will be the name on the birth certificate or, in the case of a married woman, the name of her husband (assuming she had adopted his surname). Similar principles will prima facie apply in the case of a divorced woman.

Form 14.1 Oath for executors

Oath for Executors

Extracting Solicitor

IN THE HIGH COURT OF JUSTICE

Address

Family Division

DX

*"Principal" or "District Probate". If "District Probate" add "at...........................".

The*

Registry

† If necessary to include alias of deceased in grant add "otherwise (alias name)" and state below which is true name and reason for requiring alias.

IN the Estate of †

(1) "I" *or* "We". Insert the full name, place of residence and occupation or, if none, description of the deponent(s). State the postcode of the deponent(s) and deceased's place of residence, if known.

(1)

deceased.

(2) *Or* "do solemnly and sincerely affirm".

make Oath and say,(2)

that

(3) Each testamentary paper must be marked by each deponent, and by the person administering the oath.

(1)   believe the paper writing   now produced to and marked by (3)

to contain the true and original last Will and Testament (4)

of †

(4) "with one, two (or more) Codicils", as the case may be.

of

deceased,

(5) This should be the date of birth as shown in the Register of Deaths.

who was born on the (5)   day of

(6) If exact age is unknown, give best estimate.

and who died on the   day of

(7) Where there are separate legal divisions in one country, the State, province, etc., should be specified.

aged   years (6) domiciled in (7)

and that to the best of   knowledge, information and belief there was (8) [no] land

vested in the said deceased which was settled previously to h   death (and not by h   Will

(8) Delete "no", if there was land vested in deceased which remained settled land notwithstanding his or her death.

(4)   )

and which remained settled land notwithstanding h   death

(9) Include the names of the executors who have renounced. Or delete if no executors are to renounce.

And (1)   further make Oath and say (2)

that (9)

executor(s) named in the said Will (4)

have renounced probate thereof

Notice of this application has been given to

(10) Delete or amend as appropriate. Notice of this application must be served on all executors to whom power is to be reserved unless dispensed with by a Registrar under Rule 27 (3), or unless Rule 27(1A) applies. All executors to whom power is to be reserved should be named.

the executor(s) to whom power is to be reserved, [save

](10)

And (1)   further make Oath and say (2)

that (11) (12)

(11) "I am" *or* "we are". Insert relationship of the executors to the deceased only if necessary to establish title or identification.

Execut

named in the said

(12) "The sole", *or* "the surviving", *or* "one of the", *or* "are the", or "two of the", etc.

[P.T.O.
PRO4/1

and that (1)　　　　will (i) collect, get in and administer according to law the real and personal estate (13)
of the said deceased; (ii) when required to do so by the Court, exhibit in the Court a full inventory of the said estate (13)
and when so required render an account thereof to the Court; and (iii) when required to do so by the High Court, deliver up the grant of probate to that Court; and that to the best of　　　　knowledge, information and belief

(13) If there was settled land the grant should exclude it. Insert "save and except settled land".

(14) Complete this paragraph only if the deceased died on or after 1 April 1981 and an Inland Revenue Account is not required; the next paragraphs should be deleted.

(14) [the gross estate passing under the grant does not exceed (15) £　　　　　　　　　　,
and the net estate does not exceed (16) £　　　　　　　　and that this is not a case in which an Inland Revenue Account is required to be delivered]

(15) The amount to be inserted here should be in accordance with the relevant figure shown in paragraph 1 of the PEP List.

(16) The amount to be inserted here should be the net value of the estate, rounded up to the next whole thousand.

(17) [the gross estate passing under the grant amounts to £
and the net estate amounts to £　　　　　　　　　].

(17) Complete this paragraph only if an Inland Revenue Account is required and delete the previous and following paragraph.

(18) Complete this paragraph only if the estate qualifies under paragraph 2 of the PEP List and delete the previous two paragraphs.

(18) [the gross estate passing under the grant amounts to (19) £　　　　　　and
the net estate amounts to (20) £　　　　　　and that this is not a case in which an Inland Revenue Account is required to be delivered]

(19) The amount to be inserted here is the exact amount of the gross estate.

(20) The amount to be inserted here is the exact amount of the net estate.

SWORN by

the above-named Deponent
at

this　　　　day of

Before me,

}

A Commissioner for Oaths/Solicitor.

SWORN by

the above-named Deponent
at

this　　　　day of

Before me,

}

A Commissioner for Oaths/Solicitor.

SWORN by

the above-named Deponent
at

this　　　　day of

Before me,

}

A Commissioner for Oaths/Solicitor.

Oyez 7 Spa Road, London SE16 3QQ
© Crown copyright.

Probate 4

11.2009

5073580

PRO4/2

14.21.1.2   Common problems

14.21.1.2.1   Will in 'incorrect' name

This might arise, for example, because the deceased whose full name is Jane Elizabeth Smith has made her will in the name of Jane Smith. In such a case, she should be described as 'Jane Elizabeth Smith (otherwise Jane Smith)'. It will also be necessary to swear, in the Oath (at the end of the printed form) or in a separate affidavit, that 'the true name of the deceased is Jane Elizabeth Smith but that she made and executed her will in the name of Jane Smith'. In such a case, the grant will normally issue in the true name only.

14.21.1.2.2   Property in different names

Where the deceased held property in different names, again the full true name should be given first, followed by the 'alias'. It will also be necessary, at the end of the Oath form or in a separate affidavit, to indicate which is the true name and to include a statement that the deceased held property in the alternative name(s)—identifying (at least one item of) property held in the alternative name(s). For example, at the end of the pre-printed form might be added 'And that the true name of the deceased was Jonathan Smith and that he held Black-acre in the name of John Smith'. The grant will then be issued showing both names.

14.21.2   **The applicants**

The first paragraph of the Oath identifies those who are applying for the grant. The order should be the same as that in the will, but, in practice, if it is desired to change the order (eg to place a solicitor who has been appointed first) this can be done.

14.21.2.1   Names

The true full name of each applicant should be given. If this differs from the name in the will/codicil containing the appointment, an explanation will be required.

If the discrepancy is slight, the matter is usually easily dealt with, for example 'Susan Jones (in the will called Sue Jones)'. If the name has been misspelled, again the solution is simple, for example 'Jonathan James (in the will written Jonathon James)'. If the name has changed on marriage the explanation (eg) 'Ann Evans, married woman (formerly and in the will called Ann Brown, spinster)' will suffice.

Sometimes, the Registry may require further proof of the identity of an applicant. This might arise, for example, where the will appoints 'my wife' without naming her. In such a case, the (short) further evidence needed can usually be incorporated into the Oath (eg by including a statement that the applicant 'was the lawful wife of the deceased at the date of the will').

14.21.2.2   Addresses

The full postal address (including postcode) of the true place of residence of each applicant should be given. Solicitors (and others acting in a professional capacity) may give their business addresses. Former addresses need not be given unless relevant in establishing the executor's identity (where this is an issue).

14.21.2.3   Occupations or descriptions

The occupation of each applicant, male or female, should be given (eg 'schoolteacher' or, if retired, 'retired schoolteacher'). If the applicant has no occupation, this should be stated.

14.21.3   **'… make Oath and say …'**

It is not necessary for the Oath to be sworn. Applicants may, instead, affirm—in which event, the words 'make Oath and say' whenever they appear should be deleted and replaced with 'do solemnly and sincerely affirm'. It will also be necessary to alter the jurat at the end of the form (in some prints this appears on the back of the form) by deleting the word 'SWORN' and substituting 'AFFIRMED'.

14.21.4   **'... That [I/We] believe the paper writing now produced to and marked by [Me/Us] to contain the true and original last will and testament ...'**

The purpose of this statement is to identify the document(s) which are being put forward as admissible to probate. This is achieved by 'marking' the document(s) concerned. The deponents (the applicants for the grant swearing the oath or making the affirmation) and the solicitor administering the oath or taking the affirmation sign the documents, thus exhibiting them to the affidavit evidence which the Oath comprises. If there is a codicil, after the word 'testament' there should be added 'with (one) (two, or as the case may be) codicil(s)'.

14.21.5   **Details of the deceased**

This part of the form requires basic information regarding the deceased testator. This must now include their date of birth and gender.

14.21.5.1   Name

As already discussed (in **14.21.1**) the deceased's full true name should be given here, with any alias.

14.21.5.2   Address

The last residential (postal) address (including post code, where known) of the testator should be given. If this is different from the address in the will or codicil, the previous address should be added after the words 'formerly of ...' (any intervening changes of address are ignored). If the addresses are the same, the words 'formerly of' should be deleted.

14.21.5.3   Date of birth and death

Usually, the birth and death certificates will give the relevant dates; however, it is not normally necessary to submit copies of the certificates.

14.21.5.4   Age

The testator's age should be stated (the best estimate being sufficient where this is uncertain).

14.21.5.5   Domicile

Normally, the deceased's domicile at the date of death must be included in the Oath. Where the deceased died domiciled in England or Wales domicile should be sworn as 'England and Wales'. The sworn domicile will appear in the grant; this may have important consequences in relation to the recognition of grants within the different jurisdictions in the UK.

14.21.6   **Settled land**

You will not often in practice encounter an estate where the deceased had an interest in settled land governed by the Settled Land Act 1925; this is even more unlikely now that no new strict settlements can be created (Trusts of Land and Appointment of Trustees Act 1996). However, in all cases the personal representatives must state whether there is/is not any settled land. It is quite wrong simply to delete the whole paragraph where there is no such land in the estate. In fact, the only permissible deletion is of the word '(no)' where there is, in fact, such land—for which a separate grant will be needed. In this event, it is enough to disclose in the Oath its existence: it is not necessary to give details of the settlement.

14.21.7   **Executor's title**

The purpose of this part of the form is to establish the 'capacity' in which the proving executors claim to be entitled to the grant. The discussion which follows indicates some of the more commonly met situations.

14.21.7.1   Relationship to the deceased

As we have seen (**14.4.1**), an executor's 'title' essentially depends upon appointment as executor by the will or codicil, the grant strictly only being required as evidence of that title. The fact that an executor is related to the deceased is therefore normally immaterial and need not be stated. However, it will be necessary to state the applicant's relationship to the deceased where identity is an issue, for example if the will appoints 'my daughter' without naming her. If the will appoints 'my wife' or 'my husband' without naming the spouse concerned, the Oath should include a statement to the effect that the applicant is the lawful widow(er) and was lawfully married to the deceased at the time of the making of the will.

14.21.7.2   Where all appointed are applying

The wording to be used to describe the title of the proving applicant(s) will obviously depend upon the circumstances of the particular case. For example:

Only one appointee	*the sole executor/executrix*
All male, or male and female	*the executors*
All female	*the executrixes*
Implied appointment	*the executor according to the tenor*

14.21.7.3   Not all applying

Again the wording to be used to describe the entitlement of those applying will depend upon the circumstances. For example:

Some have died	*the surviving executor(s)/executrixes*
Some have renounced	*one (or two, etc) of the executors/executrixes*

In this case it is not necessary to recite the fact of renunciation by the other executor(s), but it helps the Registry if this is done. However, the renunciation itself must be filed with the papers to lead the grant.

Power is to be reserved	*one (or two, etc) of the executors/executrixes*

In this situation, the name(s) of the executor(s) to whom power is to be reserved must be indicated: further, the Oath must normally also state (NCPR, r 27) that notice of the application for the grant has been given to such executor(s).

14.21.7.4   Partners in a firm

Where partners in a firm (eg of solicitors) are appointed by name and some have predeceased or renounced, or power is to be reserved to one or more of the named partners, the procedures described in **14.21.7.3** should be followed.

Where, however, the appointment is of partners in a firm without naming them (eg 'the partners at the date of my death in Solicitor & Co') and not all of them wish to apply, it is sufficient for the Oath to contain a statement that the applicant is/was a partner (or the applicants are/were partners) at the appropriate date. Power can be reserved to 'the other partners' without naming them, and notice need not be given to those not wishing to act (NCPR, r 27(1A)).

14.21.8   Duties of the personal representatives

In practice little needs to be done with this paragraph of the Oath, except where there is settled land (see **14.21.6**), when it will be necessary to insert the words 'save and except settled land'.

14.21.9 Value of the estate passing under the grant

This is the deceased's free estate (ie unsettled property) in the UK in respect of which a grant is needed as evidence of the personal representatives' title. Property which does not pass to the personal representatives (ie in that capacity) is not relevant here (see **13.18** to **13.22**).

In this part of the Oath the appropriate inheritance tax certificate must be completed. There are now three possibilities, depending upon whether or not the estate is an 'excepted estate' for tax purposes. As we will see, if an estate is excepted it is necessary to file a return of estate information in Form IHT 205 (see **14.27**), but a formal inheritance tax account in Form IHT 400 (see **14.28**) is not required. Where the printed form offers alternatives for completion, those not relevant to the particular case should be deleted.

14.21.9.1 Excepted estate—gross value not exceeding inheritance tax threshold
(first paragraph on the OYEZ printed form)

If the estate is excepted (ie a formal account is not required) because its gross value does not exceed the inheritance tax threshold at the date of the application (in 2017/18 this is £325,000), the gross and net figures are not stated in the Oath precisely, but rather as not exceeding:

- (in the case of the gross estate) the appropriate tax threshold; or
- (in the case of the net estate) the value of that estate, rounded up to the next whole thousand pounds.

EXAMPLE 2

If in the case of a death in 2017/18 the value of the estate passing under the will is £150,000 (gross) and £144,500 (net), the figures to be inserted would be £325,000 (gross) and £145,000 (net). The certificate must also include the words 'and this is not a case in which an Inland Revenue Account is required to be delivered'.

14.21.9.2 Estate not an excepted estate (second paragraph on the OYEZ Form 14.1)

Here, the exact gross and net values should be shown, but in this situation the words 'and this is not a case in which an Inland Revenue Account is required to be delivered' are, of course, inappropriate.

14.21.9.3 Excepted estate—gross value exceeds tax threshold but does not exceed £1 million and the chargeable estate after deducting spouse/charity exemption(s) does not exceed the tax threshold (third paragraph on the OYEZ Form 14.1)

Here, again, the exact gross and net values should be given but the certificate must also include the words 'and this is not a case in which an Inland Revenue Account is required to be delivered'.

14.21.9.4 Other matters

The blank space at the end of the printed form can be used to provide any further information which might be required, for example as to an alias (see **14.21.1**), as to the identity of the applicant (see **14.21.2**), or as to the notice required under r 27 of the NCPR (see **14.21.7.3**) if not dealt with earlier. If the matter cannot be dealt with concisely, it will be necessary to file a separate affidavit.

14.21.10 Jurat

Each deponent must swear, or affirm, the Oath before an independent solicitor (or Justice of the Peace). It is not necessary for the names of all the deponents to be inserted if they are all swearing or affirming at the same time. Otherwise, a separate jurat should be drawn and completed for each deponent.

14.22   Oath for administrators with will annexed

As we saw in **14.6.2**, a grant of letters of administration with will annexed is appropriate whenever there is a will and a grant is for some reason not going to be made to an executor (because, perhaps, none was appointed, or those appointed are all dead, or have renounced). See **Form 14.2**.

Many of the points discussed at **14.21** regarding the completion of an Oath for executors apply equally to the Oath for administrators with the will. In this section we will concentrate upon the points of difference.

14.22.1   The applicants

Entitlement to apply for a grant of administration with will annexed is determined by r 20 of the NCPR (see **14.6.2.1**). The order in which the applicants' names appear in the Oath should follow that order.

14.22.2   Minority and life interests

We have already seen (in **14.9.2**) that if a minority or life interest arises, a grant of letters of administration (whether or not with will annexed) will normally only issue to two grantees (or a trust corporation). An oath for administrators with will annexed must contain a statement as to whether or not there are minority or life interests arising—either under the terms of the will, or under the intestacy rules where the deceased died partially intestate. This part of the Oath form must, therefore, always be appropriately completed.

14.22.3   Clearing

The Oath must always 'clear off'—in effect, account for—all those who under r 20 of the NCPR have a 'better right' to the grant than the applicant(s). There is no need to account for anyone else in the same category as the applicant(s), nor to give notice of the application to any such person(s). All oaths for administration with will annexed will, therefore, have to account for the fact that no executor is applying by showing (as the case may be) that no executors were appointed, or that they are all dead or have renounced.

What further clearing is required will then depend upon how far down the list the applicant comes. Where there is a partial intestacy and an applicant is seeking a grant as a person entitled to share in the undisposed-of property under the intestacy rules, anyone under r 22 of the NCPR having a 'better' claim than the applicant will also have to be cleared. Thus, in the second example in **14.22.4**, it would be necessary to account for the fact that the deceased's spouse/civil partner (who would have a better right under r 22 than his children) was not applying.

14.22.4   Capacity

The Oath must then state the precise capacity in which the applicant claims to be entitled to the grant. This, remember, depends essentially upon entitlement to share in the estate rather than relationship to the deceased. Thus, for example:

(a) 'the residuary legatee and devisee under the said will';

(b) 'the daughters of the deceased and two of the persons entitled to share in the undisposed-of estate of the said deceased';

(c) 'one of the specific legatees and devisees named in the said will'.

Form 14.2 Oath for administrators with the Will

Oath for Administrators with the Will

IN THE HIGH COURT OF JUSTICE
Family Division

Extracting Solicitor

Address

DX

*"Principal" *or* "District Probate" .
If "District Probate" add
"at _____ "

The*   Registry

† If necessary to include alias of
deceased in grant, add "otherwise
(alias name)" and state below
which is true name and reason
for requiring alias.

IN the Estate of †

(1) "I" *or* "We". Insert the full name,
place of residence and occupation
or, if none, description of the
deponent(s). State the post code of
the deponent(s) and deceased's
place of residence, if known.

(1)

                                                                    deceased,

(2) *Or* "do solemnly and sincerely
affirm".

(3) Each testamentary paper must
be marked by each deponent, and
by the person administering the
oath.

(4) "With one, two (or more)
Codicils", as the case may be.

make Oath and say (2)

that (1)   believe the paper writing   now produced to and marked by (3)

to contain the true and original last Will and Testament (4)
of †

(5) This should be the date of
birth as shown in the Register
of Deaths.

of

(6) If exact age is unknown, give
best estimate.

                                                                    deceased,

(7) Where there are separate legal
divisions in one country, the State,
province, etc., should be stated.

who was born on the (5)   day of

(8) Complete both blanks. When
either such interest arises, two
grantees may be required unless
a trust corporation is applying.

and who died on the   day of   ,

aged   years (6) domiciled in (7)

(9) Delete "no", if there was settled
land vested in deceased which
remained settled land
notwithstanding his death.

and that (8)   minority and (8)   life interest arises in the estate of the
said deceased; and that to the best of   knowledge, information and belief there

(10) If there was settled land such
land may no longer be included
in the scope of the grant.

was (9) [no] land vested in the deceased which was settled previously to h   death
(and not by h   Will (4)   ) and

(11) Here state manner in which
all prior rights are satisfied, e.g.,
residuary legatees/devisees must
show that no executors were
appointed, or that those appointed
either died before deceased or
survived him and have since died
without taking probate, or that they
have renounced probate, or have
failed to take a grant after being
cited so to do (*the order authorising
a grant to citor being quoted*).

which remained settled land notwithstanding h   death (10)

and (1)   further make Oath and say (2)
that (11)

(12) "I am" or "we are" and state title
of applicants to the grant, including
their relationship to the deceased
only if necessary to establish title
or identification.

that (12)   ; and that

(1)   will (i) collect, get in and administer according to law the real and personal estate

(13) If there was settled land, insert
"save and except settled land".

(13)   of the said deceased;
(ii) when required to do so by the Court, exhibit in the Court a full inventory of the said
estate, (13)   and when so required

(14) Complete this paragraph only if
the deceased died on or after 1 April
1981 and an Inland Revenue
Account is not required; the next
paragraphs should be deleted.

render an account thereof to the Court; and (iii) when required to do so by the High Court,
deliver up the grant of letters of administration with Will annexed to that Court; and that
to the best of   knowledge, information and belief

(15) The amount to be inserted
here should be in accordance with
the relevant figure shown in
paragraph 1 of the PEP List.
(16) The amount to be inserted
here should be the net value
of the estate, rounded up to
the next whole thousand.
(17) Complete this paragraph only
if an Inland Revenue Account is
required and delete the previous
and following paragraphs.

(14) [the gross estate passing under the grant does not exceed (15) £   ,
and the net estate does not exceed (16) £   , and that this is not a
case in which an Inland Revenue Account is required to be delivered]

(17) [the gross estate passing under the grant amounts to £
and the net estate amounts to £   ].
†

(18) Complete this paragraph
only if the estate qualifies under
paragraph 2 of the PEP List and
delete the previous two
paragraphs.
(19) The amount to be inserted
here is the exact amount of the
gross estate.

(18) [the gross estate passing under the grant amounts to (19) £
and the net estate amounts to (20) £   and that this
is not a case in which an Inland Revenue Account is required to be delivered]

(20) The amount to be inserted
here is the exact amount of the
net estate.

[P.T.O.
PRO11/1

SWORN by

the above-named Deponent
at

this   day of
Before me,

}

A Commissioner for Oaths/Solicitor.

SWORN by

the above-named Deponent
at

this   day of

Before me,

}

A Commissioner for Oaths/Solicitor.

SWORN by

the above-named Deponent
at

this   day of

Before me,

}

A Commissioner for Oaths/Solicitor.

SWORN by

the above-named Deponent
at

this   day of

Before me,

}

A Commissioner for Oaths/Solicitor.

14.23 Oath for administrators

The grant of simple administration is appropriate where the deceased died wholly intestate. See **Form 14.3**. The entitlement to the grant essentially depends (as we saw in **14.6.3.1**) upon the applicant's relationship to the deceased. Many of the comments made in explanation of the practice in completing the Oath for executors (**14.21**) and the Oath for administrators with will annexed (**14.22**) are equally relevant in this case also. Again, we will here concentrate upon the differences.

14.23.1 The applicants

The order in which the names of the applicants are set out in the Oath should follow the order of priority in r 22 of the NCPR (see **14.6.3.1**). In the case of simple administration, no question of a discrepancy with the will can, of course, arise.

14.23.2 Clearing off

Following the words '… *domiciled in … Intestate*' it is necessary to account for those with a better right to the grant than the applicant. Specifically, three matters must here be addressed.

14.23.2.1 Status of the deceased

The deceased's marital status must first be indicated, for example:

(a) 'a bachelor/spinster';

(b) 'a married man/woman/lawful civil partner';

(c) 'a widow/widower/a surviving civil partner'; or

(d) 'a single man/woman' (where the deceased's marriage had been ended by a decree absolute of divorce). The details of the divorce (including the name of the court and the date of the decree) must be recited and it must also be sworn or affirmed that the deceased had not remarried/entered into a further civil partnership.

14.23.2.2 Clearing off those entitled under r 22 of the NCPR

It is not necessary to clear anyone entitled under this rule in the same category as the applicant (nor is it necessary to give notice of the application to any such person). Thus, for example, if the deceased had four children, an application may be made by one of them (two if a minority or life interest arises) without reference to the others. However, it is essential to account for all those who might have a better right to the grant. This is, in effect, normally done by showing that the deceased was not survived by any relative(s) in the categories higher than that of the applicant(s), or that any survivors have since died or renounced.

In the simplest case, ie where there are no surviving relatives with a better right to the grant, the wording used is as follows:

To clear	Swear that deceased died
Spouse/civil partner	a bachelor, spinster, lawful widow(er), surviving civil partner, single man/woman
Children/issue	without issue
Parents	(or) parent
Brothers/sisters/their issue	(or) brother or sister of the whole [or half] blood or issue thereof
Grandparents	(or) grandparent
Uncles/aunts/their issue	or uncle or aunt of the whole [or half] blood or issue thereof

Form 14.3 Oath for administrators

Oath for Administrators

IN THE HIGH COURT OF JUSTICE

Family Division

Extracting Solicitor

Address

DX

The*   **Registry**

IN the Estate of †

deceased,

(1)

make Oath and say (2)
that†

of

deceased,

who was born on the (3)   day of

and died on the   day of   ,

aged (4)   years domiciled in (5)

intestate (6)

(7) [or]   any other
person   entitled in priority to share in h   estate by virtue of any enactment and that
(8)   minority (8)   life interest arises under the intestacy; and
that to the best of   knowledge, information and belief there was (9) [no] land
vested in the said deceased which was settled previously to h   death and which
remained settled land notwithstanding h   death (10)

And (1)   further make Oath and say (2)
that (11)   the (12)

of the said Intestate,
and that (1)   will (i) collect, get in and administer according to law the real and
personal estate (13)
of the said deceased; (ii) when required to do so by the Court, exhibit in the Court a full
inventory of the said estate (13)
and when so required render an account thereof to the Court; and (iii) when required to
do so by the High Court, deliver up the grant of letters of administration to that Court;
and that to the best of   knowledge, information and belief

(14) [the gross estate passing under the grant does not exceed (15) £   , and
the net estate does not exceed (16) £   , and that this is not a case
in which an Inland Revenue Account is required to be delivered]

(17) [the gross estate passing under the grant amounts to £
and the net estate amounts to £   ].
†

(18) [the gross estate passing under the grant amounts to (19) £   and the
net estate amounts to (20) £   and that this is not a case in which an
Inland Revenue Account is required to be delivered]

Marginal notes:

*"Principal" or "District Probate". If "District Probate" add "at----".

†If necessary to include alias of deceased in grant, add "otherwise (alias name)" and state below which is true name and reason for requiring alias.

(1) "I" or "We". Insert the full name, place of residence and occupation or, if none, description of the deponent(s). State the post code of the deponent(s) and deceased's place of residence, if known.

(2) or "do so solemnly and sincerely affirm".

(3) This should be the date of birth as shown in the Register of Deaths.

(4) If exact age is unknown, give best estimate.

(5) Where there are separate legal divisions in one country, the State, province, etc., should be stated.

(6) Here give the status of deceased- "a spinster", "a widower", etc., and where necessary clear off the classes entitled in order of priority to applicant, e.g., "without issue or parent".

(7) The words which follow clear illegitimate, legitimated and adopted children and should be deleted if application made by surviving spouse or the civil partner (unless in the special circumstances it is necessary to clear issue) or a child. If appropriate substitute "without" for "or".

(8) Complete both blanks. When either such interest arises two grantees may be required unless a trust corporation is applying.

(9) Delete "no", if there was land vested in deceased which remained settled land notwithstanding his death.

(10) If there was settled land such land may no longer be included in the scope of the grant.

(11) "I am" or "we are".

(12) Show applicant's title, e.g., "brother of the whole blood and one of the persons entitled to share in the estate".

(13) If there was settled land, insert "save and except settled land".

(14) Complete this paragraph only if the deceased died on or after 1 April 1981 and an Inland Revenue Account is not required; the next paragraphs should be deleted.

(15) The amount to be inserted here should be in accordance with the relevant figure shown in paragraph 1 of the PEP List.

(16) The amount to be inserted here should be the net value of the estate, rounded up to the next whole thousand.

(17) Complete this paragraph only if an Inland Revenue Account is required and delete the previous and following paragraphs.

(18) Complete this paragraph only if the estate qualifies under paragraph 2 of the PEP List and delete the previous two paragraphs.

(19) The amount to be inserted here is the exact amount of the gross estate.

(20) The amount to be inserted here is the exact amount of the net estate.

[P.T.O.
PRO8/1

SWORN by

the above-named Deponent
at

this   day of

Before me,

A Commissioner for Oaths/Solicitor.

SWORN by

the above-named Deponent
at

this   day of

Before me,

A Commissioner for Oaths/Solicitor.

SWORN by

the above-named Deponent
at

this   day of

Before me,

A Commissioner for Oaths/Solicitor.

SWORN by

the above-named Deponent
at

this   day of

Before me,

A Commissioner for Oaths/Solicitor.

Where a relative in a higher category has survived but has since died/is not seeking a grant (eg having renounced) the wording of the Oath must deal with this, for example: '... Intestate leaving ... his lawful widow and the only person entitled to his estate him surviving who has since died/duly renounced letters of administration'. (In the latter case, the renunciation must be lodged with the papers to lead the grant.)

14.23.2.3   Clearing off 'any other person entitled in priority ... by virtue of any enactment'

These words are designed to clear any illegitimate, legitimated, and adopted children and remoter issue of the deceased; they cannot be used as a 'short cut' formula for clearing those entitled under r 22.

If the surviving spouse or children/issue of the deceased is making the application, these words should normally be deleted.

If the applicant is from any category in r 22 below children or other issue, the words 'or any other person entitled ... by virtue of any enactment' must always be left in.

14.23.3   Minority and life interests

The Oath for administrators must (as with the application for a grant with will annexed) contain a statement as to whether or not any such interests arise. A minority interest may of course arise whenever a beneficiary entitled to a share under the intestacy rules is under 18. Due to the enactment of the Inheritance and Trustees' Powers Act 2014, a life interest will no longer arise under the intestacy rules.

14.23.4   Capacity in which grant sought

Essentially, as we have seen, the applicant's title depends upon relationship to the deceased and entitlement to the estate. The Oath must contain a precise statement as to both these matters.

14.23.4.1   Relationship

Some of the more commonly met descriptions to be used here are:

Spouse	*Lawful husband/lawful widow*
Civil partner	*Lawful civil partner*
Child	*Son/daughter*—note that this is the appropriate description whether or not the child's parents were married at the time of the child's birth.
Adopted child	*Lawful adopted son/daughter*—note that the Oath should contain a statement giving details of the adoption order and that it is still subsisting.
Grandchild	*Grandson/granddaughter*—note that the Oath will have to show that the grandchild's parent had predeceased so as to give the grandchild a beneficial interest under the statutory trusts.
Brother or sister	*Brother/sister of the whole [or half] blood*
Nephew or niece	*Nephew/niece of the whole [or half] blood*—again, it will be necessary for the Oath to show that the applicant's parent has predeceased so as to give the applicant a share of the estate.
Parent	*Father/mother*
Grandparent	*Grandfather/grandmother*
Uncle or aunt	*Uncle/aunt of the whole [or half] blood*

Cousin	*Cousin-german of the whole [or half] blood*—again, the Oath must show that the applicant's parent has predeceased so as to give the cousin a share of the estate.

14.23.4.2   Entitlement to the estate

The Oath must show the applicant's/applicants' entitlement to the estate. For example: 'the only person(s) entitled to the estate'; 'one [two, etc] of the persons entitled to share in the estate'.

14.24   Further affidavit evidence

In the vast majority of cases, a properly completed Oath is the only affidavit evidence that the court will require. Sometimes, however, the district judge or registrar will require further affidavit evidence to be submitted before issuing a grant. Some of the situations where such additional evidence may be required are considered briefly below: in such circumstances you will need to consult relevant practitioner works and perhaps the court itself as to the nature of the evidence required.

14.24.1   Due execution (r 12 of the NCPR)

We saw in **13.3.4.2** that the inclusion in a will of an attestation clause prima facie showing compliance with the requirements of s 9 of the Wills Act 1837 raises a presumption of due execution. If no attestation clause is included, or that included is insufficient, due execution will have to be proved—as it will if there is any reason for possible doubt as to the will's due execution (eg where the signature is imperfect or appears in an unusual position). Evidence of due execution may also be required where the deceased was blind, or executed the will with a mark, or where the will was signed by someone on behalf of the testator—though in all these cases the matter is in practice most effectively dealt with by an adjustment to the attestation clause in the will. If this has not been done, an affidavit as to knowledge and approval will also be required (see **14.24.2**).

Ideally, the evidence of due execution should be given by one of the attesting witnesses or (failing this) anyone else present at the time of execution.

14.24.2   Knowledge and approval (r 13 of the NCPR)

Where a will has been signed by a blind or illiterate person, or by someone else on the testator's behalf, or if for any reason (eg signs of extreme feebleness in the signature) there is a possible doubt as to whether the testator had the necessary knowledge and approval of the contents of the will (see **13.3.3.2**), the court must be satisfied on these points before the will can be admitted to probate. These matters are (as we have already seen at **13.3.4.2**) best dealt with by appropriate adjustments to the attestation clause; if this has not been done, affidavit evidence will be required to support the application for the grant.

14.24.3   Terms, condition, and date of will (r 14 of the NCPR)

The more commonly met possibilities here are set out in what follows.

14.24.3.1   Alterations

We discussed the problems connected with alterations in **13.5**, where we saw that (except in the case of the filling in of a blank space) any unexecuted obliteration, interlineation, or other alteration is presumed to have been made after execution of the will and thus to be inadmissible. Where a will contains any such unexecuted alterations, etc it will normally be necessary (unless the district judge or registrar decides that the alteration is of no practical importance) for affidavit evidence to be provided as to whether or not each and every such alteration existed at the date of the execution of the will. Ideally, this should be given by one of the witnesses or (failing this) by anyone else present at the time of execution. A copy of the will, omitting any inadmissible alterations (and showing a blank space where an obliteration has rendered the original wording not apparent), will have to be prepared and lodged with the other papers to lead the grant.

14.24.3.2 Incorporation

Where a will refers to another document in such terms as to suggest that it should be incorporated in the will (see **13.6**) the document will have to be produced and identified by (usually) affidavit evidence.

14.24.3.3 Date

Where there is doubt as to the date upon which a will was executed affidavit evidence will normally be required (ideally from one of the witnesses or anyone else present at the time) to establish the date of its execution. If possible, this should establish the exact date of execution; however, if this is not possible it should seek to establish execution between two definite dates.

14.24.4 Attempted revocation (r 15 of the NCPR)

Where there are circumstances which suggest the possibility of attempted revocation (whether by burning, tearing, or otherwise destroying, or by possible later will or codicil—eg suggested by the presence of pin or staple marks) the court must (in effect) be satisfied that the will has not been revoked. To this end, an affidavit of 'plight and condition' will often be required.

14.25 The court's requirements: checkpoints

1. Oath for executors:
    (a) Are there any 'alias' problems (**14.21.1**)?
    (b) Are there any problems in identifying the applicant(s) (**14.21.2**)?
    (c) Do any of the applicants wish to affirm rather than swear (**14.21.3**)?
    (d) What was the deceased's domicile (**14.21.5.5**)?
    (e) What is the position regarding settled land (**14.21.6**)?
    (f) How should the title of the applicant(s) be stated (**14.21.7**)?
    (g) Have all non-proving executors been accounted for in some way and any required notices given (**14.21.7.3** and **14.21.7.4**)?
    (h) Which of the statements relating to the estate passing under the grant should be included (**14.21.9**)?
2. Oath for administrators with will annexed:
    (a) Are there any 'alias' problems (**14.21.1**)?
    (b) Are there any problems in identifying the applicant(s) (**14.21.2**)?
    (c) Do any of the applicants wish to affirm rather than swear (**14.21.3**)?
    (d) What was the deceased's domicile (**14.21.5.5**)?
    (e) Are there any minority or life interests—if so, minimum of two applicants normally needed (**14.22.2**)?
    (f) What is the position regarding settled land (**14.21.6**)?

(g)   Have those with a better right under r 20 been cleared off (**14.22.3**)?

(h)   How should the title of the applicant(s) be described (**14.22.4**)?

(i)   Which of the statements relating to the estate passing under the grant should be included (**14.21.9**)?

3.   Oath for administrators:

(a)   Are there any 'alias' problems (**14.21.1**)?

(b)   Do any of the applicants wish to affirm rather than swear (**14.21.3**)?

(c)   Have those with a better right under r 22 been cleared off (**14.23.2**)?

(d)   What was the deceased's domicile (**14.21.5.5**)?

(e)   Are there any minority interests—if so, minimum of two applicants normally needed (**14.22.2** and **14.23.3**)?

(f)   What is the position regarding settled land (**14.23.6**)?

(g)   How should the title of the applicant(s) be described (**14.23.4**)?

(h)   Which of the statements relating to the estate passing under the grant should be included (**14.21.9**)?

4.   Further affidavit evidence; are there any circumstances which may call for further evidence to be submitted, for example:

(a)   query as to due execution of will (**14.24.1**);

(b)   query as to knowledge and approval of contents of will (**14.24.2**);

(c)   alterations in will (**14.24.3.1**);

(d)   incorporation (**14.24.3.2**);

(e)   query as to date of will (**14.24.3.3**);

(f)   query as to attempted revocation of will (**14.24.4**).

14.26   HMRC's requirements

*Before studying the material in this section (**14.26** to **14.30**), you will find it helpful to have considered Chapter 7 on inheritance tax, and especially **7.9**, which relates to the charge to tax on death.*

Unless the estate is an 'excepted estate' (see **14.27**), it will not normally be possible for the personal representatives to obtain a grant of representation until they have submitted a formal inheritance tax account (see **14.28**), giving details of all the property in the deceased's taxable estate and its value, and (subject to the instalment option) paid any inheritance tax for which they are liable (Senior Courts Act 1981, s 109). The personal representatives are under a duty to deliver an account (normally) within 12 months after the end of the month of death. However, they will in practice want to be in a position to do so much earlier than this, because:

(a)   until they have paid the tax due on the delivery of the account they will be unable to obtain the grant and thus will be unable effectively to deal with the estate; and

(b)   interest will begin to run six months after the end of the month of death.

The account form currently in use is known as IHT 400, which comprises a core account (considered in **14.28**) supported by Schedules as required in the circumstances of each particular case (considered in **14.29**). The steps involved in the actual calculation of the tax are identified in **14.28.6** and **14.29**.

In order to satisfy HMRC's requirements, it will be necessary for the solicitor acting for the personal representatives to obtain details of the various assets and liabilities of the estate, including property which passes on the death otherwise than through them (see **13.18** to **13.22**). The value of all such assets and liabilities as at the date of death must be established. This is a straightforward enough process in many cases, simply involving correspondence (eg with the bank, building society, insurance company, etc) to ascertain the amount due to/from the estate. In other cases, expert assistance may be required (eg from an accountant, surveyor, or stockbroker) in order to establish the open market value of the property concerned at the date of death.

In ascertaining the extent and value of the estate, the personal representatives (and the solicitor acting for them) are required to make the fullest enquiries that are reasonably practicable in the circumstances—failure to do so may lead to penalties being imposed. Where an account is required, this must be completed to the best of the personal representatives' knowledge and belief. Again, there may be penalties (and even the liability to prosecution) for failure to disclose property on which tax may be payable.

The system is essentially one of 'self-assessment' of the taxable estate and calculation of any tax payable. The values shown in the account will ultimately have to be 'agreed' with HMRC (in the case of land with the local district valuer), but this is usually done after the grant has been issued. Where tax is payable, this must be calculated by the solicitor acting for the personal representatives, who should then send the completed account to HMRC, together with all necessary Schedules—including the probate summary (IHT 421: see **14.28.3.2**)—and a cheque for the amount of the tax (plus any interest) due from the personal representatives. If tax, etc is to be paid from the deceased's bank or building society account(s) it will also be necessary to submit a (separate) Schedule IHT 423 in respect of each such account to be used to the bank or building society concerned (see **14.15**). When IHT 421 is returned, it is lodged at the selected Registry with the other papers to lead the grant (see **14.17**). If the estate does not qualify as an excepted estate, but nonetheless in the circumstances of the case no inheritance tax is in fact payable, IHT 421 is lodged with the other papers to lead the grant, and at the same time Form IHT 400 and relevant Schedules are sent to HMRC.

14.27 Excepted estates

If the estate is an 'excepted estate' there is no requirement to file a formal account in order to obtain a grant of representation, unless:

(a) HMRC so require by notice in writing within 35 days of the issue of the grant; or

(b) it is subsequently discovered that the estate is not, after all, an excepted estate, in which event an account must be filed within six months of that discovery.

However, it will be necessary to file a 'Return of estate information'—Form IHT 205—see **14.27.2**.

In very broad terms, an excepted estate is one where no IHT is payable, either because the 'gross estate' (as defined) does not exceed the tax threshold, or does not exceed £1 million and no IHT is payable because of the operation of the spouse/civil partner and/or charity exemptions (for the detailed definition, see **14.27.1**).

The present version of the rules is to be found in the Inheritance Tax (Delivery of Accounts) (Excepted Estates) Regulations 2004 (SI 2004 No 2543) as amended particularly by the Inheritance Tax (Delivery of Accounts) (Excepted Estates) (Amendment) Regulations 2011 (SI 2011 No 214) and the Inheritance Tax (Delivery of Accounts) (Excepted Estates) (Amendment) Regulations 2014 (SI 2014 No 488).

14.27.1 Definition

An excepted estate includes one where all the following conditions are met:

(a) the deceased died domiciled in the UK; and

(b) the estate comprises only property which passes under the deceased's will or under the intestacy rules, or by statutory nomination, or beneficially by survivorship, or is settled property (not exceeding £150,000 in value) in which the deceased was entitled (immediately prior to death) under a single trust to an interest in possession; and

(c) not more that £100,000 of the gross value of such property is attributable to property situate outside the UK; and

(d) the deceased had not made any chargeable transfers (ie excluding exempt transfers but including former potentially exempt transfers ('PETs')) during the seven years prior to death, other than 'specified transfers' not exceeding in aggregate £150,000; and

(e) the total gross value (ie ignoring exemptions and liabilities) of the deceased's estate, plus 'specified transfers' and 'specified exempt transfers', does not exceed:

either

the inheritance tax threshold at the time of the application for the grant (if the application is made on/after 6 April but before 6 August in any year, the relevant figure will be the tax threshold for the previous tax year);

or

£1 million and the net chargeable estate (after deduction of any exempt transfer on death to a spouse/civil partner and/or charity (but not any other 'specified exempt transfer') and the liabilities of the estate) do not exceed the relevant tax threshold. In relation to deaths prior to 6 April 2010 it was possible for an estate to be an 'excepted estate' even though in the event the exemptions did not in fact apply because, after taking into account liabilities, etc, no property actually passed to an exempt beneficiary. This unintended anomaly has been removed for deaths on/after 6 April 2010.

'Specified transfers' are chargeable transfers (including former PETs) consisting only of cash and/or quoted shares or securities and/or an interest in land (plus furnishings and chattels intended to be enjoyed with the land) unless the property concerned is subject to a reservation of benefit or becomes settled property. Thus, for example, if the estate of the deceased includes trust property exceeding £100,000 in value or the deceased had an existing cumulative total at the date of death exceeding £100,000 the estate cannot be an excepted estate.

'Specified exempt transfers' include transfers between spouses/civil partners and gifts to charities (and also, eg, transfers to qualifying political parties or to provide maintenance funds for historic buildings, etc).

In deciding whether conditions (d) and (e) are met, neither business property relief nor agricultural property relief are taken into account in determining the value of a chargeable transfer. In respect of deaths on/after 1 March 2010, transfers within the normal expenditure out of income exemption (**7.6.3.4**) made within seven years prior to death and which exceed £3,000 in a given tax year are to be treated as chargeable transfers in determining whether the estate qualifies as 'excepted'. In determining whether condition (e) is met, where the deceased was a beneficial joint tenant, only the value of the deceased's interest is taken into account.

For deaths on/after 6 April 2010, an estate which can benefit from the transferable nil rate band (**7.9.5**) may be able to qualify as an excepted estate—see **14.27.3**. There is also a category of excepted estates for persons who have never been domiciled in the UK. In such cases, there will be no need to deliver a formal account if the deceased's UK estate is attributable solely to cash and/or quoted shares or securities the gross value of which does not exceed £100,000.

14.27.2   Form IHT 205

Although a formal account is not required, all applications for a grant in respect of an excepted estate must be accompanied by a 'Return of estate information'—IHT 205 (or IHT 207 where the deceased died domiciled abroad). The current version of this return is an eight-page document—IHT 205 (2011)—which (along with explanatory notes IHT 206 (2011)) can be downloaded from the Online Resource Centre (link at the end of this chapter) or from the website at https://www.gov.uk/government/publications/inheritance-tax-return-of-estate-information-iht205-2011.

14.27.2.1   Page 1 and 2

Question 1 requests information about the deceased.

Questions 3–8 are concerned with various issues relating to the estate and designed to ascertain (in effect) whether it is indeed an excepted estate. They require a 'No' or 'Yes' answer and identify various indicators that will mean completion of a formal account—IHT 400 (see **14.28**).

14.27.2.2   Pages 3 to 8

Question 9 relates to assets to be added to the estate for inheritance tax purposes but for which a grant is not required—lifetime transfers made within seven years of death; deceased's share of joint assets passing automatically to the surviving joint tenant; any assets held in trust for the benefit of the deceased during their lifetime; nominated assets; and assets outside the UK. Pence should be ignored. Leave blank any box where the deceased did not have assets of the type specified. The total of the figures in Boxes 9.1–9.5 is entered in Box A—'Gross value of assets for which a grant is not required'.

Question 10 relates to debts payable from the assets declared in Question 9. Again, pence should be ignored and the debts may be rounded up to the nearest pound. The total of the figures in Boxes 10.1–10.4 should be entered in Box B. This figure is then deducted from that in Box A and the result entered in Box C—'Net value of assets for which a grant is not required'.

Question 11 requests similar information about the deceased's own assets for which a grant is required, the total value of which is identified in Box D—'Gross value of assets for which a grant is required'.

Question 12 is concerned with debts of the deceased. The total is entered in Box E. The 'Net estate in the UK for the purposes of the grant' (D–E) is shown at Box F. The 'net estate for inheritance tax purposes' (Box C + Box F) is shown at Box G and the 'Gross estate for inheritance tax purposes' (Box A + Box D) is shown at Box H.

Question 13 gives an opportunity for the applicants to provide any further information asked for by HMRC or which they wish to be taken into account.

Question 14 is concerned with the deduction of exemptions for property passing to the deceased's spouse and/or charities. If the figure at Box H is less than the inheritance tax threshold, there can be no tax to pay and so it is not necessary to deduct any exemption that may be due—in which case enter '0' in Box J and copy the figure from Box G to Box K. Otherwise, the exemptions should be itemised and then totalled at Box J and at Box K show the 'Net qualifying value for excepted estates'—Box G less Box J.

The figure at Box K must not exceed the inheritance tax threshold if the estate is to be an excepted estate. If it does, Form IHT 205 is not appropriate and a formal account will be required (IHT 400—see **14.28**)—unless claiming transfer of the Nil Rate Band (see **14.27.3**).

The Declaration on page 8 is completed, and the Form signed by the applicant(s).

14.27.3   Claim to transfer unused nil rate band for excepted estates

The Inheritance Tax (Delivery of Accounts) (Excepted Estates) (Amendment) Regulations 2011 also provide for the possibility of an estate which is an excepted estate benefiting from the transfer of unused nil rate band of a pre-deceased spouse/civil partner. The effect of the claim will be to increase the available nil rate band on the occasion of the second death by 100 per cent—ie on a (second) death in 2017/18 to £650,000—and the second estate remains an excepted estate so that completion of Form IHT 205 is appropriate. A claim can be made in respect of one earlier death only.

14.27.3.1   Conditions

(a) The second deceased must have survived the earlier death of their spouse/civil partner and have been married to, or in a civil partnership with, the first deceased at the time of the earlier death.

(b) The first deceased, who must have been domiciled in the UK at the date of their death, died:

- on or after 13 November 1974 if the spouse of the second deceased; or
- on or after 5 December 2005 if the civil partner of the second deceased

(c) None of the nil rate band was used on the earlier death—so that 100 per cent is available for transfer.

(d) The first deceased's estate:

- consisted only of property passing under their will/intestacy and jointly owned assets passing to an exempt beneficiary;
- did not include foreign assets whose gross value exceeded £100,000, settled property, or gift(s) with reservation of benefit to anyone other than the second deceased;
- did not qualify for agricultural property or business property reliefs either on death or during their lifetime;
- (for deaths after 1 March 2011) did not include 'normal expenditure out of income gifts' exceeding in total £3,000 in any of the seven years prior to their death.

If any of the conditions are not met then it will be necessary to complete Form IHT 400 (see **14.28**).

14.27.3.2   The claim

If all the conditions are met, the claim to transfer the unused nil rate band is made by completing Form IHT 217 and sending it with the completed IHT 205, along with the other papers to lead the grant, to the Probate Registry. Form IHT 217 can be downloaded from the Online Resource Centre (link at end of the chapter) or from a search of the HMRC website at http://www.hmrc.gov.uk.

14.28   Form IHT 400

14.28.1   Introduction

Where the estate is not an excepted estate, this account must be completed in all cases, together with any appropriate Schedules, which will always include the probate summary—IHT 421 (see **14.28.3.2**).

The current version of the account is a 16-page document, which (along with the Schedules and explanatory notes to aid completion) can be downloaded from the Online Resource Centre (link at the end of the chapter) or from a search of the website at https://www.gov.uk/government/publications/inheritance-tax-inheritance-tax-account-iht400.

[HMRC has also produced an 'IHT Toolkit' which highlights areas of risk and identifies detailed steps to be taken in mitigation of possible issues that may arise in completing Form 400 and dealing with the IHT aspects of the estate at https://www.gov.uk/government/collections/tax-agents-toolkits].

The form contains a series of questions that must be answered; where there is nothing to be recorded in a particular box insert a dash or write in the figure '0'.

In showing the value of assets and liabilities and in identifying the taxable estate on the form, pence are ignored. Assets should be rounded down and liabilities rounded up to the nearest pound. However, when it comes to the actual calculation of tax (and any interest) due, pence are not ignored!

There are certain types of grant where it may not be necessary to fully complete IHT 400: for example, where the grant is to be limited to certain assets or is required only in respect of settled land. Such cases are beyond the scope of this book and are not considered further.

14.28.2   Pages 1 to 4 (Boxes 1–28)

Pages 1 and 2 are concerned with the deceased's details (Boxes 1–16) and page 3 requires information regarding the person(s) dealing with the estate and details relating to any will and codicil(s) (Boxes 17–26). Boxes 27 and 28 on page 4 need only be answered if there is a will.

14.28.3   Pages 4 and 5 (Boxes 29–48)

The rest of page 4 and page 5 contain a series of questions designed to identify which of the listed Schedules will be needed in the particular case. These should be completed before proceeding to the completion of the rest of IHT 400.

The information required to be included in the various Schedules is indicated in the forms and further assistance can be found in the explanatory notes. It is proposed here only to refer to three cases.

14.28.3.1   IHT 402—Claim to transfer unused nil rate band

This Schedule should be submitted by the personal representatives (not later than 24 months after the end of the month in which the deceased died) if:

- the deceased died on/after 9 October 2007; and
- their spouse/civil partner died before them; and
- when the spouse/civil partner died their estate did not use up all of the nil rate band available to it; and
- it is desired to transfer the unused amount to the deceased's estate.

For the IHT nil rate band in force at the date the spouse or civil partner died reference can be made to the Inheritance Tax Thresholds (which can be downloaded from https://www.gov.uk/government/publications/rates-and-allowances-inheritance-tax-thresholds/).

The effect of the claim is that, on the deceased's death, the nil rate band available is increased by the *percentage* of the nil rate band (not the amount) unused on the earlier death of their spouse/civil partner (see **7.9.5**).

Thus, suppose on the first death which occurred when the nil rate band was £300,000 the deceased left £120,000 to their only child and the residue (ie £180,000) to their surviving spouse who dies in May 2017 when the nil rate band is £325,000.

The percentage increase in the nil rate band available on the second death is 60% (£180,000 ÷ £300,000 × 100). The amount transferable on the second death is therefore £325,000 × 60% = £195,000. The total nil rate band available on the second death is therefore £520,000 (£325,000 + £195,000).

(If all of the estate on the first death had been left to the surviving spouse the available nil rate band on the second death would be £650,000.)

14.28.3.2   IHT 421—Probate summary

This Schedule must be completed in every case (other than an excepted estate) where application is being made for a grant in England and Wales (or Northern Ireland).

On page 2, the figures are taken from IHT 400 and Schedules. They are used to identify the 'Gross and Net estate for probate purposes' (at Boxes 3 and 5 respectively). These figures are needed to complete the appropriate Oath (see **14.21.9**); they will also appear in the grant itself when issued by the relevant Probate Registry, along with the figure for the total tax and interest paid on the account shown at Box 6.

14.28.3.3   IHT 422—Application for inheritance tax reference

This Schedule is required if there is any inheritance tax to pay on the estate: a reference number is required before a payment can be made and if it is intended to do so by cheque a payslip will also be needed. Alternatively, application can be made online.

It it is intended to pay by transferring money from the deceased's bank or building society account(s) it will also be necessary to submit a Schedule **IHT 423** in respect of each such account to be used (see **14.15**).

14.28.4   Pages 6 and 7 (Boxes 49–79)

This section of the account is concerned with the assets owned by the deceased in the UK—ie all those owned outright by the deceased and the deceased's share of jointly owned assets. Figures from the various Schedules are copied as appropriate to the various boxes. The figures in Column A (relating to property not enjoying the benefit of the instalment option for the payment of tax) are totalled at Box 77 and those in Column B (relating to property in respect of which that option is available—whether or not it is to be exercised) at Box 78. This gives, at Box 79, the 'Gross estate in the UK'.

14.28.5   Pages 8 to 10 (Boxes 80–108)

On page 8, deductions from the estate in the UK incurred up to the date of death are identified. In Box 80, details should be given of mortgages, secured loans, and other debts payable out of property or assets owned outright by the deceased and included in Column B on pages 6 and 7. Details of funeral expenses should be shown in Box 81 and other liabilities in Box 82.

A 'Deductions summary' (Boxes 83–91) occupies the first part of page 9, identifying at Box 91 the total estate in the UK.

Exemptions and reliefs are dealt with in Boxes 92–6. In Box 92 at the bottom of page 9 exemptions and reliefs claimed against assets in the deceased's sole name shown in Column A on pages 6 and 7 are identified. In Box 93 at the top of page 10 a similar exercise is conducted in relation to claims against assets in the deceased's sole name shown in Column B on pages 6 and 7. (In both cases, exemptions and reliefs relating to jointly owned assets should not be included here but deducted on IHT 404.) The section ends with the 'Total net estate in the UK after exemptions and reliefs' at Box 96.

The remainder of page 10 is devoted to identifying other assets taken into account to calculate the tax (Boxes 97–106). These are totalled at Box 107 and added to the 'Total net estate' (Box 96) to identify the 'Total chargeable estate' at Box 108.

14.28.6   Page 11 (Boxes 109–17)

This page is concerned with the calculation of the tax: if no tax is payable it can be ignored. At Box 109, any claim for reduction of the rate of IHT from 40 per cent to 36 per cent where at least 10 per cent of the estate passes to charity (see **7.9.6**) will necessitate the completion of IHT 430. At Box 110 indication must be given as to whether the instalment option (where available) is to be exercised. If so, the tax will have to be calculated using Form IHT 400 Calculation (see **14.29**).

The 'Simple Inheritance Tax Calculation' (Boxes 111–17) can be used if *all* the specified preconditions are met. Otherwise, the Form IHT 400 Calculation must be used (again, see **14.29**).

14.28.7   Pages 12 and 13 (Boxes 118 and 119)

On page 12, Box 118 is concerned with whether the direct payment scheme for the tax is to be used.

Box 119 is the declaration that all those delivering the account must complete and sign (on page 13).

14.28.8   Page 14 Checklist

This page contains a useful reminder of action to be taken and the additional information to be included when sending the forms to HMRC.

14.28.9 Pages 15 and 16

These pages identify return addresses and contact details and provide space for providing additional information.

14.29 Form IHT 400 Calculation

This form should be used where IHT 400 has been completed up to and including Box 109 and the simple tax calculation is not available to work out the inheritance tax payable.

A detailed consideration of the calculations that may be involved in completing this form is beyond the scope of this book. However, the form does contain useful brief summaries of:

- successive charges relief;
- double taxation relief;
- the calculation of interest on late payment of inheritance tax; and
- 'interest-free' instalments.

14.30 Summary

In completing, where required to do so, Form IHT 400 and any necessary Schedules, you are, in effect, presenting the details of the taxable estate and (where tax is payable) the calculation of the tax in the manner which HMRC prefer and, indeed, require. However, in essence, the process is that described in **7.9** to **7.11**. In summary, this involves:

(a) Identifying the chargeable value (ie after any available exemptions and reliefs have been claimed) of any lifetime chargeable transfers (including former PETs) within the seven years prior to the death.

(b) Identifying the value of the chargeable estate on death, which involves:

    (i) establishing the gross value of all assets within the succession estate;

    (ii) establishing the gross value of all property (of the kinds identified in **13.20**) which is not part of the succession estate but is part of the taxable estate;

    (iii) deducting the value of any allowable debts, etc;

    (iv) deducting the value of property covered by an available exemption or relief from tax.

(c) Cumulating the chargeable estate on death with the total of lifetime chargeable transfers.

(d) Applying the current inheritance tax rate scale to that (combined) cumulative total, taking account of any available unused nil rate band from an earlier death.

(e) Identifying the tax for which the personal representatives/others are accountable:

    (i) lifetime chargeable transfers (supplementary charge)—normally the trustees;

    (ii) former PETs—normally the donees;

    (iii) gifts with reservation of benefit—normally the donees;

    (iv) trust property—normally the trustees;

    (v) deceased's free estate—normally the personal representatives.

(f) Identifying the amount of tax to be paid by the personal representatives on delivery of the account:

    (i) tax on the non-instalment option property in full;

    (ii) tax on instalment option property;

        (1) if option not being exercised, in full;

        (2) if option being exercised, any instalment(s) already due;

    (iii) any interest where payment late.

14.31 HMRC's requirements: checkpoints

1. Is the estate an 'excepted estate' requiring completion of Form IHT 205—and if transfer of unused nil rate band is claimed—IHT 217 (**14.27**)?

2. If not, use Form IHT 400 and Schedules as required (**14.28**).

3. Calculate any tax due—simple tax calculation—if available (**14.28.6**); otherwise, Form IHT 400 Calculation (**14.29**).

 online resource centre Visit the Online Resource Centre for more information and useful weblinks.
www.oxfordtextbooks.co.uk/orc/foundations17_18/

Post-grant practice

15.1 Introduction

In this chapter we consider the law and practice relating to the administration and winding-up of an estate once the court has issued the grant. We will be considering:

- the duties and powers of personal representatives (**15.2** to **15.5**);
- administering the estate (**15.6** to **15.13**); and
- distributing the estate (**15.14** to **15.21**).

15.2 Duties and powers of personal representatives

As we have seen, it is generally necessary for personal representatives to obtain a grant of representation to establish title to the deceased's estate. Once the grant has been obtained, the personal representatives will need to know what duties and powers they have in the administration of the estate.

The Trustee Act 2000, which came into effect on 1 February 2001 but *in general applies to all trusts whenever created*, has significantly affected a number of the duties and powers discussed in **15.3** and **15.4**. The 2000 Act, which by virtue of s 35 *also applies to personal representatives*, does not override any express provisions of the will or trust instrument. These may extend, modify, or exclude the statutory provisions.

15.3 Duties of personal representatives

15.3.1 The fundamental duty of personal representatives

The fundamental duty of a personal representative is to 'collect and get in' the deceased's estate, and then 'to administer it according to law' (Administration of Estates Act 1925, s 25, as amended). This duty must be performed 'with due diligence'.

15.3.1.1 Duty to collect the deceased's assets

Within a reasonable time, taking such steps as may be reasonably necessary, the personal representatives must collect the monies due and other assets belonging to the deceased which vest in them. There is no absolute rule as to what is 'reasonable' in this context. Personal representatives will only be liable for loss resulting from their unreasonable conduct.

In practice, it will generally be necessary for the personal representatives to produce the original (or office copy) grant of representation to the persons who hold the deceased's assets, in order to establish entitlement to deal with such assets (see **14.4**).

15.3.1.2 Property of the deceased which does not vest in the personal representatives

The above duty only relates to the deceased's interests in property which devolve on the personal representatives. As we saw at **13.19**, certain types of property pass direct to those entitled on death and therefore do not vest in the personal representatives.

15.3.1.3   The duty to administer

Reasonable steps must be taken to preserve the deceased's estate, and within a reasonable time (prima facie within the 'executor's year'—the period of 12 months from the date of death) the personal representatives must realise any investments which it is not proper for them to retain.

Once the assets have been realised, administration of the estate thereafter involves the payment of debts, etc and any legacies, and the distribution of the residue according to the terms of the will and/or the intestacy rules (see further **15.6** to **15.21**).

15.3.1.4   Other duties

Duties imposed by s 25 of the Administration of Estates Act 1925 relate to the preparation (when required to do so by the court) of an inventory and account, and the delivery up to the court of the grant issued (eg so that it can be revoked and a new grant issued) if called upon to do so. We have seen that the various forms of Oath which constitute (in effect) the application for the grant (discussed in **14.19** onwards) contain statements acknowledging these duties.

15.3.2   The duty of care—Trustee Act 2000

Section 1 of the Trustee Act 2000 creates a defined statutory duty of care applicable to trustees and personal representatives when carrying out their functions under the Act or equivalent functions under powers conferred by the will or trust instrument. They must act with such care and skill as is reasonable, bearing in mind any special knowledge or experience they have and, for professional trustees or personal representatives, any special knowledge or experience it is reasonable to expect them to have. This duty is in addition to the existing fundamental duties of trustees—for example, to act in the best interests of the beneficiaries and to comply with the terms of the trust.

It is probable that the statutory duty does no more in effect than codify the common law duty of care so that the 2000 Act may have made little difference in practical terms.

The statutory duty is a 'default' provision that may be excluded or modified by the trust instrument. Many professionally drafted wills and trust documents contain a clause excluding liability for breach of the standard of care, and it is anticipated that this practice will continue, with the effect that the beneficiaries of professionally drafted wills and trusts may be 'entitled' to a lower standard of care than that applicable to home-made efforts or on intestacy. The (former) Solicitors' Code of Conduct 2007, Rule 2 (guidance note 67) indicated that where a solicitor/firm was considering acting as a paid executor/trustee a clause having the effect of excluding or limiting liability for negligence should not be included in the will/trust instrument without having first taken reasonable steps to ensure that the testator/settlor was aware of the meaning and effect of the clause. The Trust Law Committee (a research group based at King's College London) has gone further and recommended that paid trustees should not be able to rely on a clause excluding liability for negligence.

15.3.3   Statutory and equitable apportionments

These complex rules are no longer of concern for trusts created on/after 1 October 2013 as the Trusts (Capital and Income) Act 2013 disapplied them with effect from that date. They continue to be of relevance to trusts created before 1 October 2013, though in practice they were usually excluded by express contrary provision in wills etc. They are not considered further here.

15.3.4   Liability of personal representatives

Having accepted office, a personal representative is liable to beneficiaries or creditors for loss resulting from his own breach of duty (whether that arises from a misappropriation of estate assets, maladministration, or negligence). A personal representative is not liable for loss resulting from a breach of duty by fellow personal representatives, unless negligent in allowing such breaches to take place.

15.4   Administrative powers of personal representatives

The Administration of Estates Act 1925 confers upon personal representatives a number of powers in connection with the administration of an estate. In addition, the Trustee Act 1925, the Trusts of Land and Appointment of Trustees Act 1996, and the Trustee Act 2000 give certain powers to trustees—and since the definition of 'trustee' for the purpose of these Acts effectively includes a personal representative, personal representatives also have these powers. These statutory powers are implied in all cases, ie whether the deceased died testate or intestate. In some cases they are subject to awkward limitations, and professionally drawn wills usually give the personal representatives wider powers. The principal statutory powers are outlined at **15.4.1** to **15.4.12**, together with an indication, where appropriate, of the type of modification or express clause that will commonly be contained in a will.

15.4.1   Power of personal representative to sell, mortgage, or lease

Section 39 of the Administration of Estates Act 1925 (as amended by the Trusts of Land and Appointment of Trustees Act 1996 and the Trustee Act 2000) confers upon personal representatives wide powers enabling them to sell or exchange any property, raise money by mortgage or charge, and grant or accept surrender of leases. These wide powers are necessary to enable the personal representatives to raise monies to pay a range of administration expenses (eg the payment of debts, funeral and testamentary expenses, inheritance tax, and pecuniary legacies). The personal representatives must decide which assets should be sold (see further **15.9.2**).

15.4.2   Power to appropriate

15.4.2.1   The power

Section 41 of the Administration of Estates Act 1925 provides that personal representatives may appropriate any part of the estate in or towards satisfaction of any legacy or interest or share in the estate, provided no specific beneficiary is thereby prejudiced. The 'appropriate consents' are necessary: thus, if the beneficiary is absolutely and beneficially entitled, the consent of that beneficiary is required (or of the beneficiary's parent or guardian if a minor). The asset to be appropriated must be valued for this purpose at the date of appropriation rather than at death (*Re Collins* [1975] 1 WLR 309).

EXAMPLE 1

Tom leaves a pecuniary legacy of £5,000 to Beth. The residue includes shares now worth £3,000. Provided Beth consents, the shares can be appropriated to her in partial satisfaction of her legacy, the balance being paid in cash. However, this would not be possible if (eg) the shares concerned had been specifically bequeathed to Beatrice.

15.4.2.2   Provision in will

Wills commonly dispense with the need for the consents required by s 41 on the ground of convenience.

15.4.2.3   Application of the 'self-dealing' rule

We hope that you will recall this rule (ie that a trustee may not purchase trust property) from your earlier study of the law of trusts. The justification for the rule lies in the potential conflict of interest that may arise.

In *Kane v Radley-Kane* [1998] 3 WLR 617 it was held that this rule applies equally to personal representatives. In this case, a widow took out letters of administration to her husband's estate. The assets included some shares in a private company, which she appropriated to herself in partial satisfaction of her statutory legacy. She subsequently sold the holding for almost ten times its value at the date of appropriation. It was held that the appropriation without the consent of the court or the other beneficiaries was invalid.

Thus, it will not be possible (unless authorised in the particular case by the will) for a personal representative to make an appropriation in his/her own favour in satisfaction of a pecuniary legacy—unless the assets appropriated are cash or the equivalent of cash (eg government stocks, PLC shares).

15.4.3 Power to accept receipts for a minor's property

Unless the will provides otherwise, a minor is unable to give a valid receipt for monies or assets transferred to him or her in satisfaction of a legacy. A commonly held view is that parents (or guardians) are only able to give a valid receipt on behalf of their minor child if so authorised by the will. In the absence of such provision, the personal representatives have to retain the legacy until the minor has reached adulthood, thus preventing the estate from being wound up—for what might be a comparatively small amount of money. To overcome this difficulty, s 42 of the Administration of Estates Act 1925 enables personal representatives to appoint trustees of the property for the minor, provided the minor had a vested interest.

An alternative view, mentioned in the *Law Society's Probate Practitioner's Handbook* (6th edn, p 296 Chapter 17), is that there is no longer a problem with receipts for minors as a result of s 3 of the Children Act 1989. This section provides that persons with 'parental responsibility' under the Act have the rights and duties which a parent has in relation to a child and his property. These rights include 'the right … to receive and recover in his own name, for the benefit of the child, property … which the child is entitled to receive or recover' (s 3(3)). The parent (or guardian) would recover such monies in a fiduciary capacity for the child.

If the gift is contingent (eg on the minor attaining 18) then it cannot, of course, be paid until the contingency is satisfied.

15.4.3.1 Express provision in the will

It is not uncommon, despite the statutory provisions mentioned, for wills expressly to provide that a parent or guardian may give a valid receipt for a gift to which the minor is entitled, especially when the legacy is relatively small. Alternatively, the will may provide that the minor can personally give a valid receipt having reached a specified age (usually 16).

A further possibility is that the will directs that the legacy be held on trust for the minor. This might be particularly appropriate if significant sums are involved, and/or there are concerns about the parent, etc being able to receive the legacy on behalf of the minor.

15.4.4 Section 15 of the Trustee Act 1925

This section gives personal representatives (and trustees) wide powers to settle claims made by or against the estate. This very useful power enables personal representatives to make a reasonable compromise instead of having to litigate in order to protect themselves against claims for breach of duty—subject to them having exercised the standard of care in the Trustee Act 2000, s 1.

15.4.5 Power to insure

By s 19 of the Trustee Act 1925 (as amended by the Trusts of Land and Appointment of Trustees Act 1996 and the Trustee Act 2000, s 34) personal representatives may insure land and other property comprehensively and for its full value.

Insurance monies received under a policy of insurance are held as capital. They may be used to reinstate the property lost or damaged providing that the consent of any person whose consent is required to investment is obtained (Trustee Act 1925, s 20).

15.4.5.1   Express provision in the will

It is common for a will to provide for insurance of land and other property to full value, or reinstatement value, and against all risks. It may also provide that the property may be reinstated at the discretion of the personal representatives.

15.4.6   Power to delegate

15.4.6.1   Power to appoint agents

By s 11 of the Trustee Act 2000, personal representatives may collectively delegate all or any of their 'delegable functions' to an agent (such as a solicitor). 'Delegable functions' are any functions other than those relating to whether or in what way the estate assets should be distributed; decisions as to whether fees or other payments due should be made from capital or income; any power to appoint new trustees; and any power to delegate. By s 12, anyone (other than a beneficiary) can be appointed as agent, and if two or more people are appointed agents they must act jointly. Agents may be remunerated and employed on such terms as the personal representatives may determine (s 14) and s 15 directs that where an agent is engaged in 'asset management functions' (ie investment, acquisition, or management of trust property) there must be an agreement evidenced in writing, to include a 'policy statement'—in effect, guidance as to how the agent should act in the best interests of the trust.

15.4.6.2   Review of and liability for agents

By virtue of s 21 of the Trustee Act 2000, the will may restrict the liability of personal representatives for the acts or omissions of their agent(s)—whether appointed under the authority of the statute or of a power in the will.

Subject to any inconsistent provision in the will, by virtue of the Trustee Act 2000, s 22, personal representatives must keep under review the arrangements under which their agents act and how those arrangements are being put into effect. If asset management functions have been delegated, they have a duty to consider whether there is a need to revise or replace the policy statement (and if they consider there is such a need then to do so) and must assess whether the policy statement is being complied with by the agent(s). Further, if the circumstances make it appropriate to do so, the personal representatives must consider whether there is a need to exercise their power of intervention (in effect, to give directions to the agent(s) or to revoke the appointment), and if necessary to exercise such power.

Under s 23 of the Trustee Act 2000, personal representatives will not be liable for any act or default of the agent(s) unless they have failed to comply with the statutory duty of care applicable to them when appointing the agent or in carrying out their duties under s 22.

15.4.6.3   Section 25 of the Trustee Act 1925 (as substituted by s 5 of the Trustee Delegation Act 1999)

This allows personal representatives individually to delegate by power of attorney (on/after 1 March 2000) for a period not exceeding 12 months any of the duties, powers, and discretion vested in them. In this case, however, the personal representative remains fully liable for the acts of the delegate.

15.4.7   Indemnity for expenses

By s 31 of the Trustee Act 2000, trustees and personal representatives may reimburse themselves for all expenses properly incurred when acting on behalf of the trust or estate on or after 1 February 2001.

15.4.8   Power to run the deceased's business

The position here will depend upon whether the deceased was a sole trader or ran the business through the medium of a partnership or limited company.

15.4.8.1   Where the deceased was a sole trader

The general rule is that personal representatives have no authority to carry on the deceased's business. As an exception to this rule, however, they may do so with a view to the proper realisation of the deceased's estate, for example to enable it to be sold as a going concern. This would not enable them, normally, to carry on the business for more than the executor's year.

A power to carry on the business may be implied from the terms of the will, but it seems in such cases that personal representatives will only have authority to utilise assets used in the business at the date of death and will not be entitled to have resort to any other part of the estate for additional funds.

Personal representatives are personally liable for debts incurred in running the deceased's business after his death, though they are entitled to an indemnity from the estate.

15.4.8.2   Express provision in the will

The will may confer wider powers on the personal representatives—for instance, to run (indefinitely) the business as a going concern and to use a wider range of estate assets in running the business.

15.4.8.3   Where the deceased traded as a partner

The personal representatives will usually have no power to intervene in the business. The partnership agreement must be consulted as it will normally contain provisions relating to the succession to a deceased partner's share, which will therefore pass outside the terms of the will.

15.4.8.4   Where the deceased was a shareholder in a limited company

In such a case the company will, of course, continue despite the death of its shareholder. The Articles of Association should be consulted, as these may give other shareholders rights to purchase the deceased shareholder's shares.

15.4.9   Power to invest

15.4.9.1   The general power of investment

Like the other provisions of the Trustee Act 2000, the statutory power of investment is a default power: it is expressed to be additional to powers conferred by, but subject to any restrictions in, the trust instrument.

The 'general power of investment' contained in s 3 of the Act authorises trustees and personal representatives to make any kind of investment that they could make if they were absolutely entitled to the assets of the trust. However, it explicitly excludes investments in land other than by way of loan (though see further **15.4.9.3**).

Most professionally drawn wills (and trust instruments) are likely to contain express powers of investment in terms similar to the default power, so that this will in practice be most beneficial to older trusts lacking appropriately wide express powers, home-made wills, and cases of intestacy. It is likely that draftsmen will in future continue to use express investment clauses for a number of reasons. 'Investment' is not defined by the 2000 Act and the term will, as a result, cover whatever the common law from time to time determines. There could still, therefore, be doubt as to whether non-income-producing assets constitute 'investment'. Alternatively, the testator may wish to restrict the trustees by ethical investment clauses preventing investment in, for example, the tobacco or arms industries.

15.4.9.2   The standard investment criteria

By virtue of s 4 of the Trustee Act 2000, trustees and personal representatives (whether exercising the statutory power or one conferred by the trust instrument) must have regard to 'the standard investment criteria'. They must also from time to time review the investments and consider whether, having regard to the standard investment criteria, they should be varied.

The standard investment criteria are:

(a) the suitability to the trust of the investment; and

(b) the need (to the extent that is appropriate in the circumstances) for diversification of the trust's investments.

Unless they reasonably conclude that in all the circumstances it is unnecessary or inappropriate to do so, personal representatives, before exercising the new statutory power or one conferred by the trust instrument, must (under the Trustee Act 2000, s 5) obtain and consider proper advice about the way in which, having regard to the standard investment criteria, the power should be exercised. A similar requirement is imposed when reviewing the trust's investments. Proper advice is that of a person who is reasonably believed by the trustee to be qualified to give it.

15.4.9.3   Purchase of land

The purchase of land may be authorised by an express power. The default powers are given by s 6(3) of the Trusts of Land and Appointment of Trustees Act 1996 (as amended) and s 8 of the Trustee Act 2000. By these provisions, personal representatives are empowered to acquire freehold or leasehold land in the UK as an investment, for occupation by a beneficiary, or for any other reason. These powers are additional to any conferred by, but subject to any restriction contained in, the will.

Personal representatives are not given an express duty to take 'proper advice' when buying land, unless they are acquiring it as an investment when s 5 (**15.4.9.2**) will apply.

Again, it seems likely that professional draftsmen will continue to use express clauses relating to the purchase of land containing powers to repair, improve, and maintain property, matters which are not covered in the Act.

15.4.10   **Power to maintain a minor**

Section 31 of the Trustee Act 1925 (as amended by s 8 of the 2014 Act) provides that where property is held for a minor beneficiary and the gift carries the right to the intermediate income, the trustees or personal representatives may apply the income for the maintenance, education, or benefit of the minor, and must accumulate the income not so applied. The following points should be noted:

(a) It does not matter whether the minor's interest is vested or contingent.

(b) The trustees or personal representatives are empowered to apply such income as is reasonable and in exercising their discretion must consider the age and requirements of the minor and the circumstances of the case generally, including what other income is applicable for the same purpose.

(c) Once the beneficiary attains the age of 18, accumulated income is normally added to capital and devolves with it (s 31(2)).

(d) If, although the minor has attained 18, the interest remains contingent, the discretion to use income for maintenance, etc ceases, and henceforth the income *must* be paid to the beneficiary until such time as the contingency is fulfilled or the interest fails (s 31(1)).

(e) The statutory power is only available to permit maintenance where the gift carries the intermediate income; most testamentary gifts will (in the absence of contrary provision in the will) carry such income. However, contingent pecuniary legacies generally do not, in which event s 31 will not apply; the intermediate income belongs in this case to the residuary beneficiaries.

EXAMPLE 2

In her will Tessa leaves £100,000 to her niece, Penny, contingently upon her attaining the age of 18, and the residue of her estate upon trust for her son, Rex, contingently upon his attaining the age of 25.

Both Penny and Rex are minors when Tessa dies.

The gift to Penny is a contingent pecuniary legacy, and unless it is one of the exceptional cases, or there is specific provision in the will, the statutory power to maintain is not available. The income will form part of the residue.

So far as Rex is concerned the statutory power is available, and the trustees may choose to pay the income yielded by the residue for Rex's maintenance. Any income not so paid over must be accumulated. When Rex reaches the age of 18 the power to maintain ceases, and the trustee must pay the current income to Rex until he reaches 25, or dies without having satisfied the contingency. If Rex attains the age of 25, he is then entitled to capital and accumulations.

15.4.10.1   Express provision in the will varying s 31

The statutory power will in many, perhaps most, cases be considered adequate, but there may be circumstances where it may be prudent to include a modifying provision in the will: for example, where the gift is contingent upon the beneficiary attaining an age greater than 18, removing the right to receive income at 18.

15.4.11   Power to advance capital

Section 32 of the Trustee Act 1925 (as amended by s 9 of the 2014 Act) gives trustees and personal representatives a discretion to apply capital for the advancement or benefit of a beneficiary (whether or not a minor) who has a vested or contingent interest in capital. The following points should be noted:

(a) up to the whole of the capital money of a beneficiary's vested or presumptive share may be advanced for his or her advancement or benefit (s 9(3)(b)). This amendment applies to all interests under trusts created or arising after the coming into force of the 2014 Act (s 10(1), (4), and (5)). The trustees are able not only to pay out cash in the exercise of the statutory power of advancement but also to transfer or apply other property of the trust (s 9(2)). This amendment applies to all trusts whenever created or arising (s 10(2) of the 2014 Act);

(b) any person with a prior interest (eg a life tenant) must consent in writing to the advance;

(c) any advance made must be brought into account when the beneficiary becomes absolutely entitled;

(d) if a beneficiary contingently entitled receives an advance but fails to fulfil the contingency (eg the beneficiary dies before attaining the age specified for vesting) the amount advanced is not recoverable from the beneficiary's estate; and

(e) an advancement is a substantial payment made with a view to setting the recipient up in life: the term 'benefit' has been construed extremely widely. It may include (eg) a saving of tax: *Pilkington v IRC* [1964] AC 612.

15.4.11.1   Express provision in the will

The will/trust instrument may vary the statutory power by dispensing with the limitations in (b) and/or (c) in **15.4.11**. The statutory power does not enable advancements to be made to a life tenant, but again this power may be expressly conferred.

15.4.12   Exercise of personal representatives' powers

A sole personal representative (whether originally so appointed or by survivorship) has the same powers as two or more personal representatives. A sole personal representative may thus give a valid receipt for the proceeds of sale of land (Law of Property Act 1925, s 27). Joint personal representatives generally have joint and several authority, so that the act of one binds the others and the estate. However, there are statutory exceptions in relation to the conveyance of land and the transfer of shares: in these cases, the conveyance or transfer will normally require all living personal representatives (ie to whom a grant has been issued) to join in.

Personal representatives' powers are in nature fiduciary and, therefore, must be exercised in good faith in the interest of the estate as a whole.

15.5 Duties and powers of personal representatives: checkpoints

1. Duties of personal representatives:

    (a) to collect the deceased's assets (**15.3.1.1**);

    (b) to administer the estate according to law (**15.3.1.3**); and

    (c) statutory and equitable apportionments (**15.3.3**).

2. Powers of personal representatives:

    (a) Does the will contain modifications/additions to the statutory powers?

    (b) If not, statutory authority for power:

    (i)   to sell, etc (**15.4.1**);

    (ii)   to appropriate (**15.4.2**);

    (iii) to appoint trustees of a minor's property (**15.4.3**);

    (iv) to settle claims (**15.4.4**);

    (v)   to insure (**15.4.5**);

    (vi) to delegate (**15.4.6**);

    (vii) for indemnity (**15.4.7**);

    (viii) to run the deceased's business (**15.4.8**);

    (ix) to invest (**15.4.9**);

    (x)   to maintain a minor (**15.4.10**); and

    (xi) to advance capital (**15.4.11**).

15.6 Administering the estate

In **15.6** to **15.12**, we will begin our consideration of what happens once the personal representatives have received the grant from the issuing Registry. In **15.7** we will consider how the personal representatives may protect themselves against claims from potential beneficiaries or other claimants against the estate. In **15.8** we will outline the implications for personal representatives and solicitors acting for them of the compliance requirements under the Financial Services Act 1986 and the Solicitors' Investment Business Rules. The steps necessary to collect and realise the estate's assets are then identified (**15.9**). In **15.10** we look at the rules governing the payment of debts where the estate is solvent; the position where the estate is insolvent is outlined in **15.11**. The section concludes with a brief look at ways in which post-death changes may be effected to the deceased's dispositions (**15.12**). Figure **15.1** sets out the steps from obtaining the grant to ascertainment of the residue.

15.7 Protection of personal representatives

15.7.1 Against claims of unknown beneficiaries/creditors (Trustee Act 1925, s 27)

Even though they were not aware of the claims of a beneficiary or creditor at the time of distribution, the personal representatives remain personally liable to any unpaid beneficiary or creditor (*Knatchbull v Fearnhead* (1837) 3 M & C 122; 1 Jur 687). By complying with the requirements of s 27 the personal representatives can protect themselves against such liability. It is important, however, to appreciate that s 27 only affords protection to the personal representatives as such. Any disappointed beneficiary or creditor may recover from the person(s) to whom the personal representatives have distributed, including themselves if they are also beneficiaries.

In the case of an executor, whose authority derives from the will, advertisements under this section can (and to save time should) be made even before the grant is issued. Where the personal representatives are administrators they cannot properly do this, since they are authorised to act only by the grant itself. Once this has been issued, however, the placing of the required advertisements should be a matter of priority.

15.7.1.1   The advertisements

These are usually made by the solicitor acting for the personal representatives and on their behalf, requiring any person interested (as beneficiary or creditor) to send particulars to the personal representatives' solicitor within a stated time, which must not be less than two months from the date upon which the advertisement appears, after which time the estate will be distributed on the basis of claims of which the personal representatives then have notice (whether from a response to the advertisements or otherwise).

Such advertisements must be placed in:

(a)   the *London Gazette*; and

(b)   a newspaper circulating in the district in which any land forming part of the estate is situated (in practice, this will often be a local newspaper); and

(c)   (in effect) any other newspaper, etc (whether in this country or abroad) as might be appropriate to the particular case. Thus, for example, where the deceased had been in business it might be appropriate to advertise in a relevant trade journal. If the personal representatives are in doubt they should apply to the court for directions.

15.7.1.2   Searches

The personal representatives should also make such searches as a purchaser of land would make (s 27(2)). Searches should therefore be made in the Land Registry or Land Charges Registry; in the Local Land Charges Register; and a bankruptcy search against the deceased and also the beneficiaries (to protect against possible liability to the Trustee in Bankruptcy if a bankrupt beneficiary to whom it is proposed to make a distribution fails to pass the legacy to the Trustee in Bankruptcy—see Law Society Practice Note: 15 September 2011).

15.7.2   Against claims of missing beneficiaries/creditors

No protection, however, is afforded to personal representatives by s 27 where they are aware of the existence of claimants who simply cannot be found. In practice, the personal representatives should still make s 27 advertisements, but some further steps will be necessary to safeguard their position.

15.7.2.1   Payment into court

The personal representatives could pay the amount due to the missing beneficiary or creditor into court and distribute the rest of the estate in the normal way. The personal representatives will thereby achieve total protection, but from the viewpoint of the beneficiaries this is far from an ideal solution!

15.7.2.2   Indemnity

The personal representatives could distribute the whole of the available estate against an agreement by the beneficiaries to indemnify them in the event of the missing beneficiary or creditor subsequently appearing to claim their entitlement. This will certainly be more attractive to the beneficiaries, but is obviously risky from the standpoint of the personal representatives.

15.7.2.3   *Benjamin* Order

This is an order of the court giving the personal representatives leave to distribute the estate on the basis of an assumption set out in the order. In the case from which the order takes its name (*Re Benjamin* [1902] 1 Ch 723) the assumption was that a missing beneficiary had predeceased.

Before an application for such an order can be made, it will be necessary to make full enquiries for the missing claimant. In addition to the s 27 advertisements, the personal representatives should advertise for information in a newspaper circulating in the locality where the missing beneficiary was last heard of. The court may direct further enquiries and advertisements if it considers them to be necessary.

If the assumption in the order subsequently turns out to be wrong, the personal representatives are fully protected. The (no longer) missing beneficiary will have to seek his remedies against those to whom the estate has been distributed.

15.7.2.4   Insurance

As an alternative to a *Benjamin* Order, the personal representatives could seek cover against the risk of the missing beneficiary or creditor subsequently appearing. The insurance company will almost certainly require the same sorts of enquiries, etc as the court might require before making a *Benjamin* Order. However, where the risk is not great (eg because the sum involved is not large or the chances of a claim being made are remote) this may be a cheaper and quicker solution than an application to the court. Indeed, the use of 'missing beneficiary insurance' in the case of small estates was specifically approved in *Evans v Westcombe* (*Law Society's Gazette*, 10 March 1999) with the cost of the premium being a proper expense of the administration.

15.7.3   Other protection for the personal representatives

In relation to claims under the Inheritance (Provision for Family and Dependants) Act 1975, we have already seen at **13.25.2** that personal representatives are protected (should the court allow an 'out of time' application) if they have refrained from distributing the estate for six months after the issue of the grant. This does not, however, protect the beneficiaries to whom the assets may have been distributed.

There are a number of situations where the personal representatives need protection against other possible claims from potential beneficiaries, creditors, or other claimants. These include the following.

15.7.3.1   Future and contingent liabilities

Where personal representatives distribute with knowledge of such liabilities, they receive no protection under s 27 of the Trustee Act 1925. Where there is a known future liability, therefore, a fund should be set aside by the personal representatives to meet it.

A contingent liability might arise, for example, where the deceased had acted as a guarantor for the repayment of a loan, or there is a threat of legal proceedings against the estate. There are several possible courses open to the personal representatives to deal with such a problem:

(a) They could estimate the amount of the possible liability and set aside an appropriate amount—distributing the rest of the estate. This is really unsatisfactory on two counts:

    (i)   an accurate estimate may be difficult (even impossible) to make;

    (ii) the beneficiaries will have to wait for payment of the full amount due to them until the danger of the liability arising has passed.

(b) They could distribute the whole estate subject to an agreement from the beneficiaries to indemnify them should the liability actually materialise. This (again) is not a course which should appeal to the personal representatives for (we hope) fairly obvious reasons!

(c) If they wish to be able to distribute the whole estate (which is certainly what the beneficiaries would want) they could safely do so if they can arrange suitable (ie not too expensive) insurance cover.

(d) Failing this, the only other approach is an application to the court for directions.

15.7.3.2 Inheritance tax

The personal representatives can become liable for the inheritance tax on former potentially exempt transfers (PETs—and for the supplementary charge in respect of lifetime chargeable transfers) where the transferor dies within seven years, and the transferee has not paid the tax concerned within 12 months after the end of the month in which the transferor dies (**7.11**). A similar liability can also arise in respect of gifts with a reservation.

This potential liability is obviously something of which the personal representatives must take account. The trouble is, however, that (eg) the existence of a PET might not come to light until after they have distributed the estate (there is no obligation to report PETs in the transferor's lifetime). Further, the tax position on death may have been calculated on the assumption that there were no lifetime transfers; the discovery of the former PET may mean that the tax liability of the personal representatives in respect of the estate deemed to be transferred on death will also be increased.

The position of the personal representatives in such circumstances has been clarified by HMRC (see statement in the *Law Society's Gazette*, 13 March 1991). Broadly, it seems that the Capital Taxes Office will not normally pursue the personal representatives for any further inheritance tax where they have made 'the fullest enquiries that are reasonably practicable in the circumstances' to discover lifetime transfers, and have obtained a certificate of discharge (see further **15.16.2.4**) and distributed the estate before the former PET comes to light.

Where the personal representative is a practising solicitor, some protection may be afforded by the Solicitors' Indemnity Fund (see the *Law Society's Gazette*, 7 March 1990).

15.7.3.3 Other cases

There are a number of other situations in which the personal representatives may be afforded protection; these are described in various practitioner works which you will need to consult in appropriate circumstances. These include:

(a) s 45 of the Adoption Act 1976 (distribution of estate in ignorance of an adoption order of which they do not have notice);

(b) liability for rent and breaches of covenant where the estate includes leasehold interests; and

(c) where the court grants an application for rectification of a will under s 20 of the Administration of Justice Act 1982.

15.8 Financial services

We do not propose here to examine in any detail the framework of the Financial Services and Markets Act 2000 ('FSMA 2000') and the Financial Services and Markets Act 2000 (Regulated Activities) Order 2001 ('RAO') discussed in **Chapter 2**. Remember that, in the case of solicitors who are exempt (under Part XX of the FSMA 2000) as members of a profession regulated by a designated professional body ('DPB'), the Act must be read in conjunction with the SRA Financial Services (Scope) Rules 2001 ('the Scope Rules') and the SRA Financial Services (Conduct of Business) Rules 2001.

Our purpose here is to consider briefly the impact of the regime upon personal representatives and the solicitors acting for and advising them.

15.8.1 Personal representatives

Under s 19 of the FSMA 2000, there is a general prohibition against undertaking a 'regulated activity' (dealing, arranging, managing, or advising) in relation to investments unless the person carrying out the activity is authorised by the Financial Conduct Authority ('FCA') or is exempt. Under the RAO, Article 66 exempts personal representatives (and trustees), provided that they receive no separate remuneration for such investment business and provided (in some cases involving professional personal representatives/trustees) that they do not advertise investment services. Note, however, that Article 66 does not apply where solicitors are not themselves personal representatives/trustees but are merely acting for them.

15.8.2 Solicitors

In practice, it is highly unlikely that any firm of solicitors engaging in probate and administration work could avoid carrying out investment business as defined by the FSMA 2000. Thus, whether partners or employees of a firm are themselves the personal representatives, or are simply acting for the personal representatives, it is virtually impossible for them not to be managing investments—unless the particular estate comprised only assets that are not 'investments' for the purposes of the FSMA 2000 (eg land, works of art). Similarly, in whatever capacity partners or employees of the firm are involved, it is more likely than not that at some stage they may be called upon to give investment advice (eg as to whether to sell certain investments), or to arrange deals in investments (eg by arranging for the sale of certain shares by a stockbroker). It should be stressed that there is no bar on solicitors giving purely generic advice on investments (as opposed to advising in relation to a specific investment).

The question then arises as to whether the investment business is 'mainstream investment business'—such as advising a beneficiary on what investments to make with an inheritance received—or is 'non-mainstream investment business', namely business that is incidental to the solicitor's main work, such as selling shares in an estate that the solicitor is administering. Mainstream investment business requires regulation by the FCA. Subject to certain conditions, solicitors carrying out only non-mainstream investment business can avoid this requirement provided they fall within the exemption in Part XX of the 2000 Act for members of a profession regulated by a DPB—in the case of solicitors, The Law Society. For this exemption to apply:

(a) the investment business must be incidental to other services being provided by the solicitors which do not themselves constitute mainstream investment business;

(b) the solicitor accounts to the client for *all* commission received; and

(c) the solicitor does not hold himself/herself out as offering investment services to clients.

Further, to avoid the need for regulation by the FCA, if the solicitor does in fact arrange or advise investments, this must be on the advice of an authorised person (such as a stockbroker or an independent financial adviser).

Rule 5 of the Scope Rules sets out further restrictions. For example, solicitors relying on the DPB exemption cannot recommend clients to buy packaged products (unit trusts, life policies, and stakeholder pensions), though it is possible to arrange such a transaction where the client is relying on independent advice from an authorised person. In addition, a solicitor managing the administration of an estate/trust must be careful to delegate the day-to-day decision-making in relation to investments to an authorised person (such as a stockbroker).

15.9 Collecting/realising the assets

15.9.1 Registering the grant

On the issue of the grant, the personal representatives now have their evidence of title and should proceed apace to register the grant with the various institutions (banks, building societies, insurance companies, etc) holding the deceased's assets and obtain from them the sums due to the estate.

Office copies of the grant, bearing the seal of the Registry, should be used rather than the original: photocopies are not acceptable evidence. The original is an important document of title and therefore should so far as possible be protected from the risk of loss and kept in the file. However, HMRC certainly like to see the original.

It is hoped that you will have obtained enough office copies of the grant to enable this process to be completed swiftly. The absolute priority should be the release of sufficient funds to discharge any loan to pay the inheritance tax (**14.15**). After this has been done, normally you should aim to discharge interest-bearing liabilities first so as to minimise the 'cost' to the estate.

As we have seen, the personal representatives' duty is to 'collect and get in' all the deceased's real and personal estate (and then administer it according to law). This must be done with 'reasonable diligence'. Unsecured debts due to the deceased should be collected as soon as practicable—the personal representatives taking proceedings for their recovery if necessary. There is no need to call in or realise loans secured on mortgages of land which are authorised investments, unless the money is needed to discharge the funeral, testamentary, and administration expenses, debts, and pecuniary legacies.

Where the estate's assets include a reversionary (ie future) interest under a trust, this should not be sold unless there is some special reason for doing so (eg that there are no other funds available for the payment of the various expenses and debts of the estate).

Generally, causes of action vested in the deceased at the date of death survive for the benefit of the estate (as do those subsisting against the deceased against the estate) (Law Reform (Miscellaneous Provisions) Act 1934, s 1(1)). The main exceptions relate to contracts for the provision of personal services and the tort of defamation.

The personal representatives may also have an action to recover damages on behalf of certain dependants where the deceased's death has been caused by a wrongful act in respect of which the deceased could have sued if still alive (Fatal Accidents Act 1976). Any damages recovered under this Act do not form part of the deceased's estate for any purpose, but 'belong' to the dependants concerned.

The personal representatives (as we saw at **15.4.4**) have wide powers of settling claims made by or against the estate, so that they are not obliged to litigate every possible point or risk being held liable for not doing so.

15.9.2 Sales of assets

In order to be able to pay taxes and other liabilities, the personal representatives may have to sell assets in the estate. In principle, they are at liberty to use any assets coming into their hands for this purpose (see further **15.10**). However, in practice there are a number of 'constraints' which they should bear in mind.

15.9.2.1 The will

The terms of any will should very much influence their decision. Thus, if the will makes specific gifts the property so given should not be sold unless other assets have been exhausted. Further, beneficiaries may have indicated a wish to receive particular assets in partial or total satisfaction of (as the case may be) a pecuniary legacy or share of residue. The personal representatives should endeavour to respect those wishes and avoid selling the assets concerned, if possible to do so.

15.9.2.2 Tax implications

You will have already encountered (in **7.9.1.7** and **7.9.1.8**) what are sometimes called 'loss on sale' reliefs for land and quoted securities sold within the prescribed statutory periods for less than their probate values. Where there are assets which might qualify for such relief, the personal representatives should consider whether to sell them and thus be able to reclaim any inheritance tax paid on the 'difference'. If this relief is claimed, remember that no loss relief is available for capital gains tax purposes.

Where personal representatives sell any assets during the course of the administration, there will prima facie be a charge to capital gains tax on gains accruing since the date of death. Such gains may be relieved from charge by the annual exemption slice: personal representatives have the same exemption as an individual (in 2016/17, £11,100) for gains made on disposals in the tax year in which the death occurs and in the following two tax years. Thus, for example, if in March they are contemplating selling shares which show a gain of £15,000 since the date of death, they would be well advised to consider selling immediately sufficient to utilise the current year's exemption and the rest after 6 April.

Where personal representatives realise an allowable loss on a sale of estate assets, it may be set against their gains of that year and any amount not thereby absorbed is carried forward to be set against their gains in future tax years. Their loss cannot be passed on to the beneficiaries, so if it is possible that the personal representatives will not have sufficient gains to absorb any loss an alternative strategy should be considered. Where the asset concerned, instead of being sold, is vested in a beneficiary this is not a chargeable event and the beneficiary acquires at the value at the date of death. The beneficiary can then sell realising a loss to be set against any chargeable gains of the beneficiary.

15.10 Payment of debts (solvent estate)

A solvent estate is one where the assets are sufficient to cover in full the funeral, testamentary, and administration expenses, debts, and other liabilities. It is immaterial whether or not legacies can also be paid in full.

So far as the creditors (including secured creditors) are concerned, they are entitled to be paid what is due to them from any part of the estate available for the payment of debts. As long as they are paid, it does not matter to them upon what part of the estate the burden of the payment falls. However, this is a matter of considerable importance from the viewpoint of the beneficiaries. Thus, to take a simple example, if the will leaves Blackacre to Beatrice and the residue of the estate to Rosalind, it will matter very much to them who has to bear the burden of the debts—particularly if Blackacre is subject to a mortgage at the date of the testator's death. It is with the resolution of such problems that this section is concerned. As we shall see, the answer will depend upon whether (and what) provision is made in any will.

15.10.1 Secured creditors

We are here concerned with the situation where a debt has been charged on the deceased's property during the deceased's lifetime (eg a mortgage on Blackacre).

Subject to the testator showing contrary intention (see **15.10.4**), by s 35 of the Administration of Estates Act 1925 the property so charged is liable for the payment of that debt. So, in this example, Beatrice will prima facie take Blackacre subject to the mortgage debt. If the value of Blackacre is insufficient to cover the mortgage debt, the 'deficit' would have to be met by the residuary estate, so that Rosalind's entitlement would be correspondingly reduced.

15.10.2 Other debts: the statutory order, etc

So far as unsecured creditors are concerned (again, subject to any express provision in the will (see **15.10.4**) the order in which the estate's assets should be used is laid down by s 34(3) and Part II of the First Schedule to the Administration of Estates Act 1925. These provisions draw no distinction between realty and personalty.

The order is as follows (if there is nothing in a given 'category', or what there is proves insufficient, you move on down the list):

(a) Property undisposed of by the will (subject to the setting aside of a fund from which to pay any pecuniary legacies). Thus, where a partial intestacy arises (because the deceased's will contains no residuary gift, or where such residuary gift has totally or partially failed) the property not disposed of by the effective provisions of the will is primarily liable for the payment of the unsecured debts of the deceased. However, it is only so much of such undisposed-of property as is not set aside to pay any pecuniary legacies (see **15.15.2**) that is so liable.

(b) Residue (again, subject to the setting aside of a fund from which to pay any pecuniary legacies, ie to the extent that these are not fully covered by the retention made under (a)).

In most cases, this is as far down the order as you will need to go. However, if the assets comprised in (a) and (b) are insufficient, the list continues:

(c) Property specifically given for the payment of debts. Property is within this category if the will contains a direction that the identified property (eg Greenacre) is to be used to fund the payment of debts, but nothing is said as to what is to happen to any surplus.

(d) Property specifically charged with the payment of debts. Property falls within this category where the will contains a direction as in (c), but goes on to provide what is to happen to any surplus.

You may be pardoned for thinking that where the deceased has taken the trouble to identify specific property in the estate to fund the payment of debts, this would place such property firmly at the head of the list! Faced with the problem of reconciling logic with the statutory order, the courts have concluded that such a provision can only make the specifically given or charged property primarily liable where the will shows an intention to exonerate any property falling within categories (a) and (b) (see further **15.10.4**).

(e) The pecuniary legacy fund (retained under (a) and/or (b)). At this point, any such fund will be used to help pay the debts. Unless the testator has indicated that any such legacies are to be paid in priority, they will abate proportionately, so that each legatee bears a share of the burden of the payment.

(f) Property specifically devised or bequeathed, rateably according to the property's value (ie to the deceased) at the date of death. Thus, if Whiteacre (the subject of a specific gift in the will) is worth £100,000 and is subject to an outstanding mortgage of £25,000, its value for the purposes of this exercise will be £75,000.

(g) Property expressly appointed under a general power of appointment (again, rateably according to value). This category is rarely encountered in practice.

If needed, certain other categories of property may also be available for the payment of debts, but only after all the above categories have been exhausted. The categories include:

(a) *donationes mortis causa*;

(b) nominated property; and

(c) property in respect of which an option to purchase has been given by the will (*Re Eve* [1956] Ch 479; [1956] 3 WLR 69; 3 [1956] All ER 321).

15.10.3 Marshalling

Where (as they are entitled to do) the personal representatives discharge a debt out of property within a category which is not—as between the beneficiaries—liable to bear the burden of that debt, the equitable doctrine of marshalling can be invoked by the disappointed beneficiary so as to ensure that the debt is (at the end of the day) borne by the appropriate property. Thus, if the will makes a specific gift of some shares (within (f) in the list in **15.10.2**) to Peter and these are in fact sold to pay the debts (although the residuary estate—which is listed at (b) in **15.10.2**—is sufficient to cover them), Peter will be entitled to 'compensation' from the residue.

15.10.4 Contrary provision

The rules in **15.10.2** only apply in the absence of contrary provision in the will. What constitutes such provision?

15.10.4.1 Secured creditors

The effect of s 35 of the Administration of Estates Act 1925 can be avoided in several ways. Thus, the gift of Blackacre in our earlier example (in **15.10**) might have been expressed to be 'free of mortgage', in which event the mortgage would be repayable out of the residue.

Alternatively, the will might have contained a direction to pay debts 'including any mortgage charged on Blackacre' out of residue. It is important to appreciate, however, that a simple direction to pay 'debts' from residue without specifically mentioning the charge on Blackacre would not oust s 35. On the other hand, where the testator has identified a particular fund other than residue for the payment of 'debts', this is prima facie sufficient to cover all debts including the mortgage on Blackacre. However, Blackacre would remain charged with the payment of any deficit if the particular fund proved insufficient to discharge the debt completely.

15.10.4.2 Unsecured creditors

There are three formulae likely to be met in practice for varying the statutory order, the first two being most commonly encountered. They are:

(a) gift of residue on trust or trust for sale with a direction for payment of debts out of the proceeds (before division amongst the beneficiaries); and

(b) gift of residue 'subject to' or 'after' payment of debts.

In both of these cases, the effect will be to make the residue as a whole, including the property undisposed of by the will in the case of a partial intestacy, primarily liable for the payment of the debts.

(c) property 'given for' or 'charged with' payment of debts with intention to exonerate residue.

As we saw in **15.10.2**, without some evidence of intention to exonerate residue such property remains in the third and fourth categories in the statutory order. However, provided this intention is clear, the property given or charged will become primarily liable.

15.11 Payment of debts (insolvent estate)

An estate is insolvent if the assets are insufficient to pay in full all the funeral, testamentary, and administration expenses, debts, and liabilities. Clearly, in such a case, the beneficiaries can receive nothing, and the creditors will not be paid in full. In what order are the creditors entitled to be paid?

This is a question of crucial importance for the personal representatives because if they pay 'out of order' they will prima facie incur personal liability for debts in a higher category that have not been paid (see further **15.11.3**). As a result, if there is any risk that the estate may prove to be insolvent it is necessary to be extremely careful to observe strictly the prescribed order for payment.

15.11.1 Secured creditors

Such creditors will in practice have a choice:

(a) They may simply rely on their security. Thus, for example, the mortgagee will rely on the (eventual) proceeds of sale of the mortgaged property to obtain repayment of the loan.

(b) They may realise their security (ie sell the property) and to the extent that this proves inadequate to join the 'queue' of unsecured creditors (see further **15.11.2**).

(c) They may (without selling) place a value on their security and seek payment of any deficit as unsecured creditors.

There is, in principle, a fourth choice—unlikely in practice often to be adopted: they could surrender their security and simply be treated as unsecured creditors.

To the extent that secured creditors rely upon their security to obtain repayment, they enjoy priority over the unsecured creditors.

15.11.2   Unsecured creditors

The order of priority—which cannot be varied by the testator—is governed by the Administration of Insolvent Estates of Deceased Persons Order 1986.

The order of priority is as set out in the following paragraphs.

15.11.2.1   Reasonable funeral, testamentary, and administration expenses

By tradition, reasonable funeral expenses take precedence.

15.11.2.2   The bankruptcy order

Within each of the categories identified below debts rank equally. Personal representatives have no right to 'prefer' one creditor above the others in the same category, so that if there is insufficient to pay all the creditors in the given category in full, those debts abate proportionately, so that everyone receives (eg) 50p in the £ (see further **15.10.3**).

Under the bankruptcy order, debts rank as follows:

(a) *Preferred debts*. These include wages and salaries of the deceased's employees in the period of four months prior to the death, up to a maximum in the case of each employee of (currently) £800.

(b) *Ordinary debts*. These are all other debts (except deferred debts) including amounts owed to HMRC and the balance of any claim that does not rank as a preferred debt. Thus, for example, an employee who was owed wages of £1,000 could (subject to meeting the conditions listed earlier) claim £800 as a preferred creditor and the balance as an ordinary creditor.

(c) *Interest on preferred and ordinary debts*. The rate of interest will be the greater of the rate specified in s 17 of the Judgments Act 1838 at the date of death (currently 8 per cent) or the contractual rate applicable to the particular debt. Interest is payable from the date of death until payment, and the two categories rank equally for this purpose.

(d) *Deferred debts*. These are loans from the deceased's spouse, ie spouse at the date of death (the position at the date of the loan is irrelevant).

15.11.3   Protection of the personal representatives

If personal representatives pay (say) an ordinary debt having knowledge that there are preferred debts, the payment is an implied 'warranty' that there are sufficient assets to meet all the preferred debts of which they have notice (whether as a result of s 27 of the Trustee Act 1925 advertisements (**15.7.1**) or otherwise). If there are not sufficient funds to do this, the personal representatives are personally liable.

However, it has long been settled that they will not be personally liable where, without undue haste, they have paid an inferior debt without notice of a debt in a higher category (*Harman v Harman* (1686) 2 Show 492; 3 Mod Rep 115; Comb 35).

We have seen that personal representatives must not 'prefer' one creditor in a given category above any other in the same category. By s 10(2) of the Administration of Estates Act 1925, personal representatives are protected from liability to creditors of the same class where payment to others in that class has been made in full should the estate subsequently prove to be insolvent, provided that at the time of the payment the personal representatives were acting in good faith and had no reason to believe that the estate was insolvent. This protection is available even where a personal representative has paid a debt due to himself, unless the grant was taken as a creditor.

15.12   Post-death changes

At the beginning of the chapter we saw that the devolution of a person's estate will largely depend on whether or not that person has left a valid will. It may be, however, that when that person dies the dispositions effected by the will or intestacy, or otherwise, are unsuitable in some way. For example, they may fail to make adequate provision for the surviving spouse or another relative or dependant of the deceased; or it may be that the person entitled does not want the property which is left to them. Another possibility is that tax-saving opportunities will be wasted if the estate is distributed in accordance with the will or intestacy rules.

We have already noted (at **13.23** to **13.30**) the provisions of the Inheritance (Provision for Family and Dependants) Act 1975. There are two further methods whereby alterations can be made to the dispositions of a deceased person's property after that person's death, and generally such alterations can be achieved without adverse inheritance and/or capital gains tax consequences.

15.12.1   Disclaimers

In the much-quoted words of Abbot CJ, 'the law is not so absurd as to force a man to take an estate against his will' (*Townson v Tickell* [1819] B & Ald 31). A beneficiary under a will or intestacy can disclaim an interest that is not wanted provided no benefit has been taken from the gift. The right to disclaim is lost once any benefit has been accepted by the beneficiary, who cannot generally disclaim part only of a single gift (but may disclaim one of several gifts). All that is necessary for a disclaimer to be effective is for disclaiming beneficiaries to indicate their intention to refuse the gift either orally or in writing to the deceased's personal representatives. However, if the disclaimer is to be effective for inheritance tax or capital gains tax purposes, it must be in writing. The effect of a disclaimer is that the property will pass as if the disclaiming beneficiary had predeceased the testator or the intestate. In the case of a specific or pecuniary gift in a will, on disclaimer this will normally fall into residue. In the case of a residuary gift, the subject matter will pass under the intestacy rules (except in the case of a class gift or gift to joint tenants, when it will accrue to the other class members/joint tenants as appropriate). In both cases this is subject to contrary intention in the will.

A disclaimer of a gift under a will does not operate so as to prevent the person disclaiming receiving the property under the intestacy rules.

EXAMPLE 3

If residue is left by Tom, a widower, to his two children Ann and Ben in equal shares and Ann disclaims her share under the will, one half of the residue will pass on Tom's intestacy. Ann's disclaimer of her entitlement under the will does not operate to prevent her taking under the intestacy, however, and if this is desired she will also have expressly to disclaim her entitlement on intestacy.

As has been previously noted, the Estates of Deceased Persons (Forfeiture Rule and Law of Succession) Act 2011 came into effect on 1 February 2012 and applies to deaths on/after that date. Section 1 applies where a person is entitled to an interest in the residuary estate of an intestate but disclaims it (or would have been so entitled had he/she not been precluded by the forfeiture rule—designed to prevent convicted killers from profiting from their crimes: see the Forfeiture Act 1982). In such circumstances, the person disclaiming or subject to the forfeiture is to be treated as having died immediately before the intestate (even though, in fact, he/she is still alive). Section 2 applies in similar terms to a person entitled to interests arising under a will. These provisions are designed to overcome the problem posed by the decision in *Re DWS (Dec'd)* [2001] Ch 568, where the issue of a convicted killer could not 'stand in his place' for the purposes of intestate succession because the killer was still alive.

The disadvantage of a disclaimer is, then, that the original beneficiary has no control over the ultimate destination of the gift. If the intention is to benefit someone other than the person next entitled under the will or intestacy rules, a 'variation' (see **15.12.2**) will be more appropriate.

15.12.2   Variations

A variation is a direction by the original beneficiary to the personal representatives to transfer property that would otherwise be taken by the beneficiary to someone else. Normally a variation will be in writing, and commonly by deed.

Unlike a disclaimer:

(a) a variation is possible even though the original beneficiary has accepted a benefit;

(b) a partial variation of a gift is possible; and

(c) the original beneficiary can control the destination of the property following the variation. Those taking under the variation do not have to be other beneficiaries or members of the deceased's family.

15.12.3 Inheritance tax and capital gains tax consequences

Prima facie, a disclaimer or a variation will constitute a transfer of value (usually a PET) for inheritance tax purposes and a disposal for capital gains tax. However, under s 142 of the Inheritance Tax Act 1984 and s 62 of the Taxation of Chargeable Gains Act 1992, it is possible to effect a disclaimer or variation without either of these consequences.

The conditions to be met are:

(a) the disclaimer/variation must be:

(i) in writing;

(ii) made within two years of death;

(iii) not made for any consideration (other than another disclaimer/variation) in money or money's worth;

(b) in the case of a variation only:

(i) in the case of variations made on/after 1 August 2002, the instrument of variation should contain a statement of intent that s 142 and/or s 62 relief(s) are to apply. If the variation results in more inheritance tax being payable, a copy of the instrument must be sent to HMRC within six months, together with a statement of how much extra tax is payable;

(ii) if the variation results in more inheritance tax being payable, the personal representatives must join in the election.

If all the relevant conditions are met, then:

(a) the disclaimer/variation is not itself a transfer of value and/or disposal; and

(b) the inheritance tax and/or capital gains tax position will be determined as if the deceased had made the disposition now effected.

15.13 Administering the estate: checkpoints

1. Protection of personal representatives:
   (a) against claims of unknown beneficiaries/creditors (**15.7.1**);
   (b) against claims of missing beneficiaries/creditors (**15.7.2**);
   (c) against future or contingent liabilities (**15.7.3.1**);
   (d) against liability for inheritance tax (**15.7.3.2**);
   (e) against claims of unknown, adopted/illegitimate beneficiaries (**15.7.1**, **15.7.3.3**);
   (f) against liability for rent and other breaches of leasehold covenants (**15.7.3.3**); and
   (g) against claims under the Inheritance (Provision for Family and Dependants) Act 1975 (**13.25.2**).

2. Financial services issues:

   (a) for personal representatives (**15.8.1**);
   (b) for solicitors acting as, or advising, personal representatives (**15.8.2**).

3. Collecting/realising the assets:

   (a) registering the grant (**15.9.1**);
   (b) which assets to sell (**15.9.2**).

4. Payment of debts—solvent estate:
    (a) secured creditors (**15.10.1**);
    (b) unsecured debts—the statutory order and other property (**15.10.2**);
    (c) marshalling (**15.10.3**); and
    (d) contrary provision in will (**15.10.4**).
5. Payment of debts—insolvent estate:
    (a) secured creditors (**15.11.1**);
    (b) unsecured creditors (**15.11.2**); and
    (c) protection of personal representatives (**15.11.3**).
6. Post-death changes:
    (a) Inheritance (Provision for Family and Dependants) Act claims (**13.23** to **13.29**);
    (b) disclaimers (**15.12.1**);
    (c) variations (**15.12.2**); and
    (d) inheritance tax and capital gains tax consequences (**15.12.3**). (See also **Figure 15.1**.)

Figure 15.1   **Estate administration—from grant to ascertainment of estate available for distribution**

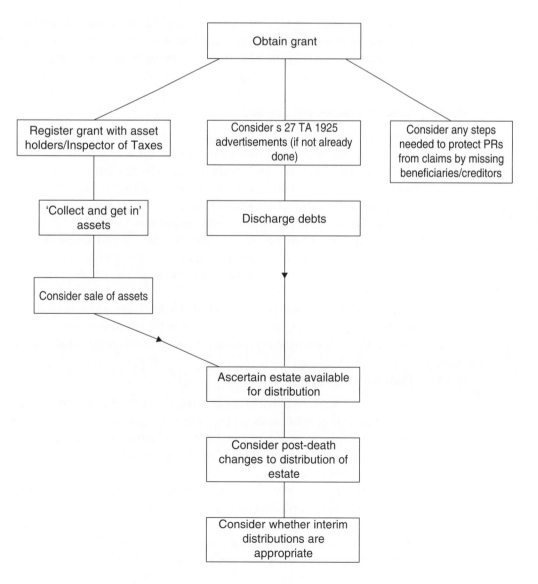

15.14 Distributing the estate

In **15.6** onwards, we examined various practical issues surrounding the early and 'middle' stages of the administration of an estate once the grant has been issued—to the point where the various debts and liabilities were discharged. We also considered how personal representatives might protect themselves against claims for breach of their duty, and how changes might be effected to the deceased's dispositions otherwise taking effect on death.

In the remainder of this section, we will now consider the 'endgame'—the distribution of the estate to those entitled under the terms of the will or the operation of the intestacy rules and the procedures are set out at **Figure 15.2**.

Although we have arbitrarily divided up our consideration in this way, it is of course an artificial division; the process of winding up an estate is a continuum with no 'natural breaks' or (necessarily) clearly definable stages (except, perhaps, 'pre-grant' and 'post-grant').

We will first look at some practical issues concerning the payment of the various legacies in any will (**15.15**). We will then consider how the residue (to which the residuary beneficiaries are entitled) is ascertained (**15.16**). Next, we will discuss estate accounts (**15.17**), assents (**15.18**), and financial services issues (**15.19**). Lastly, we will briefly discuss beneficiaries' rights and remedies (**15.20**).

15.15 Payment of legacies

Once the personal representatives are satisfied that assets are not needed for administration purposes (ie to pay the debts, etc), they can give effect to the various specific, general, and pecuniary gifts made by the will. An indication by them that a particular asset is not needed for the purposes of the administration is technically 'an assent' (see further **15.18**).

15.15.1 Specific legacies and devises

The property which has been specifically given by the will is vested in the beneficiaries entitled by the method appropriate to the assets concerned. Thus, for example, chattels will be transferred by delivery, and company shares by the completion of the appropriate stock transfer form—which, with the share certificate(s), is lodged with the company's Registrar for registration of the change of ownership and the issue of a new share certificate. In the case of land, an assent in writing will be needed (see further **15.18.2**).

Unless the will otherwise provides, beneficiaries entitled to specific gifts will have to bear the costs of the transfer of the gifted property, and also the cost of its preservation and upkeep between the date of death and assent or actual transfer (*Re Rooke* [1933] Ch 970; *Re Pearce* [1909] 1 Ch 819).

However, specific beneficiaries are entitled to the income (if any) produced by the asset since the date of death. Thus, for example, on a specific gift of shares or land, the assent retrospectively passes to the beneficiary concerned any dividends or rent arising since the date of death.

15.15.2 Pecuniary legacies

In s 55(1)(ix) of the Administration of Estates Act 1925 the term 'pecuniary legacy' is defined so as to include general legacies, demonstrative legacies insofar as they cannot be paid from the designated fund, and any general direction for the payment of money (such as the inheritance tax on a specific gift which is to be free of tax). In this section we will use the term 'pecuniary legacy' as so defined.

The problem for the personal representatives in all these cases is essentially the same: from what part of the estate should they take the money to pay the beneficiary, or to purchase the subject matter of the general legacy, or to pay the inheritance tax? We have seen that there is a similar problem for the personal representatives in relation to the payment of the various debts and liabilities of the estate (see **15.10** and **15.11**).

Unfortunately, the general law regarding the incidence of pecuniary legacies is sometimes far from clear. The problems centre upon the extent to which the pre-1926 rules have been displaced by the provisions of s 33 of the Administration of Estates Act 1925—an issue still not entirely resolved more than 90 years on.

The rules can briefly be summarised as follows.

15.15.2.1 Provision in the will

The will may (and if you ever have to grapple with the complexities which can arise you will doubtless (rightly!) conclude *should*) contain express provision as to the property to be used to fund the payment of pecuniary legacies. In practice, the formulae usually adopted for dealing with the payment of debts (**15.10.4.2**) are simply adapted to include legacies as well. So, if residue is to be the chosen source, the trust or trust for sale of the residuary estate will direct the payment out of the proceeds of 'debts and legacies' before division. Alternatively, the residue may be given 'subject to' or 'after payment of' the 'debts and legacies'. Any of these provisions will make the residue as a whole (including any lapsed share) primarily liable. Where a specific fund is identified, it can similarly be made liable for the payment of the legacies in addition to the debts.

15.15.2.2 No provision in the will

In practice, you will usually find that the rules effectively identify the residuary estate as the fund from which pecuniary legacies should be paid. However, the situation is not quite as simple as this statement implies, and there can be especially difficult problems where there is a partial intestacy. In any case where the will does not provide for which part of the estate should bear the burden of pecuniary legacies you will need to consult appropriate practitioner works to make sure you get it right.

15.15.3 Abatement

If the property identified under the rules discussed in **15.15.2** is insufficient to meet the pecuniary legacies in full, they will abate proportionately.

15.15.4 Appropriation

If a beneficiary wishes to have a particular asset from the estate in total or partial satisfaction of a pecuniary legacy given by the will, the personal representatives will normally be able to accede to the request by exercising the power of appropriation in s 41 of the Administration of Estates Act 1925, or that conferred by the will (see **15.4.2**).

15.15.5 Receipts

The personal representatives are entitled to a discharge from the beneficiaries, which normally is obtained by getting them to sign a receipt.

Beneficiaries who are under 18 cannot (unless the will otherwise provides) give a good receipt, nor (although, as we have seen at **15.4.3**, there is an alternative view) can their parent, guardian, or spouse do so for them. In such cases, it will be necessary for the personal representatives to adopt one of the following solutions:

(a) hold the gifted property until the infant attains the age of 18 (in the case of a pecuniary legacy in the meantime investing in an authorised investment);

(b) use the power of appropriation (in s 41 of the Administration of Estates Act 1925 or the will), with the infant's parent, guardian, or (if none) the court giving any necessary consent (see **15.4.2**);

(c) use the power in s 42 of the Administration of Estates Act 1925 to appoint trustees to receive and hold the property for the infant until 18 (see **15.4.3**); and

(d) obtain their discharge by payment of the legacy into court under s 63 of the Trustee Act 1925.

15.16   Ascertainment of residue

Once the various legacies have been paid, the personal representatives can direct their attention to establishing the amount available for distribution to the residuary beneficiaries. In order to do this, they will have to finalise the tax position and deal with the expenses of the administration.

15.16.1   Income tax and capital gains tax

The personal representatives will need to have dealt with two matters here.

15.16.1.1   The deceased's tax affairs

The deceased's income tax and capital gains tax liability must be finalised—with any further tax payable being paid, or any repayment due being recovered. In either event, an inheritance tax corrective account may be required (see **15.16.2.3**).

15.16.1.2   The administration period

The personal representatives must make tax returns for each of the tax years which the administration spans and discharge any assessments.

15.16.2   Inheritance tax

Various issues concerning this tax will also need to be resolved.

15.16.2.1   The deceased's liability

Where the deceased at the date of death had an outstanding liability to inheritance tax, this will need to be discharged—and if met by the estate is an allowable deduction in arriving at the taxable estate on the death.

15.16.2.2   Recovery of tax

The personal representatives may be liable to pay tax on property where the burden of the tax is in fact to be borne by the beneficiary to whom the property passes on the death. This may happen, for example, because the will expressly makes the beneficiary responsible for the tax attributable to the value of the gifted property. It may also happen where the property passes outside of the will (eg where the deceased's interest as a beneficial joint tenant accrues by right of survivorship to the surviving joint tenant(s)—though this is not a problem, of course, where it accrues to a surviving spouse). How can the personal representatives ensure that they recover for the benefit of the residuary estate the tax ultimately to be borne by others?

Where a pecuniary legacy is given 'subject to tax' the problem is easily resolved: the personal representatives simply withhold the appropriate amount and pay the net legacy to the beneficiary.

That solution is clearly not appropriate where there has been a specific legacy of, for example, Blackacre or a diamond necklace. In such cases, the personal representatives should not vest the asset in the beneficiary concerned until the tax has been paid or satisfactory arrangements have been made for their reimbursement.

If the property has passed by survivorship, the personal representatives may have a ready solution if other assets are due to the beneficiary concerned under the will or the intestacy rules: before they part with any such assets, they should ensure that they are paid, for example by deducting the amount due. Where there are no other amounts due to the beneficiary concerned, they may ultimately have to sue to recover the amount due.

15.16.2.3   Corrective accounts

Any variations in the value or content of the estate will need to be reported to HMRC on a corrective account (or by letter if the adjustments are minor). Any further inheritance tax then due will have to be paid, or any repayment due claimed.

15.16.2.4   Certificates of discharge

When the inheritance tax position has been finalised, the personal representatives should seek a discharge from any further liability to inheritance tax on Form IHT 30. This requests the issue of a Certificate of Discharge of the property in the estate and all persons liable from any further claims to inheritance tax. When given, the Certificate is an effective discharge except in the case of fraud, failure to disclose material facts, the subsequent discovery of further assets, or changes in the 'tax bill' arising as a result of any variations, etc discussed at **15.12**.

If the personal representatives have paid all the tax other than that attributable to instalment option property, a limited form of Certificate may be issued, expressed to be a complete discharge except for the outstanding tax on the instalment option property. In such cases, the personal representatives will need to ensure that there are appropriate arrangements to protect them against claims for future instalments. No Certificate of Discharge is necessary (nor should it be sought) where the estate is an 'excepted estate' (see **14.27**). In such cases, there is, as we saw, normally an automatic discharge 35 days after the issue of the grant, unless HMRC call for an account or it is subsequently discovered that the estate is not, after all, an excepted estate.

15.16.3   Administration expenses

The expenses of the administration, ie (in addition to reasonable funeral expenses) the properly incurred expenses of the personal representatives themselves in the carrying out of their duties, will have to be ascertained and met.

15.16.3.1   Reasonable funeral expenses

The estate is only liable for 'reasonable funeral expenses'; any excess will be the personal responsibility of the person incurring those expenses. What is reasonable is a question of fact; matters to be taken into account would include the deceased's position in life, religious beliefs, and expressed wishes as to funeral arrangements.

15.16.3.2   Legal costs

The personal representatives are, as we have seen, at liberty to instruct solicitors to act for them in the administration of the estate. The costs (including disbursements) of such solicitors are part of the expenses of the administration.

Solicitors' charges in non-contentious probate matters are governed by the Solicitors' (Non-Contentious Business) Remuneration Order 2009 (SI 2009 No 1931). Under the Order, a solicitor's costs must be fair and reasonable having regard to all the circumstances of the case and in particular to:

(a) the complexity of the matter or the difficulty or novelty of the questions raised;

(b) the skill, labour, specialised knowledge and responsibility involved;

(c) the time spent on the business;

(d) the number and importance of the documents prepared or considered, without regard to length;

(e) the place where and the circumstances in which the business or any part of the business is transacted;

(f) the amount or value of any money or property involved;

(g) whether any land involved is registered land within the meaning of the Land Registration Act 2002;

(h) the importance of the matter to the client; and

(i) the approval (express or implied) of the entitled person or the express approval of the testator to:

(i)   the solicitor undertaking all or any part of the work giving rise to the costs; or

(ii) the amount of the costs.

In *Jemma Trust Company Ltd v Liptrott* [2004] 1 WLR 646 the Court of Appeal considered whether it was now anachronistic and wrong for solicitors to charge a 'value element', depending on the size of the estate, in addition to an hourly rate. It was held that it was still open to solicitors to make a separate charge based on value, or a value addition to the hourly rate, provided the charges overall were fair, reasonable, and transparent.

15.16.3.3   Fees of other professionals

Where, for example, stockbrokers or surveyors are employed to assist with valuations of the deceased's assets their fees are also part of the expenses of the administration. Where such professionals have been instructed by the solicitors acting for the personal representatives, the solicitors will—as a matter of professional conduct—incur liability to meet their proper fees, which will then feature as disbursements in the solicitors' bill of costs.

15.16.4   Remuneration

Personal representatives, like trustees, are not entitled to remuneration for their services unless in some way this is authorised.

15.16.4.1   Legacy to proving executors

There is a presumption that any specific or general legacy (but not a gift of residue) given to someone appointed as executor is intended to be conditional upon that person accepting the office (*Re Appleton* (1885) 29 ChD 893). The presumption is rebuttable (eg by the testator indicating some other motive for the legacy, such as 'in recognition of a lifetime's friendship', or making it clear that the legacy should be payable whether or not the beneficiary proves the will).

15.16.4.2   Charging clause in the will

In practice, this will be the usual means by which authority to charge for their services will be conferred upon the personal representatives. Such clauses are routinely included where professionals (such as solicitors and accountants) or institutions (such as banks) are appointed.

Section 28 of the Trustee Act 2000 introduces new rules for the interpretation of charging clauses in favour of trust corporations or personal representatives acting in a professional capacity:

(a) The services for which charge may be made include those that could be provided by a lay trustee and are not confined to strictly professional services (as in the past).

(b) In the case of deaths on or after 1 February 2001, an express charging clause is not treated as a gift for the purposes of the Wills Act 1837, s 15 (see **13.7.5**).

Further, s 29 creates an 'implied' professional charging clause in certain circumstances. Trust corporations are generally entitled to receive 'reasonable remuneration' for services provided on behalf of a trust even if they could have been provided by lay trustees. Other professional trustees (but not a sole trustee) may be entitled to such remuneration provided each of the other trustees has agreed in writing.

It seems likely that draftsmen will continue to include express charging clauses both to cover sole professional trustees and to remove the need for agreement to payment by the other trustees where the professional is one of several trustees.

15.16.4.3   Agreement with beneficiaries

Remuneration can be paid to the personal representatives as a result of an agreement with the beneficiaries (being *sui juris*) out of assets to which they are entitled. There must, of course, be no hint of undue influence.

15.16.4.4   The court

The court, as part of its inherent jurisdiction, has power to authorise remuneration for the personal representatives, whether for past, present, or future services. There are also various statutory provisions which enable the court to authorise a personal representative to charge, for example s 42 of the Trustee Act 1925 (trustees to hold minor's legacy) and s 50 of the Administration of Justice Act 1985 (substituted personal representative).

15.16.4.5   Rule in *Cradock v Piper* (1850) 1 Mac & G 664

This rule applies where a solicitor (being one of two or more personal representatives) acts in connection with litigation on behalf of all the personal representatives. Such a solicitor (or his/her firm) may charge for such work provided the bill is not 'inflated' by virtue of the solicitor being one of the parties.

15.16.4.6   Foreign remuneration

Where the law of a foreign jurisdiction entitles the personal representatives to remuneration, they will, it seems, be entitled to receive it (*Re Northcote's Will Trust* [1949] 1 All ER 442).

15.17   Estate accounts

If beneficiaries are left, for example, 'Blackacre' or '£1,000' by the will, they are clearly able to identify their entitlement. Unlike pecuniary or specific beneficiaries, the residuary beneficiaries have no ready means of knowing what they are entitled to receive. The estate accounts are, in effect, the means whereby the personal representatives identify the property available for distribution to the residuary beneficiaries, and they will also show how that entitlement is to be met.

15.17.1   Form

There are no particular rules, save that the accounts should be clear and easy to follow.

15.17.1.1   The accounts

Three accounts will, in practice, be needed: an income account (**15.17.2**), a capital account (**15.17.3**), and a distribution account (**15.17.4**). In the case of small estates, the income and capital accounts will often be combined; indeed, sometimes all three are combined in a single account. This is perfectly acceptable as long as the end result is clear and easy to follow.

15.17.1.2   Apportionments

Separate income and capital accounts will certainly be needed where there is (under the will or the intestacy rules) a life interest in the residue. Unless excluded by the terms of the will, the Apportionment Act 1870 (**15.3.3**) will require the apportionment of income received after death which relates partly to a period before and partly to a period after the death: the former will be shown in the capital account and the latter in the income account. The equitable apportionment rules (unless excluded) will also affect the entries to be made in the income and capital accounts.

15.17.1.3   Commentary

The accounts are in practice often accompanied by a commentary to explain the various entries, so as to assist the beneficiaries to understand how their entitlement has been arrived at. Thus, for example, the commentary will:

(a) identify the gross and net values of the estate;

(b) indicate its disposition (whether under the terms of the will or under the intestacy rules); and

(c) deal with any other relevant matters, such as interim distributions and distributions *in specie* (eg as a result of the personal representatives exercising a power of appropriation).

15.17.2   Income account

This should essentially do three things:

(a) give details of income receipts, itemising receipts from different sources (eg building society interest, bank interest, dividends, rent, etc);

(b) itemise details of expenditure from income (eg income tax, interest paid on legacies, and legal costs properly attributable to income such as the cost of preparing income tax returns); and

(c) show the net amount available for distribution.

15.17.3   Capital account

This will in practice need to do four things:

(a) itemise all the assets of the estate at their probate values. It may be more convenient to give the details required in a schedule or schedules to the account, simply bringing in the total(s);

(b) show realisations by the personal representatives during the course of the administration. The proceeds of sale may well differ from the probate valuation of the asset(s) concerned and any such variations have to be taken on board when accounting to the residuary beneficiaries;

(c) give details of all the liabilities discharged, pecuniary and specific legacies and expenses paid, including inheritance tax, capital gains tax, and income tax; and legal costs properly attributable to capital; and

(d) show the balance available for distribution.

15.17.4   Distribution account

This should show how the beneficiary's entitlement (whether this be to income or capital) is to be met. It should show details of any interim distribution(s) and indicate how the balance is to be paid (perhaps partly *in specie* and partly in cash).

15.17.5   Discharge

The estate accounts are the personal representatives' accounts and where you or your firm are not yourselves the personal representatives they should, therefore, first be presented to them for their approval. The personal representatives' acceptance of the accounts is usually signified by an endorsement to that effect signed by them.

The approved accounts are then presented (usually in duplicate) to the residuary beneficiaries, from whom the personal representatives are entitled to a discharge. Again, this is achieved by requesting the beneficiaries to return one of the copies of the accounts sent to them with an appropriate endorsement, such as 'I ... agree to accept the amount due to me as shown by the within written accounts', duly signed. The endorsement will usually also contain a formal discharge of the personal representatives and an agreement to indemnify them against all claims and demands.

If a beneficiary refuses to approve the accounts, there are in practice ultimately only two possible solutions:

(a) an administration action for the examination of the accounts by the court may be commenced; and

(b) the personal representatives may pay the beneficiary's share into court under s 63 of the Trustee Act 1925.

It may not be possible for acceptance to be signified because the beneficiary is a minor or suffering from some other disability (eg mental incapacity).

In the case of a minor beneficiary, the solution may be the appointment of trustees under s 42 of the Trustee Act 1925 (**15.4.3**). If this section cannot be used (because the beneficiary's interest is contingent only) the personal representatives will in practice have to continue to hold the assets concerned until the beneficiary concerned attains the age of 18.

If the beneficiary is suffering from mental disability, the personal representatives should inform any deputy appointed by the Court of Protection to manage the beneficiary's affairs of the entitlement, and then proceed in accordance with the court's directions. If no deputy has been appointed, ideally application should be made for this to be done (usually by a close relative of the person concerned). If not, the personal representatives may be forced to consider payment into court to obtain their discharge.

If approval cannot be obtained because a beneficiary is missing, we saw (in **15.7.2**) that the personal representatives should (at an earlier stage of the administration) have taken steps to overcome this difficulty. In practice, this will have probably involved either obtaining a '*Benjamin* Order' or some insurance cover, so that the full amount of the residue can be distributed to the other beneficiaries.

15.17.6 Transfer of assets

Once the personal representatives have obtained their discharge, they can arrange for the transfer of the assets to the residuary beneficiaries. As we saw in **15.15**, the method of doing this will depend upon the nature of the assets concerned (see also **15.18**).

15.18 Assents

An assent occurs when the personal representatives acknowledge that they do not require an asset for the purposes of the administration (see **15.15**). Prior to this, the beneficiaries do not generally have any legal or equitable proprietary interest in the asset, but merely the right to have the deceased's estate duly administered (see further **15.20**).

15.18.1 Pure personalty

At common law, an assent may be in writing, made orally, or implied from conduct. Although the equitable title passes by virtue of such assent, if there are particular formalities needed to transfer the legal title, these must also be complied with—the personal representatives holding in the meantime as trustees for the beneficiary concerned.

15.18.2 Land

Here, the position is governed by s 36 of the Administration of Estates Act 1925. All assents relating to unregistered land are now subject to compulsory first registration under the terms of the Land Registration Act 2002 under which the duty to register (within two months of the disposition) lies with the transferee. However, if the application for registration is not made within this period, the disposition is void and the title will revert to the personal representatives who will (pending re-execution of the assent) hold it on trust for the transferee. In practice, therefore, the personal representatives should ensure that first registration takes place with the cost being a testamentary expense.

15.18.2.1 The power to assent

By s 36 of the Administration of Estates Act 1925, personal representatives are enabled to vest any interest in freehold or leasehold land in any person entitled to it—whether beneficially, as trustee, as personal representative of a beneficiary who has died before the assent can be made, or otherwise (such as a purchaser under a contract made by the deceased: *GHR Co Ltd v IRC* [1943] KB 303). An assent should not, in practice, be used where the personal representative is selling, or is asked to give effect to a contract for sale entered into by a beneficiary.

15.18.2.2 Form

By s 36(4), an assent must be in writing, signed by the personal representative(s) and naming the person(s) in whose favour it is given. Although technically a form of conveyance, an assent does not bear *ad valorem* stamp duty (except where being used to give effect to a contract).

Sometimes, a deed will in practice be needed, for example because indemnity covenants are required from the beneficiary.

It has been held that an assent complying with the requirements of s 36(4) is needed even where the personal representative is the person in whose favour the assent is being made, whether as beneficiary, trustee, or as personal representative of a deceased beneficiary: *Re King's Will Trusts* [1964] Ch 542.

15.18.2.3 Effect

By s 36(2), unless there is evidence of a contrary intention, an assent relates back to the date of the deceased's death. Thus, the beneficiary will now be entitled to rents or profits produced by the land since the date of the deceased's death.

15.18.2.4 Protection of beneficiaries

Anyone in whose favour an assent is made is entitled to require (at the expense of the estate) a memorandum of the assent to be endorsed upon the (original) grant of representation—and to call for the production of the grant to prove that this has been done (s 36(5)).

15.18.2.5 Protection of purchasers

There are two provisions affording protection to purchasers from personal representatives:

(a) Section 36(6): if a purchaser takes in good faith a conveyance from personal representatives containing a statement that the personal representatives have not previously made any assent or conveyance relating to the legal estate, the purchaser will take priority over any beneficiary in whose favour a prior assent or conveyance had been made unless notice of the earlier transaction had been endorsed upon the (original) grant. It is essential, therefore, that the purchaser ensures that the conveyance contains such a statement and that the grant is inspected to check for previous memoranda. Further, an endorsement on the grant relating to the conveyance to the purchaser should also be insisted upon.

(b) Section 36(7): the protection here is, again, afforded to the purchaser in the absence of any memorandum relating to a previous assent or conveyance endorsed on the grant. Subject to this, an assent or conveyance by a personal representative is sufficient evidence that the person in whose favour it is given or made is the person entitled to the legal estate. Thus the purchaser is not concerned, for example, to see the terms of the will to check that the recipient of the property was indeed entitled to it. However, the section does not provide that the assent or conveyance is 'conclusive' evidence, so that a purchaser in possession of information which indicates that the assent or conveyance was given or made to the wrong person will not be protected: *Re Duce and Boots Cash Chemists (Southern) Ltd's Contract* [1937] Ch 642.

15.18.2.6 Protection of personal representatives

By s 36(10), personal representatives may—as a condition of giving an assent or conveyance—require security for the discharge of any debts or liabilities to which the property is subject (such as a mortgage or liability to instalments of inheritance tax). However, personal representatives cannot refuse to give an assent once 'reasonable arrangements' have been made.

15.19 Financial services

We have seen (in **15.8**) that, in the context of probate and administration most investment business will in practice be non-mainstream investment business. However, where solicitors advise beneficiaries as to, for example, the investment of their inheritance, such advice will be prima facie mainstream business. Avoiding this consequence will normally involve taking the advice of, and making arrangements through, an authorised person.

15.20   Beneficiaries' rights and remedies

The beneficiaries will want to know that the estate is being efficiently administered by the personal representatives, and will be concerned to receive their entitlements under the will or intestacy as quickly as possible. In this section we will consider the nature of the beneficiaries' rights, and how they may be enforced.

15.20.1   The beneficiaries' right to compel due administration

The deceased's assets vest in the personal representatives 'in full ownership without distinction between legal and equitable interests' (*Commissioner of Stamp Duties (Queensland) v Livingston* [1965] AC 694).

Thus, until the administration is complete the beneficiary (whether under the will or intestacy rules) has neither a legal nor an equitable interest in the deceased's assets. It is only at this point that the personal representatives will know which of the deceased's assets have had to be sold to pay debts and administration expenses, and which are available for distribution to beneficiaries.

The beneficiary does, however, have a chose in action, the right to have the deceased's estate properly administered.

15.20.2   Date for payment of entitlement under will or intestacy

We have seen that personal representatives cannot be compelled to distribute the estate before the end of the executor's year (**15.3.1.3**). Beneficiaries will want to know whether they are entitled to income or interest between the date of death and the date of distribution. Whether the beneficiary is entitled to income from, or interest on, the value of the asset(s) during this period will depend on the provisions of any will, on the nature of the asset (ie whether or not it is income producing), and on the nature of the gift.

15.20.2.1   Specific gifts

Where the entitlement of the beneficiary is immediate, such gifts carry the right to any income accruing between the date of death and the vesting of the property in the beneficiary. The assent by the personal representatives vesting the property in the beneficiary (see **15.18**) operates retrospectively to give the beneficiary the right to such income. If the beneficiary has a contingent or future (deferred) entitlement, again such gifts carry the intermediate income which will be added to capital (and devolve with it) for so long as the rules against indefinite accumulation permit (thereafter, the income either falls into residue or passes under the intestacy rules).

15.20.2.2   Residuary gifts

Whether the beneficiary's entitlement is immediate or contingent, and whether of personalty or realty, such gifts carry the intermediate income. Where the beneficiary has a future (deferred) interest, devises (ie gifts of realty) probably carry the intermediate income: bequests (ie gifts of personalty) do not carry such right and the income passes under the intestacy rules.

15.20.2.3   Contingent pecuniary legacies

Where the will contains such a legacy, so that the sum involved has to be invested pending the fulfilment of the contingency, the gift does not normally carry the intermediate income; the income from the investment therefore belongs to the residuary beneficiaries. There are exceptions to this rule where the gift is to the child or person to whom the testator stands *in loco parentis*, and the contingency is attaining an age not greater than 18 (or earlier marriage); or where the gift is to any child made with the intention of providing for that child's maintenance.

All the rules stated earlier apply in the absence of provision to the contrary in the will.

15.20.2.4   Pecuniary legacies

As a general rule, a pecuniary legatee, general legatee, or demonstrative legatee (if the designated fund is exhausted) is entitled to interest at 6 per cent only from the date upon which such legacy is payable. In the absence of any direction to the contrary in the will, such a legacy is payable at the end of the executor's year. Any interest payable is regarded as an administration expense, payable therefore normally from residue.

Exceptionally, however, interest on such legacies is payable from the date of death (unless the will otherwise provides). For example:

(a) if the legacy is in satisfaction of a debt;

(b) if the legacy is charged on realty;

(c) if the legacy is to the testator's infant child or to an infant to whom he stands *in loco parentis*; or

(d) if the legacy is to any infant with the intention to provide for that child's maintenance.

15.20.3   Remedies available to beneficiaries

Where difficulties arise during the administration of an estate, there are a number of formal remedies available to a beneficiary. Essentially, they fall into two categories:

(a) 'Administration proceedings', designed to ensure that the administration of the estate is properly conducted. Such actions may be general, or for specific relief, and need not necessarily be 'contentious', in that the personal representatives are equally entitled to seek the court's assistance in this way.

(b) Actions to 'recover loss' suffered.

The latter include the following.

15.20.3.1   Personal action against the personal representatives

Instead of commencing administration proceedings a personal action may be brought against the personal representatives. A failure by a personal representative to carry out the duties of the office is a *devastavit*, for which the personal representative is personally liable to the beneficiaries or creditors, unless they have acquiesced in or encouraged the breach. Personal representatives may, however, be relieved from liability:

(a) by provisions in the will relieving personal representatives from liability, eg where mistakes are made in good faith;

(b) by s 61 of the Trustee Act 1925 the court may wholly or partly relieve the personal representative from personal liability where it is satisfied that the personal representative acted 'honestly, reasonably and ought fairly to be excused'; or

(c) by agreement with the beneficiaries, being *sui juris* and fully aware of the breach, the personal representatives may be released from liability.

15.20.3.2   Tracing

A beneficiary (whether under a will or the intestacy rules) or a creditor may have the right to trace and recover property of the estate (or property representing such property) from the personal representatives or any other recipient of it, other than a bona fide purchaser for value or person deriving title from such purchaser. The right to trace is also lost if the property has been dissipated, or where to allow tracing would be inequitable. This remedy may be sought whether or not a personal action has been brought against the personal representative, though insofar as such action has been 'successful' the right to trace is clearly not also going to be available.

15.20.3.3   Personal action against recipients of estate assets

Where all other remedies of a beneficiary (whether under the will or intestacy rules) or creditor have been exhausted, a personal action may be brought against a person who has wrongly received the assets of the estate (*Ministry of Health v Simpson* [1951] AC 251).

15.21 Distributing the assets: checkpoints

1. Payment of legacies:
    (a) Specific legacies/devises (**15.15.1**).
    (b) Burden of pecuniary legacies (**15.15.2**):
        (i) provision in the will (**15.15.2.1**);
        (ii) no provision in the will (**15.15.2.2**).
    (c) Abatement (**15.15.3**).
    (d) Appropriation (**15.15.4**).
    (e) Receipts (**15.15.5**).
2. Ascertainment of residue:
    (a) Finalising the tax position:
        (i) income tax and capital gains tax (**15.16.1**);
        (ii) inheritance tax (**15.16.2**):
            (1) corrective accounts (**15.16.2.3**); and
            (2) certificates of discharge (**15.16.2.4**).
    (b) Administration expenses:
        (i) funeral expenses (**15.16.3.1**);
        (ii) legal costs (**15.16.3.2**); and
        (iii) other professionals' fees (**15.16.3.3**).
    (c) Remuneration of personal representatives:
        (i) legacy to proving executors (**15.16.4.1**);
        (ii) charging clause in will (**15.16.4.2**); and
        (iii) other possibilities (**15.16.4.3** to **15.16.4.6**).
3. Estate accounts:
    (a) Income account (**15.17.2**).
    (b) Capital account (**15.17.3**).
    (c) Distribution account (**15.17.4**).
    (d) Discharge of personal representatives (**15.17.5**).
4. Assents:
    (a) Pure personalty (**15.18.1**).
    (b) Land (**15.18.2**).
5. Beneficiaries' rights and remedies:
    (a) Right to compel due administration (**15.20.1**).
    (b) Date for payment of entitlement under will/intestacy (**15.20.2**).
    (c) Remedies:
        (i) personal action against the personal representatives (**15.20.3.1**);
        (ii) tracing (**15.20.3.2**); and
        (iii) personal action against recipients of estate assets (**15.20.3.3**).

See also **Figure 15.2**.

Figure 15.2 Estate administration—the final stage

```
                        ┌─────────────────────────────┐
                        │ Estate available for distribution │
                        └─────────────────────────────┘
```

┌──────────────┐   ┌─────────────────────────┐   ┌──────────────┐
│ Testate Estate │   │ Partially Intestate Estate │   │ Intestate Estate │
└──────────────┘   └─────────────────────────┘   └──────────────┘

┌─────────────────────────┐   ┌─────────────────────────────┐
│ Pay or transfer assets to general/ │   │ Transfer personal chattels and │
│ specific legatees   │   │ statutory legacy to surviving spouse │
└─────────────────────────┘   │ (if any)   │
                                                └─────────────────────────────┘

┌──────────────────────────────────────┐
│ Finalise deceased's income tax/CGT liabilities │
└──────────────────────────────────────┘

┌───────────────────────┐
│ Finalise PRs' IHT liability │
└───────────────────────┘

┌───────────────────────┐
│ Was estate an excepted estate? │
└───────────────────────┘

(YES)   (NO) ─────────────── (Was estate liable to IHT?)

                                              (NO)   (YES)

┌───────────────────────────┐
│ Submit corrective account if needed │
└───────────────────────────┘

                                      Consider:
┌───────────────────────┐   • Collection of IHT from
│ Discharge any further IHT due │   beneficial joint tenant on
└───────────────────────┘   whom the burden of tax falls
                                       • Arrangements for discharge
┌───────────────────────┐   of IHT on instalment option
│ Obtain certificate of discharge │   property
└───────────────────────┘

┌───────────────────────────┐
│ Discharge administration expenses │
└───────────────────────────┘

┌──────────────────────────────┐
│ Prepare estate accounts for approval │
│ by PRs and residuary beneficiaries │
└──────────────────────────────┘

┌──────────────────────────┐
│ Assent assets to residuary │
│ beneficiaries or to trustees if │
│ appropriate   │
└──────────────────────────┘

Part 4

Human rights

16   Human rights   285

Human rights

16.1 Introduction

This chapter aims to provide an introduction to the following:

- the European Convention on Human Rights and the Human Rights Act 1998, taking into account the origins of the Convention and the Human Rights Act 1998 and their incorporation into UK legislation;
- general principles of European jurisprudence;
- the Articles and the Protocols themselves; and
- areas where potential breaches may occur.

When the Human Rights Act came into force on 2 October 2000 there was much anticipation and speculation on its potential ramifications. All areas of law were affected by the incorporation—in particular the areas of criminal, family, and employment law. All courts from the lowest to the highest were required to have a thorough working knowledge of the contents of the Articles and Protocols and their application. The profession needed to do more than just have an understanding of the contents of the Convention, as European case law played, and still plays, a significant part in the application of the Convention. In order to interpret and apply case law effectively lawyers and courts alike needed to have a grasp of the European jurisprudence that was current when the European Court of Human Rights came to a decision.

Seventeen years on from its incorporation into UK legislation, the political climate is substantially changed and differing forces now come to bear upon the view that is taken of the human rights legislation. The growth of terrorism and the public outcry at the mismanagement over the release from prison of foreign criminals who should have been considered for deportation have shifted the balance towards issues of security and the protection of the public as opposed to the protection of individuals seeking to uphold their specific human rights. The result was the proposal to abolish the Human Rights Act and replace it with a British Bill of Rights. The proposal formed part of the Conservative Government's 2015 manifesto but is now on hold until after Brexit and a potential General Election in 2020. There are suggestions that the plan to abolish the Human Rights Act may disappear entirely and no doubt this will be the subject of much debate in the future.

For the present, the Act remains an integral part of the judicial make-up of the UK and what is clear is that not only can legislative provisions be challenged, but also the way in which they have been applied. Practitioners should be clear about whether they are arguing that the law is incompatible, and therefore attempting to invoke s 3 or 4 of the Act, or whether they are arguing that the relevant law itself is compatible but the way in which it has been applied violates the defendant's rights under the Convention.

16.2 General principles

16.2.1 The Human Rights Act 1998

The Human Rights Act 1998 has made the Convention central to the practice of law in the UK.

Section 2(1) of the Act requires all courts and tribunals to take into account the Convention and decisions by the institutions of the Convention, whether the European Court of Human Rights, the Commission of Human Rights, or the Council.

The Act creates a general statutory requirement that all legislation (past or present) be read and given effect in a way which is compatible with the Convention. It does this by providing, in s 3, that all legislation, primary and secondary, whenever enacted, must be read and given effect in a way which is compatible with Convention rights wherever possible.

Section 6(1) and (3) require public authorities to act in compliance with the Convention unless they are prevented from doing so by statute. This means that the courts have their own primary duty to give effect to the Convention unless a statute positively prevents this. It would therefore be unlawful for public authorities to act in a way which is incompatible with a Convention right. Courts themselves are included in the definition of public authorities.

It is generally perceived that it is only the actual decision of a court in a criminal or civil case that is subject to the right of appeal. This is true, but under the 1998 Act it is not just the decision of a court that is open to challenge but the way in which the courts actually function. For example, the administrative element of the Magistrates' Court Service or clerks who are exercising judicial functions conveyed upon them by national legislation are open to challenge. Clearly the management of the court itself by the Chief Executive and the Magistrates' Courts Committee has a direct effect upon the public and public funds and those decision-making processes are also open to scrutiny. As a result, any court, committee, or individual must act compatibly with the Convention both in the decisions that it comes to and the process that it uses.

All courts and tribunals must have a working knowledge of the content of the Convention and the relevant case law to any given Article in order to be able to apply it correctly in accordance with UK legislation. To apply the decisions of cases brought down by Strasbourg, the courts and tribunals need to understand how decisions at Strasbourg are actually reached, so as to give the appropriate weight to any decision. In order to be able effectively to interpret Convention legislation and case law, the courts must understand the 'European jurisprudence' that exists when the judges come to a decision in Strasbourg.

16.3 European and international doctrines

A common misconception about the rights conveyed by the Convention is that if there is a breach by a public authority or Member State, the acts of that authority or Member State must be amended to bring them within the Convention. This is too draconian and would throw national law and procedures into a state of confusion. Although rights are conveyed to individuals, the rights contained within the Articles are rarely absolute and can be limited or qualified. The majority of rights are subject to limitations and qualifications; however, the right to freedom from torture is an absolute right and an act of torture could never be justified by acting in the interests of the state.

16.3.1 Limited rights

Some of the rights conveyed under the Articles of the Convention have limitations placed upon them so that in some circumstances an infringement of a guaranteed right does not amount to an infringement. For example, Article 2 contains the right to life. This right is limited by Article 2(2) which allows the use of force, but the amount used cannot be more than is absolutely necessary in the defence of a person from unlawful violence, to prevent escape from lawful detention, or to effect an arrest or quell a riot or insurrection. See the case of *McCann v United Kingdom* (1995) 21 EHRR 97, where suspected terrorists were shot dead in Gibraltar by British security agents. The Court held that there had been a breach of Article 2 as the state had failed to give adequate training or instructions to agents likely to use lethal force. This failure to plan and control was the central issue in deciding whether the force used had been absolutely necessary.

Article 2 is wider in its application than simply the right to life however. *Amin v Secretary of State for the Home Department* [2003] UKHL 51 which, in citing *Osman v United Kingdom* (1998) 29 EHRR 245, confirmed that the primary purpose of Article 2 involved substantive obligations—the protection and safeguarding of life—and procedural aspects, namely, the 'minimum requirements of a mechanism, whereby the circumstances of a deprivation of life by the agents of a state may receive public and independent scrutiny'. Not only should there be an effective investigation where there had been a death where agents of the state were directly responsible for the death, but also where the system itself permits or fails to prevent a death, ie in cases where there had been a life-threatening injury. This approach was confirmed in *R (D) v Secretary of State for the Home Department* [2006] 3 All ER 946, CA; [2005] UKHRR 917 where it was held that there was a duty to carry out an Article 2 investigation where there had been an attempted suicide by a prisoner. More recently the case of *Van Colle v Chief Constable of Hertfordshire* [2008] UKHL 50 confirmed that the test laid down in *Osman* was invariable and was not intended to impose a fluctuating standard to be applied on a case-by-case basis.

16.3.2   Qualified rights

Some Articles contain qualified rights, and as such the Convention permits them to be infringed in certain circumstances.

Once a victim has been shown to have established a primary right, the Convention seeks to balance the rights of the individual against other public rights. However, rights such as the right to respect for private life and the right to freedom of expression may sometimes compete with one another. Equally, some rights may be in direct conflict with public interest considerations. These sorts of rights, which impinge on the rights and freedoms of others, are necessarily qualified, and the Convention permits them to be limited by the state.

16.3.3   How far can a state limit the rights contained within the Convention?

The Convention permits these limitations only where they are:

(a) prescribed by law;

(b) intended to achieve a legitimate objective; and

(c) necessary in a democratic society (ie proportionate to the ends to be achieved).

For example, Article 8 states that, 'Everyone has the right to respect for his private and family life, his home and his correspondence'. This is a presumed right, but a number of limitations and exceptions to it are set out in Article 8(2):

There shall be no interference by a public authority with the exercise of this right except such as is in accordance with the law and is necessary in a democratic society in the interests of national security, public safety or the economic well-being of the country, for the prevention of disorder or crime, for the protection of health or morals, or for the protection of the rights and freedoms of others.

The precise terms of the limitations in respect of the Articles vary but the judicial method for considering them is the same:

(a) Is the interference prescribed by law?

(b) Does it serve a legitimate objective?

(c) Is it necessary in a democratic society?

16.3.3.1   Is the interference prescribed by law? The rule of law

No interference with a right protected under the Convention is permissible unless the citizen knows the basis for the interference because it is set out in ascertainable law. In the absence of any such detailed authorisation by the law, any interference, however justified, will violate the Convention—see *Malone v United Kingdom* (1984) 7 EHRR 14 where the applicant's telephone was tapped by the police. When this took place the only authorisation was an internal code of guidance produced by the police which was not available to the public. The European Court took the view that Mr Malone was unable to assess whether or not his telephone would be listened to, or what the basis in law for the surveillance might be. The common law position was inadequate, as could be seen from his failure in the High Court. The interference violated the Convention because it was not prescribed by law.

16.3.3.2   Does it serve a legitimate objective?

Legitimate objectives are:

(a) the interests of public safety;

(b) national security;

(c) the protection of health and morals; and

(d) the economic well-being of the country, or the protection of the rights and freedoms of others.

16.3.3.3   Is it necessary in a democratic society? Proportionality

The Convention's approach is to decide whether a particular limitation from a right is justified in the sense of being 'proportionate to the legitimate aim pursued'.

This means that even if a policy which interferes with a Convention right might be aimed at securing a legitimate social policy, for example the prevention of crime, this will not in itself justify the violation if the means adopted to secure the aim are excessive in the circumstances. *Soering v United Kingdom* (1989) 11 EHRR 439 stated:

> inherent in the whole of the Convention is a search for the fair balance between the demands of the general interest of the Community and the requirements of the protection of the individual's human rights. (para 89)

16.3.4   The margin of appreciation

A state is allowed a certain freedom to evaluate its public policy decisions, but this is subject to review by the Strasbourg institutions. The Court has to ensure that the Member State's own political and cultural traditions are respected. When determining whether a social policy aim is legitimate therefore, or whether the means adopted to achieve it are 'necessary in a democratic society', the Commission and the Court have recognised limits as to their own competence to judge the issue. They have done this by giving the state a so-called 'margin of appreciation' when assessing the extent to which a signatory has violated the Convention.

The most notable case in this area is *Handyside v United Kingdom* (1976) 1 EHRR 737. This case arose because of the intention to publish *The Little Red Schoolbook*, intended for children, but which included a chapter on sex. The books were seized by the police under the Obscene Publications Act 1959 and a forfeiture order obtained against the publishers. The publishers claimed a breach of their right to freedom of expression under Article 10.

Was the seizing of the books proportionate to the legitimate aim that the state sought to protect? The Court recognised that there was a margin of appreciation in this case which justified the interference with Article 10. It stated:

> By reason of their direct and continuous contact with the vital forces of their countries, state authorities are in principle in a better position than the international judge to give an opinion on the

exact nature of these requirements as well as on the necessity of a restriction or penalty intended to meet them. Nevertheless Article 10(2) does not give the contracting state an unlimited power of appreciation. The Court which is responsible for ensuring the observance of those states' engagements is empowered to give the final ruling on whether a restriction or penalty is reconcilable with the freedom of expression as protected by Article 10. The domestic margin of appreciation thus goes hand in hand with a European supervision.

16.3.5 Derogations and reservations

In times of war or other public emergency it is open to a Member State to enter into derogations in respect of certain obligations. These cannot be general derogations. A derogation simply allows a state not to comply with the Article in question to the legitimate extent of the derogation. However, derogations in respect of the right to life (except arising from the lawful prosecution of war) or from the prohibitions against torture are not permitted.

Reservations differ from derogations in that they are merely conditions upon acceptance of a particular Article.

16.3.6 Equality of arms

This principle, laid down in the case of *Neuminster v Austria* (1968) 1 EHRR 91, was created in order to ensure that both parties to a case, whether in civil or criminal proceedings, were not placed at a procedural disadvantage. The principle can be more easily explained with reference to a practical example.

In the case of a summary-only offence which must be tried in the magistrates' court, the defence has no right to advance information from the prosecution. This differs from an either-way offence where such information is readily available. The defence must conduct its case ignorant of evidence in the prosecution's possession and it is therefore deprived of the opportunity of investigating and testing the strength of the prosecution's case. This may well have given rise to an application in the magistrates' court that there has been a breach of Article 6 of the Convention because the principle of equality of arms has been infringed (given that the majority of summary-only offences do carry the threat of a custodial sentence). However, this potential breach is effectively dealt with by para 43 of the Attorney-General's Guidelines, Disclosure of Information in Criminal Proceedings, where such advance information is now provided.

16.3.7 Horizontality

As mentioned earlier, s 6 of the Human Rights Act 1998 incorporates courts and tribunals into the definition of public bodies. When two individuals come to court for a decision to be made about their dispute, the court needs to act compatibly with the Convention. This will therefore have an indirect effect upon the two individuals who are not themselves covered by the Convention. The court's adherence to the Convention will have a *horizontal* effect on their relationship. In *Hokkanen v Finland* (1994) 19 EHRR 139, the European Court held that where grandparents failed to abide by court orders for contact and custody in favour of the father, Article 8 imposed upon the state a positive obligation to assist, so far as possible, the father's relationship with his child.

Douglas and Others v Hello! Ltd [2001] QB 467, involving Michael Douglas and Catherine Zeta Jones, again illustrated that the court had a duty under s 6 to protect their private life. The case involved proceedings against *Hello!* magazine which threatened to publish unauthorised photographs from the couple's wedding when they had in fact sold the exclusive rights to *OK* magazine. While all three judges agreed that an injunction should be refused because the couple had in fact traded their right to private life like a commodity, the judgment is notable in confirming the effect that the Human Rights Act 1998 has had upon legal relations between individuals as opposed to legal relations between individuals and the state.

16.3.8   Living instrument

The Convention was drafted more than 60 years ago and, unlike usual pieces of legislation, it has not been amended, repealed, or replaced by more up-to-date legislation. To use the UK model of precedent would bind the court to adhere to decisions which are outmoded and probably unfair. It is primarily for this reason that the doctrine of precedent is not a main feature of Convention case law. The Convention is a 'living instrument' and cases are decided in line with the up-to-date economic and moral conditions of the Member States. Although this creates some uncertainty when relying on previous decisions handed down, it at least ensures that the decisions are modern in their approach.

16.3.9   Protocols

Protocols can be thought of as extensions to the Convention where Member States can agree to add to the rights contained within it. The procedural method for doing this is to draw up a Protocol setting out the additional rights. The First Protocol provides for rights to the peaceful enjoyment of property, to education, and to free elections. The Human Rights Act 1998 allows the government to incorporate future Protocols into national law using rules of Parliament. The rights contained within the Protocols carry as much weight as the provisions contained in the Articles themselves.

16.3.10   Where to find Convention case law

The Council of Europe publishes individual judgments and decisions under the title *Publications of the European Court of Human Rights*. Court judgments are published in Series A and the pleadings, oral arguments, and documents are published in Series B.

Decisions of the Commission and judgments of the Court can be found at http://www.echr.coe.int.

Another source is the European Human Rights Reports ('EHRR'), which publishes all judgments and important decisions. The European Human Rights Law Review ('EHRLR') appears six times a year, and has a case law section which highlights interesting cases and recent decisions.

16.4   The Convention rights

This section contains commentary on the main Articles of the Convention which affect legal practice. It should be viewed only as an introduction to some of the possible effects of the Convention and is no substitute for empirical research.

Schedule 1 to the Human Rights Act 1998 lists the Convention rights by reference to the relevant Articles of, and Protocols to, the European Convention on Human Rights, as follows.

16.4.1   Article 2—Right to life

1. Everyone's right to life shall be protected by law. No one shall be deprived of his life intentionally save in the execution of a sentence of a court following his conviction of a crime for which this penalty is provided by law.

2. Deprivation of life shall not be regarded as inflicted in contravention of this Article when it results from the use of force which is no more than absolutely necessary:

    (a) in defence of any person from unlawful violence;

    (b) in order to effect a lawful arrest or to prevent the escape of a person lawfully detained;

    (c) in action lawfully taken for the purpose of quelling a riot or insurrection.

This is a limited right: see *McCann v United Kingdom* (1995) 21 EHRR 97.

16.4.2   Article 3—Prohibition of torture

No one shall be subjected to torture or inhuman or degrading treatment or punishment.

This is an absolute right although there is a minimum level of severity required before Article 3 will be contravened. The case of *Ireland v United Kingdom* (1978) 2 EHRR 25 gave guidelines as to what constituted prohibited treatment. Torture was defined as deliberate inhuman treatment causing very serious and cruel suffering; inhumane treatment or punishment as treatment or punishment which causes intense physical and mental suffering; and degrading treatment or punishment as treatment or punishment that arouses in a victim a feeling of fear, anguish, and inferiority capable of humiliating and debasing the victim and possibly breaking his or her physical or moral resistance.

16.4.3   Article 4—Prohibition of slavery and forced labour

1. No one shall be held in slavery or servitude. [This is an absolute right.]
2. No one shall be required to perform forced or compulsory labour. [This is a limited right.]
3. For the purpose of this Article the term 'forced or compulsory labour' shall not include:
    (a) any work required to be done in the ordinary course of detention imposed according to the provisions of Article 5 of this Convention or during conditional release from such detention;
    (b) any service of a military character or, in case of conscientious objectors in countries where they are recognised, service exacted instead of compulsory military service;
    (c) any service exacted in case of an emergency or calamity threatening the life or well-being of the community;
    (d) any work or service which forms part of normal civic obligations.

16.4.4   Article 5—Right to liberty and security

1. Everyone has the right to liberty and security of person. No one shall be deprived of his liberty save in the following cases and in accordance with a procedure prescribed by law:
    (a) the lawful detention of a person after conviction by a competent court;
    (b) the lawful arrest or detention of a person for non-compliance with the lawful order of a court in order to secure the fulfilment of any obligation prescribed by law;
    (c) the lawful arrest or detention of a person effected for the purpose of bringing him before the competent legal authority on reasonable suspicion of having committed an offence or when it is reasonably considered necessary to prevent his committing an offence or fleeing after having done so;
    (d) the detention of a minor by lawful order for the purpose of educational supervision or his lawful detention for the purpose of bringing him before the competent legal authority;
    (e) the lawful detention of persons for the spreading of infectious diseases, of persons of unsound mind, alcoholics or drug addicts or vagrants;
    (f) the lawful arrest or detention of a person to prevent his effecting an unauthorised entry into the country or of a person against whom action is being taken with a view to deportation or extradition.
2. Everyone who is arrested shall be informed promptly, in a language which he understands, of the reasons for his arrest and of any charge against him.
3. Everyone arrested or detained in accordance with paragraph 1(c) of this Article shall be brought promptly before a judge or other officer authorised by law to exercise judicial power and shall be entitled to trial within a reasonable time or to release pending trial. Release may be conditioned by guarantees to appear for trial.

4. Everyone who is deprived of his liberty by arrest or detention shall be entitled to take proceedings by which the lawfulness of his detention shall be decided speedily by a court and his release ordered if the detention is not lawful.

5. Everyone who has been the victim of arrest or detention in contravention of the provisions of this Article shall have an exercisable right to compensation.

This is a limited right and will have most relevance in a magistrates' court, particularly in relation to the granting of bail. When a defendant is charged with a criminal offence he must appear before the magistrates who will decide whether or not there should be a release pending trial, with or without conditions, or a remand into custody. Article 5(3) states that he should be entitled to trial within a reasonable time or to release pending trial. The case of *Wemhoff v Germany* (1968) 1 EHRR 55 stated that the defendant was entitled to both things notwithstanding the wording and also that the defendant should be released pending trial unless there are '*relevant and sufficient*' reasons to justify continued detention. In the UK the Bail Act 1976 provides that the magistrates must be satisfied that there are substantial grounds for believing that a person should be deprived of his liberty and the exceptions to the prima facie right to bail are clearly set out in the Schedule to the Act.

Article 5(1)(c) has also been the subject of scrutiny in relation to the authorisation of the detention of claimants for over seven hours in Oxford Circus on May Day 2001. In *Austin and Saxby v Commissioner of Police of the Metropolis* [2005] HRLR 20; [2007] EWCA Civ 989; [2005] HRLR 20 the question was whether it was capable of authorising the detention of individuals whom the police neither suspected of criminality nor intended to bring before a court on reasonable suspicion of having committed an offence or to prevent them doing so. The claims made were dismissed and a subsequent appeal in 2007 was unsuccessful. However, in the case of *R (Laporte) v Gloucestershire Chief Constable* [2006] UKHL 55; [2007] 2 WLR 46 anti-war protestors were prevented from reaching an anti-war demonstration at RAF Fairford. Their coaches were stopped before they reached the site and were searched. The coaches were then forcibly escorted back to London. The House of Lords held that this was a breach of Article 5 and in addition that there had been a breach of both Articles 10 and 11 as they had prevented the protestors from reaching the demonstration when there was no imminent breach of the peace.

16.4.4.1   Disclosure and bail

Disclosure is an area which requires some consideration in relation to Article 6: the right to a fair trial and the equality of arms. However, disclosure will also be very relevant to bail applications where the prosecution is in possession of information which is not readily available to the defence. This may well prove to be a breach of the principle of equality of arms, placing the prosecution in breach of Article 5(4). Authority for this can be found in *Lamy v Belgium* (1989) 11 EHRR 529 where the applicant had been refused access to the prosecution file at both applications for bail and had bail refused. He merely had access to some information disclosed on the face of the warrant for his arrest. The European Court held that there had been a breach of Article 5(4) even though the national law at the time only allowed for disclosure 30 days after arrest. The Court then took the matter a stage further and said that not only should the information be disclosed but the applicant should have had sufficient time to consider and evaluate the material.

The case of *R (O) v Harrow Crown Court* [2006] UKHL 42; [2006] 3 WLR 195 dealt with this issue against the backdrop of the compatibility of s 25(1) of the Criminal Justice and Public Order Act 1994 with Article 5. O had been charged with rape, having previously been convicted of the same offence. An application to extend custody time limits was refused, but he was not granted bail on the basis of s 25(1). He was in custody for 22 months, 16 of which followed the expiry of the custody time limit. Whilst in custody, he had dispensed with his lawyers' services, and then had them reinstated, four times (twice, at least, causing delay). The indictment was eventually stayed as an abuse of process. The central issue on appeal here seemed to be the presumption in favour of custody indicated by s 25(1) and the presumption in favour of liberty favoured by Article 5. It is clear that the latter should take precedence. Strasbourg jurisprudence is quite clear that the decision to take away a person's liberty must be a judicial one and should take into account the presumption of innocence and 'the rule of respect for the accused's liberty'. The presumption is in favour of liberty and it is for the prosecution to bear the burden of raising exceptional circumstances.

16.4.4.2 Right to review

Note the case of *T and V v United Kingdom* (Applications 24724/94 and 24888/94) 16 December 1999, which held that the two applicants had been denied the opportunity to have the lawfulness of detention reviewed by a judicial body.

16.4.5 Article 6—Right to a fair trial

1. In the determination of his civil rights and obligations or of any criminal charge against him, everyone is entitled to a fair and public hearing within a reasonable time by an independent and impartial tribunal established by law. Judgment shall be pronounced publicly but the press and public may be excluded from all or part of the trial in the interest of morals, public order or national security in a democratic society, where the interest of juveniles or the protection of the private life of the parties so require, or to the extent strictly necessary in the opinion of the court in special circumstances where publicity would prejudice the interests of justice.

2. Everyone charged with a criminal offence shall be presumed innocent until proved guilty according to law.

3. Everyone charged with a criminal offence has the following minimum rights:

   (a) to be informed promptly, in a language which he understands and in detail, of the nature and cause of the accusation against him;

   (b) to have adequate time and facilities for the preparation of his defence;

   (c) to defend himself in person or through legal assistance of his own choosing or, if he has not sufficient means to pay for legal assistance, to be given it free when the interests of justice so require;

   (d) to examine or have examined witnesses against him and to obtain the attendance and examination of witnesses on his behalf under the same conditions as witnesses against him;

   (e) to have the free assistance of an interpreter if he cannot understand or speak the language used in court.

This Article will affect proceedings in both civil and criminal trials.

16.4.5.1 Criminal proceedings

Article 6(1) provides the right to a trial within a reasonable time and guarantees the expedition in the conduct of the proceedings themselves in order to prevent a defendant from remaining uncertain about the outcome of his fate for too long.

This has changed our approach to abuse of process proceedings. Under common law, the defence must show that the defendant has been prejudiced by the delay in order to make a successful application. However, since October 2000, there is no requirement to show prejudice as the delay, of itself, will be sufficient. In extreme circumstances the European Court may adjudge that a long-delayed trial amounts to oppression.

16.4.5.2 Article 6(2)—Reverse burden of proof

The case of *Salabiaku v France* (1991) 13 EHRR 379 was notable in that it stated that:

Article 6(2) does not therefore regard presumptions of fact or law provided for in criminal law with indifference. It requires states to confine them within reasonable limits which take into account the importance of what is at stake and maintain the rights of the defence.

Article 6(2) and the presumption of innocence has already been raised as an issue in UK proceedings, in particular the case of *R v Director of Public Prosecutions, ex parte Kebilene* [1999] 3 WLR 972. This case concerned ss 16A and 16B of the Prevention of Terrorism Act 1989 which carries with it a reverse burden of proof. The House of Lords held, in relation to the particular provision, that it was not clear that these sections were necessarily going to be contrary to Article 6(2). Two of their Lordships thought that the offence of possessing an article reasonably suspected of being possessed for terrorist purposes might well violate Article 6(2), since it required the accused to prove that the article was not in his possession for those purposes, and they proposed reinterpreting the burden on the accused as evidential only. Other members of the court disagreed and said that it was sufficient that the prosecution has the burden of showing 'circumstances giving rise to a reasonable suspicion' of terrorist purposes.

16.4.5.3   Article 6(3)(b)—Disclosure

Our present system of disclosure contains various anomalies which contravene a defendant's right to disclosure under the Convention. The main piece of legislation to be affected here is the Criminal Procedure and Investigations Act 1996 which deals with primary and secondary disclosure of unused material.

The Attorney-General's Guidelines, Disclosure of Information in Criminal Proceedings, sought to deal with some of the unfairness that had been created by the 1996 Act and by disclosure provisions in general. Indeed, in its introduction it states that the guidelines are designed to:

ensure that there is fair disclosure of material which may be relevant to an investigation and which does not form part of the prosecution case ... Disclosure which does not meet these objectives risks preventing a fair trial taking place.

Some of the dissatisfaction with the disclosure system from both a defence and a prosecution point of view has been addressed in the Criminal Justice Act 2003 which has made significant amendments to the Criminal Procedure and Investigations Act 1996.

The 2003 Act amends the original two-stage test contained in the 1996 Act and replaces it with a new objective single test for the disclosure of unused prosecution material to the defence, requiring the prosecutor to disclose prosecution material that has not previously been disclosed and which might reasonably be considered capable of undermining the case for the prosecution against the accused, or of assisting the case for the accused. It replaces the present secondary disclosure material which meets the new test. The prosecutor is specifically required to review the prosecution material on receipt of the defence statement and to make further disclosure if required under the continuing duty.

The Act also extends the remit of the defence statement. The defence will now be required to set out the nature of the defence, including any particular defences on which the defendant intends to rely and indicate any points of law he wishes to take, including any points as to the admissibility of evidence or abuse of process.

16.4.5.4   Article 6(3)(c)—Public funding

Our present provisions in relation to the granting of public funding may result in minor cases being refused legal aid. However, even minor cases may result in a term of imprisonment being imposed and in these cases a refusal of public funding would lead to a breach of this part of Article 6.

16.4.5.5   Hearsay

Historically hearsay has also been considered inadmissible evidence unless either a common law or a statutory exception to the rule was made out. Sections 114 and 115 of the Criminal Justice Act 2003 have effectively abolished this rule and provide that such evidence will be admissible on behalf of the prosecution and the defence provided certain safeguards are met. There is also an additional statutory discretion to admit into evidence out-of-court statements where it would be in the interests of justice to do so. In addition, a witness's previous statement will be more widely admissible at trial as proof of the facts contained within it and in serious cases certain witnesses may use their video recorded statements in place of their main evidence.

These significant changes place a much greater reliance upon the discretionary decision-making process exercised by the judiciary. With their discretion to admit what would have been historically inadmissible evidence comes the potential for miscarriages of justice—the main principle behind the hearsay rule was that it was inherently unreliable evidence, the 'best evidence' being oral evidence from the percipient witness. With the abolition of these strict rules of evidence the right of an individual to a fair trial may well be jeopardised. In *R v Cole, R v Keet* [2007] EWCA Crim 1924 the two defendants challenged their convictions as the prosecution's case had been based almost entirely on statements of absent witnesses which had been admitted into evidence. The Court of Appeal upheld the conviction stating that it would need to be decided on a case-by-case basis with the relevant factors set out in s 114(2) of the Criminal Justice Act 2003 taken into account.

16.4.5.6   Article 6 and inferences from silence

The Criminal Justice and Public Order Act 1994 introduced various inroads into the right to silence which had hitherto been absolute. Under s 34, in particular, if an accused failed to mention when questioned, or charged, a fact which he later relied upon in court then such inferences as appeared proper could be drawn from that earlier silence, most notably the inference of recent fabrication. It is accepted that the mere fact of drawing inference from an accused's silence will not, of itself, involve a breach of Article 6. However, the procedural safeguards involved in situations where inferences may be drawn have been subject to close scrutiny in our national courts and more recently have been challenged in the European Court (most notably in *Condron v United Kingdom* (Application 35718/97) 2 May 2000).

The Court held that there had in fact been a breach of Article 6 in that the direction given to the jury in respect of the s 34 inference had been incomplete. As a matter of fairness the judge should have directed them that if they were satisfied that the applicant's silence at the police interview could not sensibly have been attributed to their having no answer or none that would stand up to cross-examination it should not draw an adverse inference.

The problem in this case is that the Court of Appeal accepted a defect in the summing-up and also accepted that it could not know how much account the jury had taken of the defendant's silence when reaching their verdict. However, it was happy that, having looked at the other evidence before the court, the conviction of the defendant was not unsafe. This, in effect, seems to be suggesting that the Court of Appeal feels able to superimpose its own reasoning onto the trial process. It remains to be seen whether or not this attempt to override the jury's actual thought process in coming to a decision is in fact a breach of Article 6 itself.

The issue of maintaining silence upon legal advice has now advanced somewhat in the light of recent case law (see, eg, *R v Doldur* [2000] Crim LR 178 and the latest Judicial Studies Board's specimen direction). The jury must be reminded of all the relevant background considerations and directed that if they were satisfied that the applicant's silence at the police interview could not sensibly be attributed to his having no answer or none that would stand up to police questioning they should not draw an adverse inference. Therefore, cases such as *Beckles v United Kingdom* (Application 44652/98) (2003) 36 EHRR 13 (ECtHR), where the trial judge failed to emphasise the defendant's willingness to talk to the police prior to receiving legal advice and the fact that he had been prepared to provide details of the advice he had received from his solicitor at the police station, should in the future receive more careful consideration in directions given to the jury.

Inferences under s 34 are clearly not going to invalidate a trial procedure but there are procedural issues involved which will need to be carefully scrutinised.

16.4.5.7   Article 6 and public interest immunity

Public interest immunity (PII) is an exclusionary rule of evidence which allows for material falling within the definition of PII to be withheld from the defence.

16.4.5.7.1   Procedure

The procedural requirements that govern the way in which the prosecution should claim such immunity were vigorously challenged in Strasbourg in the case of *Rowe and Davis v United Kingdom* (2000) 30 EHRR 1. At trial, the prosecution decided, without informing the judge, to withhold relevant material on the grounds that it fell within the definition of PII. The Court felt that:

Such a procedure, whereby the prosecution itself attempts to assess the importance of concealed information to the defence and weigh this against the public interest in keeping the information secret, cannot comply with Article 6(1).

The subsequent review of the material by the Court of Appeal could not cure the inherent unfairness arising from the initial trial. The trial judge had never seen the material and he would have been the person in the best possible position to assess the material in the light of the evidence being given as opposed to the Court of Appeal attempting artificially to manufacture the live trial situation from a set of lifeless manuscripts.

The later case of *Atlan v United Kingdom* (Application 36533/97) [2001] Crim LR 819 (ECtHR) unanimously found a breach of Article 6(1). The Court applied the principle in *Rowe and Davis* that while Article 6(1) required in principle that the prosecution should disclose to the defence all material evidence in its possession for and against the defendant, it might be necessary to withhold certain evidence so as to preserve the fundamental rights of another individual or to safeguard an important public interest. The government, in this case, had conceded that the repeated denials of the existence of unused material and the prosecution's failure to notify the judge of its existence was inconsistent with the requirements of Article 6(1). The issue for the Court was whether the *ex parte* procedure before the Court of Appeal was sufficient to remedy that unfairness at first instance. The evidence withheld was central to the applicant's defence and the trial judge was in the best position to decide whether the non-disclosure of the evidence was unfairly prejudicial. Therefore, the prosecution's failure to lay the evidence in question before the trial judge and to permit him to rule on the question of disclosure deprived the applicants of a fair trial.

The generic issue that the Court was concerned with was the fact that in the UK the prosecution may make an *ex parte* application without notice to the judge in order to obtain PII status without the defence ever being involved in the decision-making process. This is as opposed to an *inter partes* hearing, or an *ex parte* hearing with notice, where the defence are allowed to make representation in writing or in person. Whilst the latter two options are clearly quite fair, the former *ex parte* without notice application has been severely criticised by Strasbourg and the position has yet to be clarified.

In *Fitt v United Kingdom* (2000) 30 EHRR 480 it was held that the procedures adopted with regards to disclosure, in this particular case, were Article 6(1) compliant. This was because, although the prosecution were heard *ex parte*, the defence were kept informed and permitted to make submissions and participate in those decisions as far as possible without disclosing the material the prosecution sought to withhold on PII grounds. The Court also had regard to the judge's continuing duty to monitor the situation, which it felt was an important safeguard from a defence point of view. The Court came to the same conclusion in similar terms in *Jasper v United Kingdom* (2000) 30 EHRR 441.

Consequently, care should always be taken to ensure that the trial judge is complying with the spirit of Article 6 by allowing the defence to have a role in the decision-making process, especially in cases where the prosecution adopt the *ex parte* method of application for claiming PII status. These representations can only be made, of course, where the defence is actually made aware of the fact of the application in the first place—a position that clearly did not exist in *Rowe and Davis*. Indeed, even where the defence are involved in some way in the decision-making process this will not always guarantee that the individual's rights are protected. In *R v Doubtfire* (2000) *The Times*, 28 December, the defence had been given the opportunity to explain their case to the judge, after a prosecution *ex parte* application, before he ruled, in the prosecution's favour, upon the issue of PII. Allowing the appeal, after a referral from the Criminal Cases Review Commission, the court held that it was sufficient to state that the trial had been materially unfair because there had been a failure in respect of disclosure in the context of submissions made at the *ex parte* PII application during trial, and the material in the confidential annex which the court had considered in private had not been available to the trial judge or at the earlier appeal hearing, confirming that there had been unfairness.

PG and JH v United Kingdom (2001) (Application 44787/98) *The Times*, 19 October (ECtHR) further considered the issue of non-disclosure of prosecution material. However, in this case the Court was satisfied that the defence were kept informed and allowed to participate 'as much as possible' in the judge's decision to withhold the evidence from them, and to allow the inspector to give his oral evidence before the judge in chambers. The material that was withheld from the defence formed no part of the prosecution case and never went before the jury. The need for disclosure was at all times under assessment by the trial judge. Therefore, the domestic trial court applied standards that were in conformity with the relevant principles of a fair hearing embodied in Article 6(1).

The underlying theme of these decisions is clearly turning upon the extent to which the trial judge had or had not been able to view the material and continually review the decision to withhold during the trial itself.

16.4.5.8   Article 6—Unfairly obtained evidence

Traditionally, unfairly obtained evidence may be excluded under s 78 of the Police and Criminal Evidence Act 1984, and, following the implementation of the Human Rights Act 1998, it could also be held to be a violation of an individual's rights under Article 6 or Article 8, the latter sometimes resulting in the courts determining that there had consequently been a breach of Article 6.

Section 78(1) of the Police and Criminal Evidence Act 1984 provides that the court:

> may refuse to allow evidence on which the prosecution proposes to rely to be given if it appears to the court that, having regard to all the circumstances, *including the circumstances in which the evidence was obtained*, the admission of the evidence could have such an adverse effect on the fairness of the proceedings that the court ought not to admit it. (emphasis added)

Where the evidence was excluded under s 78 it did not automatically follow that the prosecution came to an end, or that conviction, upon appeal, was necessarily unsafe. Similarly, even where a breach of Article 6 and/or Article 8 was found, it was still possible for the Court of Appeal safely to uphold a conviction.

The case of *Teixera de Castro v Portugal* (1998) 28 EHRR 101, while notable for its decision regarding unfairly obtained evidence, also states:

> The Court reiterates that the admissibility of evidence is primarily a matter for regulation by national law and as a general rule it is for the courts to assess the evidence before them. The Court's task under the Convention is not to give rulings as to whether the statements of witnesses were properly admitted as evidence, but rather to ascertain whether the proceedings as a whole, including the way in which evidence was taken, were fair.

The practical consequences of evidence obtained primarily as a result of intelligence-led policing have been clarified in the House of Lords, in *Attorney-General's Reference (No 3 of 2000)* [2002] 1 Cr App R 29 which dealt with the conjoined appeals of *R v G* and *R v Looseley*. What the House of Lords provides is a rationale for the courts to stay prosecutions based upon entrapment, described by Lord Hoffmann as a 'jurisdiction to prevent abuse of executive power' and which Lord Nicholls pronounced in greater detail as follows:

> It is simply not acceptable that the state through its agents should lure its citizens into committing acts forbidden by the law and then seek to prosecute them for doing so. That would be entrapment. That would be a misuse of state power, and an abuse of process for the courts. The unattractive consequences, frightening and sinister in extreme cases, which state conduct of this kind could have are obvious. The role of the courts is to stand between the state and its citizens and make sure this does not happen.

The House of Lords held that in *Looseley* the trial judge had been correct to refuse the application to stay the proceedings for abuse of process, as the police had reasonable grounds to suspect that the defendant was involved in the supply of Class A drugs and all the undercover officer had done was provide an opportunity for him to commit the offence; in contrast their Lordships found that the trial judge in the *Attorney-General's Reference* had been correct in staying the proceedings because there were no reasonable grounds to suspect that the defendant was involved in the supply of Class A drugs and the officer had repeatedly phoned his mobile phone number offering cheap cigarettes in return for the supply of such drugs.

This approach has been confirmed more recently in the case of *R v Moon* [2004] EWCA Crim 2872 where the court held that the proceeding should have been stayed as an abuse of process. In this case more than mere opportunity had been provided. The appellant, charged with possession with intent to supply Class A drugs to an undercover police officer, had no predisposition to deal and had no previous history of dealing. The undercover officer had made the first approach and had been persistent. In addition, the undercover operation had not been properly authorised. However, the appellate court felt that overall the operation had been bona fide and that this aberration of itself would not have been sufficient to justify a stay.

The approach adopted by the House of Lords is consistent with the reasoning of the European Court in *Teixera de Castro v Portugal*, which stated that where there was conduct amounting to entrapment, the defendant would be denied the right to a fair trial from the outset.

From a prosecution point of view, this is clearly the most serious consequence resulting from an abuse of state power; but it is not the only consequence. In cases where the court feels that a stay is inappropriate, it will still be open to the defence to make an application to exclude the evidence of the undercover officer under s 78 of the 1984 Act either because to admit it would have an adverse effect on the trial as a whole, or on grounds that could have been submitted to support an application for a stay. Even if the evidence remains, it may still be appropriate to refer to how it was obtained in the plea in mitigation.

How should the court determine what conduct should lead to the exclusion of evidence, or indeed the stay of proceedings for abuse of process? The case of *R v Smurthwaite and Gill* [1994] 1 All ER 898 has long since provided the courts with guidelines to apply in these cases in order to determine whether or not evidence ought to be excluded. Smurthwaite was convicted of soliciting to murder. The person solicited was in fact an undercover police officer who had posed as a contract killer. The prosecution's case relied upon covertly recorded conversations of meetings between the undercover officer and the defendant. The defendant appealed on the basis that this evidence should have been ruled inadmissible. The Court of Appeal held that the relevant factors to consider when applying s 78 to such circumstances included:

(a) whether the undercover officer was acting as an *agent provocateur*;

(b) the nature of any entrapment;

(c) whether the evidence consists of admissions to a completed offence, or relates to the actual commission of the offence;

(d) how active or passive the officer's role was in obtaining the evidence;

(e) whether there is an unassailable record of what occurred, or whether it is strongly corroborated; and

(f) whether the officer abused his (undercover) role to ask questions which ought properly to have been asked as a police officer in accordance with Code C of the Police and Criminal Evidence Act 1984.

In Smurthwaite's case, although there was an element of entrapment and trick, the officer had not acted as an *agent provocateur*. The tapes recorded the actual commission of the offence rather than an offence committed in the past, and they made it clear that it was the accused who was the instigator. The officer had very much taken a back seat and used no persuasion.

Both the *Attorney-General's Reference* and *Nottingham City Council v Amin* [2000] 1 WLR 1071 (see below) abandon the test of whether the officer's role is active or passive, in that they regard it as unhelpful. The basis of the distinction was not whether the officer had acted or not acted, but whether or not the extent of his involvement was acceptable to the court;

but as Lord Bingham in *Amin* stated, 'there was nothing to suggest that without [the police officers'] intervention [the offence] would have been committed'.

The decision in *Nottingham City Council v Amin*, where a driver was prosecuted for plying a cab for hire without a licence, provides the modern approach to cases involving undercover officers. The defendant's cab was licensed for an adjoining area, but not the city centre where he was driving when stopped by two plainclothes police officers. The light on his cab was not illuminated, but when the officers asked him to convey them to a specified destination he agreed, and did so for a fare. He argued that the evidence was obtained unfairly and should be excluded under s 78 of the 1984 Act. The Divisional Court held that the facts could not be construed as showing the defendant in any way being pressurised into committing the offence and that the evidence should be admitted. Confirming that it was the fairness of the proceedings as a whole that had to be looked at, the court identified two conflicting public interest points. On the one hand, it was recognised as deeply offensive to ordinary notions of fairness if a defendant were to be convicted and punished for committing a crime only because he had been incited, persuaded, or pressurised into doing so by a law enforcement officer. On the other hand, it had been recognised that law enforcement agencies had a general duty to the public to enforce the law, and it had been regarded as unobjectionable if such an officer gave a defendant an opportunity to break the law, of which he freely took advantage, in circumstances where it appeared that he would have behaved in the same way if the opportunity had been offered by anyone else. The court drew a distinction between creating an opportunity to commit an offence and inducing the commission of the offence. It would seem that positive action, beyond merely providing the opportunity to commit the offence, will be required before any breach of Article 6 becomes imminent.

16.4.5.8.1   *European perspective*

The use of participating informants was challenged in *Ludi v Switzerland* (1992) 15 EHRR 173 where the Court refused to find that the use of an undercover agent infringed the applicant's Article 8 rights as he was a suspected member of a large group of drug traffickers in possession of five kilos of cocaine and 'must therefore have been aware from then on that he was engaged in a criminal act ... and that consequently he was running the risk of encountering an undercover police officer whose task would in fact be to expose him'. In *Ludi* the drug trafficking was already underway when the undercover officer came on the scene and so the admission of evidence gathered in the course of the operation did not violate Article 6. Notable in this case was that the operation had been judicially sanctioned, and it is a weakness of our statutory scheme that certain types of covert activity do not require prior independent authorisation.

However, some cases are illustrative of the fact that covert human intelligence can be taken a stage too far, a classic example being found in the case of *Teixera de Castro v Portugal* (1998) 28 EHRR 101, where the Court ruled that the admissibility of evidence where there had been entrapment of a person not predisposed to that type of offence will not be left to regulation by national law. The applicant in this case, who had no record of drug dealing, was introduced to a third party by two police officers posing as drug addicts. They asked him to supply them with heroin. Initially he refused, but complied with a second request and supplied the officers with heroin at a profit. He maintained in his defence that he had been incited to commit an offence which, but for the intervention of the two officers, he would not have committed. The Court agreed, saying that 'the two police officers did not confine themselves to investigating criminal activities in an essentially passive manner, but exercised an influence such as to incite the commission of the offence'. The prosecution were unable to prove any predisposition to commit such a type of offence on the part of the applicant, and not even the public interest in fighting drug trafficking could justify relying on evidence obtained as a result of police incitement.

16.4.6   Article 7—No punishment without law (no retrospective criminal offences or penalties)

1. No one shall be held guilty of any criminal offence on account of any act or omission which did not constitute a criminal offence under national or international law at the

time when it was committed. Nor shall a heavier penalty be imposed than the one that was applicable at the time the criminal offence was committed.

2. This Article shall not prejudice the trial and punishment of any person for any act or omission which, at the time it was committed, was criminal according to the general principles of law recognised by civilised nations.

There is the presumption in relation to criminal offences that there will be no retroactivity and that provisions of criminal law may be argued against if they are not clear. There are various changes in our domestic legislation which may cause a problem in relation to retro-activity which can be more clearly explained in relation to case law. In *SW and CR v United Kingdom* (1995) 21 EHRR 363 the defendant was charged with raping his wife. He argued that the change in the law making rape within marriage a crime was a violation of Article 7. It was held that there was no violation of Article 7 as it was sufficiently foreseeable.

Other changes to our legislation may give rise to an application under Article 7 as well. For example, the Criminal Evidence (Amendment) Act 1997 allows the police to take DNA samples from offenders convicted before the Act came into force. This could be viewed as retroactivity and in breach of Article 7.

16.4.7 Article 8—Right to respect for private and family life

1. Everyone has the right to respect for his private and family life, his home and his correspondence.

2. There shall be no interference by a public authority with the exercise of this right except such as is in accordance with the law and is necessary in a democratic society and in the interests of national security, public safety or the economic well being of the country, for the prevention of disorder or crime, for the protection of health and morals, or for the protection of the rights and freedoms of others.

Note that in the case of *X and Y v Netherlands* (1985) 8 EHRR 235 the European Court stated that Article 8:

does not merely compel the state to abstain from interference: in addition to this primarily nega-tive undertaking, there may be positive obligations inherent in an effective respect for private and family life. These obligations may involve the adoption of measures designed to secure respect for private life even in the sphere of relations of individuals between themselves.

This imposes a secondary duty quite separate to the main function of the Article which refers to interference by a public authority. In *McVeigh, O'Neill and Evans v United Kingdom* (Applications 8022/77, 8025/77, and 8027/77) (1981) 25 DR 15 it was held that preventing the prisoners from communicating with their spouses was a breach of Article 8 even though they were held under anti-terrorist laws; if it was the case that such contact may facilitate an escape or the destruction or removal of evidence then the case may well be different.

16.4.7.1 Article 8—Intrusive surveillance

It is accepted that certain forms of intrusive surveillance adopted by the police prior to the implementation of the 1998 Act were incompatible with the rights conveyed under Article 8, not least because there was no legislative regulation of such conduct and therefore the require-ment under Article 8(2) that the surveillance be legal could not be satisfied. However, following the implementation of the Police Act 1997, Part III, and the Regulation of Investigatory Powers Act 2000, Part II, such regulation is thought to exist. However, it is feared that the potential for challenge still exists, not perhaps in terms of the validity of the procedures as a compatible piece of legislation but in relation to the doctrine of proportionality, ie that surveillance adopted is not a proportionate response to the actions complained of having regard to the legitimate aim under Article 8(2) of preventing crime.

Note that regard should be had to those undercover operations which do not fall under the umbrella of the Regulation of Investigatory Powers Act 2000 as they run the risk of being held to be prima facie unlawful.

The Regulation of Investigatory Powers Act 2000 is essentially a vehicle designed to ensure a valid legal basis is established for the use of covert human intelligence sources—be this a participating informant or an undercover police officer.

The position at common law is that the use of participating informants has always been recognised as a necessary evil by the courts. Indeed, Lord Parker stated in *R v Birtles* [1969] 1 WLR 1047:

> whilst the police are entitled to make use of information concerning an offence already laid on, and while with a view to mitigating the consequences of the proposed offence, eg to protect the proposed witness, it may be perfectly proper for the police to encourage the informer to take part in the offence, or indeed for the police officer himself to do so, the police must never use an informer to encourage another to commit an offence he would not otherwise commit.

Clearly the source should not overstep the boundaries contained in *Smurthwaite and Gill*, and when applying the position at common law regard will now have to be had to relevant European case law (see **16.4.5.8.1**).

Recently the new Investigatory Powers Act 2017 passed through the House of Lords virtually unchallenged and now provides the government and other agencies with wide ranging powers of surveillance which in summary allow them access, without direct independent supervision, to a vast array of personal information. Currently Liberty, which campaigns for civil liberties and human rights, is seeking a crowdfunded High Court judicial review of the core bulk powers which it believes breach all human rights, not just Article 8. It appears very likely that this may not be the only challenge the Investigatory Powers Act 2017 faces in the future.

16.4.8   Article 9—Freedom of thought, conscience and religion

1. Everyone has the right to freedom of thought, conscience and religion; this right includes freedom to change his religion or belief and freedom, either alone or in community with others and in public or in private, to manifest his religion or belief, in worship, teaching, practice and observance.

2. Freedom to manifest one's religion or beliefs shall be subject only to such limitations as are prescribed by law and are necessary in a democratic society in the interests of public safety, for the protection of public order, health or morals, or for the protection of the rights and freedoms of others.

16.4.9   Article 10—Freedom of expression

1. Everyone has the right to freedom of expression. This right shall include freedom to hold opinions and to receive and impart information and ideas without interference by public authority and regardless of frontiers. This Article shall not prevent States from requiring the licensing of broadcasting, television or cinema enterprises.

2. The exercise of these freedoms, since it carries duties and responsibilities, may be subject to such formalities, conditions, restriction or penalties as are prescribed by law and are necessary in a democratic society, in the interests of national security, territorial integrity, or public safety, for the prevention of disorder or crime, for the protection of health and morals, for the protection of the reputation or rights of others, for preventing the disclosure of information received in confidence, or for maintaining the authority and impartiality of the judiciary.

This is a qualified Article which has dealt primarily with political and journalistic expression. In all cases the courts must look at the restriction on the freedom of expression, and decide whether or not there is a legitimate aim which has been prescribed by law and whether or not the restriction is proportionate to the legitimate aim.

Freedom of expression was defined in *Handyside v United Kingdom* (1976) 1 EHRR 737:

> Freedom of expression constitutes one of the essential foundations of [a democratic] society, one of the basic conditions for its progress and for the development of every man. Subject to paragraph 2 of Article 10, it is applicable not only to 'information' or 'ideas' that are favourably received and

regarded as inoffensive ... but also to those that offend, shock or disturb that State or any sector of the population. Such are the demands of pluralism, tolerance and broadmindedness without which there is no 'democratic society'.

In *Observer and Guardian v United Kingdom* (1991) 14 EHRR 153, the Government obtained an interlocutory injunction against two newspapers from publishing extracts from *Spycatcher* written by former MI5 agent Peter Wright. However, once the book had been published in the US and could therefore be transported to the UK, the European Court held that the injunctions could no longer be justified because from that time confidentiality of the material had been destroyed.

There is strong protection of journalistic sources, as evidenced by the case of *Goodwin v United Kingdom* (1996) 22 EHRR 123 where the European Court stated:

Protection of journalistic sources is one of the basic conditions for press freedom. Without such protection, sources may be deterred from assisting the press in informing the public on matters of public interest ... [An order to disclose] cannot be compatible with Article 10 unless it is justified by an overriding requirement in the public interest.

Clearly issues of privacy arise here and may cause our courts some problems in the future. In the UK there has never been a right of privacy, but Article 8 clearly affords the individual some form of protection and the development of case law in this area will be drastic.

One of the most notable cases in relation to Article 8 is that of *Khan v United Kingdom* [2000] Crim LR 684. There, the court allowed evidence to be heard from a concealed listening device installed in the premises of another suspect in accordance with the Home Office guidelines on the use of equipment in police surveillance operations. Khan was convicted on the basis of this evidence. The Court held that the tape-recording was an infringement of the right to private life guaranteed by Article 8(1) but that the interference could not be justified under Article 8(2). At the time there was no statutory framework to regulate the police. The Court was not happy to accept the guidelines as they were not legally binding, neither were they directly accessible to the public. The comment was also made that they were of themselves insufficient to protect against arbitrary interference with an individual's rights under Article 8. The Court was also concerned to point out that although there had been a breach of Article 8, this did not render the trial unfair under Article 6 as it was not the function of the European Court to correct legal or factual errors made by national courts.

16.4.10   Article 11—Freedom of assembly and association

1. Everyone has the right to freedom of peaceful assembly and to freedom of association with others, including the right to form and to join trade unions for the protection of his interests.

2. No restrictions shall be placed on the exercise of these rights other than such as are prescribed by law and are necessary in a democratic society in the interest of national security or public safety, for the prevention of disorder or crime, for the protection of health or morals or for the protection of the rights and freedoms of others. This Article shall not prevent the imposition of lawful restrictions on the exercise of these rights by members of the armed forces, of the police or of the administration of the State.

16.4.11   Article 12—Right to marry

Men and women of marriageable age have the right to marry and to found a family, according to national laws governing the exercise of this right.

16.4.12   Article 14—Prohibition of discrimination (as regards the enjoyment of the rights and freedoms set out in the Convention)

The enjoyment of the rights and freedoms set forth in this Convention shall be secured without discrimination on any ground such as sex, race, colour, language, religion, political or other opinion, national or social origin, association with a national minority, property, birth or other status.

16.4.13   Article 16—Restrictions on political activity of aliens

Nothing in Articles 10, 11 and 14 shall be regarded as preventing the High Contracting Parties [the States] from imposing restrictions on the political activities of aliens.

16.4.14   Article 17—Prohibition of abuse of rights

Nothing in the Convention may be interpreted as implying for any State, group or person any right to engage in any activity or perform any act aimed at the destruction of any rights and freedoms set forth herein or at their limitation to a greater extent than is provided for in the Convention.

16.4.15   Article 18—Limitation on use of restriction on rights

The restrictions permitted under this Convention to the said rights and freedoms shall not be applied for any purpose other than those for which they have been prescribed.

The Human Rights Act 1998 also incorporates two existing Protocols in UK legislation, the First and the Sixth. They are set out as follows.

16.4.16   The First Protocol: Article 1—Protection of property

Every natural or legal person is entitled to the peaceful enjoyment of his possessions. No one shall be deprived of his possessions except in the public interest and subject to the conditions provided for by law and by general principles of international law.

The preceding provisions shall not, however, in any way impair the right of a State to enforce such laws as it deems necessary to control the use of property in accordance with the general interest or to secure the payment of taxes or other contributions or penalties.

16.4.17   The First Protocol: Article 2—Right to education

No person shall be denied the right to education. In the exercise of any functions which it assumes in relation to education and to teaching, the State shall respect the right of parents to ensure such education and teaching in conformity with their own religious and philosophical convictions.

16.4.18   The First Protocol: Article 3—Free elections

The High Contracting Parties [the States] undertake to hold free elections at reasonable intervals by secret ballot, under conditions which will ensure the free expression of the opinion of the people in the choice of the legislature.

16.4.19   The Sixth Protocol

This was ratified in 1999 and effectively outlaws the death penalty.

16.5   Judicial remedies

Section 8(1) of the Human Rights Act 1998 states that:

In relation to any act (or proposed act) of a public authority which the court finds is (or would be) unlawful, it may grant such relief or remedy, or make such order, within its powers as it considers to be just and appropriate.

But note that damages may be awarded only by a court which has powers to award damages, or to order the payment of compensation, in civil proceedings.

Where the court is required to remedy a Convention violation in relation to criminal proceedings it will be required to consider:

(a) directions in relation to the trial process;

(b) disclosure applications;

(c) an application for a stay of proceedings; and

(d) arguments in relation to the admissibility of evidence.

Where a court fails to take account of Convention provisions, individuals will be able to make use of judicial review and appeal mechanisms available under the Act and at common law. The Court of Appeal will have the right to quash a conviction in relation to an offence which of itself violates Convention rights, or where there has been a violation of an Article 6 right.

While a court may not strike down an Act of Parliament it may interpret it so as to give effect to Convention rights. Where it is not possible to construe a section to bring it within the Convention, the lower courts will have to apply the offending piece of legislation. The higher courts, including the High Court and Court of Appeal, will have the power to issue a 'declaration of incompatibility'. The government then has the power to either amend legislation or make a 'remedial order' under s 2 and Sch 2. Such a declaration would give rise to a ground for appeal against the conviction although it is only the Court of Appeal that has the power to quash a conviction.

16.6 Conclusion: checkpoints

You should now be able to:

- identify the background to the Convention and its subsequent incorporation into UK legislation;

- identify the general principles of European jurisprudence and its effect on case law interpretation;

- identify the Articles and the Protocols and where they may have an effect on UK legislation and procedure;

- correctly identify who has the right to invoke the protections afforded by the Convention;

- correctly identify potential causes of action; and

- correctly identify the procedural steps which need to be followed to enforce the rights of potential claimants under the Convention.

16.7 Bibliography

Ashcroft, P, and others, *Human Rights and the Courts* (1999) Waterside.
Starmer, K, *European Human Rights Law* (1999) Legal Action Group.
Wadham, J, Mountfield, H, and Edmundson, A, *Blackstone's Guide to the Human Rights Act 1998* (2006) Oxford University Press.

online resource centre   Visit the Online Resource Centre for more information and useful weblinks.
www.oxfordtextbooks.co.uk/orc/foundations17_18/

APPENDIX 1
ANSWERS TO SELF-TEST QUESTIONS

Chapter 2

2.5 Answers to self-test questions

A.1 The Financial Services and Markets Act 2000 ('FSMA 2000').

A.2 The Prudential Regulation Authority and the Financial Conduct Authority.

A.3 To ensure that the relevant markets function well (FSMA 2000, s 1B(2)). Section 1F of the FSMA 2000 sets out the meaning of 'the relevant markets' in s 1B(2) as, inter alia, the financial markets and the markets for regulated financial services.

A.4 (a) the consumer protection objective;
(b) the integrity objective;
(c) the competition objective.

A.5 It prohibits a person from carrying on a regulated activity unless that person is authorised under the Act (or is an exempt person).

A.6 (a) It is a criminal offence (FSMA 2000, s 23).
(b) Any agreement made in contravention is unenforceable.
(c) Action can be taken to recover money or property paid or transferred.
(d) Action can be taken for compensation for any loss.

A.7 (a) Authorised person, or
(b) An exempt person.

A.8 An exemption to members of the professions.

A.9 Section 22.

A.10 (a) be an activity of a specified kind;
(b) be carried on by way of business; and
(c) relate to a specified investment.

A.11 The Financial Services and Markets Act 2000 (Regulated Activities) Order 2001 (SI 2001 No 544). The RAO.

A.12 (a) The Financial Services and Markets Act 2000 (Regulated Activities) Order 2001 (SI 2001 No 544);
(b) Part III;
(c) The RAO.

A.13 They are activities which arise out of a solicitor's main work as a solicitor; they are incidental to that work.

A.14 A designated professional body.

A.15 (a) The SRA Financial Services (Scope) Rules 2001.
(b) The Scope Rules.
(c) The SRA Financial Services (Conduct of Business) Rules 2001.
(d) The Conduct of Business Rules.

A.16 A solicitor must account to the client for the commission.

A.17 (a) Dealing with or through authorised persons (RAO, Art 22).
(b) Arranging deals with or through authorised persons (RAO, Art 29).
(c) Funeral contract plans where the plan is covered by insurance or trust arrangements (RAO, Art 60).

A.18 Article 66.

A.19 The Scope Rules set out the conditions and restrictions with which solicitors' firms seeking to rely on the designated professional body ('DPB') regime must comply when carrying on regulated activities. Also the prohibitions which apply and the effect of a breach of the Rules. The Conduct of Business Rules set out the information clients must receive, how transactions should be effected, what records must be kept, and details of the safekeeping of clients' investments.

A.20 (a) A communication made in a face-to-face situation or in a telephone conversation.

(b) One made in writing (a letter, a publication, an email) or by email.

APPENDIX 2
INVESTMENTS

INVESTMENT	Money invested for income or profit, for a return of income or capital.
INCOME	Of a recurring nature.
CAPITAL	One-off benefit.
JARGON:	
Gross interest	Taxable but not subject to taxation direct.
Variable rate	Rate of interest paid may change—usually in line with other interest rates.
Fixed rate	Rate of interest quoted at the outset does not change—even if other interest rates do.
Index-linked	Value of the capital invested is inflation proofed (its purchasing power remains the same from beginning to end of the investment period). The value of the capital changes in line with the Consumer Price Indices (CPI) or the Retail Price Indices (RPI).
Base rate (official name— minimum lending rate)	Controlled by the Bank of England. It sets the general level of UK interest rates and is a valuable tool in managing the economy.
Tax-free	Excluded income for income tax purposes. No tax is charged either by direct assessment or deduction at source.
Tax-paid	Tax is deducted at source at the basic rate. There may be an additional liability if the taxpayer is a higher rate payer. Non-taxpayers can apply to HMRC for a tax refund.
Share	The proprietorship element in a company usually repre- sented by transferable certificates, share certificates.
Equity/equities	A share or shares which do not bear fixed interest.
Quoted shares	Shares in companies listed on a stock market.
Unquoted shares	Shares in companies *not* listed on a stock market.
Warrant	Evidence that the holder has the right to subscribe for shares or stock.
Stock	A debt due for money loaned to a company or public body (government or local authority) usually with interest being paid from the company or public body to the investor.
Gilts 'Gilt-edged' Securities	Stocks issued by the government to finance its borrowing. They are issued on the National Savings Register or through the Bank of England and can be bought and sold on the Stock Market.
Investment trust	A company whose assets are solely shares in other companies.
Unit trust	Various banks and institutions offer unit trusts. The investor hands money to the institution and is issued with a number of units. The institution uses the money to invest in shares in other companies. The units can be sold back to the institution at any time.
Bid price	The price received if the investor sells his investment (usually units in a unit trust).

Offer price		The price an investor has to pay to buy units.
Bid/offer spread		The difference in the bid price and offer price.
Par		Nominal or face value.
Repayable at par		Nominal or face value is the amount paid to the investor on maturity.
Life-assured		The person on whose life a policy is taken out. The policy will be payable on the life-assured's death if it does not mature earlier.
Joint lives		Two lives are insured under one policy and the policy will pay out either on the death of the first to die or on the second death. It is agreed at the outset which is to occur.

Types of investments

WITHOUT RISK or LOW RISK:

Bank Accounts	Current:	Money available immediately; no interest or very little (due to immediate access).
	Deposit:	Money available on specified period of notice. Differing rates of interest linked to notice period.
Building Society Accounts	Deposit:	Money available immediately. Priority on repayment if society faces difficulties. Low interest (due to security of investment).
	Share:	Money available on specified period of notice. Differing rates of interest linked to notice period and/or balance invested (tiered rates).
National Savings		Schemes offered by the government. Security of the money invested is guaranteed by the government. Return is known at the outset.
Income bonds		Penalties may be incurred if withdrawn before end of first year. Interest paid monthly. Rate of interest is variable.
Premium Bonds		Repayable on demand. No interest paid. Chance of winning a cash prize in the monthly draw.
Local Authority Bonds		Repayable only at end of term. Fixed rate of interest. Interest usually paid monthly.
GILTS		Repayable at par at end of term *but* can be sold before maturity. Fixed rate of interest. Interest usually paid half-yearly.
ISA		**Individual Savings Account**. The risk depends on category invested in. Tax-free investment income and capital gains. There is a limit on the capital that can be invested in any one tax year. For tax year 2017/18 the limit is £20,000. The savers can decide on how the amount is invested in either cash or stocks and shares. No minimum or maximum holding periods.

Life time ISA ('LISA') from 6 April 2017 the LISA can be opened by individuals from the age of 18 until they turn 40. It allows those under 50 to save up to £4,000 a year and receive a government bonus of up to £1,000 a year. Amounts invested into a Lifetime ISA can be withdrawn tax-free to put towards a first home or once the holder turns 60.

Junior ISA ('JISA') for children under 18 without a Child Trust Fund. Limit for tax year 2017/18 of £4,128 cash or shares.
Possibility of income—interest and dividends.
Possibility of capital gain—on selling stocks or shares.
Possibility of capital loss—on selling stocks or shares.

WITH RISK:

Quoted Shares	With-risk investment.
	Money available on sale of the holding, delay in monies reaching investor.
	Possibility of income (dividends) and/or capital gain/loss on selling shares.
Investment Trusts	With-risk investment.
	Money available on sale of the holding, delay in monies reaching investor.
	Possibility of income (dividends) and/or capital gain/loss on selling shares.
Unit Trusts	With-risk investment.
	Money available on sale of the holding, delay in monies reaching investor.
	Possibility of income—dividends and/or capital gain/loss on selling shares.

LIFE ASSURANCE:

Whole life	No return until death of life-assured. Life-assured or policyholder pays regular premiums. Fixed sum is paid out on the death of the life-assured.
Term assurance	No return unless life-assured dies within specified period. Life-assured or policyholder pays regular premiums. Fixed sum is paid out if life-assured dies within a fixed period of time.
Endowment assurance	No return until specified date or death if earlier. Life-assured or policyholder pays regular premiums. Sum is paid on a specified date or earlier if life-assured dies before that date. If 'with profits' sum paid is greater of fixed sum assured or value of fund in which premiums are invested.
Annuities	No return of capital.
	Capital sum is paid to the insurance company.
	Guaranteed income will be paid to the investor for life or until agreed period ends.
	Usually ceases on death but can be guaranteed for a fixed period notwithstanding death.

Stock market terminology

AIM	Alternative Investments Market.
Emerging markets	It is generally thought that the biggest stock market returns in the future will not be in the established markets but in cities such as Manila, Caracas, Lima, and Mexico City. Their economies are expected to grow faster than more mature economies.
Indices	**FT-SE 100:** an index jointly sponsored by the *Financial Times, the London Stock Exchange, and the Institute and Faculty of Actuaries. It contains shares of the top 100 UK companies ranked by market capitalisation. It is calculated every minute during the working day and shares enter and leave the index every quarter.*
	FT-SE Eurotrack 200: this contains the shares of 100 companies from continental Europe and the constituents of the FT-SE 100 index. The weighting of the 100 shares from the UK are adjusted so as not to take up an inappropriate proportion of the index. It is calculated every minute.
	DAX: this is the German share index and is published by the Frankfurt Stock Exchange. It contains 30 stocks from the main German markets. It is calculated every minute.
	NIKKEI 225: this is the original Japanese share index published by Nihon Keizai Shimbun. It is calculated every minute and contains shares from 225 companies.
	DOW-JONES INDUSTRIAL AVERAGE: the grandfather of all indices. First calculated in January 1897. It contains 30 stocks chosen by Dow-Jones and Wall Street. It is also calculated every minute.
Insider dealing	When someone trades in a company's shares using specific information that has not been made public but which would seriously affect the company's share price if it were known. It can be done by a director or a receptionist.
Derivatives	High-risk investments. Can make or break an investor or a bank. They use futures and options. An option is a bet on the future price of anything—pork bellies to ordinary shares. An investor who takes an option retains the right to buy or sell a share within a set period with the price fixed at the outset. In a futures contract the investor has to exercise the option even if the market goes against him and, as Nick Leeson and Barings know, the losses can be unlimited.
Bulls and bears	Terms describing different types of investor. Bulls are optimists about market prices and believe that they will rise in a **bull** market. There was a bull market in the mid-1980s which ended in the crash on Black Monday, 19 October 1987.
	Bears are pessimists and believe that market prices will fall. There was a **bear** market after the 1929 Wall Street Crash.

INDEX

A

abatement of legacies 271
accounting procedures
  to client 47
  estate accounts
    capital 276
    distribution 276
    distribution of estates 276
    forms 275
    income 275–6
  VAT 144–5
ademption of legacies 185–6
administration of estates *see* **probate and administration**
administrators
  effect of grant 211
  oaths
    court requirements 223
    form 224–31
    further evidence 238–9
    swearing or affirming 222
agricultural property relief 96–7
allowances *see* **reliefs and allowances**
alternative business structures (ABSs) 3–4
annual investment allowances (AIAs) 130–1
annuities
  defined App 2
  self-assessment 68
  'settlements' 160
  taxable income 73, 75
appeals
  inheritance tax cases 91
  tax cases 65
apportionments 250
appropriation 271
assents 277–8
attestation of wills 177–9
authorisation for financial services
  background to FSMA 2000 40
  Law Society as a designated exempt professional body 42–3
  need for authorisation 40–2

B

bail 292–3
balancing charge allowances
  corporation tax 131–2
  sole proprietors and partnerships 152

beneficiaries
  agreement to executors' remuneration 274
  disclaimers 267
  loans for IHT 221
  protection of PRs
    missing beneficiaries 258–9
    unknown beneficiaries 257–8
  rights and remedies
    payment of entitlements 279–80
    right to compel administration 279
  tax liabilities
    CGT 166
    income tax 168
  testamentary gifts to children 188–9
  variations 267–8
benefits in kind 75
***Benjamin* orders** 259
blind persons
  knowledge and approval of wills 178
bonuses
  ISAs App 2
  taxable income 73–4
businesses
  see also **corporation tax (CT); partnerships; sole proprietors**
  commercial and client awareness 7
  core LPC subject areas 26
  IHT relief 95–6
  PR's power to run business 253–4

C

capacity
  administrator's oath 237–8
  administrator's oath with will annexed 231
  personal representatives 214–15
  wills 175–6
capital allowances (CA)
  corporation tax 129–32
  sole proprietors and partnerships 151–2
capital gains tax (CGT)
  ascertainment of residuary estate 272
  calculation of tax 83
  capital losses 84–5
  chargeable assets 83
  checkpoints 89
  death of taxpayer 87–9

  disposal of assets 82
  exemptions and reliefs 85–7
  general principles 82
  overview 63
  parties liable 82
  post-grant practice
    effect of variations 268
    sale of assets by PRs 262–3
  rates of tax 83–4
  trusts and settlements 164–6
capital losses
  capital gains tax 84–5
  corporation tax 128–9
  sole proprietors and partnerships 153
capital punishment 303
carry forward relief 158
cars
  capital allowances for CT 132
  deductible expenses 151
  entitlement on intestacy 194
  VAT
    childrens' seats 142
    reclaims 143
    use by employee 147
Chancellor of the Exchequer 64
charitable giving
  IHT relief 95, 116
  income tax relief 79–80
charities
  calculation of IT 70
  exempt from CGT 82
  liability of trustees for IHT 164
child benefit 79
children
  administrative powers
    maintenance of minors 255–6
    receipts to PRs 252
  capacity to act as PRs 215
  entitlement on intestacy 194–5
  liability of trustees for IHT for deceased minors 162
  provision for family and dependants
    application procedure 201–2
    basis of claim 201
    categories of applicant 202–3
    checkpoints 207–8
    court orders 206–7
    inheritance tax 206–7
    property available for distribution 150
    reasonable financial provision 203–4

children (*continued*)
   statutory guidelines 204–6
   statutory provisions 201
   testamentary gifts 188–9
civil partners
   entitlement on intestacy 192–4
   nil rate band
      IHT form 243–4
      IHT relief 114–15
   provision for family and
      dependants 145
   revocation of wills 181
class gifts 189
clearing off
   administrator's oath 234
   administrator's oath with will
      annexed 231
client care
   importance 7
   practical application of OFR Code
      additional litigation Outcomes 22
      complaints 16–17
      confidentiality 20–2
      conflicts of interest 19–20
      costs 14–16
      equality and diversity 18
      instructions and resources 17–18
      Outcomes 14
      overview 14
      terms and conditions of
         business 18
close companies
   identifying 133–4
   taxation 134–6
codicils
   purpose 178
   revocation of earlier will 181–2
commercial awareness 7
commission
   taxable income 74–5
complaints 16–17
Compliance Officers 13–14
conditional fee agreements 15–16
conditional revocation of wills 182
Conduct of Business Rules (2001) 46–
      7, 50, App 2
confidentiality
   money laundering 56
   practical application of OFR
      Code 20–2
conflicts of interest
   business law and practice 26
   practical application of OFR Code
      acting with safeguards 19–20
      overview 19
      prohibition on acting 19
      property transactions 24
corporation tax (CT)
   calculation of tax 132, 136–9
   capital allowances 129–32
   capital losses 128–9
   checkpoints 139
   close companies
      identifying 133–4
      taxation 134–6
   dividends 133
   introduction 125
   overview 63–4

payment 132–3
roll-over relief 127
taxable receipts
   capital gains 126–7
   income profits 125–6
trading loss relief 128–9
costs
   administrative expenses 273–4
   practical application of OFR Code
      conditional fee agreements 15–16
      general considerations 15
      public funding 15
   time and costs recording 7–8
courts
   executors' remuneration 274–5
   payments in to protect PRs 259
   provision for family and
      dependants 206–7
   requirements for executor's oath 223
   right to a fair trial (Art 6)
      disclosure 294
      hearsay 294–5
      public funding 294
      public interest immunity 295–7
      reverse burden of truth 293–4
      right to silence 295
      text 293
      unfairly obtained evidence 297–8
creditors
   payment by PRs
      insolvent debts 265–6
      solvent estates 263–5
   protection of PRs
      missing creditors 258–9
      other liabilities 259–60
      unknown creditors 257–8
Crown entitlement on
      intestacy 195–6

D

death
   inheritance tax
      charge to tax 110–18
      deemed transfers on death 93
      liability burden and
         payment 119–20
      liability of trustees 161–4
   registration 220
death penalty 303
debts *see* **creditors**
dependants
   provision by Crown on
      intestacy 195–6
   provision for family and dependants
      application procedure 201–2
      basis of claim 201
      categories of applicant 202–3
      checkpoints 207–8
      court orders 206–7
      inheritance tax 206–7
      property available for
         distribution 150
      reasonable financial
         provision 203–4
      statutory guidelines 204–6
      statutory provisions 201

derogations from ECHR 289
destruction of wills 182
dictation 9
direct effect
   human rights 289
disclaimers 267
disclosure
   practical application of OFR
      Code 20–2
   right to a fair trial (Art 6) 294
   right to liberty and security (Art
      5) 292–3
discrimination
   practical application of OFR Code 18
   prohibition of discrimination (Art
      14) 303
distribution of estates
   checkpoints 281–2
   discharge 276–7
   estate accounts 276
   introduction 173
   overview 270
   payment of legacies 270–2
   residuary estate 272–5
   rights and remedies of
      beneficiaries 279–80
   transfer of assets 277
diversity
   practical application of OFR Code 18
   prohibition of discrimination (Art
      14) 303
dividends
   distributions 133
   taxable income 78–9
donationes mortis causa 199

E

engagement letters 18
enhanced capital allowances
      (ECAs) 130
entitlement to estates
   intestacy
      application of rules 190–1
      Crown 195–6
      issue 194–5
      other relatives 195
      surviving spouses and civil
         partners 192–4
   property not passing under will or
      intestacy 198–9
   property not taxable and passing by
      succession 200
   property passing outside will or
      intestacy 198–9
   provision for family and dependants
      application procedure 145–6
      basis of claim 201
      categories of applicant 202–3
      checkpoints 207–8
      court orders 206–7
      inheritance tax 206–7
      property available for
         distribution 207
      reasonable financial
         provision 203–4
      statutory guidelines 204–6

statutory provisions 201
taxable property not passing by
    succession 200
wills
    important provisos 174
    introduction 173
Entrepreneur's relief (ER) 86–7
equality
    practical application of OFR Code 18
    prohibition of discrimination (Art
        14) 303
equality of arms 289
estate accounts
    capital 276
    distribution 276
    distribution of estates 276
    forms 275
    income 275–6
EU law
    see also **human rights**
    impact on UK taxation and
        customs 62
    money laundering 53
    unfairly obtained evidence 299
evidence unfairly obtained 297–8
excepted estates
    defined 241–2
    Form IHT 205 242–4
    general requirements 240–1
executors
    effect of grant 211
    oaths
        court requirements 223
        form 224–31
        further evidence 238–9
        swearing or affirming 222
    power reserved 216–17
    remuneration 274–5
    renunciation of probate 216–17

F

failure of testamentary gifts
    ademption of legacies 185–6
    consequences 187–8
    date from which will speaks 184–5
    introduction 184
    lapse of legacies 186–7
    legacies generally 185
    to witnesses 187
families
    see also **children**
    entitlement on intestacy 195
    provision for family and dependants
        application procedure 201–2
        basis of claim 201
        categories of applicant 202–3
        checkpoints 207–8
        court orders 206–7
        inheritance tax 206–7
        property available for
            distribution 207
        reasonable financial
            provision 203–4
        statutory guidelines 204–6
        statutory provisions 201

right to respect for private and family
    life (Art 8) 300–1
financial services
    background to FSMA 2000 39–40
    commentary on scenarios 51–2
    conclusions and checkpoints 50–1
    financial promotions 44
    introduction 37
    investments
        definitions App 2
        financial returns 37
        meaning and scope 37
        other considerations 38
        risk 37–8
        stock market terminology App 2
        types App 2
    need for authorisation 40–2
    post-grant practice 260–1, 278
    promotions regime 47
    real and non-real-time
        communications 47
    regulation of solicitors by SRA
        designated professional body 46–7
        excluded activities 45–6
        regulatory regime 44
        relevance to solicitors 42–4
        Scope and Conduct of Business
            Rules 46–7
    self-test questions 47–9
**Financial Services (Scope) Rules
    2001** 46–7
foreign earnings 79
**free elections (First Protocol: Art
    3)** 303
**freedom of assembly and association
    (Art 11)** 302
freedom of expression (Art 10) 301–2
**freedom of thought, conscience and
    religion (Art 9)** 301–2
funeral expenses
    ascertainment of residuary
        estate 273
    financial services 41

G

gifts
    see also **legacies**
    donationes mortis causa 199
    failure of testamentary provisions
        ademption of legacies 185–6
        consequences 187–8
        date from which will speaks 184–5
        introduction 184
        lapse of legacies 186–7
        legacies generally 185
        to witnesses 187
    lifetime chargeable transfers
        charge to tax 99–105
        death of transferor within seven
            years 106–8
        gifts subject to reservation 118
        liability burden and
            payment 118–21
    potentially exempt transfers
        charge to tax 109–10
        classification 92–3

liability burden and
    payment 118–21
with reservations 199
testamentary gifts to children 188–9
grants of representation
    administrators' oaths 234–40
    administrators' oaths with will
        annexed 231–3
    checkpoints - court
        requirements 239–40
    checkpoints - HMRC
        requirements 248
    checkpoints - obtaining grant 222–3
    checkpoints - PRs 217–18
    court requirements 223
    effect of issue 211
    executors' oaths 224–31
    further affidavits 238–9
    HMRC requirements
        excepted estates 241–2
        Form IHT 205 - excepted
            estates 242–4
        Form IHT 400 - all other
            cases 244–7
        Form IHT 400 - calculations 247
        introduction 240–1
        summary 247
    IHT funding 220–2
    introduction 173
    introduction and
        background 209–10
    lodgment of papers 222
    overview of application
        procedure 218–20
    personal representatives
        capacity 214–15
        entitlement where several
            claimants 215–16
        maximum numbers 216
        renunciation/power
            reserved 216–17
    post-grant practice
        assents 277–8
        beneficiaries' rights and
            remedies 279–80
        checklist for administration 268–9
        checklist for distribution of
            assets 281–2
        distribution of estates 270–5
        duties of PRs 249–50
        estate accounts 275–7
        financial services 260–1, 278
        overview of administration 257
        payment of debts 263–6
        post-death changes 266–8
        protection of PRs 257–60
        realisation of assets 262–3
    preparation of papers 220
    registration 261–2
    registration of death 220
    situations where grant not
        necessary 211–12
    software packages 224
    solicitors duties 210–11
    swearing or affirming 222
    types of grant 212–14

grossing up
lifetime chargeable transfers 99–101

H

Handbook
background 11
dictation and note taking 9
organisation and management
skills 8
outcome-focused approach 3
Principles 11–13
structure 9–11
time and costs recording 7–8
hearsay 294–5
Her Majesty's Revenue and Customs
probate forms
excepted estates 241–2
Form IHT 400 - all other
cases 244–7
probate summary 247
HM Revenue and Customs
notification of changes 68
HM Revenue and Customs (HMRC)
administration of taxation 64–5
guidance 62
probate forms
introduction 240–1
horizontal direct effect
human rights 289
human rights
see also **EU law**
checkpoints 304
Convention rights
free elections (First Protocol: Art
3) 303
freedom of assembly and
association (Art 11) 302
freedom of expression (Art
10) 301–2
freedom of thought, conscience
and religion (Art 9) 301
limitation on use of restriction on
rights (Art 18) 303
no punishment without law (Art
7) 299–300
prohibition of abuse of rights (Art
17) 303
prohibition of discrimination (Art
14) 302–3
prohibition of slavery and forced
labour (Art 4) 291
prohibition of torture (Art 3) 291
protection of property (First
Protocol: Art 1) 303
restrictions on aliens (Art 16) 303
right to education (First Protocol:
Art 2) 303
right to a fair trial (Art 6) 293–9
right to liberty and security (Art
5) 291–3
right to life (Art 2) 290
right to marry (Art 12) 302
right to respect for private and
family life (Art 8) 300–1
death penalty 303

entitlement on intestacy 195
European and international
doctrines
case law 290
derogations 289
equality of arms 289
indirect effect 289
limited rights 286–7
living instrument 290
margins of appreciation 288–9
protocols 290
qualified rights 287
reservations 289
state limitations 287–8
general principles 286
introduction 285
judicial remedies 303–4

I

income tax
ascertainment of residuary
estate 272
sources of taxable income 73–9
trusts and settlements 167–8
income tax (IT)
allowances and rates 69
calculation of tax 69–73
charitable giving 79–80
collection and payment
income 67
notification of changes 68
self-assessment 68
tax codes 67
tax year and collection 69
time limits for returns 68
trusts and settlements 68
general considerations 65
overview 62–3
partnerships 150–1
sole proprietors 149
sources of law 67
summary of basic principles 80–1
**incorporation of wills by
reference** 183–4, 239
indirect effect
human rights 289
inheritance tax
ascertainment of residuary
estate 272–3
basic structure 90–1
charge to tax and death 110–18
chargeable transfers 91–2
checkpoints 121–2
commentary to exercises 122–4
deemed transfers on death 93
effect of variations 268
funding 220–2
gifts subject to reservation 118
liability burden and
payment 118–21
lifetime chargeable transfers 99–105
gifts subject to reservation 118
occasions to tax 93–8
potentially exempt transfers 92–3,
109–10

probate forms
Form IHT 205 - excepted
estates 242–4
Form IHT 400 - all other
cases 244–7
Form IHT 400 - calculations 247
probate summary 247
protection of PRs 260
tax planning 121
taxable property not passing by
succession 200
trusts and settlements 160–4
inheritance tax (IHT)
intestacy 196
overview 63
provision for family and
dependants 206–7
instalment options
inheritance tax 120
institutions
Financial Services Authority 44
HM Revenue and Customs
administration of taxation 64–5
notification of changes 68
HM Revenue and Customs (HMRC)
guidance 62
National Crime Agency 53
insurance
property passing outside will or
intestacy 198–9
protection of PR's against claims 259
PRs administrative powers 252–3
interest
charges on income 152
on inheritance tax 120–1
taxable income 75–7
intestacy
checkpoints 196–8
entitlement to estates
application of rules 190–1
basic position 191–2
Crown 195–6
issue 194–5
other relatives 195
surviving spouses and civil
partners 192–4
inheritance tax 196
introduction 190–1
investments
Conduct of Business Rules
(2001) 46–7
definitions App 2
dividends
distributions 133
taxable income 78–9
financial promotions 44
financial returns 37
meaning and scope 37
need for authorisation 40–2
other considerations 38
PR's powers 254–5
risk 37–8
stock market terminology App 2
taxable income 75–9
types App 2

J

judicial review
    human rights remedy 304
    intrusive surveillance 301
    right to liberty and security (Art
       5) 293

L

lapse of legacies 186–7
legacies
    see also gifts
    failure of gifts
       ademption 185–6
       lapse 186–7
       legacies generally 185
       to witnesses 187
    payment by PRs 270–2
    rights and remedies of
       beneficiaries 279–80
legal aid
    practical application of OFR
       Code 15
    right to a fair trial (Art 6) 294
legitimate objectives 288
letters of administration
    effect of grant 211
    entitlement where several
       claimants 215–16
    renunciation of grant 216–17
    types 212–14
lifetime chargeable transfers
    charge to tax 99–105
    death of transferor within seven
       years 106–8
    gifts subject to reservation 118
    liability burden and payment 119
limitation on use of restriction on
    rights (Art 18) 303
limited grants 214
limited rights 286–7
litigation
    conflicts of interest 24
    costs 15
    key professional conduct
       issues 25–6
    practical application of OFR
       Code 22
    rule in *Cradock v Piper* 275
    trustee powers 252
loans
    benefits in kind 75
    close companies 134–5
    corporation tax allowances 126
    IHT funding 221
    mortgages
       acting for borrower and
          lender 24–5
       administrators' powers 251
    PR's powers of capital
       advancement 256
    pyramid of risk 38
    sole proprietors and
       partnerships 152
    trustee powers 254

M

management skills 8
margins of appreciation 288–9
marshalling 264
mental capacity
    personal representatives 215
    wills 175–6
money laundering
    checkpoints 57
    establishment of NCA to replace
       SOCA 53
    introduction 53
    meaning and scope 53–4
    offences 54
    relevance to solicitors 55
    statutory provisions 54
mortgages
    acting for borrower and lender 24–5
    administrators' powers 251
mutual wills 180

N

National Crime Agency 53, 55
nil rate band 114–15, 243–4
no punishment without law (Art
    7) 299–300
nominations 199
non-discrimination
    practical application of OFR Code 18
    prohibition of discrimination (Art
       14) 303
note taking 9

O

oaths for executors and
    administrators
    court requirements 223
    forms
       administrator's oath 234–40
       administrator's oath with will
          annexed 231–3
       executors oath 224–31
    lodgment of papers 222
    software packages 224
    swearing or affirming 222
OFR Code
    Compliance Officers 13–14
    essential matters 9
    flexible response to changing
       needs 5
    Handbook
       background 11
       Principles 11–13
       structure 9–11
    introduction 3
    organisation and management
       skills 8
    Outcomes 13
    overview 5
    practical application
       additional litigation Outcomes 22
       client care 14–18
       confidentiality 20–2
       conflicts of interest 19–20
       equality and diversity 18
       third party relations 22–3
    significance for consumers 3
    significance for legal profession 3–4
    student membership of SRA 6–7
    time and costs recording 7–8
organisation skills 8
Outcomes
    additional litigation requirements 22
    client care 14
    mandatory compliance 13
    structure of Handbook 9–11
overlap relief 155

P

partnerships
    basis of assessment 154–5
    capital gains 153
    capital losses 153
    carry forward relief 158
    changes in membership 156–7
    checkpoints 158
    income tax 150–1
    interest on loans 152
    introduction 149
    overlap relief 155
    taxable receipts 151–2
    terminal loss relief 157–8
    trading loss relief 153–4
pensions
    property passing outside will or
       intestacy 199
    self-assessment 68
    taxable income 73, 75
personal representatives
    administrative powers
       appropriation 251–2
       capital advancement 256
       delegation 253
       indemnities for expenses 253
       insurance 252–3
       investments 254–5
       maintenance of minors 255–6
       receipts from minors 252
       running of business 253–4
       sale or mortgage 251
       settlement of claims 252
    assents 277–8
    capacity 214–15
    CGT liability 87–9
    checkpoints 257
    distribution of estates
       overview 270
       payment of legacies 270–2
       residuary estate 272–5
    duties 249–50
    entitlement where several
       claimants 215–16
    estate accounts 275–7
    financial services 260–1, 278
    liability 250
    maximum numbers 216
    payment of debts
       insolvent debts 265–6
       solvent estates 263–5

personal representatives (*continued*)
  protection against claims
    missing beneficiaries/
      creditors 258–9
    other liabilities 259–60
    unknown beneficiaries/
      creditors 257–8
  realisation of assets
    registration of grant 261–2
    sale of assets 262–3
  remuneration 274–5
  renunciation/power reserved 216–17
  sole PRs 256–7
pooling 131
potentially exempt transfers
  charge to tax 109–10
  classification 92–3
  liability burden and payment 119
power reserved for executors 216–17
presumption of innocence 293
privacy (Art 8) 300–1
privilege
  money laundering 56
  public interest immunity 295–7
probate and administration
  entitlement to estates
    basic structure 174
    intestacy 190–9
    property not passing under will or
      intestacy 198, 198–9
    property not taxable and passing
      by succession 200
    property passing outside will or
      intestacy 198–9
    provision for family and
      dependants 201–8
    taxable property not passing by
      succession 200
    wills 174–90
  grants of representation
    administrators' oaths 234–40
    administrators' oaths with will
      annexed 231–3
    checkpoints - court
      requirements 239–40
    checkpoints - HMRC
      requirements 248
    checkpoints - obtaining
      grant 222–3
    checkpoints - PRs 217–18
    court requirements 223
    effect of issue 211
    executors' oaths 224–31
    further affidavits 238–9
    HMRC requirements 240–1
    IHT funding 220–2
    introduction and
      background 209–10
    lodgment of papers 222
    overview of application
      procedure 218–20
    personal representatives 215–17
    preparation of papers 220
    registration of death 220
    situations where grant not
      necessary 211–12
    software packages 224
    solicitors duties 210–11
  swearing or affirming 222
  types of grant 212–14
  introduction 173
  post-grant practice
    assents 277–8
    beneficiaries' rights and
      remedies 279–80
    checklist for administration 268–9
    checklist for distribution of
      assets 281–2
    distribution of estates 270–5
    duties of PR s 249–50
    estate accounts 275–7
    financial services 260–1, 278
    overview of administration 257
    payment of debts 263–6
    post-death changes 266–8
    protection of PRs 257–60
    realisation of assets 262–3
  probate grants
    effect of grant 211
    entitlement where several
      claimants 215–16
    types 212
  property not passing under will or
    intestacy 198–9
professional conduct
  checkpoints 27
  core LPC subject areas
    business law and practice 26
    litigation 25–6
    property law 23–5
  history of legal ethics 4
  key requirements
    commercial and client
      awareness 7
    dictation and note taking 9
    organisation and management
      skills 8
    time and costs recording 7–8
  meaning and scope 6
  money laundering 56
  need for change 4–5
  overview 5
  solutions to activities 27–36
  treatment throughout LPC 9
profits
  investment returns 37
  taxable income 75
**prohibition of abuse of rights (Art
  17)** 303
**prohibition of discrimination (Art
  14)** 302–3
**prohibition of slavery and forced
  labour (Art 4)** 291
prohibition of torture (Art 3) 291
property law
  acting for borrower and lender 24–5
  conflicts of interest 24
  overview 23–4
  undertakings 25
proportionality 288
**protection of property (First
  Protocol: Art 1)** 303
protocols 290
public funding
  practical application of OFR
    Code 15
  right to a fair trial (Art 6) 294
public interest immunity 295–7
**punishment without law (Art
  7)** 299–300

Q

qualified rights 287
quick succession relief 112–13

R

registration
  death 220
  grants of representation 261–2
  Value Added Tax 144
reliefs and allowances
  capital allowances
    corporation tax (CT) 129–32
    sole proprietors and
      partnerships 151–2
  Entrepreneur's relief (CGT) 86–7
  income tax 130
  inheritance tax
    agricultural property relief 96–7
    charge to tax and death 110–18
    death of transferor within seven
      years 106–8
    lifetime chargeable transfers 101–5
    quick succession relief 112–13
    taper relief 106, 110
  roll-over relief (CT) 127
  sole proprietors and partnerships
    carry forward relief 158
    overlap relief 155
    start-up loss relief 158
    terminal loss relief 157–8
    trading loss relief 153–4
    woodlands relief 157–8
  trading loss relief
    corporation tax 128–9
    sole proprietors and
      partnerships 153–4
  writing-down allowances
    (WDAs) 152
remedies
  beneficiaries 280
  human rights 303–4
rents 79
renunciation of grants 216–17
reservations from ECHR 289
residuary estate
  administrative expenses 273–4
  tax liabilities 272–3
restrictions on aliens (Art 16) 303
revenue law
  administration of taxation 64–5
  appeals 65
  capital gains tax
    calculation of tax 83
    capital losses 84–5
    chargeable assets 83
    checkpoints 89
    death of taxpayer 87–9
    disposal of assets 82
    exemptions and reliefs 85–7
    general principles 82

parties liable 82
rates of tax 83–4
changing nature of system 61
corporation tax
  calculation of tax 125–7, 132,
    136–9
  capital allowances 129–32
  capital losses 128–9
  checkpoints 139
  close companies 133–6
  dividends 133
  introduction 125
  payment 132–3
  roll-over relief 127
  trading loss relief 128–9
impact of EU membership 62
income tax
  allowances and rates 69
  calculation of tax 69–73
  charitable giving 79–80
  collection and payment 67–9
  general considerations 66
  sources of law 67
  sources of taxable income 73–9
  summary of basic principles 80–1
inheritance tax
  basic structure 90–1
  charge to tax and death 110–18
  chargeable transfers 91–2
  checkpoints 121–2
  commentary to exercises 122–4
  deemed transfers on death 93
  gifts subject to reservation 118
  liability burden and
    payment 118–21
  lifetime chargeable
    transfers 99–105
  occasions to tax 93–8
  potentially exempt transfers 92–3,
    109–10
  tax planning 121
overview of main taxes
  capital gains tax 63
  corporation tax 63–4
  income tax 62–3
  inheritance tax 63
  value added tax 64
partnerships
  basis of assessment 154–5
  capital gains 153
  capital losses 153
  carry forward relief 158
  changes in membership 156–7
  checkpoints 158
  division of profits and losses 157
  income tax 150–1
  interest on loans 152
  introduction 149
  overlap relief 155
  start-up loss relief 158
  taxable receipts 151–2
  terminal loss relief 157–8
  trading loss relief 153–4
sole proprietors
  basis of assessment 154–5
  capital gains 153
  capital losses 153
  carry forward relief 158

checkpoints 158
income tax and VAT 149
interest on loans 152
introduction 149
overlap relief 155
start-up loss relief 158
taxable receipts 151–2
terminal loss relief 157–8
trading loss relief 153–4
sources of law 62
tax planning 64
trusts and settlements
  background 159–60
  capital gains tax 164–6
  checkpoints 168–9
  income tax 167–8
  inheritance tax 160–4
  introduction 159
underlying rationale 61
Value Added Tax
  accounting requirements 144–6
  calculation of tax 146–8
  checkpoints 148
  inputs and outputs 143
  introduction 140
  rates of tax 141–2
  registration 144
  sources of law 140
  tax points 144
  when charged 140–1
reverse burden of truth 293–4
revocation of wills
  civil partners 181
  codicils 181–2
  conditional revocation 182
  destruction 182
  divorce/dissolution 181
  further affidavit evidence 239
  general principles 179
  marriage 180–1
  mutual wills 180
right to a fair trial (Art 6)
  disclosure 294
  hearsay 294–5
  public funding 294
  public interest immunity 295–7
  reverse burden of truth 293–4
  right to silence 295
  unfairly obtained evidence 297–8
**right to education (First Protocol: Art
  2)** 303
**right to liberty and security (Art
  5)** 291–3
right to life (Art 2) 290
right to marry (Art 12) 302
**right to respect for private and
  family life (Art 8)** 300–1
right to silence 295
roll-over relief 127
rule of law 288

S

salaries 73–4
Scope Rules 46–7
signing of wills 177–9
social security benefits 79

sole proprietors
  basis of assessment 154–5
  capital gains 153
  capital losses 153
  carry forward relief 158
  checkpoints 158
  income tax and VAT 149
  interest on loans 152
  introduction 149
  overlap relief 155
  start-up loss relief 158
  taxable receipts 151–2
  terminal loss relief 157–8
solicitors
  financial services
    post-grant practice 261
    regulation by SRA 46–7
    relevance of FSMA 2000 42–4
  grants of representation
    later duties 211
    taking instructions 210–11
  money laundering
    key requirements 55–6
    professional conduct
      issues 56
    relevance 55
**Solicitors Regulation
  Authority (SRA)**
  introduction of OFR Code 3–4
  response to changing needs 5
  student membership 6–7
sources of law
  income tax law 67
  inheritance tax law 91
  revenue law 62
  VAT law 140
special grants 214
spouses
  entitlement on intestacy 192–4
  nil rate band
    IHT exemption 243–4
    IHT relief 114–15
  provision for family and
    dependants 145
  revocation of wills
    by divorce/dissolution 181
    by marriage 180–1
  right to marry (Art 12) 302
standards of work
  acting professionally 6
  being organised 8
  specialist services 10
start-up loss relief 158

T

taper relief 106, 110
tax avoidance 64
tax evasion 64
tax planning
  inheritance tax 121
  overview 64
terminal loss relief 157–8
**terms and conditions of
  business** 18
'Tesco law' 3
third party relations 22–3

time limits
    applications for family
        provision 201–2
    custody and bail 292
    election by spouses and civil
        partners 194
    income tax returns 68
time recording 7–8
tips
    taxable income 74–5
tracing 280
trading loss relief
    corporation tax 128–9
    sole proprietors and
        partnerships 153–4
trusts and settlements
    background 159–60
    checkpoints 168–9
    executor's oath 228
    introduction 159
    life interests 199
    statutory trusts on intestacy 191–2
    tax liabilities
        capital gains tax 164–6
        income tax 167
        inheritance tax 161–4

U

undertakings
    property transactions 25
    relationships with other solicitors 23
unfairly obtained evidence 297–8

V

Value Added Tax (VAT)
    accounting requirements 144–6
    calculation of tax 146–8
    checkpoints 148
    inputs and outputs 143
    introduction 140
value added tax (VAT)
    overview 64
Value Added Tax (VAT)
    rates of tax 141–2
    registration 144
    sole proprietors 149
    sources of law 140
    tax points 144
    when charged 140–1

W

wages
    taxable income 73–4
wills
    alterations 182–3
    charging clauses 274
    checkpoints 189–90
    codicils
        purpose 178
        revocation 181–2
    entitlement to estates 174
    failure of gifts
        ademption of legacies 185–6
        consequences 187–8
        date from which will speaks 185
        introduction 184
        lapse of legacies 186–7
        legacies generally 185
        to witnesses 187
    further affidavit evidence
        due execution 238
        knowledge and approval 238
        revocation 239
        terms, condition and date 238–9
    gifts to children 188–9
    incorporation by reference 183–4
    letters of administration with will
        annexed 212–13
    revocation
        civil partners 181
        codicils 181–2
        conditional revocation 182
        destruction 182
        divorce/dissolution 181
        general principles 179
        marriage 180–1
        mutual wills 180
    sale of assets 262–3
    validity
        capacity 175–6
        formalities 177–9
        intention 176–7
    variations 267–8
woodlands relief 112
**writing-down allowances
    (WDAs)**
    corporation tax 129–30
    sole proprietors and
        partnerships 152